COMPANY ACCOUNTS

COMPANY ACCOUNTS

ANALYSIS, INTERPRETATION AND UNDERSTANDING

Sixth Edition

Maurice Pendlebury and Roger Groves

THOMSON™

Australia • Canada • Mexico • Singapore • Spain • United Kingdom • United States

Company Accounts – Analysis, Interpretation and Understanding, Sixth Edition

Copyright © 2004 Maurice Pendlebury and Roger Groves

The Thomson logo is a registered trademark used herein under licence.

For more information, contact Thomson Learning, High Holborn House; 50–51 Bedford Row, London WC1R 4LR or visit us on the World Wide Web at: http://www.thomsonlearning.co.uk

British Library Cataloguing-in-Publication Data
A catalogue record for this book is available from the British Library

ISBN 1-86152-947-3

First edition published by Routledge in 1994
Simultaneously published in the USA and Canada by Routledge
Reprinted 1994
Reprinted by International Thomson Business Press 1996 and 1997
Fourth Edition 1999 by International Thomson Business Press
Fifth Edition 2001 by Thomson Learning
This edition published by Thomson Learning 2004

Typeset by MHL Production Services Limited, Coventry
Printed in Croatia by Zrinksi

Contents

Preface

This book provides a thorough and analytical discussion of the nature and format of published company annual reports and accounts and a full introduction to the analysis and interpretation of financial statements. It takes notice of the effects and impacts of existing legislation and regulations and all published accounting and financial reporting standards, thereby providing a relevant and up-to-date guide to this important area.

We have designed the book to be most useful for students on MBA or similar advanced-level courses in management and also to undergraduate students specializing in management and business studies who require the ability to comprehend and interpret company financial statements. In addition the book should prove extremely useful to anyone, whether they be investors, lenders, creditors or managers, who require a clear understanding of the information contained in the annual report of a company and of the techniques needed to analyse the information and assess the underlying strengths, weaknesses and potential of the company.

In Part One, we provide a systematic description of the nature and role of the company annual reports and accounts and a detailed discussion of the impact of British legislation and regulation and of professional practices and recommendations. In Part Two, we provide a detailed examination of the principal and subsidiary financial statements of a leading British company, and an explanation of how the information contained in these statements, together with other publicly available data, can be used to provide a structured approach to the interpretation and analysis of that company's performance. In addition, the final chapter of Part Two provides a discussion of the major research findings and practical applications concerning the use of ratio analysis in assessing the performance and financial position of a company. This chapter will be more particularly appropriate for MBA and other management students. The appendices include the complete text of the company's financial statements, together with a glossary of accounting terms and a glossary of ratios.

We are grateful to the directors of The BOC Group plc for permission to reproduce an extensive extract from the company's annual report for the year ended 30 September 2002. It is worth pointing out that The BOC Group and its directors have consistently been at the forefront of progress in information provision and disclosure. The authors of this book are particularly pleased to be able to acknowledge here the very marked contribution that the company and its executives have made to financial reporting in the UK. We are also grateful to Jordans Limited for permission to reproduce an extract from their FAME information service.

As teachers and researchers, we are deeply appreciative of the considerable assistance given by successive generations of students who have permitted us to try out our ideas and refine our teaching practices with their cooperation. Our colleagues at the Cardiff Business School have demonstrated continued support and interest, and we are especially grateful to Julie Roberts for her unfailing goodwill and dedication in the task of turning a number of drafts into a cohesive finished typescript.

Maurice Pendlebury
Roger Groves

1 The purpose, regulation and format of company reports

Many people are affected by and are properly interested in the activities and influences of the modern company: investors (whether equity or preference shareholders), creditors and lenders (whether debenture or mortgage holders, trade suppliers or bank officials), employees and their representatives, government officials and administrators (whether tax collectors or statisticians) and members of the local, regional and national communities within which the corporation operates. Each of these parties has a clear right, in law or otherwise, to have reasonable access to certain levels of information about the company's activities and prospects. This chapter sets the scene by discussing the accountability and stewardship aspects of a company's reporting practices and by outlining some of the legal and professional background for those practices. The considerable increase of legislative demands upon limited companies has led to a widening of the range of information that a company must provide. The even greater increase in the ethical and professional requirements imposed by accountants, stock market administrators and others, and more recently the significant amount of media attention given to the unexpected failure of some major companies, has brought about a burgeoning succession of standards and pronouncements with which a company is obliged to comply, and these will be examined in Part One.

Types of company

Although much business activity in the UK is carried out by sole traders or partnerships, the most important form of business entity is undoubtedly the limited liability company. Limited liability companies have a legal status quite separate and distinct from that of their owners, and the liability of owners is limited to the amount of money they have invested in a company. The ownership of a company is divided into shares of equal value, and every company must have at least two shareholders, but there is no upper limit and some companies have many thousands of shareholders. Companies with such large numbers of shareholders would almost certainly be *public* limited companies and would almost certainly be *quoted*. A public limited company is one in which shares can be owned by the general public, and since 1981 the name of such a company has been followed by the abbreviation plc (public limited company). (Companies registered in Wales have the option of using ccc – cwmni cyfyngedig cyhoeddus.) A 'quoted' or 'listed' company is one whose shares can be bought and sold on a stock exchange. The BOC Group plc, for example, is both a public and a quoted company.

Only public companies can have a stock market quotation, but not all of them choose to do so. There are over 14,000 public companies in existence but only about 2,000 of these are quoted. A company that is not public is known as a private company and is not allowed to sell its shares to the public. The vast majority of limited companies are private companies, with over 1,500,000 currently in existence, and yet it is the relatively few public companies that contribute most to the economic activity and employment opportunities of the country. The shares in private companies tend to be traded infrequently and are usually held by only a small number of shareholders. Shareholders in private companies also tend to be much more closely involved with company management than is typically the case with a public company. It is in fact the separation of the ownership of a public company (which rests solely with its shareholders) from its day-to-day control (which rests largely with its full-time directors and managers) which underpins the requirement for proper accountability and stewardship, and the need for a framework of regulation and supervision of limited companies generally.

Accountability and stewardship

The separation of ownership from the management of a company, combined with substantial protection afforded to company directors and managers by the concept of limited liability, has meant that those responsible for the financial and trading activities of a company are required to report conscientiously and honestly on the affairs of the company and its current and prospective status.

Shareholders assign to a board of directors the duties and obligations of running their company from year to year, while retaining the legal duties and obligations of owning shares in a company. Some directors act in a part-time or non-executive capacity, which means that in effect the affairs of the company will often be under the routine control of a handful of executive directors. Executives must report on their stewardship of what may be very considerable assets and on their management of very substantial operations.

Without delving too deeply into company law, the legal control and ownership of a limited company resides in the shareholders in a general meeting. For many companies, this may involve nothing more than the directors and their immediate families. For one of the 2,000 or so quoted public companies in the UK, this general meeting could potentially involve some 40,000 or 50,000 separate shareholders. In practice, company general meetings rarely attract more than 100 or 200 actual participants. Nevertheless, as the steward of an estate is responsible to its owner, so the directors of a company are responsible to its shareholders.

The whole question of the direction and control of companies was put into sharp focus following a series of spectacular company failures and in May 1992 the 'Cadbury Committee' was set up to examine the financial aspects of corporate governance. The Committee's report was published in December 1992, and contained a code of best practice which companies are expected to follow. This work was further developed by the Hampel Committee, which was set up to promote high standards of corporate governance. The Hampel Committee report was published in 1998, and led to the acceptance by the London Stock Exchange of a 'Combined Code' which contained principles of good corporate governance and a code of best practice. This Combined Code was based on the work of the Cadbury Committee, the Greenbury Committee on directors' remuneration and the Hampel Committee. The rules of the Stock Exchange require listed UK companies to disclose in their annual reports and accounts how the principles of the Combined Code have been applied, and whether or not the provisions of the Combined Code have been followed.

The Cadbury Report of 1992 pointed out (p. 16) that its code of best practice was based on the principles of openness, integrity and accountability. The importance of openness as the basis of the confidence which needs to exist between business and all those who have a stake in its success, was emphasized. Integrity was defined as 'both straightforward dealing and completeness'. On the issue of accountability, they commented:

> Boards of directors are accountable to their shareholders and both have to play their part in making that accountability effective. Boards of directors need to do so through the quality of the information which they provide to shareholders, and shareholders through their willingness to exercise their responsibilities as owners.

In general terms, that accountability is served by reporting to the shareholders on the sales and other activities of the company during a stated period (usually a twelve-month fiscal or calendar year, supplemented by half-yearly reports) and on the profits (or losses) generated by those activities. Such reports will take the form of a financial statement (the trading and profit and loss account) reporting the money value of those activities and their results, and a further statement (the balance sheet) reporting the position in money terms of the company at the year end and revealing the impact of the previous year's activities on the company's assets and liabilities. The directors also provide further statements revealing the cash flows of the company (see Chapter 4) and the total recognized gains and losses of the company (see Chapter 5).

Additionally, these financial statements will be accompanied by a review by both the chairman and the chief executive of the important events of the past year and expectations for the future (see Chapter 6) and also supported by a qualitative report by the directors and an operating and financial review (see Chapter 7) which amplify the statements and report certain additional information.

Where legally or institutionally necessary, the directors' reports and statements are accompanied by a report from the company's auditors (whose qualifications are prescribed by law) attesting the reasonable reliability and apparent truth and fairness of the company's financial statements. The nature and implications of the auditors' opinion are discussed more fully in Chapter 8; it has to be recognized that an 'unqualified' auditors' report (i.e. one in which no reservations are expressed on the grounds of uncertainty or disagreement) is not the equivalent of a guarantee that the company's affairs are wholly sound and its future secure.

Although the law currently says little about the statutory duties of auditors, the various professional bodies of accountancy have laid down certain minimal standards which must be complied with. All those who rely on financial statements, whether as shareholders, creditors, regulators or similarly interested parties, are closely affected by auditors' work and a proper appreciation of the nature and scope of an audit is essential to a full understanding of the purpose and characteristics of company accounts.

Regulation and supervision

The process of providing the various financial statements, supporting notes and reports is known collectively as financial reporting. If this is to have an important part to play in the accountability of companies, then some form of regulation and supervision is necessary. Although some would argue that financial reporting does not need to be regulated at all, most governments throughout the world ensure that a regulatory framework does exist. However, the regulation of financial reporting is not undertaken solely by governments; often, it is seen as a joint responsibility of government on the one hand and private sector organizations, such as the accountancy profession and the Stock Exchange, on the other. Thus in the UK there are several sources of regulation, including the following.

Parliament is responsible for the legislation which directly affects financial reporting, e.g. the Companies Act 1985.

Government not only initiates the legislative process but also exerts considerable influence through the activities of the Department of Trade and Industry (DTI).

The Financial Reporting Council develops policy on accounting standards and guidance on work programmes and issues of public concern.

The Accounting Standards Board (ASB) issues exposure drafts of proposed accounting standards as part of a process leading to Financial Reporting Standards (FRSs). (Before August 1990 standards were set by the Accounting Standards Committee (ASC) and were known as Statements of Standard Accounting Practice (SSAPs).) The ASB is assisted by an Urgent Issues Task Force (UITF) which attempts to obtain a voluntary and speedy consensus on the accounting treatment that should apply in situations where unsatisfactory or conflicting interpretations have developed.

The Financial Reporting Review Panel examines the accounts of companies which do not appear to comply with the requirement to show a true and fair view.

The Stock Exchange produces rules concerning the financial disclosure of listed companies. Listed companies are those public companies whose shares are quoted and can be traded on the Stock Exchange's markets. The Stock Exchange expects listed companies to comply with accounting standards and reasons for noncompliance must be disclosed.

The International Accounting Standards Board (IASB) has the objective of working generally for the improvement and harmonization of regulations, accounting standards and procedures relating to the presentation of financial statements. The ASB supports the IASB in this and each FRS contains a section explaining how it relates to the International Accounting Standard dealing with the same topic. For accounting periods beginning on or after 1 January 2005 all European Union *listed* companies will be required to produce consolidated financial statements that comply with International Accounting Standards.

Other influences include various pressure groups, organizations and individuals which have some influence on the content of Companies Acts and accounting standards, including government departments, employer organizations (such as the Confederation of British Industry (CBI)) and other professional bodies (such as the Law Society).

A major issue which emerges out of this regulatory partnership between public and private sectors concerns the precise role of each partner. There are different types of regulation and these can be classified as those concerned with:

- disclosure of information;
- the format in which information is to be disclosed;
- the measurement and valuation of information.

In the past it could be said that regulations from the public sector (e.g. Companies Acts) were concerned mainly with disclosure, whereas those from the private sector (e.g. accounting standards) were concerned mainly with format, measurement and valuation. However, there have always been some examples of this distinction being breached and towards the end of the twentieth century these have become much more frequent. Thus, for example, the Companies Act 1981 introduced a requirement for specific formats to be used for the profit and loss account and the balance sheet. Similarly, from 1975 until 1992 there was an accounting standards requirement to disclose a source and application of funds statement. This has now been superseded by a requirement to disclose a cash flow statement. The impact of the various sources of regulation on financial reporting practices is described fully and discussed in Part One (Chapters 2–8), but it is useful here to examine in a little more detail the major constituents of the regulatory framework outlined above.

Legal regulation

The legal regulation of accounting can be traced as far back as the Joint Stock Companies Act of 1844, but the statutes which have had the greatest influence on the current state of company financial reporting are the more recent Companies Acts of 1948, 1967 and 1981. The provisions of these Acts (and also the Companies Acts of 1976 and 1980) were consolidated into the Companies Act 1985, which, as amended by the Companies Act 1989, contains the overall legal framework.

The Acts of 1948 and 1967 were very important in laying down the basic disclosure requirements which still apply today. The 1948 Act also introduced the requirement for auditors to report on whether the accounts give a true and fair view of the company's financial position at the end of an accounting period and of its profit or loss for that period. As a result of the 1981 Companies Act, the need for accounts to give a true and fair view became an 'overriding consideration'. This means that information not specifically required by law must be provided in order to give a true and fair view. Similarly, departure from the specific requirements of the law is permitted in situations where compliance with the law would prevent a true and fair view being shown. (Where departure does occur, full particulars must be given, together with reasons for that departure and an explanation of the effect of such a departure.) The 1981 Act was also very much concerned with the need for disclosure, and a notable example of this was a new requirement for cost of sales information to be given in the profit and loss account. However, the most important features of the 1981 Act were that it prescribed the formats that could be used for presenting company financial information and that it required some basic accounting principles to be written into the law. Both of these features are examples of the increasing influence of the European Community (EC) on the regulatory framework of accounting in the UK.

One of the objectives of the EC is to harmonize company law in member states. This is achieved through the development of directives, which, when approved and adopted by the EC Council of Ministers, are meant to be binding on the member states. The EC directive with the greatest impact on accounting has been the Fourth Directive. This was adopted by the EC in 1978 and it contains detailed regulations concerning the format, content, valuation methods and publication of accounts; these regulations were reflected in the requirements of the Companies Act 1981. Because the provisions of the 1981 and earlier Acts are now consolidated into the Companies Act 1985 (as amended by the Companies Act 1989) it is this amended 1985 Act that will be referred to in the chapters that follow.

Regulation by the accountancy profession

Until 1 August 1990, the principal means by which the accountancy profession contributed to the regulation of financial reporting was through the ASC. This was an organization made up of representatives of the six major professional accounting bodies in the UK, together with the preparers and users of accounting information. The objectives of the ASC were to define accounting concepts, to reduce differences in financial accounting and reporting practices and to codify generally accepted best practice in the public interest. One of the ways in which it achieved these objectives was by issuing SSAPs. During its existence the ASC issued twenty-six SSAPs, some of which were subsequently revised. All the SSAPs were preceded by exposure drafts to permit full consultation on proposed standards and a total of fifty-five exposure drafts were issued.

On 1 August 1990 the ASC was replaced by the ASB and the twenty-two SSAPs that were then extant were adopted by the ASB. The ASB, like the ASC before it, embodies a substantial amount of technical expertise, with nine members including a full-time chairman and a Technical Director, and its funding and membership is drawn from the accountancy profession, the financial community and the government.

The ASB is guided on its work programme and on issues of public concern by the Financial Reporting Council, whose chairman is appointed jointly by the Secretary of State for Trade and Industry and the Governor of the Bank of England. The Financial Reporting Council also provides a high level of support for accounting standard setting and operates through a Financial Reporting Review Panel to examine and question examples of material departure from accounting standards. The 1985 Act (as amended) requires companies (other than small or medium-sized companies) to disclose whether their accounts have been prepared in accordance with applicable standards and to give particulars of, and reasons for, material departures from standards. Compliance with accounting standards will normally be required for accounts to show a true and fair view but if in exceptional circumstances compliance with an accounting standard is inconsistent with the need to give a true and fair view then departure from the requirements of the standard is permitted.

Where the accounts of a company do not comply with the requirements of accounting standards the Financial Reporting Review Panel can consider these and decide what action to take. At the time of writing approximately 50 cases that have been considered by the Financial Reporting Review Panel have been publicized. Although these have, for the most part, been limited to obtaining an agreement from the companies concerned that they will amend the practice complained of in subsequent years, the Panel can ask that the accounts of a company be revised and apply to the courts for an order requiring the directors of the company to do so.

The ASB issued its statement of aims in 1991 and these are as follows:

The aims of the Accounting Standards Board are to establish and improve standards of financial accounting and reporting, for the benefit of users, preparers and auditors of financial information.

The ASB intends to achieve its aims by:

- developing principles to guide it in establishing standards and to provide a framework within which others can exercise judgement in resolving accounting issues;
- issuing new accounting standards or amending existing ones, in response to evolving business practices, new economic developments and deficiencies being identified in current practice;
- addressing urgent issues promptly.

The ASB approached the development of these principles piecemeal in seven separate chapters. These were combined and published as a draft *Statement of Principles for Financial Reporting* in November 1995. The draft attracted considerable criticism, mainly because of its strong support for current cost accounting and the importance it attached to the statement of total recognized gains and losses at the expense of the profit and loss account. A revised exposure draft was published in March 1999, and was followed in December 1999 by the publication of the final version of the *Statement of Principles*.

The ASB states that its primary purpose in developing principles for financial reporting is to provide a coherent frame of reference which should clarify the conceptual underpinnings of proposed accounting standards, and enable standards to be developed on a consistent basis by reducing the need to debate fundamental issues each time a standard is developed or revised.

The final version of the *Statement of Principles* has eight chapters:

1 The objective of financial statements
2 The reporting entity
3 The qualitative characteristics of financial information
4 The elements of financial statements
5 Recognition in financial statements
6 Measurement in financial statements
7 Presentation of financial information
8 Accounting for interests in other entities

An outline of the contents of each of the above chapters is provided in the Appendix to this chapter (see pages 17–19).

The standards issued by the ASB are called Financial Reporting Standards (FRSs). As with the ASC, wide consultation is seen as an important part of the standard setting process. All accounting standards are preceded by the issue of an exposure draft. Those issued by the ASB are called Financial Reporting Exposure Drafts (FREDs). Several FRSs and FREDs have already been issued by the ASB as well as a number of discussion documents, which provide an even earlier stage of consultation than exposure drafts.

The way in which the ASB addresses urgent issues promptly is through the UITF: The authority and scope of the UITF was explained in a 1991 ASB pronouncement to be 'a committee of the Accounting Standards Board comprising a number of people of major standing on the field of financial reporting'. Its main role is to consider situations where unsatisfactory or conflicting interpretations of accounting standards or

Companies Act provision have developed or are likely to develop. Where such situations occur a voluntary consensus as to the appropriate accounting treatment is sought and this is then issued as a consensus pronouncement. The ASB in its 1991 pronouncement states that

> Consensus pronouncements should be considered part of the corpus of practices forming the basis for determining what constitutes a true and fair view. Such pronouncements consequently may be taken into consideration by the Financial Reporting Review Panel in deciding whether financial statements call for review.

It is clear therefore that UITF pronouncements, which are issued in the form of abstracts, are intended to be complied with by companies when preparing financial statements. The UITF has already issued several of these abstracts.

Regulation by the Stock Exchange

The Council of the Stock Exchange requires that the published financial statements of listed companies (i.e. those public companies whose shares are quoted and can be traded on the Stock Exchange's markets) contain certain types of information. Although much of this information is already required, either by law or accounting standard, the Stock Exchange also imposes additional disclosure requirements. An example of these is the requirement for UK incorporated listed companies to include in their annual report and accounts a statement as to whether or not they have complied with the Cadbury Committee's code of best practice. Listed companies are also expected to comply with the provisions of accounting standards (SSAPs and FRSs) and companies are required to give reasons for any significant departures from standard accounting practice.

The International Accounting Standards Committee (IASC)

The IASC was set up in 1973 with a membership drawn from nine countries; by 1999 it had members in 103 countries. In its attempt to harmonize international financial reporting, the IASC formulated and published international accounting standards (IASs) and promoted their world-wide acceptance and observance.

Initially, the standards produced by the IASC tended to permit alternative ways of measuring or disclosing financial information. Compliance was voluntary and so permitting more than one acceptable way of dealing with a specific accounting issue was a means of ensuring support for the standard. The main impact was therefore the prohibiting of the more undesirable accounting practices rather than achieving real harmonization. Although the IASC had, over time, attempted to reduce the number of permitted alternative accounting treatments, the influence of the IASC in the UK had, until recently, been relatively minor. However, the influence of the IASC increased significantly following an agreement, in 1995, for the IASC to produce a set of core IASs which could be accepted by the International Organization of Securities Commissions (IOSCO) as the accounting rules to be used by multinational companies for the purpose of cross-border security issues and listings. The use of those accounting rules would permit multinational companies to be listed on a foreign stock exchange, say New York or London, without having to comply with specific US or UK accounting standards. The IASC completed the production of the set of core IASs by 2000 and these have now been endorsed by IOSCO, subject to some qualifications. International Accounting Standards issued from 2002 onwards will be referred to as International Financial Reporting Standards or IFRSs.

In 2000, a major review of the structure of the IASC led to it being reconstituted as the International Accounting Standards Board (IASB) and the role of this body in international accounting standard setting increased further in 2002 with the acceptance by the European Union Council of Ministers of the requirement for EU listed companies to comply with IASs when preparing consolidated accounts for accounting periods commencing on or after 1 January 2005.

Other influences on regulation

With the continuing growth of pressure groups, such as those concerned with environmental issues, racial and ethnic minorities, disabled or disadvantaged groups and political ideologies, more attention has been paid to companies' published accounts as a source of information on those companies' social and environmental impacts. Equally, many companies have taken the opportunity to include with their financial statements detailed information designed to rebut or forestall criticism or pressure on social and environmental grounds.

Legal requirements on the disclosure of information on matters relating to employment, health and safety at work, training and the employment of disabled people, for example, have been considerably extended in recent years and have forced the wider disclosure of many employee-related matters. In 1975, the Accounting Standards *Steering* Committee (the body which preceded the Accounting Standards Committee) produced a discussion document in which it advocated the production of an increased series of reports and statements. The Committee's proposals received a mixed reception, but some of its more beneficial suggestions have been adopted, as discussed in Chapter 7.

In addition, the activities of chemical companies, mineral-extraction companies and the like have come in for closer scrutiny by lobbyists and campaigners. That increased scrutiny has, almost invariably, resulted in enhanced or widened disclosure of relevant financial and non-financial information.

The suggestion has often been made that companies should move away from the traditional, solely financial, orientation of company reports and introduce a wider degree of disclosure in respect of all the resources used in a company's business, including human and environmental resources. This method of presenting information has been labelled 'social accounting' or 'social reporting', and it has attracted some support from both academic and practising accountants. A growing number of large companies now produce stand-alone reports providing information about their social and environmental performance. Social reporting is, of course, entirely voluntary but many companies now recognize that there are benefits in confirming that they are aware of their ethical, social and environmental responsibilities and are therefore willing to report on their actions and achievements.

A further influence on the regulation of financial statements has been the growth of the use of off-balance-sheet finance and window-dressing schemes by companies. In a statement issued by the Institute of Chartered Accountants in England and Wales (Technical Release 603, December 1985), off-balance-sheet finance was defined as

> The funding or refinancing of a company's operations in such a way that, under legal requirements and existing accounting conventions, some or all of the finance may not be shown on its balance sheet.

Window dressing was defined as

> Transactions, the purpose of which is to arrange affairs so that the financial statements of the concern give a misleading or unrepresentative impression of its financial position.

It is clear from these definitions that off-balance-sheet financing and window-dressing schemes provide the opportunity to mislead the users of financial statements. The problem facing the regulatory process was to decide on the best way to prevent the use of such schemes. One approach would have been to introduce a series of specific requirements aimed at restricting each scheme. However, given the wide range of opportunities for off-balance-sheet financing and window dressing, this would require a significant number of detailed provisions, with no guarantee that they could keep pace with the development of new schemes by imaginative preparers of accounts. An alternative would be to issue a general standard based on the concept of 'substance over form'. This concept would require that the accounts of a company should reflect the economic reality of the underlying transactions, rather than their legal form. Although some would argue that the concept of substance over form must always apply if accounts are to give a true and fair view, not all would agree. The Law Society, for example, in 1986 issued a paper entitled 'Off-balance sheet finance and window-dressing' in which concern was expressed that reliance on substance over form could introduce too much subjectivity into the preparation of accounts. The Law Society argued that the analysis of the legal position in relation to assets and liabilities provides the most objective basis because it gives a clear point of reference, whereas a subjective evaluation of the economic or real effect of a transaction does not.

However, the ASB (and before it the ASC) is very clearly supportive of the concept of substance over form. The ASC issued two exposure drafts (ED 42 in 1988 and ED 49 in 1990) which proposed that transactions should be accounted for in accordance with their substance. The ASB then withdrew ED 42 and ED 49 and replaced them with FRED4, which reiterated the commitment to substance over form. FRS 5 ('Reporting the substance of transactions') was issued in April 1994 and this showed only minor changes from FRED4. Although FRS 5 is drafted in terms of general principles rather than a series of rules it does provide detailed Application Notes to clarify the application of the Standard to the specific topics of: consignment stock; sale and repurchase agreements; factoring of debts; securitized assets; and loan transfers.

These are the most frequently encountered areas where the distinction between the legal ownership of assets and the substantive ownership might give rise to off-balance-sheet financing opportunities. FRS 5 makes it clear that it is the substance and economic reality of transactions that should be reported in financial statements. This emphasis on substance and economic reality is now evident in the ASB's Statement of Principles. Accounts preparers and auditors are expected to ensure that accounts do not simply follow a set of detailed rules but are consistent with the underlying principles. This differs from the requirement in the USA where, in spite of the existence of a conceptual framework containing the broad principles for accounting and financial reporting, the emphasis has been for accounting standards to prescribe detailed and complex rules to be followed when preparing accounts. This difference in emphasis has led to the UK approach to standard setting being characterized as 'principles based' and the US approach as 'rules based'. The problem with a rules based approach is that it might be possible through accounting and financial 'engineering' to account for transactions in a way that does not break the rules, but quite clearly fails to reflect the underlying economic reality. The collapse of Enron does seem to confirm the limitations of a rules based approach, with special purpose entities being put together in such a way that the rules governing consolidation did not apply, with the result that the full extent of Enron's liabilities did not appear in the group accounts. The supporters of a principles based approach would argue that the requirement for the accounts to be consistent with the underlying principles would have ensured that the special purpose entities were included in the group accounts.

Generally Accepted Accounting Practices (GAAP)

All of the influences outlined above on the form and content of the published accounts of a company gave rise to what is often referred to as 'UK GAAP'. In some countries, e.g. USA and Canada, the term GAAP has a very clear meaning and definition. In the UK the term is used much more loosely and includes all practices that are considered to be permissible or legitimate, either through support by statute, accounting standard or official pronouncement, or through consistency with the needs of users and of meeting the fundamental requirement to present a true and fair view, or even simply through authoritative support in the accounting literature. GAAP is therefore more than just the requirements of accounting standards and the law; it is a dynamic concept which changes in response to changing circumstances. The accounting concepts that are discussed below also represent an important part of GAAP.

Accounting concepts

The regulatory framework of accounting that was outlined earlier provides the disclosure and measurement rules that have to be followed by companies. In addition, the financial accounts of business organizations are based on a set of generally accepted assumptions which are known as accounting concepts. Accounting concepts are not a set of rigid rules but are practices which currently have general acceptability but which could change and evolve to reflect changes in accounting development. The accounting concepts that are considered most important are as follows:

- the entity concept;
- the money measurement concept;
- the going concern concept;
- the cost concept;
- the realization concept;
- the accruals concept;
- the matching concept;
- the periodicity concept;
- the consistency concept;
- the prudence concept;
- the materiality concept.

The entity concept

Under company law a company is a separate legal entity which is quite distinct from its owners. For other types of business organizations it is an accepted principle of financial accounting that a business should be regarded as a separate entity. A business has assets and liabilities and the difference between the two is the capital or equity of a business. This belongs to the owners and under the entity concept the capital of a business is regarded (and accounted for) as the amount a business owes to its owners.

The money measurement concept

Under the money measurement concept only those events to which a monetary value can be attached appear in the accounts. Thus the *quality* of a workforce is not usually capable of being expressed as a monetary amount and is therefore not shown in the accounts. However, the amount paid to the workforce is a monetary value and so does appear. Likewise the amounts spent on recruiting and training the workforce are accounted for. Money is an obvious standard of measurement and by restricting accounting information to the monetary value of transactions, the concept limits the type of information that might be recorded and provides a basis for comparisons to be made. However, there are problems associated with the money measurement concept.

In the first place the value of money does not remain constant over time. At times of inflation the value of money declines and so the monetary values of transactions of earlier years are not equivalent to the monetary values of today. Also, limiting information to monetary values only means that the accounts, and particularly the balance sheet of an organization, are unlikely to disclose all of the relevant information about a business. For example, most successful businesses enjoy an element of goodwill, which might be based on reputation or be due to operational efficiencies. Because of this a business might well be worth more than the value of all of its assets less liabilities that do have monetary values, such as buildings, equipment, vehicles, stock, etc. This 'extra' value is goodwill, but because it is so difficult to attach a monetary value to this goodwill element it is only accounted for when a business is purchased and a market value is then determined. For most of the time that a business exists, therefore, the goodwill is not accounted for because its monetary value is not known.

The money measurement concept provides a good example of how accounting concepts are not rigid rules but are capable of evolving and developing, and another example of this is the treatment of brand names. One obvious reason for goodwill existing in a business is when the products of a company have brand names which contribute significantly to product demand and therefore profitability. Until recently brand names were not thought of as being capable of having a monetary value attached to them and were not included in the balance sheets of businesses. In recent years, however, several major companies have now decided to place a monetary value on brand names and include these as assets in the balance sheet.

The going concern concept

The assumption under the going concern concept is that a business will continue to operate in the foreseeable future and is not about to be closed down. Immediately some types of assets are brought into use their disposal value is very low relative to their acquisition cost. The going concern concept means that the underlying disposal value of an asset can be ignored and the acquisition cost can be spread over the years that benefit from the asset's use.

The cost concept

The cost concept is often referred to as historic cost accounting because of the reliance for accounting purposes on the original acquisition cost of assets. One of the reasons for using the original acquisition cost is that it is an easily verifiable and therefore objective value. However, when prices are not stable the use of historic cost can mean that the asset values used when preparing final accounts might be quite different to current market values and therefore a misleading picture of the business is provided. Proposals for moving away from the cost concept to some form of market valuation basis have been made and experimented with over the years, but the cost concept still predominates. However, many companies periodically revalue certain of their fixed assets so that they then reflect the market value at the time of valuation; this is known as modified historic cost accounting.

The draft Statement of Principles issued by the ASB (see Appendix to this chapter on pages 17–19) reveals a distinct preference for companies to move away from historic cost accounting and make greater use of current value accounting.

The realization concept

There is a very close link between the realization concept and the cost concept. Although the assets of a business may increase in value, there is no certainty that the profit will be realized until the asset is sold. Thus only when the sale is made will the profit be recognized. This is a clear example of the caution that is inherent in accounting. However, it is not deemed necessary to wait for cash to be received before recognizing a profit. Once a sale is made a legally enforceable contract exists and the profit can be recognized at that point.

The accruals concept

The accruals concept is consistent with the realization concept in that revenues and costs are recognized as they are earned or incurred, not as money is received or paid. This distinguishes accruals accounting from cash accounting. Under cash accounting it is the time of payment or receipt of cash that determines in which accounting period a transaction should be accounted for. Under accruals accounting it is the time an expense is incurred or revenue is earned that determines the accounting period in which the transaction is accounted for. The accruals concept, when combined with the matching concept, provides the basis for the determination of profit and loss.

The matching concept

The matching concept requires the revenues earned by a business to be matched with the expenses incurred in earning those revenues. In reality the revenues of a specific transaction are not matched with the expenses of that transaction but the revenues of each accounting period are matched with the expenses of that period. The difference between the two is the profit or loss for the period. The difficulty associated with this is of course identifying which accounting period benefits from certain types of expense. For example, an asset such as plant or machinery that will enable revenues to be earned over several accounting periods should be charged as an expense in the form of depreciation to each period that will benefit. How to do this in a manner that exactly reflects the benefits of each period is probably impossible for many types of asset.

The periodicity concept

Under the periodicity concept accounts are prepared for a specific period. The specific period is usually one year and for companies this is the period required by law. Annual reporting is now firmly established for most organizations. However, not all transactions are conveniently completed within one year and this gives rise to the problems discussed under the matching concept of determining an *accurate* means of allocating expenditure and revenue between different periods. For example, a major civil engineering construction contract may take several years to complete and yet for the purposes of the annual accounts it will be necessary to show the proportion of the expenses, revenues and profit (or loss) that should be recorded each year in the accounts of the construction company.

The consistency concept

In accounting there are often several acceptable ways of determining asset values and the proportion of the cost of assets that should be borne by each accounting period. Examples of different methods of valuing closing stock and determining depreciation expenses are given in Chapter 2. The consistency concept requires there to be consistency of treatment of like items within each accounting period and from one period to the next. In other words once one of the generally accepted methods is chosen this method should usually be used consistently from year to year. However, if there are compelling and justifiable reasons for changing the method of valuing a particular item, e.g. closing stock, then this is permitted under the consistency concept, but the impact of the change on current year profit and the impact the change would have had on the accounts of the previous year should be reported to provide comparability.

An important qualitative characteristic of financial information that has been identified in the ASB's *Statement of Principles* is that of comparability (see Appendix to this chapter on pages 17–19). The consistent application of accounting methods throughout an enterprise and through time is a key requirement for comparability.

The prudence concept

The prudence concept is often referred to as the conservatism concept. The preparation of accounts requires judgements to be made about the future and because of the uncertainties associated with this a prudent or cautious approach is required for profit determination. Under this concept all expected losses should be taken into account immediately they are known about, whereas expected gains are not recognized until actually realized. An example of the widespread use of the prudence concept is in closing stock valuation. The normal rule is that closing stock should be valued at cost, but if the market value of the stock falls below cost then the market value should be used. This is the 'lower of cost or net realizable value' that is generally applied to all stock valuations. The prudence concept is clearly useful in terms of preventing over-optimistic calculations of profit to be reported. Overstatement of profit might lead to excessive dividend payments being made or to incorrect investment decisions being taken. However, the concept of prudence should not be taken to excess because the understatement of profit which would result might be just as misleading as the overstatement and might discourage investment unnecessarily.

The materiality concept

Under the materiality concept only information that is essential to the decisions being taken by the users of accounting reports is required to be included. In other words information is material if its omission or misstatement would affect the economic decisions taken by users of financial statements. If too much detail is provided in financial statements the ability to reveal a true and fair view might well be impaired. On the other hand if too little information is given then this would create difficulties. Materiality requires a judgement to be exercised on striking the appropriate balance. Materiality can only be considered in relation to context. In a small business a transaction of £100 might be material whereas in a large company £1 million might not be material. Those responsible for preparing accounts have to make a professional judgement on which items and amounts are likely to influence the decisions of users of accounting information.

Summary

The accounting concepts outlined above do not ensure uniformity in the preparation of accounts. There are still a wide range of generally accepted valuation and measurement bases that companies might choose to use and the concepts of accounting do not eliminate or restrict such a choice. Accounting concepts are simply the main assumptions underpinning accounts preparation and it is important to the understanding and interpretation of financial statements that users are aware of these assumptions. The concepts tend to emphasize the reliability of information rather than usefulness and many would argue that reliability should be the overriding characteristic of financial accounting. However, because the concepts are not rigid rules they are capable of evolving and changing to reflect changes in the requirements and needs of the day.

Format

There are two related considerations in respect of the format of published accounts and reports: the actual format of the accounts themselves (i.e. their content and structure as ordained by law or best practice) and the format of the document in which they are published (i.e. its characteristics and usual form). In broad terms, the first of these considerations applies to virtually all companies, while the second varies markedly from company to company.

Content and structure of financial statements

In accordance with the Companies Act 1985, balance sheets and profit and loss accounts must be presented in conformity with one of the prescribed formats. Two alternative formats are permitted for the balance sheet, allowing either a horizontal or a vertical presentation of specific minimum levels of information. Four alternative formats are permitted for the profit and loss account, allowing for either a horizontal or a vertical presentation and for either an 'operational' or an 'expenditure' basis of calculation. These alternative formats are described and discussed more fully in Chapters 2 and 3, and pro forma examples are presented in illustration.

Once a particular format has been selected, it should be adopted consistently in subsequent periods unless there are special reasons for not doing so. In each case, comparative figures for preceding periods must be in a compatible format.

For any given format, the order in which the items are listed, and the headings and subheadings describing them, are strictly delineated. Subject to those statutory requirements, items may be shown in greater detail than is laid down, new headings may be introduced, items may be combined where they are not individually material, certain items may be shown in the notes rather than on the face of the accounts and arrangements and headings may be adapted where the special nature of a company's business requires it.

The discussion in the following chapters draws on the published report and accounts of The BOC Group plc for the year to 30 September 2002. The full text of the company's financial review is reproduced in Appendix A and many examples from its reports and accounts appear throughout the book.

Published reports and accounts

Leaving aside the statutory definition of the 'publication' of company accounts (which covers the delivery of certified copies of the financial statements and auditor's report to the Registrar of Companies and the transmission of copies to the shareholders of limited companies), the conventional view of a company annual report and set of accounts is a glossy booklet, generally of A4 size, illustrated with photographs of the company's directors and some of its activities, containing a chairman's statement and other promotional or publicity material and supplemented by a closely printed section carrying complex and detailed financial data.

The annual report and accounts offers a unique opportunity of providing not only the statutory legal and financial information and notices but also important corporate reports, statements and background information. Against that has to be weighed the very considerable costs of designing, printing, producing and distributing each annual report to very large numbers of shareholders.

For the majority of companies, the annual report and accounts document is little more than the bare provision of statutory information and a brief statement from the chairman or the directors. For the 2,000 or so companies listed on the Stock Exchange, the yearly document is generally more informative.

Faced with the ever-increasing costs of reproducing and then mailing the very many items of information now required to be included in company accounts and reports it has often been argued that companies should be permitted to send a simplified version to shareholders. The Companies Act 1985 made provision for regulations to be made which would permit companies to send summarized financial statements to shareholders. Such regulations now exist (The Companies [Summary Financial Statement] Regulations 1990), and companies are now permitted to send summarized financial statements, the form and content of which are specified in the regulations, to their shareholders, but with the full version of the annual report and accounts being available to those shareholders who request it.

Equally, simplified or extracted financial statements are often made available to employees and their representatives. In most cases, those employee reports consist of highlighted paragraphs or inserted pages in the normal employee newspaper or bulletin. In some instances, employee reports are prepared specifically and issued separately.

Both these areas of reporting, to shareholders and to employees, are crucially important. Of their nature, both those sets of readers are relatively unsophisticated in the interpretation and manipulation of accounting and financial data, and might therefore prefer to receive a simplified set of accounts. However, it is clear that the safeguards embodied in various statutes and professional recommendations cannot lightly be abandoned in the pursuit of 'readability' or 'relevance' and full, detailed and wide-ranging statements must continue to be available.

Conclusion

As W. T. Baxter has said (Lee 1981), the original purpose of company reports is still fundamental and

> even if reports help decision making in only an indirect way, we have no cause to feel apologetic about them. They are important. Their original task . . . was to provide evidence that the accounting records have been kept properly, and to show what has happened to the owners' wealth. This they still do. They are the culmination of complex and exacting work. Much of it may have become routine, yet it is essential for business survival.

What accounting reports and financial statements give, then, are items of background information. They provide a framework against which may be judged the stewardship of a company's directors and managers and the viability and health of the company.

Appendix

The development of principles has been addressed by the ASB in its *Statement of Principles for Financial Reporting* (Accounting Standards Board) which consists of the following eight chapters:

1 *The objective of financial statements.* This is defined as the provision of information about the reporting entity's financial performance and position that is useful to a wide range of users for assessing the stewardship of the entity's management and for making economic decisions. The Statement of Principles goes on to note that this objective can usually be met by focusing exclusively on the information needs of present and potential investors and that investors need information to enable the evaluation of an entity's cash generating ability and financial adaptability.

2 *The reporting entity.* This chapter sets out two principles: firstly that an entity should prepare and publish financial statements if there is a legitimate demand for the information and it is a cohesive economic unit; and secondly that the boundary of a reporting entity is determined by the scope of its control. Control can be achieved by the direct control of assets (e.g. as a result of direct ownership) or indirectly through the control of another entity that has direct control of the assets.

3 *The qualitative characteristics of financial information.* The information provided by financial statements has to be *relevant* and *reliable*. Information is *relevant* if it has the ability to influence the economic decisions of users because of its predictive or confirmatory value. It has predictive value if it helps in the evaluation of past, present or future events. Information has confirmatory value if it helps in the confirmation or correction of past evaluations. *Reliable* information can be depended on by users to represent faithfully what it purports to represent, is free from deliberate or systematic bias and material error, is complete and reflects the need for a degree of caution to be exercised when making judgements and estimates under conditions of uncertainty. Information in financial statements also needs to be comparable and understandable. *Comparability* points to the need for the consistent use of accounting methods through time and adequate disclosure of accounting policies. *Understandability* requires the clear classification and presentation of information. There is an assumption that users of financial information have a reasonable knowledge of business and economic activities and accounting and a willingness to study with reasonable diligence the information provided. A further characteristic is that of *materiality*. Information whose omission or misstatement could influence the economic decisions of users is material. *Materiality* is therefore a threshold quality that is required of all information. If information is not material then the other characteristics do not have to be considered.

4 *The elements of financial statements.* The following seven elements are defined: *assets* – these are 'rights or other access to future economic benefits controlled by an entity as a result of past transactions or events'; *liabilities* – 'obligations of an entity to transfer economic benefits as a result of past transactions or events'; *ownership interest* – 'the residual amount found by deducting all of the entity's liabilities from all of the entity's assets'; *gains* – 'increases in ownership interest not resulting from contributions from owners'; *losses* – 'decreases in ownership interest not resulting from distributions to owners'; *contributions from owners* – 'increases in ownership interest resulting from transfers from owners in their capacity as owners'; *distribution to owners* – 'decreases in ownership interest resulting from transfers to owners in their capacity as owners'.

5 *Recognition in financial statements.* Assets and liabilities are to be included in financial statements if there is sufficient evidence that rights or access to future economic benefits or obligations to transfer economic benefits have occurred and a monetary amount can be established with sufficient reliability. If there is sufficient evidence that the amount of an asset or liability has subsequently changed and the new amount can be measured with sufficient reliability then the asset or liability should be recorded at the changed amount. If there is sufficient evidence that the asset or liability has either been eliminated or the monetary amount can no longer be measured with sufficient reliability then the asset or liability should cease to be recognized in the financial statements.

6 *Measurement in financial statements.* This chapter sets out the measurement bases that could be used in financial statements. A single measurement basis could be used for all assets and liabilities using either a *historical cost* basis or a *current value* basis. Alternatively a *mixed measurement* system could be used, with some assets measured on a historical cost basis and some on a current cost basis. This is frequently referred to as *modified historical cost* and the ASB envisages that this is the system that will be used.

7 *Presentation of financial information.* The statement of financial performance, the statement of financial position (the balance sheet) and the cash flow statement are identified as the primary financial statements. The profit and loss account and the statement of total recognized gains and losses are examples of statements of financial performance.

8 *Accounting for interests in other entities.* This chapter contains a discussion of the issues surrounding accounting for business combinations and consolidated financial statements.

Part One

Published financial statements

2 The profit and loss account

In essence the profit and loss account (often known as the income statement) summarizes the results of the company's activities during the financial period under review. It reports sales or turnover, operating expenses, exceptional items, interest payments, taxation charges and dividends paid and proposed. It has a particular attraction for most users of accounts, in that it reports a 'bottom line' figure – the proflt or loss for the financial year – which can be used as a shorthand performance measure.

This chapter examines the alternative formats for the profit and loss account that are permitted by the 1985 Act, as amended, and describes and discusses the various items to be included on the face of the accounts or in the notes thereto. In addition, the provisions and requirements of accounting standards, and in particular the requirements of FRS 3 ('Reporting financial performance'), will be linked with the legal requirements.

Formats

Schedule 4 to the 1985 Act, as amended, sets out the permitted formats for financial statements. These formats were first prescribed by the 1981 Act and, although the use of standardized formats had been common practice in European countries for a number of years, their introduction into the UK was a significant departure from previous practice. There are advantages and disadvantages in standardizing format. On the one hand, it encourages greater consistency of treatment between one financial period and another, and facilitates comparison between the results of one year and another. It also ensures that different companies follow much the same disclosure practices, in terms of the nature of the items and the extent of the information disclosed. On the other hand, the prescription of standard formats removes some of the otherwise welcome flexibility that companies had adopted in presenting their results, allowing them to present their individual accounts in what they considered the most appropriate way. By and large, however, such considerations applied with more force to balance sheets than to profit and loss accounts. On the whole, the introduction of standardized formats and enhanced minimum levels of disclosure is to be welcomed.

Four alternative formats are now permitted for a company's profit and loss account. Tables 2.1–2.4 reproduce the four alternative profit and loss account formats. Formats

Table 2.1   Profit and loss account – format 1

1   Turnover
2   Cost of sales
3   Gross profit or loss
4   Distribution costs
5   Administrative expenses
6   Other operating income
7   Income from shares in group undertakings
8   Income from participating interests[a]
9   Income from other fixed asset investments
10 Other interest receivable and similar income
11 Amounts written off investments
12 Interest payable and similar charges
13 Tax on profit or loss on ordinary activities
14 Profit or loss on ordinary activities after taxation
–   Minority interests[b]
15 Extraordinary income
16 Extraordinary charges
17 Extraordinary profit or loss
18 Tax on extraordinary profit or loss
–   Minority interests[b]
19 Other taxes not shown under the above items
20 Profit or loss for the financial year

Notes: [a]In group accounts, this item is replaced by
                  Interests in associated undertakings
                  Other participating interests
            [b]Group accounts only.

1 and 2 are vertical arrangements, while formats 3 and 4 are double-sided or horizontal arrangements. The essential difference between the alternative formats is in their classification of the presented information. Formats 1 and 3 classify income and operating expenses by function, whereas formats 2 and 4 classify information by type of income and expense.

This essential difference can be shown summarily as follows. Formats 1 and 3 require operating expenses to be separated into:

■ cost of sales;
■ distribution costs;
■ administrative expenses;

leading to the identification of operating profit perhaps more easily than other alternative arrangements. Formats 2 and 4 require operating expenses to be separated into:

■ change in stocks of finished goods and in work in progress;
■ own work capitalized;
■ raw materials and consumables;
■ other external charges;
■ staff costs;
■ depreciation and other amounts written off tangible and intangible fixed assets;
■ exceptional amounts written off current assets;
■ other operating charges.

Table 2.2   Profit and loss account – format 2

---

1   Turnover
2   Change in stocks of finished goods and in work in progress
3   Own work capitalized
4   Other operating income
5   (a) Raw materials and consumables
   (b) Other external charges
6   Staff costs:
   (a) wages and salaries
   (b) social security costs
   (c) other pension costs
7   (a) Depreciation and other amounts written off tangible and intangible fixed assets
   (b) Exceptional amounts written off current assets
8   Other operating charges
9   Income from shares in group undertakings
10 Income from participating interests[a]
11 Income from other fixed asset investments
12 Other interest receivable and similar income
13 Amounts written off investments
14 Interest payable and similar charges
15 Tax on profit or loss on ordinary activities
16 Profit or loss on ordinary activities after taxation
–   Minority interests[b]
17 Extraordinary income
18 Extraordinary charges
19 Extraordinary profit or loss
20 Tax on extraordinary profit or loss
–   Minority interests[b]
21 Other taxes not shown under the above items
22 Profit or loss for the financial year.

Notes: See Table 2.1.

Formats 2 and 4 make the calculation of cost of sales and gross profit less easy than under alternative formats. In the case of many companies, gross profit is a significant performance measure and its calculation under formats 2 and 4 is possible only if substantial further information is provided in respect of such items as depreciation, employment costs and other operating charges.

Companies and their advisers are able to adopt the format that they consider most appropriate, but it is considered that the vertical formats have rather more to commend them than do their horizontal counterparts. The range of permitted formats reflects the differences in the practices followed in different European countries. In the UK most of the larger companies tend to follow format 1.

Before turning to an examination of the various permitted components of the alternative formats, it is necessary to set out the rules by which modification or extension of the permitted formats is allowed. Items to appear in statutory balance sheets and profit and loss accounts are denoted by either letters (A, B, C etc.), Roman numerals (I, II etc.) or arabic numbers (1, 2, 3 etc.). Every balance sheet and profit and loss account must show the items denoted by letters or Roman numerals in the respective formats. As can be seen from Tables 3.1 and 3.2 (in Chapter 3) the standard formats for balance sheets include items that are prefixed by letters, Roman numerals and arabic numerals and items prefixed by the letters and Roman numerals must be

Table 2.3   Profit and loss account – format 3

A	Charges	B	Income
1	Cost of sales	1	Turnover
2	Distribution costs	2	Other operating income
3	Administrative expenses	3	Income from shares in group undertakings
4	Amounts written off investments	4	Income from participating interests[a]
5	Interest payable and similar charges	5	Income from other fixed asset investments
6	Tax on profit or loss on ordinary activities	6	Other interest receivable and similar income
7	Profit or loss on ordinary activities after taxation	7	Profit or loss on ordinary activities after taxation
–	Minority interests[b]	–	Minority interests[b]
8	Extraordinary charges	8	Extraordinary income
		–	Minority interests[b]
9	Tax on extraordinary profit or loss	9	Profit or loss for the financial year
–	Minority interests[b]		
10	Other taxes not shown under the above items		
11	Profit or loss for the financial year		

Notes: See Table 2.1.

shown in the order and under the headings and sub-headings given (unless the amounts are nil for both this financial year and the preceding financial year). However, the profit and loss accounts formats 1 and 2 contain only arabic number items and these can therefore be combined on the face of the accounts if the amounts involved are not material to an assessment of the company's profit or loss for the relevant period, or if such a combination would facilitate that assessment. In the latter circumstances, the individual amounts must be disclosed separately in the notes to the account.

The Act specifically requires only three items to be shown on the face of the profit and loss account:

1 the amount of the company's profit or loss on ordinary activities, before taxation;
2 the amount of any transfers to or withdrawals from the company's reserves, both completed and proposed;
3 the aggregate amount of any dividends paid and proposed.

As all items listed in the prescribed formats are prefixed by arabic numbers, this allows a company's directors to adapt the arrangement and headings of those items in the manner most appropriate to the company's affairs. There is also the flexibility mentioned earlier – that of combining the items on the face of the account.

This flexibility must be used sensibly. It is unlikely that directors would be justified in combining all the items making up profit or loss on ordinary activities before taxation and showing just one amount on the face of the account, with the individual items making up that amount relegated to the notes. In fact greater detail than is prescribed by the permitted formats can be given and new items or headings can be introduced for matters not otherwise covered. A significant development in this respect has been the introduction of FRS 3 ('Reporting financial performance'). FRS 3 has taken advantage of the permitted flexibility to bring about a major reshaping of the profit and loss account. The standard requires all profit and loss items from turnover down to operating profit to be analysed between continuing operations (sub-divided into acquisitions and other) and discontinued operations. As a minimum the analysis in

Table 2.4   Profit and loss account – format 4

A	Charges	B	Income
1	Reduction in stocks of finished goods and in work in progress	1	Turnover
2	(a) Raw materials and consumables	2	Increase in stocks of finished goods and in work in progress
	(b) Other external charges	3	Own work capitalized
3	Staff costs:	4	Other operating income
	(a) wages and salaries	5	Income from shares in group undertakings
	(b) social security costs	6	Income from participating interests[a]
	(c) other pension costs	7	Income from other fixed asset investments
4	(a) Depreciation and other amounts written off tangible and intangible fixed assets	8	Other interest receivable and similar income
	(b) Exceptional amounts written off current assets	9	Profit or loss on ordinary activities after taxation
5	Other operating charges	–	Minority interests[b]
6	Amounts written off investments	10	Extraordinary income[b]
7	Interest payable and similar charges	–	Minority interests[b]
8	Tax on profit or loss on ordinary activities	11	Profit or loss for the financial year
9	Profit or loss on ordinary activities after taxation		
–	Minority interests[b]		
10	Extraordinary charges		
11	Tax on extraordinary profit or loss		
–	Minority interests[b]		
12	Other taxes not shown under the above items		
13	Profit or loss for the financial year		

Notes: See Table 2.1

respect of turnover and operating profit must be reported on the face of the profit and loss account. FRS 3 also requires the disclosure of exceptional items (see page 41). Three specific categories of non-operating exceptional item must be disclosed on the face of the profit and loss account. Other types of exceptional items should appear under the statutory format heading to which they relate and disclosed either on the face of the profit and loss account or by way of note. One consequence of this is that many of the items that would often have been disclosed on the face of the profit and loss account prior to the issue of FRS 3 now appear in the notes so as to make space for the new required format.

The logic behind the distinction between continuing and discontinued operations is that where financial statements are used to assess the likely future performance of a company then the results from those operations that the company no longer owns or runs need to be excluded because it is only the continuing operations that will affect the future. Similarly, if the actual results of a period are to be sensibly compared with forecasts made for that period, then the contributions from any operations acquired during the year need to be eliminated so that like can be compared with like.

The consolidated profit and loss account for The BOC Group plc for the year ended 30 September 2002 (see Table 2.5) provides an example of the disclosure requirements of FRS 3. As can be seen the Companies Act format 1 has been followed, but not all of the items denoted by arabic numbers have been included. The information required by FRS 3 on continuing and discontinued operations and on exceptional items has been

Table 2.5   The BOC Group plc – consolidated profit and loss account for the year ended 30 September 2002

	Notes	2002 Before exceptional items (£ million)	Exceptional items (£ million)	After exceptional items (£ million)	2001 (restated) Before exceptional items (£ million)	Exceptional items (£ million)	After exceptional items (£ million)
Turnover							
Continuing operations		3,890.8	—	3,890.8	4,159.2	—	4,159.2
Acquisitions		127.1	—	127.1	—		—
Turnover, including share of joint ventures and associates	1	4,017.9	—	4,017.9	4,159.2	—	4,159.2
Less: Share of turnover of joint ventures		324.1	—	324.1	340.0	—	340.0
Share of turnover of associates		36.1	—	36.1	46.3	—	46.3
Turnover of subsidiary undertakings		3,657.7	—	3,657.7	3,772.9	—	3,772.9
Cost of sales	2(a)	(2,089.7)	(15.1)	(2,104.8)	(2,164.2)	(44.6)	(2,208.8)
Gross profit		1,568.0	(15.1)	1,552.9	1,608.7	(44.6)	1,564.1
Net operating expenses	2(a)	(1,142.4)	(58.9)	(1,201.3)	(1,150.3)	(61.1)	(1,211.4)
Operating profit							
Continuing operations		421.2	(67.8)	353.4	458.4	(105.7)	352.7
Acquisitions		4.4	(6.2)	(1.8)	—	—	—
Operating profit of subsidiary undertakings		425.6	(74.0)	351.6	458.4	(105.7)	352.7
Share of operating profit of joint ventures		63.8	(0.5)	63.3	59.0	(2.2)	56.8
Share of operating profit of associates		10.7	—	10.7	13.2	(0.4)	12.8
Total operating profit including share of joint ventures and associates	1	500.1	(74.5)	425.6	530.6	(108.3)	422.3
Loss on termination/disposal of businesses – continuing operations	2(b)	—	(20.2)	(20.2)	—		
Profit on disposal of fixed assets – continuing operations	2(b)	—	—	—	—	3.6	3.6
Profit on ordinary activities before interest		500.1	(94.7)	405.4	530.6	(104.7)	425.9
Interest on net debt	3(a)			(103.1)			(123.4)
Interest on pension scheme liabilities	6(e)			(106.1)			(107.2)
Expected return on pension scheme assets	6(e)			139.1			166.9
Net interest				(70.1)			(63.7)
Profit on ordinary activities before tax				335.3			362.2
Tax on profit on ordinary activities	4(a)			(106.2)			(104.6)
Profit on ordinary activities after tax				229.1			257.6
Minority interests – equity				(26.2)			(33.5)
Profit for the financial year				202.9			224.1
Dividends	12(a)			(186.6)			(180.3)
Retained profit for the financial year				16.3			43.8
Earnings per 25p	2(d)						
Ordinary share, basic							
– on published earnings				41.36p			46.03p
– on exceptional items				14.58p			11.48p
– before exceptional items				55.94p			57.51p
Earnings per 25p	2(d)						
Ordinary share, diluted							
– on published earnings				41.21p			45.87p
– on exceptional items				14.53p			11.44p
– before exceptional items				55.74p			57.31p

All turnover and operating profit arose from continuing operations.

provided. Also, presumably because the amounts of exceptional items relating to the ordinary activities of cost of sales and operating expenses are very large in both 1999 and 1998, BOC have chosen to disclose these separately on the face of the profit and loss account rather than by way of note as in previous years. This extracted account will form the basis for the following discussion of the usual profit and loss account components.

Contents

The following sections describe and discuss the various items to be included either on the face of the profit and loss account or in the notes thereto. Reference is made to three complementary sets of requirements: the statutory requirements contained in the Companies Acts; the professional requirements contained in accounting standards and accountancy bodies' recommendations; the supervisory requirements imposed on public listed companies by the Council of the Stock Exchange.

Turnover

All formats given in the fourth schedule to the 1985 Act, as amended, require the disclosure of turnover. In the case of consolidated financial statements, turnover should exclude intra-group transactions.

FRS 3 requires turnover to be analysed between continuing operations, acquisitions and discontinued operations, with acquisitions being presented as a component of continuing operations. Discontinued operations are defined as operations of the reporting entity that are sold or terminated either in the reporting period or before the earlier of three months after the commencement of the subsequent period and the date on which the financial statements are approved. Terminated operations must have ceased permanently to be treated as discontinued. Also sales or terminations must be material and any assets, liabilities, results of operations and activities must be clearly distinguishable, physically, operationally and for financial reporting purposes, if they are to be categorized as discontinued.

Acquisitions are defined in the FRS as operations of the reporting entity that are acquired in the period. In effect this means operations that are purchased rather than operations that a company builds up itself. Thus, for example, if a company decides to move into a new product line by purchasing another entity this would be an acquisition, whereas building up the new product line by itself would not. The BOC Group's disclosure of its turnover for 2002, with comparative information for 2001, is provided in the consolidated profit and loss account as shown in Table 2.5. The note at the foot of the consolidated profit and loss account states that all turnover and operating profit arose from continuing operations (including acquisitions) and therefore BOC does not report any turnover from discontinued operations.

In addition, the Companies Act 1985 requires turnover to be reported (by way of a note to the accounts) in respect of each substantially different class of business carried on by the company and each geographical area in which the company operates. If a class of business or geographical segment is significant to the company as a whole its turnover should be reported. SSAP 25 ('Segmental reporting') states that a segment will normally be regarded as significant if its turnover to third parties is 10 per cent or more of total turnover to third parties. SSAP 25 also requires geographical segmental disclosure to distinguish between turnover by origin (i.e. the geographical area from which products or services are supplied) and turnover by destination (i.e. the geographical area to which goods or services are supplied).

The reasons for requiring companies to disclose segmental information of this nature is that users of financial statements are able to assess the contribution of each segment to overall turnover, and can then employ judgements about the relative risk and growth potential of each segment. BOC provides information on turnover by class of business and by geographical area and also by country of origin and country of destination in note 1 to its accounts (see Appendix A). The analysis of BOC's 2002 turnover is as follows:

	Process Gas Solutions	*Industrial and special products*	*BOC Edwards*	*Afrox hospitals*	*Gist*	*Total Group by origin*	*Total Group by destination*
	(£ million)	*(£ million)*	*(£ million)*	*(£ million)*	*(£ million)*	*(£ million)*	*(£ million)*
Europe	257.1	399.3	150.0	—	263.2	1,069.6	1,055.3
Americas	528.1	464.8	298.9	—	—	1,291.8	1,240.1
Africa	23.6	158.4	—	259.0	—	441.0	443.3
Asia/Pacific	391.8	582.8	239.3	—	1.6	1,215.5	1,279.2
	1,200.6	1,605.3	688.2	259.0	264.8	4,017.9	4,017.9

Cost of sales

Formats 1 and 3 of the Companies Act require the disclosure of cost of sales as a separate item. It was pointed out earlier that, following the introduction of FRS 3, all items from turnover down to operating profit must be analysed between continuing operations, acquisitions and discontinued operations. The analysis for cost of sales is shown in note 2 to the profit and loss account (see Appendix A, pages 240–1). Cost of sales will normally include all direct elements of the cost of ordinary activities, and will typically include:

■ opening stocks and work in progress;
■ direct materials;
■ other external charges;
■ direct labour;
■ fixed and variable production overheads;
■ depreciation or diminution in value of productive assets;
■ research and development costs;

and adjustments will be made for closing stocks and work in progress.

In a retail business the most important element of the total cost of sales figure will probably be the cost of direct materials purchased for resale. In a manufacturing organization, where raw materials are turned into finished goods, the expenditure on manufacturing wages and the depreciation of manufacturing equipment will also be significant elements. Although it is not the intention of this book to explain the techniques and rules of accounting, it is useful at this stage to provide a brief illustration of how the permitted variety in accounting measurement method might affect the calculation of the cost of direct materials and the charge for depreciation.

Direct materials

When materials are purchased, either for resale or as raw material input to a manufacturing process, they become an asset known as stock. This stock will eventually be sold and then replaced by a further purchase of materials which will in turn be sold, and so on throughout the accounting period. At the end of the accounting period it will then be necessary to determine the cost of direct materials sold. This is usually calculated as the cost of stock at the beginning of the period, plus the purchases made during the period, less the cost of stock held at the end of the period. Because stock is constantly being depleted and then replaced, it is often impossible to identify particular items of stock as belonging to a specific batch purchased, and there is usually no attempt to do so. Where the cost of materials purchased does not change throughout the accounting period, then this practice presents few problems. However, where price changes do occur, and it is not possible to identify which items in stock were bought at which price, then the only way in which a value can be placed on closing stock is by making an assumption about the pattern of stock flows into and out of the business. The three most widely recognized methods of accounting for stock are FIFO (first in first out), LIFO (last in first out) and weighted average.

FIFO assumes that the items carried at the oldest prices will be the first to be sold. LIFO assumes that the items acquired at the most recent prices will be the first to be sold. Weighted average calculates the cost of each stock item sold as the average of all items of that type held in stock at the time of sale. The following simple example illustrates the use of each of these three methods.

Example 2.1

The Plastic Products company started business on 1 January 20X1. It purchases one particular type of plastic valve which it shapes and polishes and then sells. The purchases and sales that took place during the year were as shown in Table 2.6. The cost of direct materials sold under each of three alternative methods would be calculated as shown in Tables 2.7–2.9. Under all three methods there is a different closing stock figure. Every time issues are made under the FIFO system, the earliest prices are used up first. For example, on 31 March 3,000 units were issued. Of these,

Table 2.6 Purchases and sales for the Plastic Products company

Date	Purchases		Sales	
	Units	Price per unit (£)	Units	Price per unit (£)
1 January	3,000	12		
31 January			2,000	21
1 March	4,000	13		
31 March			3,000	22
1 July	4,000	14		
31 July			5,000	23
1 November	5,000	15		
30 November			3,000	25

Table 2.7   FIFO method of accounting for stock

Date	Received	Issued		Value (£)
1/1	3,000 @ £12			
31/1		2,000	@ £12	24,000
1/3	4,000 @ £13			
			1,000 @ £12	
31/3		3,000		38,000
			2,000 @ £13	
1/7	4,000 @ £14			
			2,000 @ £13	
31/7		5,000		68,000
			3,000 @ £14	
1/11	5,000 @ £15			
			1,000 @ £14	
30/11		3,000		44,000
			2,000 @ £15	
31/12	Cost of sales			£174,000
31/12	Closing stock	3,000	@ £15	£45,000

Table 2.8   LIFO method of accounting for stock

Date	Received	Issued		Value (£)
1/1	3,000 @ £12			
31/1		2,000	@ £12	24,000
1/3	4,000 @ £13			
31/3		3,000	@ £13	39,000
1/7	4,000 @ £14			
			1,000 @ £13	
31/7		5,000		69,000
			4,000 @ £14	
1/11	5,000 @ £15			
30/11		3,000	@ £15	45,000
31/12	Cost of sales			£177,000
			1,000 @ £12	
31/12	Closing stock			£42,000
			2,000 @ £15	

1,000 are assumed to be the units remaining in stock after the 31 January issue and are therefore priced at £12 per unit. This is the earliest price available. The balance of 2,000 units are assumed to come from the units received on 1 March priced at £13, i.e. the next earliest price available. At 31 December there are 3,000 units remaining in stock and these are assumed to be from the 5,000 purchased on 1 November at £15 each.

Under the LIFO system, issues are made first from the most recent prices available. Thus, for example, the issue of 5,000 units on 31 July is priced on the assumption that

Table 2.9 Weighted-average method of accounting for stock

Date		Units	Cost (£)	Average cost per unit (£)	Value (£)	Cost of sales (£)
1/1	Received	3,000	12	12	36,000	
31/1	Issued	2,000		12	24,000	24,000
	Balance	1,000		12	12,000	
1/3	Received	4,000	13		52,000	
	Balance	5,000		12.8[a]	64,000	
31/3	Issued	3,000		12.8	38,400	38,400
	Balance	2,000		12.8	25,600	
1/7	Received	4,000	14		56,000	
	Balance	6,000		13.6[b]	81,600	
31/7	Issued	5,000		13.6	68,000	68,000
	Balance	1,000		13.6	13,600	
1/11	Received	5,000	15		75,000	
	Balance	6,000		14.77[c]	88,600	
30/11	Issued	3,000		14.77	44,310	44,310
1/12	Balance	3,000		14.77	44,290	
31/12	Cost of sales					174,710

Notes: [a]Weighted average = 64,000/5,000 = £12.8.
 [b]Weighted average = 81,600/6,000 = £13.6.
 [c]Weighted average = 88,600/6,000 = £14.77.

4,000 of them were the units received on 1 July at £14: this is the latest price available. The balance of 1,000 were the units remaining unsold after the issue on 31 March; these had cost £13 each. The closing stock of 3,000 units is therefore made up of the 2,000 remaining out of the 5,000 received on 1 November at £15 each, and for the balance of 1,000 units it is necessary to go right back to the 1 January purchases at £12 per unit to find the most recent price still available.

Under the weighted-average approach, a new price is calculated every time new stock is received. For example, after the 31 January issue there are 1,000 units in stock at £12 each. Then on 1 March, 4,000 more units are received at a cost of £13 each. The new weighted-average price at 1 March is therefore calculated as $(1{,}000 \times £12 + 4{,}000 \times £13)/5{,}000 = £12.8$. The closing stock at 31 December is simply the weighted average of £14.77 per unit that was calculated after the 1 November receipt of 5,000 units, multiplied by the 3,000 units remaining in stock.

This example shows that when the three different approaches are applied to an identical set of data it is possible to obtain three different figures for closing stock and therefore three different figures for the cost of materials sold. The Companies Act permits the use of any of the above methods, but the appendix to SSAP 9 ('Stocks and long-term contracts') points out that LIFO is unlikely to provide a sufficiently close approximation to actual cost to be permissible. It can be seen from this example that, at times of rising prices, LIFO will result in a higher cost of sales and therefore a lower reported profit figure.

The use of FIFO produces the opposite effect, and this perhaps explains why FIFO is permitted as a basis for calculating taxable profit, whereas LIFO is not. Although weighted average appears to offer a useful compromise, it does require more calculations to be made, because a new weighted-average figure is required each time new stock is received.

Depreciation

Fixed assets, such as buildings, plant and machinery, vehicles etc., are usually expected to be used by a business for several years, and yet it has to be recognized that they will eventually wear out or become obsolete. Some method of spreading the cost of such assets over their useful economic life is therefore needed, and this is what depreciation is intended to do. The four profit and loss account formats require the disclosure of depreciation provisions, either in a note to the financial statements (under formats 1 and 3) or on the face of the account (under formats 2 and 4). FRS 15 ('Tangible fixed assets') is consistent with the requirements of the 1985 Act and states that the cost or revalued amount of fixed assets, less any estimated residual value, should be charged to the profit and loss account on a systematic basis that reflects as fairly as possible the pattern in which the asset's economic benefits are consumed over its 'useful economic life'. (The useful economic life of an asset is defined as the period over which the present owner expects to derive economic benefit from the asset).

The assessment of depreciation calls for the estimation of at least three factors:

1 the cost or valuation of the asset;
2 the probable realizable value on disposal at the end of the asset's working life (the residual value) in the business of the company;
3 the expected length of the asset's working life (or useful economic life) to the business of the company.

Thus, even before different measurement methods are considered, any calculation of depreciation demands a considerable amount of judgement, particularly in respect of the likely residual value and the estimated working life. There are then several methods that might be used to determine a depreciation charge for each accounting period. Two of the most widely used of these are the *straight-line* method and the *reducing-balance* method. The straight-line method assumes that an asset will be used up evenly throughout its useful life and therefore allocates a uniform amount of depreciation to each accounting period. The reducing-balance method assumes that the loss in value is heaviest in the early years of an asset's life and therefore allocates a high proportion of the depreciation expense to those years. Example 2.2 illustrates the use of both these methods.

Example 2.2

Suppose that the Plastic Products company of Example 2.1 also purchased special shaping and polishing equipment on 1 January 20X1. The equipment cost £30,000 and it was estimated that it would last for five years, with an expected trade-in value after that time of approximately £5,000.

Straight-line method   The annual charge is calculated as

$$\frac{\text{Cost} - \text{Residual value}}{\text{Number of years' life}}$$

Therefore,

$$\text{Annual charge} = \frac{£30,000 - £5,000}{5} = £5,000$$

The depreciation charge would therefore be £5,000 for each of the five years' life.

Reducing-balance method   What is required here is a percentage rate which, when applied to the balance at the end of each period, will reduce the book value of the equipment to approximately £5,000. This rate can be found by trial and error, or from the following formula:

$$\text{Percentage rate} = 1 - \sqrt[n]{\left(\frac{\text{Salvage value}}{\text{Cost}}\right)}$$

where n is the number of years of expected useful life. Applying this formula to the data from the Plastic Products company gives

$$\text{Percentage rate} = 1 - \sqrt[5]{\left(\frac{5,000}{30,000}\right)} = \text{approximately 30 per cent}$$

The annual depreciation charge for each of the five years is then as shown in Table 2.10.

At the end of the five-year period the net book value of the equipment will be more or less the same under both methods (i.e. £5,000 with the straight-line method and £5,042 with the reducing-balance method) but the pattern of annual charges for each of the five years will be quite different.

If the different cost-of-materials-sold figures obtained in Example 2.1 and the different depreciation charges calculated in Example 2.2 are considered together, then the impact these differences have on gross profit can be determined, and this is illustrated in Example 2.3 below. For the purpose of this example, the sales revenue for the year 20X1 has been calculated from the data given in Example 2.1 to be £298,000 (2,000 × £21 + 3,000 × £22 + 5,000 × £23 + 3,000 × £25), and it has also been assumed that the other cost of sales expenses on such items as 'direct labour' and 'other external charges' amounted to £50,000 for the year to 31 December 20X1.

Table 2.10   Annual depreciation charges for the Plastic Products company

Year	Book value at beginning of year (£)		Percentage rate		Annual depreciation charge (£)	Book value at end of year (£)
20X1	30,000	×	30%	=	9,000	21,000
20X2	21,000	×	30%	=	6,300	14,700
20X3	14,700	×	30%	=	4,410	10,290
20X4	10,290	×	30%	=	3,087	7,203
20X5	7,203	×	30%	=	2,161	5,042

Table 2.11   Gross profit of the Plastic Products company

Accounting method	Turnover (£)	Cost of direct materials (£)	Depreciation (£)	Other expenses (£)	Gross profit (£)
FIFO/straight line	298,000	174,000	5,000	50,000	69,000
LIFO/straight line	298,000	177,000	5,000	50,000	66,000
Weighted average/ straight line	298,000	174,710	5,000	50,000	68,290
FIFO/reducing balance	298,000	174,000	9,000	50,000	65,000
LIFO/reducing balance	298,000	177,000	9,000	50,000	62,000
Weighted average/ reducing balance	298,000	174,710	9,000	50,000	64,290

Example 2.3

The gross profit of Plastic Products for the year to 31 December 20X1 is given in Table 2.11. As can be seen from this table, by applying just three different accounting methods for stock valuation and two different methods for depreciation to the same basic set of data, it is possible to obtain six different gross profit figures. All of these figures could be justified as being the appropriate one to report for Plastic Products, because they are all based on permitted methods of accounting measurement. However, there are methods of calculating depreciation in addition to the two illustrated here, and there are many other areas where a choice of measurement method is permitted, so the accounting process could derive many different profit figures from a single set of data, and all of these could be thought of as 'correct'. The facility to choose from a range of permitted measurement methods is both a strength and a weakness of financial reporting. It is argued that without some degree of flexibility it would be difficult to select the methods that are most likely to reflect a true and fair view. On the other hand, such flexibility can lead to difficulties in interpreting accounting information and in obtaining an accurate picture of a company's financial performance. It can also lead to difficulties when comparing one company with another, and an essential part of any examination of company accounts is the careful scrutiny of information disclosed concerning the accounting policies used by a company.

Distribution costs

Distribution costs are required to be shown separately and to be analysed between continuing operations, acquisitions and discontinued operations (if any). As BOC did not have any discontinued operations in 2002 an analysis of its distribution costs between continuing operations and acquisitions, and also exceptional items, is provided in note 2(a)(ii). Broadly, such costs include all costs of holding goods for sale, promotional, advertising and selling costs and costs of transferring goods to customers. The following elements of cost will be included:

■ sales salaries, commissions and bonuses and related employment costs (including social security and pension costs);

■ advertising and promotion costs;
■ warehousing costs;
■ transportation costs (including depreciation on vehicles);
■ sales outlet costs (including depreciation and maintenance costs);
■ sales discounts.

Administrative expenses

Similarly required to be disclosed separately and analysed in accordance with FRS 3, administrative expenses include operational costs other than those associated with the production and distribution of goods and services (which are required to be shown separately, as mentioned earlier). Typically, administrative expenses will include the following:

■ administrative staff salaries, bonuses, etc. and related employment costs (including social security and pensions costs), also included are directors' executive salaries and related employment costs;
■ administration buildings costs (including depreciation and maintenance);
■ professional fees;
■ amounts written off in respect of bad debts.

Note 2(a)(ii) to the BOC financial statements shows that administrative expenses, which are analysed between continuing operations, acquisitions and exceptional items, totalled £861.4 million, but only a small number of the individual expense items making up that total are separately identifiable. Thus, for example, directors' remuneration, which includes salaries, bonuses, pension contributions and provision for share incentive schemes, is disclosed in the report of the management resources committee (see pages 220–7) and totals £6.426 million. Similarly, that part of professional fees that relates to the fees paid to auditors has to be disclosed separately, distinguishing between fees for audit work and fees for non-audit work. Note 2(c) to the accounts (page 242) reveals that the fees paid to auditors were as follows:

	(£ million)	*(£ million)*
Audit fees		1.0
Non-audit fees:		
tax advice and compliance	2.5	
expatriate tax administration	1.4	
acquisition related work	0.8	
other advice	0.4	
Total non-audit fees		5.1
Total fees paid to auditors		7.0

However, most of the items of expenditure that make up the total of administrative expenses (and also the total of cost of sales and the total of distribution costs) are only reported as aggregated expenditure items. For example, BOC reports its employee costs as follows (note 6(c) page 252).

	(£ million)
Wages and salaries	813.9
Social security costs	77.7
Other pension costs	66.3
	957.9

Part of this total of £957.9 million will relate to cost of sales, part to distribution costs, part to administrative expenses and part to research and development but an analysis along these lines is not provided. Similarly, depreciation expenses (see note 8(a), page 261) are analysed by class of fixed asset but not by the category of expenditure to which they relate.

Research and development

Many companies are active in researching, designing and developing new products and SSAP 13 ('Accounting for research and development') requires public companies to disclose the total amount of research and development expenditure charged to the profit and loss account. A footnote to note 2(a)(i) to the BOC Group's 2002 accounts reports that the total for administrative expenses includes research and development expenditure for the year of £47.0 million.

Other operating income

Other operating income is required to be disclosed separately under all four formats. Included in this category are all other income sources associated with a company's ordinary activities – with the exception of interest receivable and investment income, which are required to be disclosed separately. However, if income from investments or interest receivable is not material, it is permissible for it to be included under this heading. Examples of such other operating income might be:

- rental income from surplus premises or facilities;
- sales income from canteen or recreational facilities.

For most companies, such income is unlikely to be significant, and BOC do not report any income under this heading.

Income from shares in group companies

Companies can and frequently do hold shares in other companies. If this results in one company having effective control over the activities of one or more other companies, then a group relationship exists. The company that exercises control is known as a parent company, with the companies over which control is exercised being known as subsidiaries. A key requirement for determining whether a group exists or not is therefore that of control, and there are two quite distinctly different approaches to this question. The first is the 'legal control' approach, which defines control as being the ownership of more than 50 per cent of the voting rights of a company. The second approach places more emphasis on the 'economic reality' of the relationship between one company and another. Thus if one company has the power to exert a 'dominant influence' over another company and exercises that power, even though it owns less than 50 per cent of the voting rights, then there is effective control. A 'dominant influence' is defined in FRS 2 ('Accounting for subsidiary undertakings') as 'influence that can be exercised to achieve the operating and financial policies desired by the holder of the influence, notwithstanding the rights or influence of any other party'.

The Companies Act 1989 recognizes both of these approaches to determining whether control exists. The right to exercise a dominant influence, either through the existence of written control contracts or through provisions in the subsidiary's memorandum of association, creates a parent–subsidiary relationship. Similarly, if an investing company has a 'participating interest' in another company and actually exercises a dominant influence over the investee company or if the two companies are managed on a unified basis, then a parent–subsidiary relationship exists. A participating interest occurs where a company invests in the shares of another company with the intention of exercising influence or control as a result of that investment. A holding of 20 per cent or more of the shares of another company can be presumed to be a participating interest.

Where a group relationship exists, then group accounts must be prepared. In other words, the group has to be accounted for as though it were a single economic entity. A group relationship is nowadays very common and the annual reports of a large number of companies are group accounts. The 1989 Companies Act provides that group accounts will normally consist of a single set of consolidated accounts. Consolidation is simply a process of aggregation whereby the financial statements of the holding company and all of the subsidiary companies of a group are combined into a single set of financial statements. This means that corresponding items of assets, liabilities, revenues and expenses are added together on a line by line basis so as to show the *total* amounts that are under the control of the group as a separate legal entity. If any of these items are in fact not 100 per cent owned by the group, then the amounts not owned are reported separately as minority interest.

Because the consolidated profit and loss account of a group of companies will show the total turnover, the total expenses and the total profit or loss of the group (after eliminating any intra-group transactions), then there will be no need to report separately the 'income from shares in group undertakings'. In fact the only time this item would appear in *group* accounts would be on the relatively rare occasions when subsidiaries had not been consolidated. This item would appear in the separate profit and loss account of the parent company, but it is rare for this to be published in addition to a consolidated profit and loss account. This is because the Companies Act permits its omission provided the consolidated profit and loss account reveals certain minimum information about the profit that is dealt with in the separate accounts of the parent company.

Income from interests in associates and joint ventures

The requirement for investments in subsidiaries to be consolidated into group accounts arises because of the very close relationship between parent and subsidiary companies. There are two other types of investment, which, although not satisfying the criteria for a parent–subsidiary relationship, do require special accounting treatment because of the closeness of the involvement. These are associates and joint ventures.

Associates

Income from interests in associated undertakings is required to be shown separately in group accounts under all four formats. The Companies Act, 1985 defines an associated undertaking as one in which an investing company has a 'participating interest' and over which the investing company has a 'significant influence'. The Act states that where a company holds 20 per cent or more of the voting shares of an entity it can be presumed to have a participating interest and exercise a significant influence unless the contrary is shown. FRS 9 ('Associates and joint ventures'), which introduces the term 'associates' rather than 'associated undertakings', follows the Companies Act requirement for a participating interest to be held and a significant influence to be exercised but moves away from the '20 per cent or more' rule for determining their existence. A participating interest is defined as one in which the investor has a *long-term* interest for the purpose of securing a contribution to the investor's activities. A significant influence arises when the investor is *actively involved and influential* in the direction of its investee. In other words, even though an investing company may own 20 per cent or more of the shares of an entity this will not result in the entity being regarded as an associate unless the holding is long-term and brings about active and beneficial involvement in the direction of the entity.

The exercise of a significant influence over associates does not presume a parent–subsidiary relationship (as was pointed out above, this would require a dominant influence to be exercised). The accounts of the investee company are therefore not consolidated with the accounts of the investor company but are included under the 'equity' method of accounting. FRS 9 defines the equity method as:

> A method of accounting that brings an investment into its investor's financial statements initially at its cost, identifying any goodwill arising. The carrying amount of the investment is adjusted in each period by the investor's share of the results of the investee less any amortisation or write-off for goodwill, the investor's share of any relevant gains or losses, and any other changes in the investee's net assets including distribution to its owners, for example by dividend. The investor's share of its investee's results is recognized in its profit and loss account. The investor's cash flow statement includes the cash flow between the investor and its investee, for example relating to dividends and loans.

Equity accounting therefore differs from normal consolidation by requiring disclosure of only the group's *share* of profits etc. of the associates. Under normal consolidation it is the *total* amount of the subsidiaries turnover profit, assets etc. that is included in the consolidated accounts, with the interests of minority shareholders shown as a separate item.

Joint ventures

As well as investing in associates, companies may choose to enter into a relationship with one or more other companies whereby they jointly control an entity. This gives rise to a joint venture. FRS 9 defines a joint venture as an entity in which the reporting company holds an interest on a long-term basis and which is jointly controlled by the reporting company and one or more other venturers under a contractual arrangement. Under a joint venture the venturers exercise their joint control for their mutual benefit, with each venturer playing an active role in setting the operating and financial policies of the joint venture.

Joint ventures are required to be accounted for under the 'gross equity' method. The gross equity method extends the equity method defined above, so that the investor's share of the aggregate gross assets and liabilities underlying the investment is shown on the face of the balance sheet and the investor's share of the turnover of the joint venture is shown in the profit and loss account.

The effect of this on the profit and loss account is that the investor's share of its joint ventures' turnover should be shown, and in the segmental analysis of turnover the share of joint ventures' turnover should be clearly distinguished from the turnover for the group itself. The investor's share of the profits or losses of joint ventures and associates should be shown in the consolidated profit and loss account immediately after the group operating profit or loss. Any amortisation or writing down of goodwill arising on the acquisition of associates should be shown at this point.

BOC uses the gross equity method for both associates and joint ventures, and BOC's share of the turnover and the operating profit of its joint ventures and associates can be clearly seen in Table 2.5. BOC also provides a segmental analysis of the performance of its joint ventures and associates (see note 1(d) page 239).

BOC provides information on the subsidiary companies, associates and joint ventures of the group showing the country of domicile, the percentage of shares held by the group and the nature of the business (see pages 272–3).

Other investment income

All formats call for the separate disclosure of income from other fixed asset investments and other interest receivable and similar income. Income from listed securities must be reported. Listed companies are those that are quoted on a recognized stock exchange and note 9(c) to the BOC accounts (page 264) shows the income from listed and unlisted securities and, after deducting the dividends received from associates and joint ventures, reveals that the income from other fixed asset investments was £4.2 million.

Operating profit

FRS 3 requires the operating profit of a company to be analysed between continuing operations (sub-divided into acquisitions and other) and discontinued operations. The term operating profit is not used in the Companies Acts and although it is not *defined* in FRS 3, the standard does state that the normal meaning of operating profit is profit before income from shares in group undertakings. As can be seen from Table 2.5, BOC reports the operating profit before exceptional items from its subsidiary companies as £425.6 million and then reports its share of the operating profit from its joint ventures (£63.8 million) and associates (£10.7 million) separately, to give an overall operating profit of £500.1 million. This amount is then analysed by class of business and geographical region in notes 1(b) and 1(c) to the financial statements (see pages 238–9).

Exceptional items

FRS 3 defines exceptional items as

> Material items which derive from events or transactions that fall within the ordinary activities of the reporting entity and which individually or, if of a

similar type, in aggregate, need to be disclosed by virtue of their size or incidence if the financial statements are to give a true and fair view.

Following from FRS 3 there are in effect two categories of exceptional items as follows:

1 those that are included under the relevant heading of the profit and loss account to which they relate (cost of sales, distribution costs etc.) and disclosed either on the face of the account or in the notes;
2 those that are required to be disclosed on the face of the profit and loss account *after operating profit and before interest*. These are as follows:
    (a) profits or losses on the sale or termination of an operation;
    (b) costs of a fundamental reorganization or restructuring having a material effect on the nature and focus of the reporting entity's operations; and
    (c) profits or losses on the disposal of fixed assets.

These items have to be analysed between continuing and discontinued operations. Table 2.5 shows that BOC discloses exceptional items under both of these categories. In 2002 exceptional cost of sale items are shown as £15.1 million and exceptional net operating expenses are £58.9 million. These are reported against the profit and loss account headings to which they relate. In addition there is an extraordinary loss of £0.5 million affecting the share of operating profit from joint ventures. These three amounts total £74.5 million and represent the exceptional items charge under the first of the above categories in arriving at the 'all-inclusive' operating profit (including share of joint ventures and associates) of £425.6 million. This can be summarized as follows:

	£ million
Total operating profit (including share of joint ventures and associates) *before* exceptional items	500.1
Less *operating* exceptional items	74.5
Total operating profit (including share of joint ventures and associates) *after* exceptional items	425.6

Note 2(b) to the BOC financial statements provides an analysis of the *operating* exceptional items total of £74.5 million.

The second category of exceptional items total £20.2 million (an analysis of this total is provided in note 2(b)(iii)) and these are then deducted to leave an amount of £405.4 million as the profit on ordinary activities before interest but *after* exceptional items.

Interest payable and similar charges

Interest payable, and similar charges, are also required to be disclosed separately under all four formats. This heading should include:

- interest charged and payable on borrowings;
- imputed interest element of financing leases and cognate obligations;
- amounts amortized on discounts or premiums on bills, debentures, etc.;
- commitment and procurement fees on loan arrangements and credit facilities;

and the Companies Act requires an analysis of other interest and similar charges to show separately the aggregate interest on bank loans, overdrafts and loans wholly repayable within five years (whether by instalments or not) and on any other loans. In that way, interest on short-term loans is separated from that on medium- and long-term loans.

The capitalization of interest on borrowings to finance assets in the course of their construction is a permitted accounting treatment but one over which there is much controversy. On the one hand it could be argued that interest costs incurred during the period of construction of an asset are just as much a part of the total cost as any other item of expenditure incurred on that asset and therefore spreading these costs over the useful life of the asset is perfectly consistent with the matching concept. On the other hand it could be argued that it is illogical to distinguish interest costs in this way and that identical assets could be valued at different amounts simply because of the way they were financed. FRS 15 ('Tangible fixed assets'), which was effective for accounting periods ending on or after 23 March 2000, permits the capitalization of finance costs. BOC discloses in note 3(a) to its accounts that interest of £2.0 million was capitalized in 2002.

Many companies net off against interest payable any interest receivable. This is the practice of BOC and note 3 reveals that the interest payable by BOC and its subsidiaries was £103.2 million, from which is deducted the interest receivable of £22.6 million and the interest capitalized of £2.0 million to arrive at a net amount payable of £78.6 million. The share of the interest payable by joint ventures of £23.2 million and associates of £1.3 million is added to this giving an amount of £103.1 million which is charged as an expense to the 2002 profit and loss account.

Profit or loss on ordinary activities before taxation

A company's profit or loss on ordinary activities before taxation must be shown on the face of the profit and loss account. The figure reported must represent the balance of all the previously mentioned items, including exceptional items, that relate to the ordinary activities of the company, but excluding taxation and extraordinary items (see later).

Taxation

The treatment of taxation in the profit and loss account is governed both by the provisions of the 1985 Act (as amended) and by the requirements of FRS 16 ('Current tax') and FRS 19 ('Deferred tax'). In addition, other standards contain matters pertinent to the treatment of taxation in the course of their statements on other topics.

The profit and loss account formats prescribed under the 1985 Act (as amended) require the disclosure of three essential taxation items:

1 tax on profit or loss on ordinary activities;
2 tax on extraordinary profit or loss;
3 other taxes not shown under the above items.

Tax on profit or loss on ordinary activities

The disclosure of charges or provisions under this heading should take account of the following items:

- UK corporation tax on the profit for the period;
- double taxation relief;
- deferred taxation;
- overseas taxation;

- income tax;
- associated and joint venture companies' corporation tax and deferred taxation;
- changes to taxation provisions for prior periods.

The basis on which corporation tax has been computed and the amount of tax charge have to be disclosed. The BOC accounts (note 4(a) to the financial statements) report a charge of £51.7 million at the rate of 30 per cent on taxable profit in respect of corporation tax for the year ended 30 September 2002.

Deferred taxation is defined variously by different authorities. In terms of FRS 19, deferred taxation is taxation attributable to 'timing differences'. These are the differences between profits calculated for financial statement purposes and those calculated for taxation purposes. Items of income and expenditure are included in taxation computations in periods different from those in which they were or will be included in financial statements. These timing differences are created in four major ways:

1 timing differences arising from the use of different bases for taxation and reporting statements (i.e. receipts and payments basis for taxation and accruals basis for financial accounts);
2 differences between the depreciation charges for financial reporting purposes and the capital allowances permitted by the Inland Revenue;
3 fixed asset revaluation arising from differences between asset values and original costs;
4 fixed asset disposal arising from taxation liability on 'profits' from fixed asset disposal.

Adjustments to the deferred taxation balance can arise also from changes in the rate of tax.

Overseas taxation should be disclosed separately and the amount reported should include all overseas taxation charged in the financial statements of the overseas branch or company, whether relieved or not.

For a more detailed treatment of company taxation readers are recommended to consult a specialist text, such as *Tolley's Corporation Tax*.

As an example of the reported tax on ordinary activities BOC discloses, on the face of its profit and loss account, a 2002 taxation charge of £106.2 million. A summary of the analysis that is provided in note 4(a) to the accounts (page 249) is as follows:

Tax on profit on ordinary activities

	(£ million)	*(£ million)*
Current tax:		
Payable in the UK:		
Corporation tax	51.7	
Double tax relief	(19.7)	32.0
Payable overseas:		
US – federal tax	(1.0)	
– state and local taxes	0.6	
Australia	14.6	
South Africa	18.0	
Japan	8.3	
Other countries	30.9	71.4
Total current tax		103.4

	(£ million)	*(£ million)*
Deferred tax:		
Origination and reversal of timing differences	3.4	
Effect of change in tax rate	(0.6)	2.8
		106.2

Note that double taxation relief occurs because BOC has overseas subsidiaries which pay tax in the overseas countries on profits earned there. If tax was also charged in the UK on those profits then there would have been double taxation. The UK government has agreements with many countries that effectively provide relief against double taxation by permitting the total UK tax liability to be partially reduced by tax paid overseas.

Tax on extraordinary profit or loss

As a consequence of FRS 3 extraordinary items (see later) have now been virtually eliminated and so this item should appear relatively rarely. However, if there are extraordinary items the tax on these should be shown separately. FRS 3 requires that the taxation attributable to extraordinary items should be calculated by computing the tax charge on the profit or loss for the period as if the extraordinary items did not exist. This notional tax charge can then be compared with the total tax charge, with the difference being attributed to extraordinary items.

Tax on exceptional items

FRS 3 requires the notes to the financial statements to show the effect on tax of the three forms of exceptional item that have to be disclosed on the face of the profit and loss account (see the discussion on exceptional items on pages 41–2).

Extraordinary items and prior period adjustments

There is no statutory definition of what constitutes an 'extraordinary item', but FRS 3 provides the following definition:

> Extraordinary items are material items possessing a high degree of abnormality which arise from events or transactions that fall outside the ordinary activities of the reporting entity and which are not expected to recur. They do not include exceptional items nor do they include prior period items merely because they relate to a prior period.

FRS 3 goes on to provide a very wide definition of 'ordinary activities' and the effect of this is that extraordinary items have almost completely disappeared from the accounts of companies. Prior to the introduction of FRS 3, many of the items that are now categorized as exceptional might have been categorized as extraordinary. The all-important 'bottom-line' performance indicator of profit after taxation would therefore have included exceptional items (i.e. they appeared 'above the line') and excluded extraordinary items (i.e. they appeared 'below the line'). The reason for this was that it enabled the reported after-tax profit figure to include only those items that were expected to occur regularly or frequently. Items that were expected to occur infrequently were reported 'below the line' as extraordinary items so as to avoid the distortions and wide fluctuations in after-tax profit that might result from the inclusion of these unusual items. However, the distinction between exceptional items and extraordinary items lacked precision and this permitted the opportunity for other distortions of reported after-tax profit. For example, if, at the extreme, a company chose to classify all of its unusual items of profit as exceptional (i.e. above the line) and all of its unusual losses as extraordinary (i.e. below the line), then this would boost reported profit and thereby give a misleading signal about the company's financial performance. FRS 3 now significantly restricts such opportunities, with virtually all items being required to be included above the line.

One consequence of removing extraordinary items from the profit and loss account is that there is now a tendency for attention to shift to the profit from continuing operations *before exceptional items* (see pages 41–2). This is particularly so in the case of the items that have to be disclosed on the face of the profit and loss account and could lead to these being thought of as something that should be set aside when considering performance. This is precisely the problem that used to occur with extraordinary items and that FRS 3 aimed to remove.

Prior period adjustments are required where it is necessary to correct a fundamental error in the accounts of a prior period or because of changes in accounting policies. A fundamental error is one which is so significant that it would destroy the true and fair view and hence the validity of the financial statements. It does not include the normal recurring corrections and adjustments of estimates made in previous years. FRS 3 requires prior period adjustments to be accounted for by restating the comparative figures for the preceding period in the accounts and notes and adjusting the opening balance of reserves for the cumulative effect.

Minority interests

Where a parent company holds less than 100 per cent of the shares of a subsidiary, then the shares not held by the parent represent a minority interest in that subsidiary. Thus, for example, if a parent company holds 80 per cent of the shares of a subsidiary, then the holders of the remaining 20 per cent are minority shareholders in that subsidiary. Even though the subsidiary is not 100 per cent owned by the parent, the consolidated accounts include 100 per cent of the subsidiary's turnover, expenses and profit. The part of the consolidated profit that belongs to the minority shareholders in subsidiary companies is reported as minority interests. The Companies Act 1989 requires the amount of any profit or loss on ordinary activities attributable to minority interests to be shown separately in the consolidated profit and loss account after group profit or loss on ordinary activities after tax. If a company reports any extraordinary items then any minority interest in these must also be reported.

Dividends

Although the item 'dividends' is not included in any of the four prescribed formats, the 1985 Act (as amended) does require the aggregate amount of any dividends, paid and proposed, to be disclosed on the face of a company's profit and loss account. This straightforward requirement disguises an area of considerable confusion and complexity – the determination of 'distributable profits'. There are also the difficulties of calculating a company's 'realized' and 'unrealized' profits and losses.

Realized profits are those determined in accordance with generally accepted accounting principles at the time of preparation of the financial statements in question. Generally, this has been interpreted to mean that, where a specific accounting standard requires an item of profit to be recognized in the profit and loss account, then this should normally be treated as a realized profit. Also, profits determined in accordance with the two concepts of accruals and prudence, set out in both SSAP 2 ('Disclosure of accounting policies') and the 1985 Act (as amended), would normally be 'realized'. Under the accruals concept, the financial statements must reflect all items of income and expenditure that relate to the financial year in question: in other words, as these items are earned or incurred and not as money is received or paid. Under the prudence concept, profits should not be anticipated and should only be recognized in the profit and loss account when realized in the form of cash or other assets (including a commitment to pay, or other obligation). Losses are provided when an amount is known with certainty or is a best estimate in the light of the circumstances and available information.

Basically, any company that wishes to make a distribution must have profits available for that purpose. They are the accumulated realized profits that have not previously been either distributed or capitalized, less any accumulated realized losses that have not been previously written off. In addition, a public company must satisfy the further condition that the amount of its assets, after making a distribution, must be at least equal to the aggregate of its called-up share capital and undistributable reserves. Undistributable reserves are:

- the share premium account;
- the capital redemption reserve;
- the excess of accumulated unrealized profits over accumulated unrealized losses;
- any other reserve which is not distributable (e.g. because of provision in the memorandum or articles of association of a company).

The situation is complicated further when revalued assets and associated depreciation charges play a part in the net asset position of a company. Readers are referred to a textbook on advanced financial accounting for a fuller treatment (see, for example, Alexander and Britton 2001: 184–90).

Employee information

In respect of employees, the total average number of employees must be disclosed and that total should be broken down on the same basis as the organization of the company's activities. Staff costs must be disclosed under the following separate headings:

- wages and salaries paid or payable for the year;
- social security costs that the company has incurred on behalf of its employees (e.g. employer's national insurance contribution);
- other pension costs that the company has incurred on behalf of its employees (this will include contribution to any pension scheme other than the state scheme).

The Act permits considerable flexibility in the manner in which categories of staff should be reported. This can be by function (sales, production, distribution, administration and so on) or by activity (motor assembly, construction, oil exploration etc.) or by a geographical region. The BOC Group provide both an activity-based classification and a regional classification (see note 6 to the financial statements).

One of the more controversial aspects of reporting employee costs relates to the appropriate accounting treatment of pension costs. In November 2000 the ASB issued FRS 17 ('Retirement benefits') and this was intended to apply for accounting periods ending on or after June 2003. The implementation date was subsequently deferred to June 2005 to permit amendments to the IASB's standard on employee benefits (IAS 19) to be considered. Until then the provisions of SSAP 24 apply, although companies are encouraged by the ASB to adopt FRS 17 as early as possible. The BOC Group fully adopted the requirements of FRS 17 in its 2002 accounts. Pension schemes are classified as either defined contribution schemes or defined benefit schemes. In a defined contribution scheme, the employer makes an agreed contribution to a pension scheme, and the benefits paid out of the scheme will depend on the funds available from these contributions plus any investment earnings thereon. The cost to the company can therefore be measured with reasonable certainty. In a defined benefit scheme, the benefits to be paid will typically depend upon the final pay of the employee. This means it is impossible to be certain in advance that the contributions to the scheme, plus any investment earnings, will be sufficient to cover the benefits that will have to be paid. The final cost of a defined benefit scheme is subject to considerable uncertainty and, because of the very long-term nature of pension commitments, it is necessary to make use of actuarial calculations to help determine the pension cost charge.

For defined contribution schemes, both SSAP 24 and FRS 17 require simply the disclosure of the accounting policy followed, the pension cost charge for the period and any outstanding or prepaid contribution at balance sheet date. For a defined benefit scheme, the disclosure requirement is much wider. The assets of a defined benefit scheme are the investments that have been purchased from contributions to the scheme. FRS 17 requires these assets to be valued at their market value. The liabilities of a defined benefit scheme are the present value of the pension benefits that will be paid out to employees. FRS 17 requires the market value of a company's pension scheme assets and the present value of the company's pension schemes liability to be reported in the balance sheet of the company. Actuarial gains and losses on the assets and liabilities of a defined benefit scheme are reported in the Statement of Total Recognised Gains and Losses (see Chapter 5). The amounts to be included in the profit and loss account are:

1 the current service costs (the increase in the present value of the liabilities of the scheme expected to arise from employee service in the current period);
2 an interest charge (the increase in the present value of the liabilities of the scheme due to the liabilities being one year closer to payment;
3 a credit representing the expected return on the assets of the scheme during the year.

In addition any improvements in the benefits of the scheme or the awarding of new benefits for past service will result in an immediate increase in the liabilities of the scheme and this increase should be charged to the profit and loss account. An analysis of BOC's pension charges for 2002 is provided in note 6(e) (pages 254–9).

The current service cost and past service cost are analysed by geographical segment and result in a total operating charge of £56.7 million and this is included in the overall employment costs for the year. The expected return on net assets (£139.1 million) and the interest charge for the year (£106.1 million) are also analysed by geographical region and result in a net surplus of £33.0 million. FRS 17 requires the expected return on net assets and the interest charge to be presented as finance costs/income rather than operating costs and these items are therefore reported separately on the face of BOC's consolidated profit and loss account (see Table 2.5), where they form part of the net interest total and appear immediately before the sub-total for 'profit on ordinary activities before tax'.

Directors' emoluments

The Companies Act requirements relating to the disclosure of directors' emoluments have been amended significantly following The Company Accounts (Disclosure of Directors' Emoluments) Regulations 1997 (SI 1997/570). For accounting periods ending on or after 31 March 1997 disclosure is no longer required of the emoluments of the Chairman or of the number of directors whose remuneration falls into bands of £5,000. However, if the aggregate emoluments of all directors exceed £200,000 per year then the emolument of the highest paid director must be disclosed.

There have in addition been a number of other developments affecting the disclosure of directors' remuneration. The Study Group on Directors Remuneration (the Greenbury Committee) which reported in July 1995 made a number of recommendations. In 1994 the Urgent Issues Task Force of the ASB issued Abstract 10 ('Disclosure of directors' share options'). In January 1998 the report of the Committee on Corporate Governance (the Hampel Committee) was published and led to the production of 'The Combined Code – Principles of Good Corporate Governance and Code of Best Practice' in June 1998. The London Stock Exchange requires listed companies to follow the provisions of the Combined Code when disclosing directors' remuneration. The requirements are very detailed, but can be broadly summarized as including the following items of information for each director:

- basic salary and fees;
- estimated monetary value of benefits (for example company cars, subsidized accommodation, etc.);
- annual and deferred bonuses;
- compensation for loss of office and payments for breach of contract or other termination payments;
- information on share options;
- details of any long-term incentive schemes other than share options;
- detailed information on pension contributions and accrued pension benefits.

BOC provides comprehensive information on directors' remuneration in the Report on remuneration (see pages 220–7).

Comparative amounts

The corresponding amounts for the previous year of items in the profit and loss account, balance sheet, cash flow statement, statement of total recognized gains and losses and notes to the accounts are required to be reported. In the profit and loss account the comparative figures have to be analysed into continuing and discontinued activities in the same way as the current year's results. The continuing activities category of the comparative figures should include only the results of activities continuing in the *current* year. The discontinued activities category of the comparative figures will include the results of the activities that were discontinued in both the current and previous year. There will not normally be an acquisitions category in the comparative figures because the acquisitions of the previous year will be the continuing activities of the current year and so to help comparison between the two years will be included as continuing activities in the comparative figures.

Earnings per share

FRS 14 ('Earnings per share') requires all companies whose ordinary shares or potential ordinary shares are publicly traded and companies that are in the process of issuing ordinary shares to report, on the face of the profit and loss account, a figure for both basic and diluted earnings per share. The basis of the calculation must be shown in the notes to the financial statements and details of the earnings figure and the numbers of shares used in the calculations must be given. FRS 14 defines basic earnings per share as 'a measure of past performance. Calculated by dividing the net profit or loss attributable to ordinary shareholders by the weighted average number of shares outstanding during the period.'

All items of income and expense that are recognized in the period, including tax, exceptional and extraordinary items, minority interests and appropriations in respect of non-equity shares (e.g. preference dividends) are included in the determination of the net profit or loss for the period. Because the profit figure used in the EPS calculation is inclusive of any exceptional items it is possible that the earnings per share could fluctuate quite widely from period to period. FRS 14 therefore permits companies to calculate and disclose a further earnings per share figure which could, for example, be based on normal or maintainable profit, i.e. a profit figure which excludes the distortions caused by abnormal items (such as exceptional items) in a particular year. This is often referred to as the 'headline profit'. This additional earnings per share should not be presented more prominently than the basic earnings per share required by FRS 14, and a reconciliation of the two figures is required. BOC reports a basic earnings per share based on its published earnings and an additional earning per share based on its earnings before exceptional items. The calculation of earnings per share is discussed further in Chapter 10.

Exemptions and modifications

The Companies Act of 1967 abolished the status of 'exempt private company' and for a number of years all limited companies were required to conform to the same basic auditing, disclosure and filing provisions, although differences in status (between 'public' and 'private', or 'parent' and 'subsidiary') led to differences in additional disclosure requirements. The 1985 Act, however, permits reduced disclosure in the documents to be filed with the Registrar of Companies. Two points need to be emphasized: first, the implementation of reduced disclosure is permitted without being demanded; second, the permission extends only to those documents to be delivered to the Registrar and does not cover the documents to be delivered to members of the company in question. Members must receive full accounts, prepared wholly in accordance with the act's requirements.

Two categories of limited company may opt to apply the exemptions from full public disclosure:

1 medium-sized companies;
2 small companies;

and the Act lays down certain criteria for determining the category into which a company falls. It is perhaps best to consider first those companies that cannot be classified as either medium-sized or small. They are:

- public companies;
- member companies of a group of companies containing a public company;
- banking or insurance companies;
- member companies of a group of companies containing a banking or insurance company;
- member companies of a group of companies containing a non-British corporate body that may lawfully offer its securities to the public;
- member companies of a group of companies containing a non-British corporate body that is a recognized bank or insurance company.

If a company does not fall into any of those categories, it may be eligible to be considered as either medium-sized or small, and those classifications depend entirely on size, as follows. Medium-sized companies are those that fulfil at least two of the following three conditions in respect of the current financial period:

1 turnover did not exceed £11.2 million;
2 total assets did not exceed £5.6 million;
3 average weekly number of employees did not exceed 250.

Similarly, the conditions for being considered a small company are that two or more of the following conditions are satisfied:

- turnover did not exceed £2.8 million;
- total assets did not exceed £1.4 million;
- average weekly number of employees did not exceed 50.

'Total assets' refers to the balance sheet total of fixed and current assets, as specified in the prescribed balance sheet formats, without deduction of any liabilities.

The exemptions for a medium-sized company are limited. It is permitted to omit only the following: turnover; cost of sales information; other operating income; analyses of turnover and profit amongst different classes of business; and analyses of turnover amongst different markets. The whole of the balance sheet and supporting notes, together with the rest of the notes to the profit and loss account, have to be given in full.

The exemptions for a small company are extensive. It is permitted to omit the following: the whole profit and loss account; the directors' report; particulars of the emoluments of directors and higher-paid employees; all of those items in the balance sheet that are not identified with Roman numerals (see Chapter 3); and considerable portions of the notes to the financial statements.

However, these are disclosure exemptions. Given that a smaller company, like any company, has to prepare financial statements that give a true and fair view then it could be argued that they must also follow the requirements of accounting standards. It has been argued that this requirement places a considerable burden on smaller companies and the ASB has responded by issuing, in December 2001, a revised version of Financial Reporting Standard for Smaller Entities (FRSSE). This may be applied to all companies that meet the conditions outlined above for being considered a small company. The FRSSE consists of a simplified summary of the whole body of existing accounting standards. If companies choose to comply with the requirements of FRSSE then they are exempt from complying with other SSAPs or FRSs or UITF abstracts (unless they are preparing consolidated financial statements in which case a limited number of other standards will still apply).

3 The balance sheet

Perhaps best described as a 'position' statement, the balance sheet reports the position at the close of business on a given day, detailing the values of assets and liabilities at the balance sheet date and offering considerable scope for the analysis of the relationship between the different classes of assets and liabilities. The bases on which assets and liabilities are valued are, of course, of crucial importance.

This chapter examines the alternative formats permitted under the 1985 Act (as amended) by describing and discussing the various items to be included on the balance sheet or in the related notes, and by examining certain wider-ranging topics associated with particular balance sheet entries.

Formats

There are two permitted formats for a company's balance sheet; these are reproduced in Tables 3.1 and 3.2. The first format arranges the balance sheet items vertically (the practice most prevalent amongst UK companies), while the second format arranges those items horizontally (although the presentation does not necessarily have to be side by side).

Headings given Roman letters or numerals must be shown in the order, and under the headings and sub-headings, set out in the prescribed formats; no flexibility is permitted. The prescribed formats do, however, include a number of additional sub-headings, labelled with arabic numerals, which enjoy greater flexibility. These additional sub-headings will be described in the appropriate sections below, and their arrangement and description are adaptable to meet the particular needs or nature of a company's business. They may be combined to facilitate the better assessment of a company's affairs, but the fact of such combination must be stated and the details of such combined items must be disclosed in the notes to the financial statements.

Before turning to the detailed examination of the individual categories and their components, it is useful to consider two actual examples of balance sheets prepared under the provisions of the Act. Table 3.3 presents a modified extract from the balance sheet of The BOC Group plc, as at 30 September 2002; the full version may be seen in Appendix A to this book.

The descriptions and discussions following will deal with the various items in this order:

Table 3.1   Balance sheet – format 1

A   Called-up share capital not paid
B   Fixed assets
    I Intangible assets
    II Tangible assets
    III Investments
C   Current assets
    I Stocks
    II Debtors
    III Investments
    IV Cash at bank and in hand
D   Prepayments and accrued income
E   Creditors: amounts falling due within one year
F   Net current assets (liabilities)
G   Total assets less current liabilities
H   Creditors: amounts falling due after more than one year
I   Provisions for liabilities and charges
J   Accruals and deferred income
–   Minority interests[a]
K   Capital and reserves
    I Called-up share capital
    II Share premium account
    III Revaluation reserve
    IV Other reserves
    V Profit and loss account
–   Minority interests[a]

Note: [a]Group accounts only. This item to be treated as one to which a letter is assigned. Under this format the minority interests are normally shown after 'capital and reserves' rather than after 'accruals and deferred income'.

Table 3.2   Balance sheet – format 2

Assets	*Liabilities*[a]
A Called-up share capital not paid	A Capital and reserves I Called-up share capital

B   Fixed assets
    I Intangible assets
    II Tangible assets
    III Investments
	II Share premium account
	    III Revaluation reserve
	    IV Other reserves
	    V Profit and loss account
	    – Minority interests[b]

C   Current assets
    I Stocks
    II Debtors
    III Investments
    IV Cash at bank and in hand
	B Provisions for liabilities and charges
	
	C Creditors

D Prepayments and accrued income	D Accruals and deferred income

---

Notes: [a] 'Liabilities' may alternatively be shown below 'Assets' or be shown on a separate page.
[b] Group accounts only. This item to be treated as one to which a letter is assigned.

Table 3.3 The BOC Group plc – consolidated balance sheet as at 30 September 2002

	Notes	2002 (£ million)	2001 (restated) (£ million)
Fixed assets			
Intangible assets	7	150.7	48.1
Tangible assets	8	3,027.4	3,168.6
Investment in joint ventures			
share of gross assets		616.2	615.2
share of gross liabilities		(410.7)	(410.4)
		205.5	204.8
loans to joint ventures		111.8	97.6
Investment in associates			
share of net assets		57.5	47.1
loans to associates		6.2	9.1
Investment in own shares		42.5	59.5
Other investments		45.1	31.7
Investments	9	468.6	449.8
		3,646.7	3,666.5
Current assets			
Stocks	10(a)	260.0	275.2
Debtors falling due within one year	10(b)	733.8	713.3
Debtors falling due after more than one year	10(c)	28.3	21.3
Investments		38.8	43.2
Cash at bank and in hand	10(d)	185.5	233.5
		1,246.4	1,286.5
Current liabilities			
Creditors: amounts falling due within one year			
Borrowings and finance leases	10(e)	(390.1)	(486.4)
Other creditors	10(f)	(857.8)	(795.3)
		(1,247.9)	(1,281.7)
Net current (liabilities)/assets		(1.5)	4.8
Total assets *less* current liabilities		3,645.2	3,671.3
Long-term liabilities			
Creditors: amounts falling due after more than one year			
Borrowings and finance leases	11(a)	(1,121.0)	(1,019.9)
Other creditors		(58.0)	(59.4)
		(1,179.0)	(1,079.3)
Provisions for liabilities and charges	11(b)	(407.5)	(419.2)
Total net assets excluding pension assets and liabilities		2,058.7	2,172.8
Pension assets	6(e)	54.3	107.0
Pension liabilities	6(e)	(311.0)	(56.0)
Total net assets including pension assets and liabilities		**1,802.0**	**2,223.8**
Capital and reserves			
Equity called up share capital	12(b)	124.3	123.6
Share premium account	12(c)	362.1	335.8
Revaluation reserves	12(c)	27.8	47.9
Profit and loss account	12(c)	1,304.8	1,400.3
Pensions reserves	12(c)	(256.5)	47.1
Joint ventures' reserves	12(c)	88.1	98.1
Associates' reserves	12(c)	33.5	33.4
Equity shareholders' funds		1,684.1	2,086.2
Minority shareholders' equity interests		117.9	137.6
Total capital and reserves		**1,802.0**	**2,223.8**

The financial statements were approved by the board of directors on 22 November 2002 and are signed on its behalf by: **A E Isaac** Director **R Médori** Director

- fixed assets;
- current assets;
- creditors;
- provisions for liabilities and charges;
- capital and reserves;
- minority shareholders.

Valuation rules

The fourth schedule to the 1985 Act (as amended) lays down certain rules for the valuation of balance sheet items. These general valuation rules are discussed here, and the rules applicable to specific assets are discussed in the sections that follow. Broadly, the rules permit companies to draw up their financial statements under either the pure historical cost convention or the alternative conventions of historical cost modified to include certain assets at a revalued amount, or current cost. The BOC Group's accounts are based on the historical cost accounting convention.

The general rules may be summarized as follows. Under the historical cost convention, gross value shall be purchase price or production cost. Under the alternative conventions, gross value shall be either market value determined at the most recent valuation date or current cost. For example, tangible fixed assets shall be valued at market value or at current cost, stocks shall be valued at current cost, investments included in fixed assets shall be valued at market value or at a value determined by the directors on any basis considered appropriate in the circumstances, and investments included in current assets shall be valued at current cost.

Provisions for reduction in value shall be made in respect of all fixed assets where the reduction is expected to be permanent. Where investments are concerned, a provision for diminution in value may be made even where the reduction in value is not expected to be permanent. Fixed assets with finite economic lives shall be subject to depreciation charges as discussed in Chapter 2. Current assets shall be written down to a net realization value where that value is lower than cost or alternative valuation. Conversely, where a provision for reduction in value is no longer necessary, the provision shall be written back (via the profit and loss account) to the extent that it is no longer necessary.

Current cost accounting

The requirement to prepare and publish current cost accounting statements was contained in SSAP 16 ('Current cost accounting'), which was issued in March 1980. In June 1985 the mandatory status of SSAP 16 was suspended and in April 1988 it was formally withdrawn. In 1986 the ASC issued 'Accounting for the effects of changing prices: a handbook', and this is an authoritative reference work on current cost accounting. The 1985 Act does not define current cost and, therefore, where a company chooses to adopt the alternative accounting rules and value some assets at their current costs, then the principles set out in the ASC's handbook would normally be followed.

The basic requirement of current cost accounting is to ensure that the net operating assets of a company, and the calculation of profit, reflect the impact of price changes on the input prices of goods and services used and financed by a company.

When prices are rising, for example, the historical cost accounting profit will need to be adjusted to reflect the additional depreciation, cost of sales and monetary working capital that will be required to maintain the operating capability of a company. These are the basic current cost accounting adjustments. Also, when prices are rising, a company that is partly financed by loans, overdrafts or other fixed monetary liabilities will benefit from the fact that these will be repaid out of a depreciated currency. A gearing adjustment that reduces the total of the basic current cost accounting adjustments by the proportion that is effectively being financed by net monetary liabilities is therefore required. This leads to asset valuations that reflect the 'value to the business' or 'current cost' of an asset. The ASC's definition of *current cost* in its 1986 handbook on accounting for the effect of changing prices and the ASB's definition of *value to the business* in its 1995 statement of principles are identical. Both the *value to the business* of an asset and the *current cost* of an asset are defined as the lower of the replacement cost and the recoverable amount, with the recoverable amount being the higher of value in use and net realizable value. The mechanics of calculating the actual adjustments of current cost accounting are not described here in detail; readers are referred to a textbook on advanced financial accounting. Alexander and Britton (2001: chapters 5–8) for example, provides a comprehensive coverage of this topic.

Revaluation of assets

When assets are revalued a gain or loss on revaluation will arise. The Act requires a separate reserve called a valuation reserve to be used to account for such gains or losses and for these to be disclosed separately in the accounts. Thus, for example, if land which cost £400,000 is revalued at £600,000, then the unrealized gain of £200,000 cannot be taken to the profit and loss account but would be credited to a revaluation reserve. Also, following the introduction of FRS 3 ('Reporting financial performance') the unrealized gain of £200,000 would be disclosed in a statement of total recognized gains and losses for the period (see Chapter 5). If in a subsequent period the land is sold for £650,000 then the unrealized gain has become a realized gain and would be transferred out of the revaluation reserve and into the profit and loss reserve. The profit or loss on disposal is the difference between the sales proceeds and the carrying value. In this case the sales proceeds are £650,000, the carrying value is £600,000 and so the profit is £50,000. This can be included in the profit and loss account for the year. The carrying value for an asset is its revalued amount less any depreciation. If the land had been sold for £550,000 then a loss on disposal of £50,000 would be included in the profit and loss account. Prior to the introduction of FRS 3, the entry in the revaluation reserve of £200,000 could have been reversed and the profit would then have been based on the land's original cost of £400,000. Assuming that the land sold for £550,000, then this would have enabled a profit of £150,000 to be included in the profit and loss account.

In reality relatively few companies in the UK use a pure form of historical cost accounting when preparing financial statements. Even fewer use current cost accounting. The practice that has grown up is to use a modified historical cost approach, which is a mixture of historic cost for some assets and market values or current cost for others. This resulted in a lack of consistency in revaluation practices, because companies were not obliged to revalue all assets or update previous revaluations; this in turn led to a lack of comparability of the financial statements of different companies. Because of this companies are required under FRS 3 ('Reporting financial performance') to publish a note of the profits or losses on an unmodified historical cost basis. Such a note is intended to enable a fair comparison to be made between companies' profits.

The ASB has also responded by issuing FRS 15 ('Tangible fixed assets'). One of the main objectives of FRS 15 is to ensure that where a company chooses to revalue tangible fixed assets the valuation is performed on a consistent basis and kept up to date, with gains and losses on revaluation recognized on a consistent basis. Where a policy of revaluation is adopted for a specific asset then all fixed assets of the same class (i.e. those assets that have a similar nature, function or use as the asset being revalued) must also be revalued. The valuations of revalued assets should be their current value at the balance sheet date. This does not mean that annual revaluations are required. FRS 15 indicates that for property a full revaluation at least every five years with an interim valuation in the third year would normally be sufficient. For assets other than property (e.g. vehicles, machinery) the use of indices may provide a reasonably reliable valuation. If this is not possible then valuations by a qualified valuer at least every five years with an update in year three would be required.

Contents

The prescribed contents of balance sheets under the alternative formats are summarized below in the order outlined earlier.

Fixed assets

The 1985 Act (as amended) defines fixed assets as those intended for use on a continuing basis in the company's activities. Other assets must be taken to be current assets. In each of the prescribed formats, fixed assets must be subdivided into three groups:

1 intangible assets;
2 tangible assets;
3 investments.

In addition, the notes to the financial statements are required to disclose information in the standard format about the cost (or revaluation or current cost) at the beginning and end of the financial year of each item shown as a fixed asset and also the effect on that item of:

■ acquisitions during the year;
■ disposals during the year;
■ transfers during the year;
■ any revision of the amount due to the application of the alternative accounting bases.

Details must also be disclosed for each fixed asset category of the accumulated provision for depreciation and diminution in value at the beginning and end of the financial year, any provisions made in the financial year and any adjustments to the provisions resulting from either the disposal of fixed assets or for any other reason, during the year.

A diminution in value may arise because of impairment of the asset. Impairment occurs because something has happened either to the fixed asset itself (e.g. damage or obsolescence) or to the economic environment in which the asset is operated. Where this occurs FRS 11 ('Impairment of fixed assets and goodwill') requires the asset to be recorded in the balance sheet at no more than its recoverable amount and that the losses due to impairment are measured and recorded in a consistent manner.

The calculation of depreciation was discussed briefly in Chapter 2 and it was shown how different methods could affect the annual charge for depreciation. FRS 15 ('Tangible fixed assets') requires companies to disclose the depreciation method used for each class of tangible fixed asset and also the useful economic lives or depreciation rates used and the financial effects, if any, of a change during the period in the estimate of the useful economic lives or residual values of assets. If there has been a change in the depreciation method used then the effect of this and the reason for the change must be disclosed. The BOC accounting policies in respect of tangible fixed assets and depreciation are shown on page 236. Also, note 8(a) to the financial statements (see page 261) provides information on the gross book value of tangible fixed assets at the beginning of the accounting year (1 October 2001), which is then adjusted for any acquisitions, revaluations and disposals during the year, to give the gross book value at the end of the year (30 September 2002). The depreciation at the beginning of the year is then shown, together with the depreciation charge for the year and any adjustments for impairments, revaluations and disposals, to give the cumulative amount of depreciation at the end of the year. This is then deducted from the gross book value of the tangible fixed assets to arrive (after adjusting for leased assets) at an overall figure of £3,027.4 million at 30 September 2002. This is the amount that is reported on the face of the consolidated balance sheet in Table 3.3.

Intangible assets

Intangible assets must be included on the face of the balance sheet under a main heading, with the following sub-headings included either on the face of the balance sheet or in the notes to the financial statements:

- development costs;
- concessions, patents, licences, trade marks and similar rights and assets;
- goodwill;
- payments on account.

The Act lays down that only in special circumstances may an amount be included in the balance sheet in respect of 'development costs', although it does not define those circumstances. In general, research and development costs may not be capitalized; where they are, a reason must be stated. In most respects, the provisions of the schedule are closely similar to those presented in SSAP 13 ('Accounting for research and development'). SSAP 13 provides certain criteria for the capitalization of development costs and those criteria may be considered analogous to the Act's 'special circumstances'. They include: the clear identification of a project; the related expenditure is separately identifiable; the outcome of the project has been assessed with reasonable certainty as to technical feasibility and commercial viability; the future revenues can be reasonably expected to exceed the aggregate costs; and adequate resources exist to complete the project.

'Goodwill' is not defined in the 1985 Act, but is generally thought to mean the difference between the *overall* value of a company and the aggregate of the fair value of all the company's other identifiable assets and liabilities. Goodwill will therefore exist in most businesses. This is the *internally generated goodwill*, but because it is often volatile and difficult to identify – and even more difficult to value – it does not appear in the balance sheet of a company. However, when one company acquires another and the cost of the acquisition differs from the fair values of the assets and liabilities acquired, then goodwill arises and has to be accounted for. This is *purchased goodwill*. FRS 10 ('Goodwill and intangible assets') states that purchased goodwill is the difference between the cost of an acquired entity and the aggregate of the fair value of the entity's identifiable assets and liabilities. Purchased goodwill is required to be capitalized and classified as an asset on the balance sheet. Internally generated goodwill should not be capitalized.

Having acquired purchased goodwill, it is then necessary to determine whether the goodwill is likely to have a definite or an indefinite useful economic life. The presumption of FRS 10 is that purchased goodwill has a definite useful economic life of not more than 20 years and should therefore be amortized (normally on a straight-line basis) over the period of the economic life. If it can be demonstrated that the goodwill is likely to have a useful economic life of more than 20 years then the amortization can be spread over this longer period. Similarly, if it can be demonstrated that the goodwill has an indefinite useful economic life, then amortization is not necessary. In both of these cases, however, the goodwill must be capable of continued measurement so that an annual impairment review can be undertaken.

An issue that is closely related to the question of accounting for goodwill is that of accounting for other intangibles, such as brand names. Until the issue of FRS 10, companies were permitted to write-off any purchased goodwill directly to reserves rather than requiring it to be capitalized and then amortized. This often meant that other intangibles such as brand names were written off with the goodwill. However, brand names can add significant value to a company, and many companies began to isolate the brand names element of purchased goodwill as separately identifiable intangible assets in their balance sheets. The practice of including brand names in balance sheets then spread to internally generated brands. As a result of the introduction of FRS 10, any brand names that are acquired as a part of the goodwill will now be capitalized along with the purchased goodwill which should remove much of the pressure for separately identifying brand names in the balance sheet. FRS 10 permits any intangible assets acquired as part of an acquisition to be capitalized separately from goodwill if their value can be measured reliably on initial recognition. Intangible assets that cannot be measured reliably are to be subsumed within the goodwill. Internally developed intangible assets can be capitalized, but only if they have a readily ascertainable market value. Intangible assets also have to be amortized in accordance with their useful economic lives in the same way as goodwill.

FRS 10 requires the cost or revalued amount of capitalized goodwill and intangible assets at the beginning and end of the accounting period to be disclosed, together with the cumulative amounts for amortization at the beginning and end of the period and any amortization or other adjustments made during the period. FRS 10 came into effect in December 1998. BOC explains its accounting policy in respect of goodwill on page 236. Any goodwill arising after 1 October 1998 is now capitalized and amortized on a straight-line basis over its useful economic life (generally up to a maximum period of 20 years). Note 7 to the financial statements discloses details of goodwill and intangible assets capitalized during the year and amortizations during the year. Goodwill arising before 1 October 1998 was written off to reserves. As permitted by FRS 10, this policy has not been reversed and the goodwill will remain written off to reserves until such time as it is impaired or the businesses whose acquisition gave rise to the goodwill are disposed of.

BOC's policy with regard to other types of intangible assets (such as patents and trademarks) of capitalizing their acquisition cost and amortizing over useful economic lives was already consistent with the requirements of FRS 10.

Tangible assets

The amounts of the following fixed assets must be shown either on the face of the balance sheet or in the notes thereto:

- land and buildings;
- plant and machinery;
- fixtures, fittings, tools and equipment;
- payments on account and assets in course of construction.

The category 'land and buildings' must be further divided into freeholds, long leaseholds (more than 50 years unexpired life remaining) and short leaseholds.

An important issue affecting the accounting treatment of fixed assets is the measurement of the cost of the assets. FRS 15 ('Tangible fixed assets') states that a tangible fixed asset should initially be measured at the costs that are directly attributable to bringing the asset into working condition for its intended use. The cost of a fixed asset will therefore include its purchase price plus other directly attributable costs such as: acquisition costs (e.g. stamp duty, import duties); site preparation and clearance costs; delivery and handling costs; installation costs; professional fees; and dismantling and removal costs. If an asset is constructed, then in addition to the costs outlined above, the costs of work subcontracted, plus the costs of materials, labour and directly traceable overheads should be included.

Interest charges on capital borrowed to finance the construction of tangible fixed assets may also be capitalized and the disclosure requirements of FRS 15 must then be followed. These were discussed earlier in Chapter 2 (see page 43).

Leased assets

SSAP 21 ('Accounting for leases and hire purchase contracts') requires the financial statements of a company to reflect the full impact of leasing transactions. The accounting treatment adopted for a leased asset depends on whether the lease is a finance lease or an operating lease. SSAP 21 defines a finance lease as one that transfers to the lessee substantially all of the risks and rewards of owning an asset, with all other leases being classed as operating leases. Assets leased to a company under a finance lease must be accounted for in a way similar to owned assets. Thus a finance lease will appear in a lessee's balance sheet as both an asset and an obligation to pay future rentals, and the asset should be depreciated over the shorter of the lease term and its useful life. At the inception of the lease the amount to be regarded both as the asset and the obligation should be the present value of the minimum lease payments (calculated by discounting at the interest rate implicit in the lease).

In Chapter 1 the concept of substance over form was discussed (see page 10). SSAP 21, which was issued in 1984 and amended in 1997, was the first accounting standard to apply this concept. Assets obtained under a finance lease are not legally owned and yet they are required to be accounted for as though they are. Prior to the introduction of SSAP 21 companies could avoid disclosing assets and the associated liabilities on their balance sheets by simply obtaining them under a lease agreement rather than buying them. SSAP 21 prevented this for assets leased to a company under a finance lease agreement.

The precise rules for accounting for finance leases are complex and somewhat outside the scope of this book. Readers who wish to obtain a fuller understanding of the accounting techniques are referred to a textbook on advanced financial accounting (see, for example, Alexander and Britton, 2001: chapter 19).

SSAP 21 requires disclosure for each major class of fixed asset held under a finance lease of the gross amount, the related accumulated depreciation and the depreciation allocated for the period. Alternatively, this information may be included within the totals disclosed by each major class of asset for owned assets, provided that the total of the net amount of assets held under finance leases and the total amount of depreciation allocated for the period in respect of finance leases are disclosed separately. The BOC Group adopts the latter approach as can be seen from note 8(a) on page 261.

Investments

Under the two alternative formats, investments appear in either fixed or current assets. Under the heading 'fixed assets', the following must be shown either on the balance sheet or in the notes to the financial statements:

- shares in group companies;
- loans to group companies;
- participating interests;
- loans to undertakings in which the company has a participating interest;
- other investments *other* than loans;
- other loans;
- own shares.

In group accounts, participating interests are to be replaced by two items: interests in associated undertakings and other participating interests. Under the heading 'current assets', the following must be disclosed on the face of the balance sheet or in the notes:

- shares in group undertakings;
- own shares;
- other investments.

In general terms, the distinction between the two headings relates to the basis on which investments are held. Those held on a relatively short-term basis would be included under 'current assets'.

As mentioned earlier in this chapter, there are alternative valuation bases for these assets – cost, market value or determined value. Listed investments must be distinguished, sub-divided between those listed on a recognized stock exchange and those listed elsewhere.

Where an investment in shares exceeds 10 per cent of the allotted share capital of the subject company or of the nominal value of any class of equity share capital, or where the value of the investment exceeds 10 per cent of the assets of the investing company, the notes must give additional information:

- the name of the subject company;
- its country of incorporation and/or registration;
- the identity and proportion of the nominal value of each class of shares held.

Companies listed on the Stock Exchange must give additional information, including the principal country of operation of the subject company and the percentage of each class of loan capital attributable to the investing company's interest (direct or indirect).

In its financial statements, The BOC Group presents information that reveals the total book value of investments in joint ventures, associates, other investments and own shares, net of provisions to be £468.6 million (see note 9(b) on page 264). That net value is analysed as:

	(£ million)
Listed on stock exchanges in the UK and overseas	91.1
Unlisted – equity at directors' valuation	244.9
– other at directors' valuation	132.6
	468.6

The item 'own shares' in note 9(a) refers to BOC's own shares held for satisfying options under the company's share-based incentive schemes. Many companies have taken advantage of the tax incentives available for employee share ownership and have established schemes that enable employees to be allocated free shares under a profit-sharing scheme or give employees the option to buy shares at a favourable price. The shares that are needed for this can be either new shares or existing shares acquired by a trust and held for the employees. The shares acquired in this way are usually financed by a loan from the company or through a bank loan guaranteed by the company. BOC discloses the shares held for share-based incentive schemes as a fixed asset investment at an acquisition cost of £42.5 million.

Current assets

Stock

Stocks are required to be disclosed as a main heading in the balance sheet. The word 'stocks' must be used; alternatives are not permitted. The category will require the following sub-headings:

- raw materials and consumables;
- work in progress;
- finished goods and goods for resale;
- payments on account.

A company should normally follow the above categorization, but the directors may adapt the format where the special nature of a company's business makes such an adaptation appropriate. SSAP 9 ('Stocks and long-term contracts') requires that the accounting policies adopted with respect to stocks and work in progress must be disclosed. The value to be used in respect of stocks is their purchase price or production cost, unless their net realizable value is lower, in which case that lower amount is used.

The 1985 Act (as amended) permits several methods of determining the cost of stock to be used, i.e. FIFO, LIFO, weighted average or any other similar method. An example of the use of these methods was considered in Chapter 2. Detailed consideration of the valuation of work in progress and long-term contracts is not appropriate here, and readers are referred to SSAP 9 and a relevant accounting textbook, such as Alexander and Britton (2001: chapter 20).

The BOC balance sheet (see Table 3.3) shows a value for stocks of £260.0 million and an analysis of that total is provided in note 10(a) (see page 264) as follows:

	(£ million)
Raw materials	67.8
Work in progress	47.8
Gases and other finished goods	159.0
Payments on account	(14.6)
	260.0

Note 10 also provides similarly detailed information about the other categories of current assets and liabilities referred to below.

Debtors

Debtors must be disclosed as a main heading on the balance sheet and the following items must be disclosed either on the face of the balance sheet or in the notes thereto:

- trade debtors;
- amounts owed by group undertakings;
- amounts owed by undertakings in which the company has a participating interest;
- other debtors;
- called-up share capital not paid;
- prepayments and accrued income.

While shown under separate main headings on the alternative formats, the two final items above ('called-up share capital not paid' and 'prepayments and accrued income') may be included under 'debtors' when the amounts are not material.

'Trade debtors' will include amounts owed by customers, suppliers' debit balances, contract retentions etc., less any provision for bad and doubtful debts, credits for returns, allowances, cash discounts and rebates.

'Other debtors' will include amounts in respect of debts arising from non-trading or lending activities – amounts due from the sale of fixed assets, insurance claims, refundable deposits and the like. Additionally, the Companies Acts require disclosure under this heading of the following:

- loans to finance share purchases, where such loans are lawful;
- loans to directors;
- loans to officers other than directors.

The amounts shown under debtors will normally include all amounts due within one year of the balance sheet date. The accounting treatment of amounts due beyond one year is less clear. Strictly speaking these should be recorded as fixed assets, but this accounting treatment may not be appropriate and might even be misleading for situations where the terms of trade of an industry allow customers longer periods than one year in which to pay. BOC discloses the amounts due from debtors within one year and the amounts due beyond one year separately on the face of its balance sheet.

Cash at bank and in hand

Cash at bank and in hand should not include deposits with building societies or time deposits with banks and the like, which should be shown as current asset investments. However, all other cash and near-cash items should be shown in this category: legal tender, cheques, postal orders, credit card vouchers, demand deposits and the like.

Creditors

Format 1 requires that creditors must be separated into those falling due within one year and those falling due after more than one year. Format 2 provides only one heading for creditors, but the amounts must be shown separately – within one year and after more than one year – and in aggregate. The Act lays down that 'creditors' must be shown under the following sub-headings either on the face of the balance sheet or in the notes to the balance sheet:

- debenture loans;
- bank loans and overdrafts;
- payments received on account;
- trade creditors;
- bills of exchange payable;
- amounts owed to group undertakings;
- amounts owed to undertakings in which the company has a participating interest;
- other creditors including taxation and social security;
- accruals and deferred income.

The last heading is shown separately on the alternative formats, but may be included under creditors where not material.

In general terms, the categories above are straightforward and the calculation of the amounts to be reported is fairly easy. However, care should be taken not to confuse the item 'other creditors including taxation and social security' with the item 'taxation, including deferred taxation' which appears under the heading of 'provisions for liabilities and charges' (see later). UK corporation tax, and tax on profits that is payable to overseas governments, should appear under creditors. This is because these liabilities are certain as to the amount and date when payable and therefore do not fall within the definition of a 'provision'.

The BOC balance sheet for 2002 (see Table 3.3) shows that the creditors falling due within one year, which are also referred to as current liabilities, consisted of borrowings and finance leases of £390.1 million and 'other creditors' of £857.8 million (i.e. a total of £1,247.9 million). Notes 10(e) and 10(f) to the financial statements provide an analysis of these amounts as follows:

Borrowings and finance leases	*(£ million)*
Bank loans and overdrafts	196.7
Loans other than from banks	182.3
Finance leases	11.1
	390.1

Other creditors	*(£ million)*
Deposits and advance payments by customers	41.5
Trade creditors	367.3
Taxation – UK	69.0
– Overseas	78.5
Other taxes and social security	27.3
Other creditors	130.0
Accruals and deferred income	144.2
	857.8

Separate disclosure is also required of amounts due to creditors after more than one year (also described as long-term liabilities) and for 2002 the total amount due is reported as £1,179.0 million. This total is made up of borrowings and finance leases amounting to £1,121.0 million and other creditors of £58.0 million. Information on the maturity dates of the long-term borrowings is required to be disclosed and BOC provide this information in note 3(c)(ii) to the financial statements.

Provisions for liabilities and charges

Provisions for liabilities and charges must be shown on the face of the balance sheet as a main heading; the following sub-headings must be disclosed either on the face of the balance sheet or in the notes thereto:

- pensions and similar obligations;
- taxation, including deferred taxation;
- other provisions.

Provisions for liabilities or charges is defined in the Act as 'Any amount retained as reasonably necessary for the purpose of providing for any liability or loss which is either likely to be incurred, or certain to be incurred but uncertain as to amount or as to the date on which it will arise'.

FRS 12 ('Provisions, contingent liabilities and assets') defines a provision as simply a liability that is of uncertain timing or amount. A provision is therefore different from a liability such as a trade creditor because a trade creditor liability presents no uncertainty as to the amount. FRS 12 provides several examples of provisions. The first of these is where a manufacturer gives warranties to purchasers of its products whereby any defects that become apparent within three years from the date of sale will be made good. On past experience it is likely that there will be some claims under the warranties. The sale of the products gives rise to a liability, but as the amount and timing of the liability is uncertain, this is a provision. The amount recognized as a provision should be the best estimate of the expenditure required to make good the obligation at the balance sheet date. In this example the provision would be the estimated cost of making good any products sold before the balance sheet date.

FRS 14 requires the disclosure for each different class of provision of the amount of the provision at the beginning and end of the accounting period and any changes in the provision during the accounting period. BOC in note 11(b) provides information on the following different classes of provision: deferred tax; incentive and other employee provisions; uninsured losses; restructuring provisions; environmental; and others. The total of these provisions at 30 September 2002 was £407.5 million.

Information on pension assets and liabilities is required under FRS 17 ('Retirement benefits') to be presented separately on the balance sheet.

Pension assets and liabilities

BOC operates defined benefits pension schemes for its employees and following BOC's implementation of the requirements of FRS17 the consolidated balance sheet for 2002 (see Table 3.3) presents information on the assets and liabilities of the pension schemes. It can be seen from this that the schemes show an overall deficit of £256.7 million (£54.3 million − £311.0 million). Note 6(e) to the financial statements provides a geographical analysis of this deficit and reveals that the overall relationship between the market value of the pension scheme assets and the present value of the pension scheme liabilities is as follows:

	(£ million)
Total market value of assets	1,473.3
Present value of scheme liabilities	(1,825.4)
Irrecoverable surplus	(11.0)
Deficit in the scheme	(363.1)
Reduction in deferred tax liability	106.4
Net deficit in the schemes	(256.7)

Much of the controversy surrounding the introduction of FRS 17 is that it forces companies to disclose the existence of any surplus or deficit in defined benefit pension schemes. Since FRS 17 was introduced in November 2000 there has been a sustained fall in the value of equities leading to a fall in the market value of many pension scheme assets. Also, revisions to the life expectancy data used by actuaries has led to increases in the present value of the liabilities of many schemes. The result for very many of the companies operating defined benefits schemes is that their schemes are likely to be in deficit. The full implementation of the requirements of FRS 17 will result in such deficits being clearly disclosed and the accounts for BOC for 2002 are a good example of this. The surplus or deficit of a pension scheme will fluctuate in line with fluctuations in the market value of the assets of the scheme and so unless a deficit becomes significant or sustained it should not necessarily signal any concerns over a company's operational viability.

Capital and reserves

Share capital and share premium

The 1985 Act (as amended) and its schedule require the disclosure of the following items:

- the amount of the authorized share capital;
- the amount of the allotted share capital;
- the amount of the called-up share capital that has been paid;
- the number and aggregate value of each class of allotted shares;
- the earliest and latest redemption dates of any redeemable shares and associated details;
- the reasons for and details of any allotment of shares during the period in question;
- the number, description and amount of any share options;
- the amount and period of any arrears in respect of fixed cumulative dividends;
- details of any holdings of the company's securities by subsidiaries or their nominees.

Where companies issue shares for a consideration in excess of their par or face value, the excess is to be placed in a share premium account. For example, if a company issues 400,000 £1 shares at £3 each, then it must credit £800,000 to a share premium account. Once a share premium account has been established it may be used only for purposes laid down in the Act: the issue of fully paid bonus shares, the writing-off of any preliminary or formation expenses, the writing-off of any expenses, commissions or discounts in connection with the issue of shares or debentures, or the provision of any premium payable on the redemption of debentures. Apart from those specific uses, the share premium account has to be treated as if it were part of the paid-up share capital of a company.

Certain types of shares have features which make them economically similar to debt. The basic distinction between debt and equity is that debt carries an obligation to pay interest, whereas there is no obligation to pay anything to equity. The holders of equity may receive a dividend if there are sufficient profits but there is no *entitlement*. The share capital of a company will consist of equity but might also consist of other types of shares (such as preference shares) which have an *entitlement* to a dividend and therefore are more akin to debt. However, company law requires these types of non-equity shares to be included as part of the share capital of a company rather than as a liability. FRS 4 ('Capital instruments') requires the shareholders' funds of a company to be analysed between the amounts attributable to equity interests and the amount attributable to non-equity interests. Disclosure of each class of non-equity share is required together with a summary of the rights to dividends, the date of and amount due on redemption, priority on the winding up of the company and voting rights.

The BOC Group balance sheet (see Table 3.3) reveals that the nominal value of the equity share capital is £124.3 million. Note 12 to the financial statements (see pages 266–7) confirms that there are no non-equity shareholders' interests in the share capital and resources of the Group.

Other reserves and profit and loss account

'Other reserves' will generally be capital redemption reserves or own share redemption reserves. Additionally, a company's articles of association may stipulate the creation of other reserves for specific purposes.

The 1985 Act (as amended) formats require that the retained balance on profit and loss account should be shown on the face of the balance sheet, and movements on profit and loss account must be disclosed. Note 12(c) to the financial statements reports movements on all reserves for the year, including movements on the share premium account, and also reports the impact on reserves of the deficit in the defined benefits pension scheme.

Minority interests

Minority interests are required to be disclosed on the face of the balance sheet. Minority interest, as a balance sheet item, is defined as the amount of capital and reserves attributable to shares in subsidiary undertakings included in the consolidation and held by or on behalf of persons other than the parent company and its subsidiaries. The consolidation process requires 100 per cent of a subsidiary's assets and liabilities to be aggregated with those of the parent company, even though only, say, 60 per cent of the shares of the subsidiary might be held by the parent. The remaining 40 per cent of the shares are held by minority shareholders and it is the value of their share of the subsidiary undertakings, assets and liabilities that is represented by the item minority interests. FRS 2 ('Accounting for subsidiary undertakings') requires the assets and liabilities of a subsidiary undertaking to be attributed to minority interests on the same basis as those attributed to group interests. Dividends due to minority interests should be shown as liabilities under the heading of 'other creditors including taxation and social security'. FRS 4 ('Capital instruments') requires minority interests to be analysed between equity interests and non-equity interests.

Contingencies and commitments

Contingencies

It is appropriate here to mention the matter of contingent liabilities and assets. Contingencies are conditions that exist at a balance sheet date, but of which the future outcome is uncertain and only confirmed on the outcome of one or more uncertain future events – law suits, guarantees, taxation and the like. The Act requires that, for any contingent liability which has not been provided for in the financial statements, the notes must disclose the amount or estimated amount of that liability, its legal nature and the particulars of any security given. FRS 12 ('Provisions, contingent liabilities and assets') clarifies the distinction between a provision (see above, page 66) and contingent liabilities. Provisions must be recognized as liabilities because they are obligations which will lead to a probable transfer of economic benefits, even though the amount and timing of the transfer is uncertain. Contingent liabilities are not recognized as liabilities in the balance sheet of a company because they are either obligations that are unlikely to lead to the transfer of economic benefits or are only possible obligations which have yet to be confirmed. FRS 12 requires a brief description of the nature of contingent liabilities to be disclosed in the notes, together with, where practicable, an estimate of the amount of the contingent liability.

Note 13(b) to the BOC accounts (see page 268) reveals that 'other guarantees and contingent liabilities' amounted to £38.7 million. The note goes on to report that:

> various group undertakings are parties to legal actions and claims, some of which are for substantial amounts. While the outcome of some of these matters cannot readily be foreseen, the directors believe that they will be disposed of without material effect on the net asset position as shown in these financial statements.

Commitments

The Act requires disclosure of the following financial commitments:

- capital commitments (expenditure contracted for or authorized at the balance sheet date);
- pension commitments (those that are provided for in the balance sheet and those that are not provided for);
- other financial commitments (purchase commitments in excess of normal requirement, exposed foreign currency positions, lending or guarantee commitments).

In broad terms, these details are given in respect of any financial commitments that have not been provided for and are relevant to an assessment of the company's affairs.

Post balance sheet events

There is now a requirement to report post balance sheet events, generally defined as events that become apparent only between the balance sheet date and the date of the signing of the balance sheet on behalf of the board of directors. Both the Act and SSAP 17 ('Accounting for post balance sheet events') contain requirements in this respect. SSAP 17 makes a distinction between events that require adjustment of the financial statements ('adjusting events') and those that require disclosure but do not require adjustment to the financial statements ('non-adjusting events'). Examples of adjusting events would include the bankruptcy of a debtor after the year-end; a fall in the selling price of a product, causing net realizable value of stocks to fall below cost; changes in the rate of taxation on profits taken up in the financial statements; or the discovery of errors or fraud showing the financial statements to be incorrect. Non-adjusting events might include a fall in the value of property or investments, a change in foreign exchange rates, the issue of shares or the acquisition or disposal of a business.

An example of the disclosure of non-adjusting events is found in this extract from the notes to the 2000 accounts of BAE Systems plc:

> *Airbus.* An integrated joint Airbus company was formed with effect from 1 January 2001 to take on the combined operations of the Airbus Industrie GIE partners, BAE SYSTEMS and EADS, together with Airbus Industrie GIE itself. BAE SYSTEMS will hold a 20% interest in the new company with EADS holding the balance.
>
> *Business divestments.* In February 2001 agreement was reached for the sale of the company's 54% subsidiary BAE SYSTEMS Canada Inc. to ONCAP, an investment fund located in Toronto, Canada. The transaction, which is subject to both Canadian and US regulatory approvals, is expected to complete in the first half of 2001.
>
> In February 2001 the company reached agreement to sell its Flight Simulation and Training business based in Tampa, Florida, to CAE, Toronto, Canada. Completion of this transaction is expected in the first half of 2001, subject to regulatory approval in the US.

The Act requires disclosure in the directors' report of particulars of important events affecting the company and its subsidiaries that have occurred after the year end. It is clearly a matter of very fine judgement as to whether a post balance sheet event is a 'non-adjusting event', which SSAP 17 requires to be disclosed in the notes (as in the BAE Systems example) or an 'important event' which the Companies Act requires to be disclosed in the directors' report.

The approach adopted in the 2001 accounts of Cadbury Schweppes is to include a note to the financial statements and a note in the directors' report which states that 'details of the three acquisitions made by the Group since 30 December 2001 are given in the Description of Business ...'.

The Description of Business section of the annual report then states

> *2002.* In February, the Group announced that its open offer to acquire the outstanding 49% minority in Cadbury India Ltd had closed. At a price of 500 Rupees per share, the offer valued the minority at 8,749 million Rupees (£128 million). Approximately 14 million shares were tendered in the open offer, taking Cadbury Schweppes' holding above 90% of the paid-up capital of Cadbury India Ltd. In accordance with the SEBI Takeover Code, Cadbury Schweppes will make another offer at the same price as the original offer within three months.
>
> In February, the Group announced that it had agreed to purchase Squirt, the eighth largest carbonated soft drinks brand in Mexico, from Refremex AG for an undisclosed sum. The Squirt brand had concentrated sales of US$23 million (£16 million) in 2001.

In February, the Group announced that it had agreed to acquire a 51% equity interest in Kent, Turkey's leading sugar confectionery manufacturer, together with a majority equity interest in its distribution arm, Birlik, for £67 million (US$95 million).

The date of approval of the financial statements of The BOC Group is shown on the face of the balance sheet to have been 22 November 2002.

4 The cash flow statement

In September 1991 the ASB issued FRS 1 ('Cash flow statements') requiring all companies (except for small companies, wholly owned subsidiaries, building societies and mutual life assurance companies) to publish a cash flow statement. Prior to the introduction of FRS 1, companies had been required by SSAP 10 to provide a statement of source and application of funds.

The basic purpose of a cash flow statement is simply to report the cash receipts and the cash payments of an accounting period. As such it is claimed to be objective and understandable and to avoid many of the allocations that are needed for conventional profit determination. The matching concept requires the matching of the income of a period with the expenses of a period, with the difference between the two being profit or loss. Because many income and expense items do not conveniently fall into a particular period but have an impact on several periods it is necessary to allocate such items over the periods that are affected. As was seen in Chapter 2 there are a range of permitted methods for determining closing stock values and periodic depreciation charges and each method produced different costs for each accounting period. These are just two of the very many examples where items have to be allocated on an arbitrary basis to specific accounting periods. Cash flow statements avoid the need to make such periodic allocations.

However, a cash flow statement that simply reported the aggregate of cash receipts and the aggregate of cash payments would probably not be particularly useful. The original FRS 1 therefore required cash flows to be classified under the standard headings of: operating activities; returns on investment and servicing of finance; taxation; investing activities; and financing.

The requirements of FRS 1 were undoubtedly a major development in financial reporting and although it generally worked quite well there were some criticisms, particularly in relation to the requirement for cash flow statements to report the 'inflows and outflows of cash and cash equivalents'. The definition of cash as cash in hand and deposits repayable on demand with any bank or other financial institution was relatively straightforward. However, the definition of cash equivalents did cause problems. The inclusion of cash equivalents was an attempt to recognize that cash over and above that immediately needed would not be held in the form of cash but would be invested in short-term investments. Providing these investments were highly liquid, could be converted into known amounts of cash and were not subject to significant changes in value because of interest rate changes then they were accountable for as cash equivalents. To ensure that changes in interest rates would not bring about a significant change in the value of an investment, a cut-off date of not more than three months to maturity was imposed. This arbitrary cut-off date was difficult to defend and in October 1996 the ASB published a revised version of FRS 1 that contained a much tighter and much purer definition of cash. Cash is now defined as:

> Cash-in-hand and deposits repayable on demand with any qualifying financial institution, less overdrafts from any qualifying financial institution repayable on demand. Deposits are repayable on demand if they can be withdrawn at any time without notice and without penalty or if a maturity or period of notice of not more than 24 hours or one working day has been agreed.

The revised FRS 1 requires the cash flow statement to be classified under eight standard headings as follows:

1 operating activities;
2 returns on investment and servicing of finance;
3 taxation;
4 capital expenditure and financial investment;
5 acquisitions and disposals;
6 equity dividends paid;
7 management of liquid resources; and
8 financing.

The first six headings should follow the above sequence but the last two can be combined under a single heading providing that the cash flows that relate to each are shown separately and that separate sub-totals are given.

Where a group relationship exists a consolidated cash flow statement should be produced. If an investor company has investments in associates or joint ventures (see Chapter 2, pages 39–41), then FRS 9 ('Associates and joint ventures') requires an additional standard heading to be included in the consolidated cash flow statement. The additional standard heading is 'dividends from joint ventures and associates' and should be placed immediately after 'operating activities'.

The BOC Group's cash flow statement for 2002, and the comparatives for the previous year, is reported in Table 4.1. This provides the classification of cash flows in the format required by the revised FRS 1, together with the additional standard heading required by FRS 9.

Cash flow statement components

Operating activities

The net cash flow from operating activities is the cash surplus or deficit for the period that results from the items that normally make up the operating profit of the profit and loss account. It will therefore include the cash receipts from sales; the cash payments to suppliers, employees, providers of services, etc. It will be different from the operating profit because it will not include non-cash transactions such as credit sales, credit purchases and depreciation.

Table 4.1   The BOC Group plc–consolidated cash flow statement for year ended 30 September 2002

	Notes	2002 (£ million)	2001 (restated) (£ million)
Net cash inflow from operating activities	14(a)	759.3	787.8
Dividends from joint ventures and associates			
Dividends from joint ventures		30.5	19.4
Dividends from associates		3.4	4.1
Dividends from joint ventures and associates		33.9	23.5
Returns on investments and servicing of finance			
Interest paid		(89.6)	(95.4)
Interest received		18.5	23.1
Dividends paid to minorities in subsidiaries		(13.9)	(7.7)
Interest element of finance lease rental payments		(5.7)	(7.2)
Returns on investments and servicing of finance		(90.7)	(87.2)
Tax paid		(96.2)	(100.6)
Capital expenditure and financial investment			
Purchases of tangible fixed assets		(352.1)	(349.8)
Sales of tangible fixed assets		31.6	47.1
Purchases of intangible fixed assets		(0.1)	(0.3)
Net sales/(purchases) of current asset investments		4.3	(6.5)
Purchases of trade and other investments		(19.7)	(10.2)
Sales of trade and other investments		11.5	7.8
Capital expenditure and financial investment		(324.5)	(311.9)
Acquisitions and disposals			
Acquisitions of businesses	15(a)	(207.3)	(145.9)
Net overdrafts acquired with subsidiaries		(7.4)	—
Disposals of businesses	15(a)	10.6	2.7
Investments in joint ventures		(12.6)	—
Divestments/repayments from joint ventures		—	10.8
Investments in associates		(0.5)	(2.7)
Divestments/repayments from associates		1.7	1.5
Acquisitions and disposals		(215.5)	(133.6)
Equity dividends paid		(186.6)	(180.3)
Net cash outflow before use of liquid resources and financing		(120.3)	(2.3)
Management of liquid resources			
Net sales of short-term investments		52.6	102.8
Financing			
Issue of shares		25.0	16.9
Increase/(decrease) in debt	14(d)	64.1	(51.3)
Net cash inflow/(outflow) from financing		89.1	(34.4)
Increase in cash		21.4	66.1

A reconciliation of the increase in cash to the movement in net debt in the year is given in note 14(b).
Liquid resources are defined as short-term deposits.

FRS 1 requires operating cash flows to be reported by using the indirect method but permits the information required by the direct method to be reported as well. Under the direct method the cash book is analysed into the various types of cash receipts and payments of the period and these are reported in the statements of operating cash flows. Under the indirect method it is only the net cash flow from operating activities that is reported and this is arrived at by starting with the operating profit and then adjusting this for all non-cash items.

As can be seen from Table 4.1, BOC uses the indirect method and reports simply the net cash flow from operations of £759.3 million. However, FRS 1 requires a note showing the reconciliation of this figure to the operating profit. This is provided in note 14(a) (see page 269) as follows:

	2002
Net cash inflow from operating activities	*£ million*
Total operating profit before exceptional items	500.1
Depreciation and amortization	330.9
FRS 17 retirement benefits charge	49.9
Operating profit before exceptional items of joint ventures	(63.8)
Operating profit before exceptional items of associates	(10.7)
Change in stocks	13.7
Change in debtors	(38.4)
Change in creditors	57.3
Exceptional cash flows	(67.3)
Other	(12.4)
Net cash inflow from operating activities	759.3

Even if the direct method is used to report cash flows from operations, a statement showing the reconciliation with operating profit is still required.

Dividends from joint ventures and associates

This is required by FRS 9 to be included in the consolidated cash flow statement of an investor company which has investments in joint ventures and/or associates. Only the dividends received from joint ventures and associates should be included under this heading. Any other cash flows between the investor and its joint ventures and associates should be included in whichever of the other headings is appropriate for the activity giving rise to the cash flows.

Returns on investment and servicing of finance

The purpose of this category is to capture all of the cash flows that result from payments to the providers of finance and from ownership of investment. In Table 4.1 BOC report interest paid; interest received; dividends paid to minorities in subsidiaries; and the interest element of finance lease payments. Dividends relating to equity shares appear under a separate heading in the cash flow statement. If the returns on investment and servicing of finance classification were not provided, these types of cash flows would have to be categorized as relating to either operating activities or financing activities or capital expenditure and financial investment activities or acquisitions and disposals activities. At times such a distinction might be difficult to make. Also, by categorizing interest payments under this heading the cash flows from operating activities are not affected by the way in which a company is financed and this should improve comparability. Any interest paid in the year that has been capitalized should be reported under this heading (rather than part of capital expenditure and financial investments).

Taxation

The use of this category avoids the need for arbitrary allocations of taxation to other categories such as cash flows from operating activities. Cash flows in respect of taxation on profits tend to arise because of the activities of previous periods rather than the current period and so this provides a further rationale for a separate category for taxation. It follows from this that it is only tax flows relating to payments (or refunds) of tax on profits that is reported here. Cash flows in respect of VAT, property tax (business rates) or other taxes not assessed on profits should not be reported under this heading. VAT and property tax, for example, will normally form part of the cash flows from operating activities. The usual accounting treatment is for cash flows to be reported net of VAT with only the net amount of cash due to or from the VAT authorities included as an operating cash flow.

Capital expenditure and financial investment

This category includes all cash flows relating to the acquisition or disposal of fixed assets (including investments). The following cash inflows should be separately disclosed:

- receipts from sales of property, plant and equipment;
- receipts from the repayment of loans made to other entities (other than receipts forming part of a disposal or a movement in liquid resources (see below);
- receipts from the sale of debt instruments of other entities (other than receipts forming part of a disposal or movement in net liquid resources).

The cash outflows that are required to be disclosed are as follows:

- payments to acquire property, plant and equipment;
- loans made by the reporting entity to other entities (other than payments forming part of acquisition or a movement in liquid resources);
- payments to acquire debt instruments of other entities (other than payments forming part of an acquisition or a movement in net liquid resources).

Table 4.1 shows that BOC's net cash outflow from capital expenditure and financial investment for the year to 30 September 2002 was £324.5 million.

The purchase of fixed assets on credit can complicate the classification of the associated cash flows. If a fixed asset is paid for in cash or a down payment of part of the total acquisition cost is made in cash, then these are clearly capital expenditure and financial investment flows. Subsequent repayments of what is essentially a loan from the seller of the fixed asset are financing cash flows. The treatment would also apply to the acquisition of assets under hire purchase contracts or where assets are obtained under a finance lease, with the payments of principal being classified as financing cash flows rather than capital expenditure and financial investment cash flows. (A short-term difference between the time when an asset is acquired and the subsequent payment would not of course change the cash flow classification from capital expenditure and financial investment to financing.

Acquisition and disposals

This heading covers cash receipts from the disposal of any trade or business or from the sale of investments in an entity that as a result of the sale ceases to be either an associate, a joint venture or a subsidiary. Likewise any payments to acquire any trade or business or for investing in an entity that would result in the entity becoming an associate, joint venture or subsidiary is also covered by this heading.

The revised version of FRS 1 requires any balances of cash and overdrafts acquired on the purchase of subsidiaries or any balances of cash and overdrafts transferred as part of the sale of subsidiaries to be disclosed separately.

The complication caused by the purchase of fixed assets on credit as discussed above also applies when the payment to acquire a subsidiary is deferred. When the deferred payment is eventually made the question that then arises is whether this should be treated as a financing cash flow or as an acquisition and disposal. The revised FRS 1 is silent on this point.

BOC reports several items under the heading acquisitions and disposals and also shows separately the cash balances and overdrafts on the acquisition and disposal of subsidiaries. The amounts of £207.3 million paid for acquisitions of businesses and £10.6 million received from the disposals of businesses are analysed further in note 15(a) to the financial statements.

Equity dividends paid

The amounts to be included under this heading are the dividends paid on the company's equity shares, excluding any related tax credit.

Management of liquid resources

The cash flows included under this heading are defined in FRS 1 (para. 2) as those related to 'current asset investments held as readily disposable stores of value'. The standard makes it clear that 'readily disposable' means an investment that could be disposed of without curtailing or disrupting the business of the entity. This in turn means investments that are either readily convertible into known amounts of cash at, or close to, their carrying amounts (which would tend to exclude any that are more than one year from maturity at acquisition), or traded in an active market.

FRS 1 requires the separate disclosure of:

- cash inflows from withdrawals from short-term deposits not qualifying as cash;
- cash inflows from the disposal or redemption of other investments held as liquid resources;
- cash outflows for payments into short-term deposits not counting as cash;
- cash outflows to acquire any other investments held as liquid resources.

The items can however be netted off for presentation purposes if the cash inflows and outflows are due to the high turnover occurring from the rollover or reissue of short maturity items. BOC has obviously taken advantage of this netting-off provision and reports simply the net purchase of short-term investments as £52.6 million.

Financing

Included in this category are the receipts from and payments to providers of finance. Only the principal amounts involved are included, with interest, dividends, etc. appearing under returns on investments and servicing of finance. The cash inflows that are required to be disclosed under this heading are:

- receipts from issuing shares or other equity instruments; and
- receipts from issuing debentures, loans, notes and bonds and from other long- and short-term borrowings (other than overdrafts).

The financing cash outflows include the following and these also are required to be separately disclosed:

- repayments of amounts borrowed (other than overdrafts);
- the capital element of finance lease rental payments;
- payments to re-acquire or redeem the entity's shares; and
- payments of expenses or commissions on any issue of shares.

One complication arises with the premium payable on redemption of loans or shares. Where a premium payable on redemption is in the nature of interest then presumably this should be classified under the returns on investments and servicing of finance heading. BOC provides an analysis of the increase in debt of £64.1 million in note 14(d) to the financial statements.

Usefulness of cash flow statements

The requirement to include a cash flow statement in the annual report of a company is a relatively recent one and the extent to which users of financial statements find it useful still has to be established. The statement which it replaced, the funds flow statement, was generally perceived to be helpful in answering questions concerning the resources that a company had available to it and the use it made of those resources. However, funds flow statements were based on movements in working capital rather than cash and this could obscure movements relevant to the liquidity and viability of an entity. An example of this provided by FRS 1 is where a significant decrease in cash is masked by an increase in stocks or debtors. Companies might therefore run out of cash while reporting increases in working capital. Similarly a decrease in working capital does not necessarily indicate a cash shortage. Also a wide variety of funds flow statements were presented, with some companies reporting movements in net liquid funds and others reporting movements in working capital, net borrowings or total external financing.

The ASB feels that by concentrating on cash flows only, the cash flow statement, in conjunction with the balance sheet, provides information on liquidity, viability and financial adaptability that is easier to understand than information on changes in working capital. Also, the cash flow statement and its associated notes do not simply reorganize existing opening and closing balance sheet information (as was the case with the source and application of funds statements) but provides new data.

In addition cash flows have the advantages mentioned earlier in this chapter of being more objective and less dependent on arbitrary allocations than conventional accruals-based financial statements. The cash flow statement might be expected therefore to become one of the prime sources of information about the financial performance and financial position of a company.

In an attempt to bring out the distinction between cash flow statements and the conventional accruals based profit and loss statements an illustration drawn from the following simple set of information has been provided.

Example 4.1

Suppose that New Company Limited was formed on 1 January 20X0 and commenced in business on that date as manufacturers of central heating thermostats. Because they were a new start-up company they were offered brand new factory premises by the local industrial development agency for a low start rent of £15,000 per year payable quarterly in advance. On 1 January 20X0 the four owners of the company each invested £25,000 of their own money to provide a total of £100,000 of equity share capital. Also on that date New Company Limited obtained a medium term loan of £100,000 at an interest rate of 11½ per cent per annum from the local industrial development agency. During the year to 31 December 20X0, the following nine transactions took place:

1 Purchased manufacturing plant and equipment for £175,000. All of this had been paid for by the end of the year but none of the installation costs of £17,500 had been paid.
2 The rent for the year had been paid and in addition the rent for the first quarter of 20X1 had been paid early in December 20X0.
3 Six months interest on the loan had been paid by 31 December 20X0.
4 Wages and salaries expenses totalling £220,000 were incurred and paid for during the year.
5 Raw materials amounting to £217,000 had been purchased during the year but only £193,000 of this had been paid for by 31 December 20X0.
6 The stock of raw materials that had not been used by 31 December 20X0 was valued at £21,500 and the stock of finished goods was valued at £36,200. There was no work in progress.
7 Heating, lighting and miscellaneous expenses totalling £92,450 were paid for during the year.
8 It was decided that no dividend would be paid to the shareholders for the first year of business and no taxation was due.
9 The sales value of central heating thermostats sold during the year was £560,020. This amount includes £33,400 that had not been received from customers by 31 December 20X0.

Shortly after the end of the financial year it was noted that an invoice amounting to £11,207 for electricity that had been consumed in December 20X0 for heating and lighting the factory had not been paid. It was estimated that the plant and machinery would have a useful life of seven years and no residual value. It was also estimated that approximately 20 per cent of the amounts due from debtors at 31 December 20X0 might never be recovered.

Table 4.2   Cash flow statement – New Company Limited

Cash Flow Statement – Year ended 31 December 20X0	£	£
Operating cash flows		
Cash received from customers		526,620
Less		
Wages	220,000	
Raw materials	193,000	
Rent	18,750	
Heating, lighting, miscellaneous	92,450	524,200
Cash flow from operating activities		2,420
Returns on investments and servicing of finance – interest paid		(5,750)
Taxation		—
Capital expenditure and financial investments		
Manufacturing plant and equipment		(175,000)
Acquisitions and disposals		—
Equity dividends paid		—
Net cash outflow before use of liquid resources and financing		(178,330)
Financing		
Issue of shares	100,000	
Issue of debt	100,000	200,000
Increase in cash		21,670

From this data the cash flow statement shown in Table 4.2 has been prepared by simply classifying the data for actual cash outflows or inflows under the appropriate standard heading. The direct method of determining the operating cash flow has been used, and the format follows the revised version of FRS 1.

The statement in Table 4.2 does, of course, make no adjustment for non-cash items. For example the value of central heating thermostats sold was £560,020 but only £526,620 of this was received from customers in the form of a cash receipt. The remaining £33,400 is the amount due from debtors, i.e. customers who have bought the thermostats on credit terms but not yet paid the amount they owe. The cash flow statement only recognizes the cash received from customers. Similarly, the total expenditure on heating, lighting and miscellaneous expenses was not simply the cash paid during the year on these items of £92,450 but also included the amount of £11,207 in respect of electricity consumed during the year but not paid for by the end of the year. However, the cash flow statement simply focuses on the cash payment of £92,450. The cash flow statement therefore ignores the accruals concept discussed in Chapter 1.

An alternative way to examine the performance of New Company Limited is to prepare a conventional profit and loss account that does follow the accruals (and also the matching) concepts. Under this approach all income from the sale of thermostats, irrespective of whether the cash has been received, will be recorded and all expenditure that relates to the year will be included, even though some of the items have not been paid for by the end of the financial year.

This does, however, bring into play the need to consider other concepts. It has to be recognized that not all of the amounts due from customers, which in the case of New Company Limited total £33,400, might be received and therefore the concept of prudence or conservatism would require an adjustment to be made. In this case it is estimated that 20 per cent of the total debtors of £33,400, i.e. £6,680 might never be recovered. Recognizing the possibility of bad debts is also consistent with the matching concept. If no adjustment were made in 20X0, then the period in which it became certain that the amounts were irrecoverable, which might be 20X1 or 20X2, would have to bear the cost of bad debts that relate to the 20X0 accounting year. This would be in conflict with the matching concept which requires expenses to be charged to the period that gave rise to the expenses, which in this case is clearly 20X0, the year in which the sales were made.

If these concepts of accruals and matching are followed then the closing stocks of raw materials and finished goods should not be an expense of 20X0 because they have not been sold in 20X0 and the cost of plant and equipment will be spread over the years that benefit from its use through an annual depreciation charge. This was discussed in Chapter 2.

A 'conventional' profit and loss account, which is based on the accounting concepts outlined in Chapter 1, for New Company Limited is shown in Table 4.3.

If the cash flow statement and the profit and loss account for New Company Limited are now compared it can be seen that they both provide different kinds of information about the performance of the company. The cash flow statement is based on information that is entirely objective. It makes no assumptions about whether debtors

Table 4.3   Profit and loss account – New Company Limited

Profit and Loss Account – Year Ended 31 December 20X0

	£	£
Sales		560,020
Cost of sales – purchases	217,000	
Less closing stock	57,700	159,300
Gross profit		400,720
Heating and lighting	103,657	
Wages and salaries	220,000	
Interest (£100,000 × 11½%)	11,500	
Rent	15,000	
Depreciation (175,000 + 17,500) ÷ 7	27,500	
Bad debts provision (33,400 × 20%)	6,680	384,337
Profit for year		16,383

Note
(i) The closing stock of £57,700 is made up of raw materials valued at £21,500 and finished goods valued at £36,200.
(ii) The purchase price of the plant and equipment was £175,000 to which has been added the installation costs of £17,500 to give a total cost of £192,500. The plant and machinery has an estimated useful life of seven years with no residual value and so a straight line depreciation charge of £192,500 ÷ 7, i.e. £27,500 has been made.

will or will not pay or how the costs of long-lived assets should be spread over their useful life. It simply works on the basis that if cash is received or paid it will be recorded in the cash flow statement. The operating cash flow surplus of £2,420 might therefore be thought of as an objective and reliable measure of the ability of the company to generate cash from its ongoing day-to-day activities. The cash flow statement also provides very clear information concerning the liquidity of the company and about the sources and uses of cash.

However, as a performance measure the cash flow statement is flawed because it does not tell the whole story. It does not show the total of the benefits or revenues earned by the company in 20X0, or the expenses incurred by the company in 20X0 to achieve those revenues. This is the role of the profit and loss account. The profit of £16,383 for New Company Limited for 20X0 might therefore represent a more relevant measure of performance because it is the balance that remains after taking into account all of the revenues and all of the expenses for 20X0. But is it reliable? Had the depreciation expense been allocated over a different period, say 6 or 8 years, or had a reducing balance method of calculating the annual charge been used, then a different amount to £27,500 would have been charged. Similarly, the closing stock might have been valued differently and the bad debts provision might have been estimated at higher or lower than 20%. All of these adjustments are based on estimates or judgements about uncertain future events. Providing the methods used comply with generally accepted accounting practices, then the different amounts would be defensible and the different profit or loss amounts that would result would be equally defensible. The example of depreciation charges and inventory valuation for the Plastic Products company, that was included in Chapter 2, showed that choice in accounting measurement can produce different measures of profit or loss for the same underlying economic events. This is the dilemma of conventional accruals-based accounting. Conceptually, profit or loss is a very sound measure of performance. In reality, it suffers from the fact that it is based on a series of estimates and judgements and had different but equally valid estimates and judgements been made then the resultant profit or loss would have been different. On the other hand the cash flow statement, which avoids the estimates and judgements and therefore is more reliable, fails to take into account the full range of events that affected performance. The obvious answer is to use both statements together to obtain as clear a picture as possible of the underlying strengths and weaknesses of a company.

Questions

The following 2 questions provide further examples of the distinction between cash flow statements and conventional profit and loss statements. The solutions to these questions can be found in Appendix E (pages 301–9).

Question 4.1

Poppy Field commenced trading as a florist on 1 March 20X2. She rented shop premises from that date at an annual rental of £18,000 which she paid quarterly in advance. Also on 1 March 20X2 Poppy paid £25,000 of her own savings into a new bank account for the florist business, borrowed £24,000 from the bank at a fixed rate of interest of 10% per annum and purchased a delivery van for £12,000. The delivery van was paid for by cheque and Poppy estimates that it will last for 3 years at which time its expected disposal value will be £1,500. During the first two weeks of March 20X2 the shop was equipped with display counters and other fittings for a total cash payment of £30,000. Poppy estimates that these will need replacing in about 6 years time when their disposal value will be negligible.

During the year to 28 February 20X3, the following transactions were recorded:

1 £50,800 paid for flowers, plants and other items for sale;
2 £102,120 received from sale of flowers, plants and other items;
3 £14,680 paid for wages for two part-time assistants;
4 £3,800 paid for advertising charges;
5 £10,200 paid for heating, lighting, telephone and postage;
6 £3,640 paid for miscellaneous items (including delivery van running costs)

It was noted that at 28 February 20X3 Poppy owed the suppliers of flowers £8,070 and that the cost of unsold stock was £4,600. It was also noted that an invoice for £420 for telephone charges for February 20X3 and invoices for £2,640 for heating and lighting charges in January and February 20X3 had not been paid. Bank interest is due monthly in arrears and the interest had been paid every month except February 20X3. This was not paid until early March 20X3. Finally, it was noted that Poppy was owed £6,820 by credit card companies for flowers sold during the year and a further £8,600 from a small number of customers whom Poppy had allowed to purchase flowers on credit. Poppy has decided to use a straight-line basis of depreciation for the delivery van and the shop's display counters and fittings. She has been advised to make a bad debts provision of at least 20% of the £8,600 due from customers who purchased flowers on credit.

From the above information prepare Poppy Field's draft cash flow statement and profit and loss account for the year ended 28 February 20X3. Poppy feels that it is very important for her to show a profit for her first year of trading and asks you to explain how the 'bottom line' of the draft profit and loss account you have prepared could be legitimately improved.

Question 4.2

Alibarba Limited, a company providing advice for society weddings, was formed by two friends, Ali and Barbara, each investing £2,000 in cash as initial capital on 1 May 20X2. During the year ended 30 April 20X3 the following transactions took place.

(a) Acquired on 1 May 20X2 a 5 year lease on office premises for a payment of £7,500. The annual rental on the office premises is £12,000, payable in 4 equal instalments in arrears. The payment due on 30 April 20X3 was not paid until 5 May 20X3.
(b) Paid for advertising in the local and national press at a cost of £16,660.
(c) Paid heating and lighting costs of £3,300.
(d) Paid wages to two part-time assistants at a cost of £6,530 each per annum.
(e) Incurred and paid expenses in respect of stationery and miscellaneous expenses at a cost of £3,550. An invoice for headed paper for £250 was received on 2 May 20X3 for goods received and used in April.
(f) Provided advice for fourteen weddings at the standard fee of £4,680 per wedding.

At 30 April 20X3 they are half way through advising on their fifteenth wedding arrangement and have invoiced the couple for half of the fee, although they still await payment. One of the weddings previously arranged had problems with the recommended photographer and hence the couple concerned had withheld £1,000 of the fee. Ali and Barbara hope to receive half the outstanding fee, but feel the rest is unlikely to be recovered. All other fees have been received in full except that of the Smythes. This is because the Smythes had separated before paying the fee and Ali and Barbara have since been pursuing payment without success. Solicitor's fees of £300 have been incurred for chasing the unpaid fee and these also remain outstanding. Ali and Barbara are optimistic about recovering some of the fee, but feel a 50% provision would be appropriate at this time.

About half way through the financial year, Ali and Barbara decided that the business was taking off sufficiently to allow them to run a company car to help in visiting clients and contacts. A second hand car was purchased and paid for on 1 November 20X2 at a cost of £7,200. They expect it to last three years when it will be worthless.

When they set up the company, they arranged an overdraft facility of up to £15,000 with the local bank. In the early months of the business the bank overdraft facility had been used and net interest of £420 had been paid on this. An invoice for £1,420 for advertising in a society magazine in March and April 20X3 had not been paid by 30 April 20X3. As the car was acquired half way through the year, Ali and Barbara are advised to charge a half-year's depreciation, using a straight-line basis, for the year ending 30 April 20X3.

From the above information prepare a cash flow statement and a profit and loss account for Alibarba Limited for the year ended 30 April 20X3.

5 Other reports and statements

The impact of FRS 3 ('Reporting financial performance') on the profit and loss account of a company has already been discussed in Chapter 2. FRS 3 also introduced a requirement for further reports and statements as follows:

- a statement of total recognized gains and losses;
- a note of historical cost profit or losses; and
- a reconciliation of movements in shareholders' funds.

Statement of total recognized gains and losses

This statement provides additional information on financial performance and is reported alongside the profit and loss account, balance sheet and cash flow statement. This statement recognizes that the profit and loss account of a company is primarily concerned with the *realized* profit or losses of a period. In addition there are unrealized gains and losses, such as an increase in the value of assets, which do not form part of the calculation of profit. The FRS points out that it is necessary to consider all gains or losses recognized in a period when assessing the financial performance of a company and it is this that has led to the requirement for the statement of total recognized gains and losses. The purpose of this statement, therefore, is to report the total of all gains and losses of the reporting entity that are recognized in a period and are attributable to shareholders. The ASB defines gains as increases in equity, other than those relating to contributions from owners, and losses as decreases in equity, other than those relating to distributions to owners.

Where an unrealized but recognized gain or loss is realized in a subsequent period, then it cannot be included as profit for that period, otherwise this would be tantamount to reporting the gain or loss twice – once through the statement of total recognized gains and losses when the gain or loss was first recognized and once through the profit and loss account when the gain or loss was subsequently realized. Thus, for example, as was pointed out in Chapter 3 (page 57), if an asset such as land is revalued in 20X1 from its original acquisition cost of £400,000 to £600,000, then the increase in value of £200,000 is an unrealized but recognized gain which is reported in the statement of total recognized gains and losses for the year 20X1. If the land is sold in a subsequent

Table 5.1 The BOC Group plc – statement of total recognized gains and losses (year ended 30 September 2002)

	Notes	2002 (£ million)	2001 (restated) (£ million)
Profit for the financial year		202.9	224.1
Actuarial (loss)/gain recognized on the pension schemes		(431.2)	(464.9)
Movement on deferred tax relating to actuarial loss/(gain) on pensions		134.0	154.5
Unrealized loss on write down of revaluation reserve		(11.5)	—
Exchange translation effect on:			
results for the year of subsidiaries		(5.2)	(3.9)
results for the year of joint ventures		(2.6)	(1.5)
results for the year of associates		(0.3)	(0.1)
foreign currency net investments in subsidiaries		(114.6)	(55.8)
foreign currency net investments in joint ventures		(11.9)	(1.6)
foreign currency net investments in associates		(1.7)	0.4
Total recognized gains and losses for the financial year	12(c)	(242.1)	(148.8)
Prior year adjustment		(220.1)	
Total recognized gains and losses since last annual report		(462.2)	

period, say 20X3, for an amount of £650,000 then there is a total realized gain at that point of £250,000. Of this amount only £50,000 would be recorded in the profit and loss account for the year 20X3 because the original revaluation gain of £200,000 has already been reported in the statement of total recognized gains and losses for the year 20X1. Prior to the introduction of FRS 3, as was pointed out in Chapter 3, it was possible for the earlier revaluation surplus to be reversed in the year of sale so that the profit on sale could be reported as £250,000 in 20X3.

Any capital contributed to a company by shareholders or any dividends or capital repayments to shareholders or movements in reserves do not represent gains or losses and are not included in the statement.

The statement of total recognized gains and losses for the BOC Group is reported in Table 5.1. From this it can be seen that the statement is dominated by the actuarial loss of £431.2 million on the pension schemes. The principal components of this actuarial loss are reported in note 6 as the difference between the expected and actual return on the pension scheme assets, caused mainly by the decline of £328.6 million in the market value of the investments, and changes in the actuarial assumptions underlying the scheme liabilities, amounting to £94.3 million.

Note of historical profit or loss

It was pointed out in Chapter 3 that companies are allowed to draw up their accounts on either a pure historical cost basis or on one of the alternative bases. An alternative basis that is widely used is that of historic cost modified by the revaluation of certain assets. Where a company uses this basis and this results in a profit or loss that is materially different to the profit or loss that would have resulted from the use of unmodified historical cost, then a note of the historical cost profits and losses is required. The note of historical cost profit or loss must be reported immediately after either the profit and loss account or the statement of total recognized gains and losses.

The FRS offers two reasons for requiring disclosure of profit or loss on the unmodified historical cost basis. The first of these is that as long as there is discretion over the timing or scale of revaluations included in financial statements then the unmodified historical cost basis will give a profit or loss figure that is more comparable with that of other companies. The second reason is the wish of some users to assess the profit or loss on the sale of assets that is based on the historical cost of the assets sold rather than the revalued amount.

The note of historical cost profits and losses will therefore typically include such items as:

- the difference between an historical cost depreciation charge and the depreciation charge actually used in the profit and loss account that was based on the revalued amount; and
- gains reported in the statement of total recognized gains and losses of previous periods and realized in the current period. In this case the note would show the difference between the profit on disposal of an asset calculated using the depreciated historical cost of the asset and the profit based on the revalued amount of the asset.

BOC do not provide a note of historical cost profit or loss for the year to 30 September 2002 and a footnote to the statement of total recognized gains and losses confirms that this was not materially different from the reported profit.

Reconciliation of movements in shareholders' funds

FRS 3 requires the presentation of a note which reconciles the opening amount of shareholders' funds with the closing amount for the period. This reconciliation can be

Table 5.2   The BOC Group plc – reconciliation of movements in shareholders' funds (year ended 30 September 2002)

	2002 (£ million)	2001 (restated) (£ million)
Profit for the financial year	202.9	224.1
Dividends	(186.6)	(180.3)
	16.3	43.8
Other recognized gains and losses	(445.0)	(372.9)
Shares issued	24.6	16.9
Credit in relation to share options	2.0	4.4
Net (decrease)/increase in shareholders' funds for the financial year	(402.1)	(307.8)
Shareholders' funds at 1 October – previously reported	2,306.3	2,273.6
Prior year adjustment	(220.1)	120.4
Shareholders' funds at 1 October — restated	2,086.2	2,394.0
Shareholders' funds at 30 September	1,684.1	2,086.2

presented either as a primary statement or as a note to the accounts. BOC have reported it in the form of a primary statement and this is reproduced in Table 5.2. The profit or loss for the period and the other recognized gains or losses are two of the items that will bring about a change in the shareholders' funds and these are included in the reconciliation. In addition the reconciliation will include other items as follows:

- dividends for the period;
- capital contributions from shareholders or repaid to shareholders during the period, e.g. the amount received in respect of new shares.

6 The chairman's statement and the chief executive's review

The chairman's statement

The statement to members by a company chairman is an influential part of the annual report and is widely read by shareholders. In essence the statement offers an opportunity for a chairman to report in unquantified and unaudited terms on the performance of a company during the past financial period and on likely future developments. The chairman will usually take the opportunity to comment on directors and other employees, and on the efforts of the management team and the workforce. Quite often, the statement will be used to make political or social comments about government, taxation, accounting standards or whatever else exercises the chairman at the time of writing.

There is no format, other than the general one that the statement is usually addressed to the shareholders and is conventionally signed and dated by the chairman, and there are no standard or even recommended contents.

Chairmen's statements range in length from half a printed page to more than seven or eight pages. In the latter case, the contents will include a reasonably thorough description of each of the main areas of activity.

Although the chairman's statement is not audited as such, the auditors would be expected to review it to ensure that the information disclosed is neither misleading nor incompatible with the financial statements. However, whether audited or not, there is little doubt that the users of annual reports find the chairman's statement to be of real value in assessing a company and its prospects. Lee and Tweedie (1981) found that professional institutional investment specialists considered the chairman's statement to be an important part of the annual report. The most important were the profit and loss account and the balance sheet, and the chairman's statement was next. It is salutary to add here that the auditors' report was considered the least important part of the annual report. Of the 214 readers of annual reports surveyed by Lee and Tweedie, all except one read the chairman's statement briefly or thoroughly; of those readers, the great majority did not read the auditors' report at all. Confirmation that the chairman's statement continues to be the most widely read part of the annual report is provided by more recent surveys of private shareholders (see Bartlett and Chandler 1997; 1999).

This relatively wide readership of the chairman's statement led the Committee on the Financial Aspects of Corporate Governance ('Cadbury Report' 1992) to note (p. 34) that 'it is therefore of special importance that it [the chairman's statement] should provide a balanced and readable summary of the company's performance and prospects and that it should represent the collective view of the board'.

The Cadbury Report also noted that the chairman should be able to stand back from the day-to-day running of the company to ensure that the board is in full control of the company's affairs and alert to its obligations to shareholders. There is no doubt that, divorced from the strict requirement of the law and the regulatory bodies, the tone and approach of a chairman's statement are valuable indicators of a company's 'state of mind' and as such the statement is clearly helpful to readers.

The role of the chairman of a company was, in the past, often combined with the role of chief executive. However, a chief executive is someone who is actively involved in the implementation of board decisions and the day-to-day management of a company, which is in direct contrast with the role of a chairman who is meant to be able to stand back from all of this. The Cadbury Report therefore recommended in its code of best practice that the roles of chairman and chief executive should be split with 'a clearly accepted division of responsibilities at the head of a company, which will ensure a balance of power and authority, such that no one individual has unfettered powers of decision'. Although this was not a requirement, most major companies have separated the roles of chairman and chief executive and it is usual for each to provide a statement or review.

BOC follows this practice and includes in its 2002 report and accounts both a statement by the chairman (Mr Rob Margetts) and a review by the chief executive (Mr Tony Isaac). Neither of these are reproduced in full in Appendix A and so it might be useful to consider extracts from these here.

Rob Margetts became chairman in January 2002 and in his statement he notes that following the lapsed joint bid for BOC from Air Liquide and Air Products the company has reviewed all aspects of strategy, performance and governance and that the objective is to deliver superior returns to shareholders, both in the form of dividends and in share price increases. The statement provides a graphical comparison to illustrate the superiority of the performance of BOC since October 2000 (the first full year following the lapsed bid) over the performance of FTSE 100 companies and its major competitors.

The chairman also comments on the continued strengths of the compressed gases component of the Industrial and Special Products division. The cyclical nature of the semiconductor industry is also noted but it is felt that this industry is an excellent long-term market and one that BOC Edwards is well equipped to serve. Underperforming assets are either improved to an acceptable level or attempts are made to dispose of them.

The chairman also welcomed two new non-executive directors to the board and thanked the highly committed staff for their achievements. He concluded that the foundations for future prosperity are firm and that the board is confident of the continuing success of BOC.

The chief executive's review

The chief executive points out that the company adopted the new UK standards FRS 17 and FRS 19 and that operating cash flow before exceptional items remained strong at £826.6 million. This is made up of the operating cash flow of £759.3 million reported in Table 4.1, plus the exceptional cash flows of £67.3 million reported in the reconciliation of operating profit and operating cash flow (see page 76). The chief executive also refers to the success of the Process Gas Solution division and the joint venture established in China in April 2002 with Yangtze Petrochemical Corporation, a subsidiary of Sinopec, China's leading petrochemical company. This is seen as giving BOC a head start in Nanjing, the chemicals capital of China.

The chief executive repeats the concerns of the chairman over the difficulties facing the semiconductor industry and the impact on BOC Edwards. However, BOC Edwards took advantage of what is thought to be the low point in the cycle to make a number of acquisitions, including the turbomolecular pumps business of Seiko Instruments Inc. Elsewhere in the report the chief executive points out that BOC completed a record number of acquisitions during the year, involving an amount of £207.3 million. In addition BOC has announced its intention to merge its Japanese gases business, OSK, with Air Liquide Japan. This is dependent on clearance from the Japanese competition authorities.

The chief executive finally points out that although growth and the financial health of the group are key priorities, BOC also attempts to fulfil its wider responsibilities to communities and the environment and pays particular attention to the development and well being of employees and to safety performance. The chief executive thanks BOC's customers and suppliers and the shareholders for their support through a difficult year for stock markets.

7 The directors' report and the operating and financial review

The basic purpose of the directors' report is to provide a narrative supplement to the financial information. The 1985 Act (as amended) requires certain information to be included in the directors' report. Additionally, the Listing Agreement of the Stock Exchange occasionally calls for wider disclosure than that required by statute or accounting standard, and more recently the Cadbury and Hampel Reports have recommended specific items that should be reported on by directors.

There are no formats specified, but the directors of a company are required to give details of, and information on, the company's activities, its directors, substantial holdings of its shares, its employees and its charitable and political donations in the year under review. The quantity of those details and information vary considerably from company to company. However, all companies are required to present a directors' report and the same broad pattern is followed by most.

Activities and trading results

The directors are required to give details of the principal activities of the company and its subsidiaries during the year, and of any significant changes in those activities. Definitions or examples of principal activities are available, and the following offers a useful guide.

Principal activities are usually taken to mean important categories of diversification, generally in terms of distinct classes of industrial or commercial activity – engineering, leisure, retailing, etc. Vertical classification is not required.

In terms of changes to the company's activities, it is generally suggested that a positive statement be made if there has been no change or that sufficient details be given of any major changes, such as withdrawal from an industrial sector or a significant class of business.

Where a company that is quoted on the Stock Exchange has published a forecast of its performance and subsequent trading results reveal a material difference from the forecast, then the report of the directors should provide an explanation for the difference.

The operating and financial review

Additionally, the directors are required to give a fair review of the development of the company and its business during the period, and the position of the company and its subsidiaries at the end of the period. They must give details of any important occurrences affecting the company during the year, and present an assessment of likely future developments.

Although the Companies Act gives no guidance as to what constitutes a fair review, the Cadbury Report's code of best practice notes that the report and accounts of a company should contain a coherent narrative, supported by the figures, of the company's performance and prospects. The Cadbury Report went on to recommend that the directors of a company should provide a forward looking operating and financial review (OFR) along the lines of the ASB's statement of best practice ('Operating and Financial Review') which was published in 1993 and revised in January 2003. This statement, which is persuasive rather than mandatory, makes it clear that the OFR is intended as a report on the year under review, not a discussion of future performance. It should nevertheless draw out those aspects of the year under review that are relevant to an assessment of future prospects.

The operating review

The purpose of the operating review is to identify and explain the main factors that underlie the business and any past changes or expected future changes in these factors. It should include a discussion of:

- the significant features of the operating performance for the period including changes in market conditions, new products and services introduced, changes in market share, changes in turnover and margins, changes in exchange rates, and new and discontinued activities;
- the factors that might have a major effect on future results including dependence on major suppliers or customers, scarcity of raw materials, skills shortages, patents licences or franchises, product liability, health and safety, environmental protection costs, exchange rate fluctuations;
- the extent to which directors have sought to maintain and enhance future income by capital expenditure, marketing and advertising campaigns; pure and applied research, training programmes, maintenance programmes and new product development;
- the overall return to shareholders in terms of dividends and increases in shareholders' funds and the contributions of different business units;
- the dividend policy of the directors;
- any subjective judgements, including the application of accounting policies, to which the financial statements are particularly sensitive;
- the extent to which information from the financial statements has been adjusted for inclusion in the OFR, together with a reconciliation back to the financial statements;
- the measures that are used by the directors as key performance indicators in managing the business.

The financial review

The purpose of the financial review is to explain the capital structure of a company, its treasury policy and its sources of liquidity, including the implications of the financing requirements arising from capital expenditure plans. It should include a discussion of:

- the capital structure of the company;
- the capital funding and treasury policies and objectives including the management of interest rate and exchange rate risks, and the maturity profile of borrowings;
- the reconciliation between the actual and standard tax charges;
- the cash from operations and other cash inflows and any special factors affecting these;
- liquidity at the end of the period;
- restrictions on the ability to transfer funds between different parts of the group;
- debt covenants and breaches of covenant;
- the ability to remain a going concern;
- the strength and resources of a company whose value is not fully reflected in the balance sheet.

Prior to the implementation of the Cadbury Code of best practice, a discussion of many of the above items would have been contained in the directors' report. BOC do not, in fact, include in their annual report for 2002 a statement that bears the title 'Directors' Report'. However they do provide a thirteen page performance review and a seven page finance and treasury review (pages 208–14). In addition there is a report on remuneration, an extensive group profile and sections on employees, safety, health and the environment, research, development and information technology, and risk factors. It is these pages that contain the disclosure of the items discussed in this chapter.

Directors

The Companies Acts and other regulatory pronouncements are quite clearly concerned with ensuring the disclosure of all significant information about the directors of a company and their relationship with it. The basic requirements are as follows:

- the names of all directors at any time during the period in question;
- the interest of directors in shares and debentures of the company and/or its subsidiaries at the beginning of the period and at the end.

Listed companies must distinguish between beneficial and non-beneficial holdings, and information about the interests of directors' close families is usually provided.

Details must be given of a director's service contract with the company – usually when he or she is eligible for re-election. Full details of all transactions and arrangements with directors – particularly loans, quasi-loans and credit facilities – must be presented in the financial statements.

Directors' remuneration

In Chapter 2 we saw that the recommendations of the study group on Directors' Remuneration (the Greenbury Committee) and the subsequent report of the Hampel Committee on Corporate Governance resulted in the publication in 1998 of 'The

Combined Code – Principles of Good Corporate Governance and Code of Best Practice'. The Combined Code's disclosure requirements for directors' remuneration were summarized in Chapter 2. The combined code establishes 'principles of good governance', and a 'code of best practice'. One of the principles requires companies to establish a formal and transparent procedure for developing policy on executive remuneration and for fixing the remuneration package of individual directors. The best practice provision is for the remuneration of executive directors to be determined by a remuneration committee made up of independent non-executive directors and that the remuneration committee should make an annual report to shareholders to be included in the annual report and accounts. BOC includes an eight-page report on remuneration in its annual report (pages 220–8). It explains that the main function of the remuneration committee is to set the company's overall policy on executive employment conditions and to determine the specific remuneration benefits and terms of employment for each executive director, including the chief executive and the chairman. The report also explains the remuneration policy of BOC. The report on remuneration provides detailed disclosure of the remuneration of each individual director, including their pension contributions and benefits and their interests in the company's share options and share incentive units.

Employees

In note 6 to the financial statements (see pages 252–9) BOC provides information about the number of employees in each line of business and geographical region and also information on the costs of employees, share options and incentives held by employees and employee retirement benefits. A further two pages of information is also provided by the directors covering such issues as the employment policy of BOC and the training and development and reward and recognition of employees. The directors also state that the group is committed to maintaining 'a workplace free from discrimination for reasons of race, creed, culture, nationality, religion, gender, sexual orientation, age or marital status'. They also confirm that 'disability is not considered a barrier to employment, and as far as local conditions allow, employees are selected on the basis of their ability to perform the job'.

Creditor payment policy

Amendments to the 1985 Companies Act were introduced in 1996 and 1997 (SI 1996/189 and SI 1997/571) by means of statutory instruments which have the effect of requiring a company to disclose its policy for making payments to suppliers. There is also a requirement to disclose in the directors' report the number of days represented by the amount of trade creditors due for payment at the end of the year compared to the total amount invoiced by suppliers during the year. The method of calculating this is as follows:

$$\text{Number of days} = \frac{\text{Trade creditors at the end of the year}}{\text{Amounts invoiced during year by suppliers}} \times 365$$

BOC discloses its supplier payment policy as part of its Finance and Treasury Review (see page 214) and it can be seen that its number of creditor days at 30 September 2002 was 52.

Donations

The directors are required to report political and charitable donations by the company or group of companies, where those donations exceed £200. In addition, where donations are for a political purpose, the name of the recipient and the individual amount paid must be disclosed. There are considerable areas of confusion about the proper definition of a 'political purpose', but in general terms such payments are readily identified and should be reported. Given the degree of interest in the political donations of British companies, many reports make a point of stating categorically that no payments are made or donations given for political purposes.

Auditing and taxation matters

The appointment of a company's auditor is a matter for the shareholders in general meeting, but it is customary for the directors' report to refer to the auditor's willingness to be reappointed or, if appropriate, to mention and explain any proposed change to current auditing arrangements. Although the 1985 Act (as amended) does not require the directors' report to be audited, there is a requirement for auditors to draw attention in their reports to any inconsistency they find between the directors' report and the company's financial statements.

Where a company is held to be subject to the close company taxation liability of any company, that fact should be included in the directors' report; listed companies must report whether or not they are subject to close company provisions.

Corporate governance

The influence of the Cadbury Report – and more recently the Hampel Report – on corporate governance has been significant. The Hampel Report (the report of the committee on corporate governance) was published in 1998 and led to the further publication, in co-operation with the Stock Exchange, of the 'Combined Code'. Much of the Combined Code retains the substance of the recommendations of the Cadbury Report and the Greenbury Report on directors' remuneration. The Combined Code contains two parts. Part 1 deals with principles of good governance, and Part 2 covers a code of best practice. Each part is split into two sections. Section 1 contains the corporate governance principles and best practice provision for all *listed companies*. Section 2 contains the corporate governance principles and best practice provisions for *institutional shareholders*, covering such issues as voting, discussions with companies and the evaluation of a company's corporate governance arrangements. The Stock Exchange listing rules require companies to disclose how they have applied the principles of Section 1 of the Combined Code and their compliance with the best practice provisions of Section 1.

One of the principles of the Combined Code requires the directors of a company to present a balanced and understandable assessment of the company's position and prospects. The best practice provisions for achieving this state that the directors should explain their responsibility for preparing the accounts and there should be a statement about their reporting responsibilities.

The Cadbury Report specified that the statement of directors' responsibilities should cover the following points:

- the legal requirement for directors to prepare financial statements for each financial year which give a true and fair view of the state of affairs of the company (or group) as at the end of the financial year and of the profit and loss for that period;
- the responsibility of the directors for maintaining adequate accounting records, for safeguarding the assets of the company (or group) and for preventing and detecting fraud and other irregularities;
- confirmation that suitable accounting policies, consistently applied and supported by reasonable and prudent judgements and estimates, have been used in the preparation of the financial statements;
- confirmation that applicable accounting standards have been followed, subject to any material departures disclosed and explained in the notes to the accounts. (This does not obviate the need for a formal statement in the notes to the accounts disclosing whether the accounts have been prepared in accordance with applicable accounting standards.)

The Combined Code also requires directors to report on the company's system of internal control and on whether they consider the company to be a going concern. With regard to the internal control, the best practice provisions state that:

> The directors should, at least annually, conduct a review of the effectiveness of the group's system of internal control and should report to shareholders that they have done so.

For a going concern the requirement is for the directors to report that the business is a going concern, with supporting assumptions or qualifications as necessary.

BOC include a section in their annual report on Corporate Governance. This contains a statement on internal controls which explains the system of controls that the company has developed and explains that the internal control system is monitored and supported by an internal audit function that reports to management and the audit committee. The statement confirms that the effectiveness of the internal control process is regularly reviewed throughout the year by the audit committee and concludes by stating that:

> The directors therefore believe that the Group's system of internal financial control provides reasonable but not absolute assurance that assets are safeguarded, transactions are authorized and recorded properly and that material errors and irregularities are either prevented or would be detected within a timely period. Having reviewed its effectiveness, the directors are not aware of any significant weakness or deficiency in the Group's system of internal financial control during the period covered by this report and accounts.

The finance and treasury review of BOC's annual report and accounts contains a statement which confirms that the directors are confident that the Group has adequate resources for the foreseeable future. For this reason, they continue to adopt the going concern basis in preparing the accounts.

8 The auditors' report

The audit of the accounts of a company by independent experts has, for many years, been a key feature of corporate accountability and it is a statutory requirement that auditors' reports must accompany the annual financial statements that are presented to the shareholders of all companies above a certain size. Until recently there was a requirement for every company registered in the UK, whatever its size, to have an annual audit, but this is no longer a requirement for companies with an annual turnover of less than £350,000 and a balance sheet total of less than £1.4 million.

An audit is defined by the Auditing Practices Board as 'an independent examination of, and expression of an opinion on, the financial statements of an enterprise'. The audit provides an objective verification to shareholders and other users that the financial statements have been prepared properly and in accordance with legislative and regulatory requirements, that they present the information truthfully and fairly and that they conform to best accounting practice in their treatment of various measurements and valuations. A key phrase in the above definition is that of 'independent examination', and a continuing controversy surrounds the extent to which the auditor is, or should be, independent. Auditors may act for the same client for many years leading to the possibility of auditors becoming too trusting of management. Also auditors often provide significant amounts of non-audit work for the audit client. The possibility of the loss of fees from this additional work might affect the willingness of auditors to confront management over accounts preparation and auditing concerns. The debate over auditor independence has intensified following the collapse of Enron and calls have been made for compulsory auditor rotation and limitations, or even a total ban, on the ability of auditors to provide non-audit services to audit clients.

Note 2(c) to BOC's financial statements reports that the total fees paid to auditors was £7.0 million, with £1.9 million representing the audit fee and £5.1 million representing non-audit fees. If all of these fees were paid to the company's auditors, PricewaterhouseCoopers, then this illustrates the significance of non-audit work. However, BOC report in their statement on corporate governance (page 216) that they are fully aware of the impact this may have on independence when they state:

> To enhance further the confidence of investors in the independence of the independent auditors and their report, the board of BOC has introduced a

policy that defines which other services PricewaterhouseCoopers may or may not provide to BOC. The policy requires the provision of these services to be approved in advance by the audit committee of the board.

The auditors' duty is to the shareholders of a company and although the extent to which this duty does or should extend to other users of financial statements has frequently been debated, the issue would seem to have been clearly resolved by the ruling in the 1990 'Caparo Case'. In this case (*Caparo Industries plc* v. *Dickman and Others* (1990) 1 All ER 568) the House of Lords ruled that unless there are special features the auditors do not have a duty of care to prevent loss to anyone relying on their report except (a) the company and (b) the shareholders as a body. In other words no duty of care is owed to individual shareholders, to purchasers of shares, to lenders to the company or to those doing business with the company. Until this ruling it had been widely accepted that third parties could rely on the audit report to enhance the integrity of financial statements. Also it was felt that if auditors had this duty to a wide range of users then this provided a means of ensuring the effectiveness of the audit process because auditors would strive to avoid negligence claims against them by being diligent in their duties. The ruling did very little to enhance the role of the audit and many commentators felt that the benefits of having accounts audited would become very questionable. However, it was also clear that the full extent of the auditors' responsibilities needed to be clarified and the House of Lords felt that to hold auditors liable to anyone who might rely on the audit report would be far too onerous. The potential magnitude of the liability would be out of all proportion to the size of the audit fee. Also it is the duty of the directors to produce true and fair view accounts and so to make the auditors carry all of the liability would seem to be unfair. It should be noted though that the House of Lords ruling could be affected if any 'special features' are present. An example of a special feature might be where the auditors know or can reasonably foresee that third parties would rely on the audit report when making specific decisions. Under such circumstances the auditors' duty of care could well extend to the third parties involved and from a number of recent cases it is clear that the legal position is not quite as straightforward as the Caparo ruling might indicate.

The Cadbury Report accepted the Caparo ruling and stated that 'it is unable to see a practical and equitable way in which the House of Lords could have broadened the boundaries of the auditors' legal duty of care without giving rise to a liability that was indeterminate in scope, time and amount, nor does it consider that the decision should be altered by statutory intervention at the present time.'

The Auditing Practices Board

Until 1991, the contribution of the accountancy profession to the development of auditing guidelines and standards was provided through the Auditing Practices Committee. In 1991 the Consultative Committee of the six principal accounting bodies in the UK and Ireland (the CCAB) established the Auditing Practices Board (APB) to replace the Auditing Practices Committee. The membership of the APB includes representatives of the accountancy and auditing professions and also representatives of the Bank of England, the Stock Exchange, the Department of Trade and Industry, the National Audit Office, the Audit Commission and the Securities and Investment Board.

The objectives of the APB are contained in a May 1993 statement ('The scope and authority of APB pronouncements') and are as follows:

- to establish high standards of auditing;
- to meet the developing needs of users of financial information; and
- to ensure public confidence in the auditing process.

The APB intends to achieve these objectives by:

- taking an active role in the development of statutes, regulations and accounting standards which affect the audit profession;
- promoting ways of increasing the value of audits and of ensuring their cost effectiveness;
- consulting with the users of financial information to ensure that the APB provides an effective and timely response to their developing needs and to issues raised by them;
- advancing the wider public's understanding of the roles and responsibilities of auditors; and
- establishing and publishing statements of the principles and procedures with which auditors are required to comply in the conduct of audits and other explanatory material to assist in their interpretation and application.

The pronouncements of the APB take the form of statements of auditing standards (SASs), practice notes and bulletins.

SASs contain the basic principles and essential procedures with which auditors are expected to comply. SASs also include material which is not meant to be prescriptive, but to help in interpreting and applying auditing standards. The Companies Act 1989 requires auditors of companies to be registered with a recognized supervisory body. If auditors fail to comply with SASs they make themselves liable to action by their recognized supervisory body, which could include the withdrawal of eligibility to perform company audits. Before SASs are introduced the APB issues exposure drafts and may also issue other consultative documents in order to provide the opportunity for widespread consultation on proposed standards.

Practice notes are intended to assist auditors when applying standards which have been written in general terms to the requirements of specific circumstances and industries.

Bulletins are intended to provide auditors with timely guidance on new or emerging issues. They are persuasive rather than prescriptive but are indicative of good practice.

Usefulness of audit reports

The objectives of the APB as outlined above are an attempt to counter much of the criticism that has been directed at external auditing in recent years. To some extent this criticism has occurred because of the gap between the public's expectations of what the audit achieves or should achieve in terms of assurances about financial statements and what the audit actually does achieve. This has become known as the expectations gap. For example, it is not the responsibility of auditors to guarantee that the financial statements are correct or that the company will not fail or that there has been no fraud, and yet there is strong evidence to show that a significant proportion of the public believes that the purpose of the audit is to provide reassurances about these matters.

The financial statements of a complex organization can never be 'correct' in the sense that there is only one set of figures that is 'correct'. The judgements and valuations required to prepare the accounts of a company mean that a range of possible outcomes could be generally accepted as 'correct'. The directors of a company are therefore not required to prepare accounts that are 'correct', but accounts that give a true and fair view. The responsibility of the auditors is to give an opinion on whether the accounts give a true and fair view and have been prepared in accordance with the requirements of company law.

Similarly, it would be clearly impossible for the directors or auditors to guarantee that a company will not fail given the risks and uncertainties inherent in the business environment. However, perhaps auditors should be expected to form an opinion on the going concern assumptions on which the accounts are based.

Finally, if auditors were required to guarantee that material fraud had not occurred then the audit costs arising from the very detailed checking that would be required would probably be unacceptably high. Even if every transaction were checked the existence of collusion could still lead to a fraud going undetected and so the expectation that an audit guarantees the absence of fraud is generally felt to be unreasonable. However, it might be appropriate for auditors to contribute to fraud minimization by reporting on the adequacy of internal control systems.

The Cadbury Report considered the above causes of the expectations gap and made the following recommendations:

- the APB should be encouraged to expand the format and content of audit reports so that a description of the key features of the audit process is provided together with a clear statement of the auditors' responsibilities for reporting on the financial statements;
- the directors should state in the report and accounts that the business is a going concern, with supporting assumptions or qualifications as necessary, and the auditors should report on this statement;
- the directors should make a statement on the effectiveness of their system of internal control and the auditors should report on this statement.

Format and content of audit reports

The APB issued in May 1993 SAS 600 ('Auditors' reports on financial statements'), which had the purpose of establishing standards and providing guidance on the form and content of auditors' reports. The basic elements of the auditors' report are as follows:

- an identification of the report's addressee(s);
- an identification of the financial statements audited;
- separate sections dealing with:
  (i) respective responsibilities of directors and auditors,
  (ii) the basis of the auditors' opinion,
  (iii) the auditors' opinion on the financial statements;
- the signatures of the auditors;
- the date of the audit report.

In an attempt to overcome the expectations gap the audit report should include an explanation that the financial statements are the responsibility of the directors and a statement that the auditors' responsibility is to express an opinion on the financial statements.

Auditors' reports should contain a clear expression of opinion on the financial statements and should explain the basis of their opinion by including in their report:

- a statement of their compliance or otherwise with auditing standards;
- a statement that the audit process includes:
  - (i) the examination, on a test basis, of evidence relating to the amounts and disclosures in the financial statements;
  - (ii) the assessment of the significant estimates and judgements made by the reporting entity's directors;
  - (iii) the consideration of whether the accounting policies are appropriate, consistently applied and adequately disclosed;
- a statement that they planned and performed the audit so as to obtain reasonable assurances that the financial statements are free from material mis-statement, whether caused by fraud or other irregularity or error, and that they have evaluated the overall presentation of the financial statements.

The report of the auditors to The BOC Group is contained in Appendix A (page 229) and it can be seen that this follows the above requirements. The BOC audit report is an example of an unqualified opinion that the financial statements give a true and fair view and have been properly prepared in accordance with the requirements of the Companies Act 1995.

However, there are occasions when the view given by the financial statements might be affected by an inherent uncertainty which, in the opinion of the auditors, is fundamental. In such cases the auditors should include an explanatory paragraph which draws attention to the fundamental uncertainty. Providing the fundamental uncertainty is adequately accounted for and disclosed in the financial statements then the auditors might still be capable of giving an unqualified opinion. However, if the disclosures about the fundamental uncertainty are inadequate then a *qualified* opinion will have to be given. There are various circumstances that might give rise to the need for a qualified opinion and various forms that qualified opinions can take. These are outlined below.

Qualified opinion – disagreement   This occurs when the auditors disagree with the treatment or disclosure of a matter in the financial statements. The audit report explains the area of disagreement and states that except for this the accounts give a true and fair view.

Qualified opinion – adverse opinion   This occurs where the effect of the disagreement is so material or pervasive that the auditors conclude that the financial statements are seriously misleading. In these circumstances they would state that the accounts do not give a true and fair view.

Qualified opinion – except for limitation of scope   Where the scope of the audit is limited by the inability to obtain sufficient evidence or explanations or because proper accounting records have not been kept and this prevents an unqualified opinion being given then the opinion should be qualified.

Disclaimer of opinion   Where the possible effect of a limitation of scope is so material or pervasive that the auditors have not been able to express an opinion as to whether or not the financial statements give a true and fair view then a disclaimer of opinion is required. If the effect of the limitation is not so material or pervasive as to require a disclaimer then an opinion that the financial statements give a true and fair view, except for the possible adjustments that might have been necessary had the limitation not existed, is appropriate.

Examples of the wording that could be used for the various forms of qualified and unqualified audit report are provided in SAS 600 ('Auditors' reports on financial statements'). This standard also gives an example of the qualified opinion that should be used when a primary statement required by financial reporting standards has not been included in the financial statements.

Going concern statement

The Cadbury Report recommended that the directors should satisfy themselves that the going concern basis is appropriate and report accordingly to shareholders. This remains a requirement of the Combined Code. The responsibility of the auditors is to '. . . assess the consistency of the directors' going concern statement with the knowledge obtained in the course of the audit of the financial statements . . .' (APB Bulletin 196/3). Auditors are required to evaluate explicitly whether there are uncertainties over an entity's ability to continue as a going concern, and also to assess the adequacy of the disclosures about uncertainty in the financial statements. If the auditors consider that the uncertainties are not adequately disclosed then a qualified opinion will be required, with the form of qualified opinion depending on the level of inadequacy of the disclosure.

Internal control

The internal control systems of an organization cover a range of rules and procedures which provide the necessary checks and balances to ensure the early detection of errors or frauds. Examples might include systems for the safeguarding of assets or for the proper authorization of expenditure or for ensuring that all income is received and accounted for. Any well run organization will have such procedures and through the use of internal auditing or other forms of internal monitoring will attempt to ensure that the rules and procedures for effective internal control are complied with. The authors of the Cadbury Report were convinced that effective systems of internal control are essential for the efficient management of a company. The Combined Code requires the directors of a company to conduct a review, at least annually, of the effectiveness of the system of internal control and report to the shareholders that they have done so. The auditors are required to undertake a review of compliance with the Combined Code, but are not expected to form an opinion on the effectiveness of the internal controls.

The Combined Code

The Combined Code, which came into effect for accounting periods ending on or after 31 December 1998, contains 45 provisions which should be followed as part of the corporate governance requirements. Seven of these are what might be thought of as 'objective' provisions, i.e. those for which compliance is relatively easy to determine, and these must be reviewed by the auditors. The auditors are not required to report a satisfactory review but to report on any non-compliance which has not been disclosed by the directors. The seven provisions of the Combined Code that require review by the auditors cover:

- the establishment of an audit committee;
- a statement of directors' and auditors' reporting responsibilities;
- the election of directors;
- the appointment of non-executive directors;
- the review by directors of internal controls;
- procedures for seeking professional advice;
- and a schedule of items specifically reserved for decision by the board.

Given the relatively narrow scope of the review by the auditors, it is no longer necessary to provide a separate report on compliance with corporate governance issues and a combined audit report is now recommended. The report of the auditors for BOC (see page 229) provides a good example of the scope and content of an audit report.

Part Two

Interpretation and assessment

9 Financial statement analysis and comparison

Objectives

Having described and examined the principal components of published financial statements, it is now time to focus attention on the means by which those statements may be analysed to extract information that will be useful in making financial decisions or judgements about a company. The principal tools of financial statement analysis have been developed over a long period and consist, in general, of first identifying the important items of both financial and non-financial data and then relating these to one another and also to factors external to the company. This process is usually referred to as ratio analysis. The ratios calculated can then be used in conjunction with other information such as the annual review and performance report or external analyst's reports. On their own, ratios, like the figures in the published financial statements, do not necessarily provide answers, but rather suggest questions that require answering. Perhaps they have identified that significant changes have occurred, but identification of the cause is still required.

But first, just as in the preparation of the accounts, it is necessary to identify the purpose of the financial analysis. The structure and strategy of a review is described in some depth in Chapter 14. The selected purpose will influence the approach and the extent of the analysis. This will provide part of the basis of the selection of critical items in the profit and loss account, cash flow statement and balance sheet. Size of item will also be another factor since a 10 per cent change in £500 million is much larger and thus possibly more important than a 100 per cent change in £1 million.

In general, key items in the profit and loss account are turnover, operating profit and net profit after tax. In the balance sheet total assets and capital employed are important, particularly as they represent, respectively, the total resources working to earn the profit and the total long-term funds invested in the company to earn the return. There are several key items in the cash flow statement, including the net cash inflow from operations and the net cash inflow/outflow from financing, which indicate the extent of internal and external financing. The outflows are also reflected in the amounts spent on returns on investments and servicing of finance, capital expenditure and financial investment and equity dividends paid. Having made a cursory assessment of the key variables the more rigorous assessment can be made by ratio analysis.

Ratio analysis

The decisions facing different users may be quite varied, e.g. lenders will be interested in credit-worthiness, employees in information for wage-bargaining purposes and the security of their jobs, shareholders in profits and dividend prospects and so on. Potential and existing shareholders are concerned about the profitability of the company, the return on the shares, the availability of cash to pay the dividends, to name but three items. Strategic information is just as important to shareholders as it is to the company's management as it helps in the selection of ratios that help them in their daily operations. It is also worth remembering that management usually has access to more information concerning the company and its competitors than persons external to the company. Nevertheless, it is true to say that just about all users will be interested in evaluating the current performance and financial position of the company and in making predictions about its future. It is necessary, therefore, to consider the role that financial statement analysis has to play in this process.

The figures contained in the financial statements – turnover, profit, current assets, total assets etc. – are absolute amounts that may not by themselves be very meaningful indicators of good or bad performance, or of a satisfactory or unsatisfactory position. For example, the balance sheet of a company may reveal that the current assets figure is £150,000 and the current liabilities figure is £75,000. Individually these items may not tell us very much. However, if they are related to one another in the form of a ratio, i.e. £150,000 to £75,000, the resultant 2:1 (or simply 2) may indicate whether there is a sufficient cushion of short-term funds in the business. Similarly, it is possible to take two profit and loss account items, such as net pre-tax profit of £40,000 and sales of £800,000, and examine their relationships. Any informational value that these two items may have when considered in isolation will be greatly enhanced by calculating the profit to sales ratio of £40,000 to £800,000, or 0.05:1. This ratio is usually expressed as a percentage, in this case 5 per cent, which indicates the net profit percentage being earned on each pound of turnover value. Further ratios can be obtained by relating items from both the profit and loss account and the balance sheet. For example, the net profit figure used above was £40,000 and an examination of the balance sheet may reveal a figure of £400,000 for total assets employed. By themselves, these figures are difficult to interpret, but if they are related to each other in the form of a ratio, i.e. £40,000 to £400,000, a ratio of 0.1:1 or 10 per cent is obtained. This may indicate the adequacy of the profit figure when considered against the total value of the assets available for earning such a profit.

Reducing the large number of financial statement items to a relatively small number of key ratios in this way can help to begin to answer the following questions about the economic aspects of a company:

- Is the profit that is being earned satisfactory?
- Is the management of working capital (cash, debtors, stock, creditors) efficient or at least adequate?
- Is the long-term capital structure suitable?
- Is efficient use being made of assets and other resources?

To answer these sorts of questions does require comparison with acceptable benchmarks, some of which will be discussed shortly. It is also true that the ratios calculated following a standardized procedure may throw up further questions that require investigation, such as the following:

- Why have certain expenses grown as a proportion of sales?
- Why has the proportion of production carried in stock declined?
- Are the loans still well covered?
- Why has the profit growth target not been achieved?
- Why has the sales growth outstripped that of the competition?

Like all financial information, ratios can also be used as targets and projections, just as absolute targets of profit or sales are made. As we shall see, ratio analysis can be as simple or as sophisticated as the user wishes it to be.

One general approach is to break the analysis down into two series: one being the horizontal or line-by-line comparison of the accounts with those of the previous year. This is sometimes called common size analysis. The second series is called vertical analysis, where each item in the balance sheet or profit and loss account is expressed as a percentage of the total. Horizontal analysis provides, over a number of years, a trend of changes, growth or decline, in these elements of the accounts. We can get annual percentage growth rates in profits, sales, stock or any other item for this approach. The vertical analysis on the other hand will provide evidence of structural changes in the accounts: increased profitability through more efficient production would show up in the profit and loss account, while from the balance sheet could be discovered greater dependence on borrowing to finance new investment etc.

Another approach is to make use of what is in effect a pyramid structure of ratios to select the level of detailed analysis required. Thus, for example, if profitability is being considered, then the ratio at the apex of the pyramid would be return on capital employed. This can then be broken down into its constituent elements of return on sales and asset turnover, as explained in Chapter 10. Each of these ratios can then be broken down further into more detailed ratios such as cost of sales to sales, administration cost to sales and research and development to sales.

Comparison of financial ratios

The calculation of ratios is only the first step in financial statement analysis. Although ratios provide a useful means of relating individual items in the financial statements to other items, some standard is needed against which those ratios can be assessed. Unfortunately, there is no such thing as an 'ideal' or absolute standard measure for this purpose. For example, it is not possible to state categorically that the ratio of net pre-tax profit to total assets for all companies should be 10 per cent and therefore that anything less than 10 per cent is 'bad' and anything greater is 'good'.

The lack of absolute ratio criteria has been overcome in practice in a number of ways. The first – and the one most frequently adopted – is to calculate the average ratios for all the companies in a particular industrial or commercial sector. This gives an 'industry' standard against which the ratios of a particular company can be evaluated. The second method involves calculating the relevant ratios for the company under analysis for each of a number of preceding years and using these ratios as a basis for assessing those for the current period as part of a trend or as a deviation from a trend.

Figures for immediately preceding years are available in the current year's financial statements. In addition, the more important items are shown in summarized form for at least the past five years by all listed public companies. Perhaps useful trends will emerge from this.

From a strategic view it is necessary to make comparisons with similar and competing companies. Thus it may be possible to take published information for such companies, compute their ratios and make comparisons. The use of ratio analysis is not restricted to publicly available information. The managers of companies and other organizations make widespread use of ratio analysis techniques for internal control and evaluation purposes, and in these circumstances will have budgeted figures and ratios to use as standards or targets.

However, these 'standards' do have certain limitations. There is still no clear guide as to the optimal size of a particular ratio. For example, assume that the industry average for the ratio of current assets to current liabilities is 1.5. If a particular company in that industry has a ratio of 0.5, it is well below the 'standard' and can perhaps be thought of as 'bad'. However, another company in the same industry with a ratio well in excess of the industry average, say 2.5, cannot categorically be thought of as 'good'. Such a high ratio might be the result of cash being allowed to lie idle or of stock levels being higher than necessary. Both of these practices could be instances of bad management of current assets. The answer, therefore, might seem to be to evaluate a company in terms of its deviation below or above the average for the industry. Unfortunately, it is not so simple. Even within the same industry, companies have to face different situations that may justify a substantial deviation from the industry average. Thus, if a particular ratio is out of line with the average for the industry, such a deviation merely indicates an area for further examination. Moreover, it could be argued that the industry average is not the most appropriate standard. After all, the average incorporates the ratios of the best and the worst companies in the industry. Perhaps it might be better to have industry standards based on the ratios of the most successful companies in the industry. This is a form of benchmarking, using the best as a comparator or target. If this is not possible, then the groups can be broken up into quartiles to help as a guide. It should also be borne in mind that where the ratios making up the statistics for a particular industry are drawn mainly from the larger public companies, then the resultant standard is of limited relevance for smaller companies. A similar problem is encountered if the 'standard' is based on the ratios of the company in earlier years. Conditions are unlikely to be stable over time and the ratios obtained in previous years may be wholly inappropriate to the current environment in which the company has to operate. Thus, a deviation from the previous years' ratios does not permit instant 'good' or 'bad' classifications but might, depending on the size of the deviation, suggest that further examination is necessary.

By themselves, ratios are of limited value. It seems clear that if absolute ratio criteria did exist then ratio analysis would be a mechanical procedure requiring very little expertise. It is because there are no absolute criteria and because of the imperfections in the surrogate 'standards' that a great deal of skill and judgement are required in the evaluation and interpretation of ratios.

Similarly, individual ratios taken in isolation can be misleading; they need to be combined in order to present a composite picture of a firm. In Chapters 14 and 15, the uses and limitations of both inter-firm and intra-firm ratio comparisons are considered further.

Ratio calculation

When calculating ratios, a logical connection between the items being related to each other is essential. For example, the ratio of net profit to total assets is economically meaningful and the resultant statistic can be used in the evaluation of those profits against the asset base available. A ratio relating the income tax charge in the profit and loss account to the total assets employed, on the other hand, is of doubtful significance. The implications of this for financial statement analysis are that a few key ratios are in reality all that is needed. Additional support for the view that only a limited number of ratios are required stems from the high degree of correlation among the various ratios. This is mainly because many ratios are made up of items that also appear in other ratios from the pyramiding effect, and so correlation might be expected.

A further requirement that is often proposed for ratio calculation is that the components of the ratios should be determined in a consistent manner. For example, a frequently calculated ratio is that of sales to debtors, i.e. the debtor turnover ratio. However, the debtors figure occurs as a result of credit sales, while the reported sales figure usually includes both credit sales and cash sales. So the same valuation basis is not being used. Such an inconsistency in the method of calculating the components of a ratio does not necessarily invalidate it, but merely suggests care in its interpretation.

It is often argued that the components of the ratios should have relationships that vary with each other; in other words, the components should be functionally related. For example, when calculating the ratio of net profit to sales (turnover), the profit figure is arrived at by deducting from the sales figure all the manufacturing and operating expenses of the company. Some of those expenses will vary more or less directly with the level of sales, but others will be fixed, whatever the level of sales. Thus, the resultant profit figure is not linearly related to the sales figure.

Depending on the length and positioning of time periods used for the analysis, it is possible that short-run fluctuations are hidden. Similarly, there might be a situation where rapidly changing prices affect different items at different rates. In these cases caution is needed in the interpretation of the ratios, particularly when trying to assess trends.

Ratios, do not, of course, have to be restricted to financial items. In recent years, much more use has been made of non-financial data. Employee-related data are an obvious example of this, and ratios of sales per employee or profit per employee are now quite common. Other ratios of a similar nature will depend on the types of activity carried on by a company. For a road haulage company, for example, a useful ratio for comparative purposes might be profit per road mile travelled or per ton carried, for an airline, profit per passenger mile or costs per passenger mile might be useful statistics. The BOC Group plc provides evidence in their annual report of the use of non-financial ratios. In particular these relate to management of safety, health and the environment by the company. In consideration of the importance of these areas the company indicates it set up 'Project Review' with various non-financial targets, such as zero fatalities, reductions in the lost workday case rate and passenger car avoidable accident rate.

Internally, companies make much more use of non-financial ratios. For example, when measuring the level of quality; the percentage of output requiring reworking or the percentage of output scrapped might be useful; or for the marketing activity, ratios concerned with market share or market penetration could be calculated. Obviously in the case of BOC this approach is extensively used internally.

Problems in ratio analysis

Some of the problems surrounding ratio calculation and finding suitable bases for comparison have been mentioned earlier. In this section, attention is focused on some of the other frequently cited problems in ratio analysis.

Lack of uniformity in accounts preparation

It was shown in Part One that accountants preparing financial statements are free, within broad limits, to choose from a wide range of generally accepted accounting principles. Thus, two firms that are identical in every respect may show quite different figures for profit and balance sheet valuations, owing to the use of differing accounting policies. The efforts of the Accounting Standards Board and its predecessor body have done much to reduce the range of permitted accounting policies, but choices still exist for the valuation of stocks and work in progress, depreciation methods, deferred tax treatment of intangibles and goodwill, accounting for leases and many other areas. The consequences for ratio analysis are readily apparent. Comparisons are a very important feature of ratio analysis, yet without uniformity in the preparation of financial statements it is impossible to determine whether variations in ratios are due merely to accounting policy differences or to real economic differences.

Even if uniformity of accounting policies existed (e.g. a mandatory requirement for straight-line depreciation in all circumstances), differences in estimates of asset lives would still result in variations in depreciation charges. Thus, only total uniformity, with both depreciation method and asset lives being prescribed, would produce truly comparable bases for ratio preparation. Such requirements would, of course, be anathema to the British business community. Different companies do use identical assets in different ways and, therefore, in reality, there will be differences in asset lives. Accounting for economic reality, and not simply accounting in accordance with the rules, is a cornerstone of accounting philosophy in the UK.

Furthermore, because of the need for speedy reporting by companies, many of the figures incorporated in the published accounts are based on an element of estimation. Buildings being valued by different professional valuers can produce significantly different results. Although the company and the auditors may believe the valuation to be a true and fair view estimate, it does mean that the accuracy of the ratios cannot be guaranteed any more than that of the underlying data.

Finally it must be recognized that the use of historic cost accounting has also, during times of rapidly changing prices, had the effect of making ratio comparison an exercise of doubtful validity. Using, once again, the ratio of net profit to total assets as an example, it is evident that the denominator of the ratio (total assets) will be different for a firm with assets purchased more recently than it would be for a firm with equivalent assets purchased some time ago at lower prices.

Diversified companies and multinationals

The growth by acquisition and merger of companies still continues. The merger boom of the 1960s and early 1970s started a movement which has produced a large number of highly diversified companies. Because, by definition, diversified companies operate in different industries with different degrees of risk and different expected profitabilities, the calculation of ratios based on the aggregated figures is of limited use in financial statement analysis. The problems of aggregating the results of diversified companies have been recognized for a long time. The obvious solution is to report separately the results of the segments of a company that operates in different industries. That will facilitate comparisons by permitting the calculation of ratios not only for the diversified group as a whole but for each of the industrial sectors in which the company operates. The recent SSAP 25 provides detailed guidance on the provision of segmental information. However, there are still difficulties in terms of ratio analysis, one of which is the allocation to individual segments of costs that are common to the whole company. Head office administrative costs, interest charges on loans and so on, are examples of common costs that are incurred by the company and have to be allocated on an arbitrary basis to each segment. Such a requirement can significantly distort the results of a particular segment. Nevertheless, thanks to the passage of time, greater consistency has come about in the methods and bases used by companies for their segmental reporting, and this has helped.

The 1990s have also brought about changes in corporate strategies based upon the concept of refocusing companies to a limited range of products or services. This has led to the breakup of many of the conglomerates into a number of separate entities, e.g. Thorn EMI became Thorn and EMI. But even within these newly separated and refocused companies there are still individual segments so the accounting problems still exist even if the scale is not as great.

A further development has been the large increase in the numbers of multinational companies. These companies with subsidiary operating companies based in many foreign countries, buy and sell in currencies other than pounds sterling. The annual combining of the accounts of those companies based in different local currencies into one consolidated group set of accounts in one currency, sterling, is not without its difficulties, in particular when exchange rates with sterling have not been particularly stable during a year.

These problems and difficulties of using financial information for ratio analysis reinforce the need for the analyst to make full use of the details provided in the notes to the accounts and not just take the figures in the balance sheet and profit and loss account at face value.

Lack of conceptual foundation

It was claimed earlier that the purpose of financial statement analysis is to extract information useful for decision making purposes. It was also stated that ratio analysis is the principal tool of financial statement analysis. It might therefore be reasonable to assume that ratio analysis would figure largely in microeconomic theories about asset valuation and in theories about securities analysis. However, an examination of the literature in those areas reveals that this is not the case. This is because of the lack of any conceptual foundation surrounding ratio analysis and decision making. It has been assumed that ratios will be useful without ever establishing that usefulness. Moreover, the strong support for the efficiency of capital markets, which argues that share prices at any time always reflect fully all publicly available information, implies that securities analysis is of little use in assessing share prices.

That statement is too sweeping and thus somewhat misleading since it is only in the long term that the market reflects the information. Some of the information is that which is derived from fundamental analysis, that is, ratio and other analysis. There are plenty of examples of how, in the short term, users of this type of information have made gains.

So ratio analysis is still used in practice. In spite of its apparent limitations, a great deal of time and effort is spent on calculating and comparing ratios. In fact, as will be described in Chapter 15, decision models consisting of a combination of ratios have proved very effective in making predictions about companies. However, before considering these it is necessary to examine in detail the mechanics of ratio analysis; this is done in the next four chapters, before combining this knowledge in a structured approach to ratio analysis in Chapter 14.

As previously, the financial information prepared and produced by The BOC Group plc is used as the basis and source for the ratios computed, explained and analysed in the next few chapters. Appendix A includes a complete copy of The BOC Group plc annual financial report which includes the group five year record, the finance and treasury review, the statements on corporate governance, the reports of the auditors and the management resources committee and the financial statements and accompanying notes. Appendix B is a copy of the print-out of the financial information on BOC Group plc found on the FAME (Financial Analysis Made Easy) database. This is prepared and sold commercially by Jordans Ltd.

In Appendix B, which is derived from the annual financial accounts and notes of BOC Group plc, can be found both basic financial information and sets of ratios based upon that information. Five years of information is provided and analysed. Note as you go through the next few chapters that you will find differences between the values computed for a few ratios and those explained here. This is due to alternative interpretations and methods being chosen and used in the two places. This is a good chance therefore to remind readers that if and when they use financial information prepared by others they comprehend the basis upon which it has been prepared. Reference will be made to pages in Appendices A and B for source material and/or comparisons as we go through the next few chapters.

10 Profitability and performance

In Chapter 2 it was shown how information concerning the profit of a company is presented in the annual financial report. Although such information is useful in establishing the absolute level of profit earned during a period, it fails to indicate the performance of a company because it does not take account of the resources available for the generation of the profit. A measure of profitability is therefore required that relates profit earned to other relevant factors. There are several widely used indicators of profitability; this chapter introduces some of the more important of these.

Return on capital employed

Return on capital employed, which is usually expressed as a percentage, is calculated as

$$\frac{\text{Profit}}{\text{Capital employed}} \times 100$$

This ratio concentrates on the efficiency with which capital employed has been utilized. Thus, if two companies are being compared and the reported profit of Company A is £10,000 and that of Company B is £15,000, then Company B has clearly earned the greater profit. However, if it is then observed that the capital employed of Company A was £50,000 and that of Company B was £150,000, the return on capital employed for each company is as follows:

$$\text{Company A} \quad \frac{10,000}{50,000} \times 100 = 20 \text{ per cent}$$

$$\text{Company B} \quad \frac{15,000}{150,000} \times 100 = 10 \text{ per cent}$$

It is now apparent that, when the profits earned by the two companies are related to their respective investment bases, Company A achieved the better return on capital employed and might therefore be regarded as the more successful. It is at this point, however, that the problem is first encountered of establishing precisely what is meant by the components of financial ratios, and also the methods by which these components may be calculated. Both 'capital employed' and 'profit' can quite sensibly have different meanings attached to them, and, before comparisons between the ratios of different companies can be made, it is obviously essential to ensure that like is being compared with like.

Capital employed is usually taken to be either the total assets of the company, i.e. fixed assets plus current assets, or the net total assets, i.e. fixed assets plus current assets minus current liabilities. If the amount of total assets is used, the resultant profitability measure is intended to focus attention on the efficiency with which all of the resources available to the managers of the company have been utilized. The argument for the use of net total assets is that the level of current assets is inextricably linked with the level of current liabilities and is very much dependent on the working capital policy of the company. In other words, only the net total assets can be thought of as a resource that is completely at the disposal of management. Any distortions caused by variations in working capital policy will be minimized by netting off current liabilities against current assets, so that a more comparable asset base is obtained. These are the assets financed by long-term funds such as the shareholders' capital and long-term loans. Therefore, using return on net total assets can be regarded as assessing the return by the business to the long-term investors in the business. Hence it is also called return on capital employed or ROCE.

In the examples that follow, ratios of return on capital employed have been calculated for The BOC Group plc, based on each of the alternative definitions discussed above. One point concerning capital employed relates to the date at which this should be calculated. Because the numerator of the ratio represents a flow of profit earned over the entire accounting period, the denominator ought to reflect the average amount of capital employed during the period. It is usually sufficient for this purpose to take an average of the amounts of capital employed at the beginning and end of the accounting period.

It is also evident that the basis on which the assets have been valued will have important implications for profitability analysis. At times of rising prices, the historical cost of the assets will usually be lower than their current values. This can make comparisons extremely difficult between firms with different asset age structures.

During the late 1970s and early 1980s, many companies included in their annual reports supplementary financial statements prepared according to the principles of current cost accounting. This enabled ratios based on current cost as well as historic cost to be prepared. Following the adoption of FRS 15, tangible assets, particularly land and buildings, are no longer revalued. Any revaluations done prior to FRS 15's adoption are treated as historic cost at that date of adoption. In the case of BOC this was 1 October 1999 and for reference see Accounting Policies and Note 8(d) to the Accounts of the BOC Group plc in Appendix A, pages 236 and 262, respectively.

The detailed financial review of The BOC Group plc for the year ended 30 September 2002 is reproduced in Appendix A (pages 206–73). As the profit and loss account (see page 230), balance sheet (see page 231) and cash flow statement (see page 232) are referred to extensively during this and succeeding chapters, they are reproduced in this section in Tables 10.1, 10.2 and 10.3 respectively.

Before calculating a company's ratios, it is useful to read through the statement on the accounting policies used by the company in its preparation of the figures. This is important to help maintain comparability between firms or time periods, since firms do change policies from time to time and also may have some variations from those of the

Table 10.1 The BOC Group plc – consolidated profit and loss account for the year ended 30 September 2002

	Notes	2002 Before exceptional items (£ million)	2002 Exceptional items (£ million)	2002 After exceptional items (£ million)	2001 (restated) Before exceptional items (£ million)	2001 (restated) Exceptional items (£ million)	2001 (restated) After exceptional items (£ million)
Turnover							
Continuing operations		3,890.8	—	3,890.8	4,159.2	—	4,159.2
Acquisitions		127.1	—	127.1	—	—	—
Turnover, including share of joint ventures and associates	1	4,017.9	—	4,017.9	4,159.2	—	4,159.2
Less: Share of turnover of joint ventures		324.1	—	324.1	340.0	—	340.0
Share of turnover of associates		36.1	—	36.1	46.3	—	46.3
Turnover of subsidiary undertakings		3,657.7	—	3,657.7	3,772.9	—	3,772.9
Cost of sales	2(a)	(2,089.7)	(15.1)	(2,104.8)	(2,164.2)	(44.6)	(2,208.8)
Gross profit		1,568.0	(15.1)	1,552.9	1,608.7	(44.6)	1,564.1
Net operating expenses	2(a)	(1,142.4)	(58.9)	(1,201.3)	(1,150.3)	(61.1)	(1,211.4)
Operating profit							
Continuing operations		421.2	(67.8)	353.4	458.4	(105.7)	352.7
Acquisitions		4.4	(6.2)	(1.8)	—	—	—
Operating profit of subsidiary undertakings		425.6	(74.0)	351.6	458.4	(105.7)	352.7
Share of operating profit of joint ventures		63.8	(0.5)	63.3	59.0	(2.2)	56.8
Share of operating profit of associates		10.7	—	10.7	13.2	(0.4)	12.8
Total operating profit including share of joint ventures and associates	1	500.1	(74.5)	425.6	530.6	(108.3)	422.3
Loss on termination/disposal of businesses – continuing operations	2(b)	—	(20.2)	(20.2)	—	—	—
Profit on disposal of fixed assets – continuing operations	2(b)	—	—	—	—	3.6	3.6
Profit on ordinary activities before interest		500.1	(94.7)	405.4	530.6	(104.7)	425.9
Interest on net debt	3(a)			(103.1)			(123.4)
Interest on pension scheme liabilities	6(e)			(106.1)			(107.2)
Expected return on pension scheme assets	6(e)			139.1			166.9
Net interest				(70.1)			(63.7)
Profit on ordinary activities before tax				335.3			362.2
Tax on profit on ordinary activities	4(a)			(106.2)			(104.6)
Profit on ordinary activities after tax				229.1			257.6
Minority interests – equity				(26.2)			(33.5)
Profit for the financial year				202.9			224.1
Dividends	12(a)			(186.6)			(180.3)
Retained profit for the financial year				16.3			43.8
Earnings per 25p	2(d)						
Ordinary share, basic							
– on published earnings				41.36p			46.03p
– on exceptional items				14.58p			11.48p
– before exceptional items				55.94p			57.51p
Earnings per 25p	2(d)						
Ordinary share, diluted							
– on published earnings				41.21p			45.87p
– on exceptional items				14.53p			11.44p
– before exceptional items				55.74p			57.31p

All turnover and operating profit arose from continuing operations.

Table 10.2 The BOC Group plc – consolidated balance sheet as at 30 September 2002

	Notes	2002 (£ million)	2001 (restated) (£ million)
Fixed assets			
Intangible assets	7	150.7	48.1
Tangible assets	8	3,027.4	3,168.6
Investment in joint ventures			
share of gross assets		616.2	615.2
share of gross liabilities		(410.7)	(410.4)
		205.5	204.8
loans to joint ventures		111.8	97.6
Investment in associates			
share of net assets		57.5	47.1
loans to associates		6.2	9.1
Investment in own shares		42.5	59.5
Other investments		45.1	31.7
Investments	9	468.6	449.8
		3,646.7	3,666.5
Current assets			
Stocks	10(a)	260.0	275.2
Debtors falling due within one year	10(b)	733.8	713.3
Debtors falling due after more than one year	10(c)	28.3	21.3
Investments		38.8	43.2
Cash at bank and in hand	10(d)	185.5	233.5
		1,246.4	1,286.5
Current liabilities			
Creditors: amounts falling due within one year			
Borrowings and finance leases	10(e)	(390.1)	(486.4)
Other creditors	10(f)	(857.8)	(795.3)
		(1,247.9)	(1,281.7)
Net current (liabilities)/assets		(1.5)	4.8
Total assets *less* current liabilities		3,645.2	3,671.3
Long-term liabilities			
Creditors: amounts falling due after more than one year			
Borrowings and finance leases	11(a)	(1,121.0)	(1,019.9)
Other creditors		(58.0)	(59.4)
		(1,179.0)	(1,079.3)
Provisions for liabilities and charges	11(b)	(407.5)	(419.2)
Total net assets excluding pension assets and liabilities		2,058.7	2,172.8
Pension assets	6(e)	54.3	107.0
Pension liabilities	6(e)	(311.0)	(56.0)
Total net assets including pension assets and liabilities		**1,802.0**	**2,223.8**
Capital and reserves			
Equity called up share capital	12(b)	124.3	123.6
Share premium account	12(c)	362.1	335.8
Revaluation reserves	12(c)	27.8	47.9
Profit and loss account	12(c)	1,304.8	1,400.3
Pensions reserves	12(c)	(256.5)	47.1
Joint ventures' reserves	12(c)	88.1	98.1
Associates' reserves	12(c)	33.5	33.4
Equity shareholders' funds		1,684.1	2,086.2
Minority shareholders' equity interests		117.9	137.6
Total capital and reserves		**1,802.0**	**2,223.8**

The financial statements were approved by the board of directors on 22 November 2002 and are signed on its behalf by: **A E Isaac** Director **R Médori** Director

Table 10.3 The BOC Group plc – consolidated cash flow statement for year ended 30 September 2002

	Notes	2002 (£ million)	2001 (restated) (£ million)
Net cash inflow from operating activities	14(a)	759.3	787.8
Dividends from joint ventures and associates			
Dividends from joint ventures		30.5	19.4
Dividends from associates		3.4	4.1
Dividends from joint ventures and associates		33.9	23.5
Returns on investments and servicing of finance			
Interest paid		(89.6)	(95.4)
Interest received		18.5	23.1
Dividends paid to minorities in subsidiaries		(13.9)	(7.7)
Interest element of finance lease rental payments		(5.7)	(7.2)
Returns on investments and servicing of finance		(90.7)	(87.2)
Tax paid		(96.2)	(100.6)
Capital expenditure and financial investment			
Purchases of tangible fixed assets		(352.1)	(349.8)
Sales of tangible fixed assets		31.6	47.1
Purchases of intangible fixed assets		(0.1)	(0.3)
Net sales/(purchases) of current asset investments		4.3	(6.5)
Purchases of trade and other investments		(19.7)	(10.2)
Sales of trade and other investments		11.5	7.8
Capital expenditure and financial investment		(324.5)	(311.9)
Acquisitions and disposals			
Acquisitions of businesses	15(a)	(207.3)	(145.9)
Net overdrafts acquired with subsidiaries		(7.4)	—
Disposals of businesses	15(a)	10.6	2.7
Investments in joint ventures		(12.6)	—
Divestments/repayments from joint ventures		—	10.8
Investments in associates		(0.5)	(2.7)
Divestments/repayments from associates		1.7	1.5
Acquisitions and disposals		(215.5)	(133.6)
Equity dividends paid		(186.6)	(180.3)
Net cash outflow before use of liquid resources and financing		(120.3)	(2.3)
Management of liquid resources			
Net sales of short-term investments		52.6	102.8
Financing			
Issue of shares		25.0	16.9
Increase/(decrease) in debt	14(d)	64.1	(51.3)
Net cash inflow/(outflow) from financing		89.1	(34.4)
Increase in cash		21.4	66.1

A reconciliation of the increase in cash to the movement in net debt in the year is given in note 14(b).
Liquid resources are defined as short-term deposits.

firm to which they are being compared. For BOC the note on accounting policies is given on pages 235–7.

From this it can be seen that the accounts are based on the traditional historical cost accounting convention, but they include the revaluation of certain land and buildings. BOC plc revalues its land and buildings periodically, basing the revised value on the purchase cost in the open market for the type of property, which is then depreciated to reflect the age of the buildings. This year there have been some changes in some accounting policies or treatments. Two new accounting standards, FRS 17 – retirement benefits – and FRS 19 – deferred tax, have been fully adopted in the 2002 accounts. Following the full adoption of FRS 17, the regular service cost of providing retirement benefits to employees during the year is charged to operating profit in the year, instead of being disclosed just as a note to the financial statements. This has led to a restatement of the comparative figures for 2001 and 2000 from those shown in their original accounts. For example, in note 6(c) (Appendix A page 252) the total restated comparative employment costs for 2001 are £908.8 million, an increase from the £823.5 million stated in the 2001 report.

As far as the profit component of the ratio is concerned, comparability will be improved by using a profit figure that reflects the sustainable ordinary trading activities and excludes the effects of any extraordinary and exceptional items that may have occurred. Analysts and financial reports call this the headline earnings. They argue that their approach, though at odds with that of the FRS, provides a more standardized approach to reported profit from trading. The approach is perceived to provide a sharper focus on the results from a company's ongoing trading activities.

By showing exceptional items separately it highlights to the reader the material costs or revenues from within the ordinary trading activities caused by some significant event(s). One such event for BOC Group plc was the announcement in August 2001 of a major restructuring. The total provision made in the 2002 profit and loss account amounted to £74.5 million, which included, *inter alia*, £47.2 million for restructuring and £21.2 million for write-down and impairment of assets (Table 10.1). A more detailed explanation of these charges, the forecast annual savings of £55 million that should arise, and the accounting treatment of them can be found in the Finance and Treasury review in Appendix A (page 208). The five-year record can give the reader an indication of the trend of the headline earnings and the regularity/or otherwise) of the incidence of these exceptional items. Clearly, the inclusion of the exceptional items can significantly affect the trend.

FRS 3 treats the profit on ordinary activities before interest, which are post exceptional items, as the company's profits from its year's commercial activities, but it is not the sustainable profit figure. The debate as to which profit figure, operating profit or profit on ordinary activities before interest, to use as the numerator, continues but analysts still tend to focus on the operating profit before exceptional items. Note how the BOC five-year trend in operating profit and earnings per share (EPS) is affected by the exceptional items.

Comparability is similarly improved by using a profit figure before deductions for interest and taxation. The amount of taxation paid by a company depends on a variety of circumstances, not all of which are under the control of the company. Distortions caused by differences in liabilities to taxation can therefore be avoided by concentration on the before-tax position. The rationale for excluding interest charges is that the resultant profit figure is then consistent with the calculation of capital employed. If capital employed is taken to represent the total assets of the company, then it is evident that these have been partially financed by the creditors; therefore the profit figure should be the amount before any interest payments to creditors have been deducted. If capital employed is taken to represent the net total assets, then strictly speaking it would be correct to exclude only the long-term interest payments. The interest paid on current liabilities, or received on current assets, should be included in the calculation of profit.

BOC, in note 3(a) (page 243) to the financial statements, give some details concerning interest paid and received, but this does not include information on interest paid to short-term creditors on loan, etc., maturing within one year. Therefore any adjustment to the operating profit for short-term interest paid has to be ignored because it cannot be made through lack of information. With many companies the amounts involved in interest paid on short-term creditors is small and thus ignored.

Return on total assets

The formula for return on total assets is

$$\frac{\text{Trading profit before interest paid, taxation and exceptional items}}{\text{Average total assets for the period}} \times 100$$

The average total assets for the period can be determined from Table 10.2. The total assets figure at the end of the period (30 September 2002) is the sum of the fixed assets of £3,646.7 million and the current assets of £1,246.4 million, i.e., a total of £4,893.1 million. Similarly, the total assets figure at the beginning of the period (30 September 2001) is made up of fixed assets of £3,666.5 million and current assets of £1,286.5 million, i.e. a total of £4,953.0 million.

The trading profit before interest, taxation and exceptional items can be obtained by referring to Table 10.1; it consists of the amount shown as 'operating profit' of £500.1 million.

The return on total assets (ROTA) can now be calculated as

$$\text{ROTA} = \frac{500.1}{0.5(4,893.1 + 4,953.0)} \times 100 = 10.16 \text{ per cent}$$

Return on net total assets

The formula for the return on net total assets, which is also called the return on capital employed (ROCE), is

$$\frac{\text{Trading profit before interest, taxation and exceptional items}}{\text{Average net total assets for the period}} \times 100$$

The net total assets figure is the same as the capital employed figure; the latter being made up of the sum of the long-term liabilities and the capital and reserves, i.e. the long-term funding element of the total assets. In 2002 the capital employed for BOC from Table 10.2 is made up of the sum of the long-term liabilities of £1,843.2 million plus capital and reserves of £1,802.0 million, which is £3,645.2 million; the same as the total assets less current liabilities. Thus, the alternative but preferred name to return on net total assets is return on capital employed.

The net total assets are referred to in Table 10.2 as 'total assets less current liabilities'. At the end of the period these amounted to £3,645.2 million and at the beginning of the period to £3,671.3 million. The operating profit for the year was £500.1 million.

The return on net total assets is

$$\text{ROCE} = \frac{500.1}{0.5(3,645.2 + 3,671.3)} \times 100 = 13.67 \text{ per cent}$$

Where inter-firm comparisons are being made it is not possible to state categorically which of the alternatives of return on total assets or return on net total assets is the 'correct' one to use. It all depends on the particular aspects of the company on which the analyst wishes to concentrate, either long-term capital employed, or the complete economic unit. Provided that the components of the ratios are defined in the same way for the companies being compared, then the comparisons should be meaningful. It is also usual to compare the performance of a particular company over time, and ideally a sequence of the above ratios calculated for BOC for 2002 and earlier years would enable the establishment, or otherwise, of a trend in the return on capital employed (see Table 14.2).

However, BOC has its own method of calculating net total assets/capital employed and as the only information available for years prior to 2001 is that given in the five-year record on pages 206–7, it will be necessary to use the BOC definition for the purpose of time series comparisons. The BOC definition for capital employed differs from that in the balance sheet in Table 10.2 in so far as all short-term borrowings and finance leases are included, but are reduced by the deposits and cash. It also excludes the pension assets and liabilities. It is shown in BOC's five-year record (see page 207).

The calculation of the capital employed figure used by BOC for 2002 is as follows:

		(£ million)
Total assets less current liabilities		3,645.2
Add		
Borrowings and finance leases falling due within one year (see notes 3 and 10(c))		390.1
		4,035.3
Less		
Deposits and cash (see notes 3 and 10(d))	185.5	
Pension liabilities (see note 6(e))	256.7	442.2
BOC capital employed		3,593.1

The figure of 'capital employed' for 2002 and the corresponding figures for the four previous years are to be found in the five-year review on page 207. Because of the adjustments to the net total assets figure by BOC indicated above, the operating profit figure given in the profit and loss account in the five-year review needs no further adjustment. Therefore, using the BOC review figures, for 2002 and 2001 the returns on average capital employed have been calculated as follows:

$$\text{ROCE 2002} = \frac{500.1}{0.5(3,593.1 + 3,974.5)} \times 100 = 13.22 \text{ per cent}$$

$$\text{ROCE 2001} = \frac{530.6}{0.5(3,974.5 + 4,453.2)} \times 100 = 12.59 \text{ per cent}$$

If the analysis is extended to years prior to 2001 the improvement in the return on capital employed since 1998 is not evident, with an overall decline of 0.2 per cent. But over the same five-year period, headline operating profit has fluctuated, starting at £479.9 million in 1998 and rising over three years, before a decline to £500.1 million in 2002. Trend analysis is used in Chapter 14 (see Table 14.2 for an example) and is discussed more fully as a concept in Chapter 15. (In 1997 BOC added a further degree of sophistication not available to the external reader by calculating the average capital employed on a monthly basis. This resulted in a different average capital employed than the simple averaging of the opening and closing capital employed as used in the above calculation, and produced a return on average capital employed of 12.3 per cent).

Some analysts argue that a number of firms use bank overdrafts as a form of long-term borrowing, and that this is particularly true of small firms. In such cases it is suggested that the bank overdraft should be included as part of the capital employed, and any cash-in-hand balances should be netted off against the overdraft and 'short-term' borrowing, with no interest being deducted from the operating profit. This would also appear to be BOC's logic. BOC has included all interest bearing borrowings in its capital employed less any deposits and cash held.

In the above ratios the numerator used was described as trading profit before interest, taxation and exceptional items. This is also known as EBIT – earnings before interest and tax. Some analysts have proposed an alternative numerator, EBITDA, which is EBIT with the depreciation and amortization expenditure added back. It is supposed to provide a gross return on the assets used or capital employed and reduces the potential for variation in methods used to compute profits by companies. We would argue that this places the EBITDA-based ratio part way between the EBIT-based ones above and the cash flow return on capital employed (page 135) which conceptually are the preferred ones.

Return on equity

The purpose of the return on equity ratio is to show the profitability of the company in terms of the capital provided by the owners of the company, i.e. the ordinary shareholders. Return on equity is usually calculated as follows:

$$\frac{\text{Profit after interest and preference dividends but before tax}}{\text{Average ordinary share capital, reserves and retained profit for the period}} \times 100$$

This ratio therefore focuses attention on the efficiency of the company in earning profits on behalf of its ordinary shareholders, by relating the profits to the total amount of shareholders' funds employed in the company. As with return on capital employed, it is usually more appropriate to take the figure of profit before tax, to avoid distortions caused by differences in the taxation liability of different companies.

In the following ratios, calculated for BOC for 2002, the numerator is the amount described in each of the consolidated profit and loss accounts as profit before tax minus any preference dividend. The denominator is the average of the opening and closing amounts described in each of the consolidated balance sheets as shareholders's funds in the 'capital and reserves' section. As it is the intention to concentrate on the returns attributable to the shareholders in BOC, the minority shareholders' interests (i.e. the interest of outside shareholders in consolidated subsidiary companies) should not be included in the calculation. The minority interest of £26.2 million in the 2002 profits of BOC has therefore been deducted.

$$\text{Return on equity} = \frac{335.3 - 26.2}{0.5(1,684.1 + 2,086.2)} \times 100 = 16.40 \text{ per cent}$$

In Appendix B, page 282, the ratio Return on Shareholder Funds (Return on Sh. F) can be found. This is another name for return on equity. However the numbers above and on pages 277–83 differ because of small differences in defining the numerator and denominator. FAME have made no adjustments for the minority interest in profit and the dividends and, in the past, the capital of the preference shareholders.

This is a good example of two interpretations of the same ratio. We would argue ours is more conceptually sound, but more time consuming to compute.

Earnings per share

Earnings per share (EPS) is a much more widely used variation of the return on equity indicator of profitability. The numerator of this represents the total amount of earnings available to ordinary shareholders after all deductions have been made, i.e. the profit after exceptional and extraordinary items, interest, taxation, minority interests and preference dividends. The denominator represents either the number of ordinary shares issued by the company at the year-end or, if substantial changes have taken place during the year, the average number of shares outstanding during the year. It is now standard practice for EPS information to be given in the published accounts of a company (as required by FRS 14); it is therefore normally unnecessary for the analyst to have to calculate this ratio. However, it might be useful to consider briefly the steps that are involved in this calculation. In the group five-year record, as shown on pages 206–7, various different EPS figures are given.

Details of the computation of BOC's EPS can be found in note 2, page 242. The profit for the financial year has been calculated in accord with FRS 14 and is thus the net profit after exceptional and extraordinary items, interest, tax and any preference dividends, i.e. the net profit (or loss) for the period attributable to ordinary shareholders. It is possible for the profit for the year to be materially influenced by the size of the exceptional item(s). This was the case for BOC in 1998. There was an overall charge of £240.6 million for restructuring, which was partially offset by the profit on disposal of the health business of £144.0 million. In 2002 the restructuring costs treated as exceptional totalled a smaller £47.2 million, with some other costs such as write-down and impairment of assets bringing the total net of tax exceptional costs to £71.4 million. These amounts are shown in the profit and loss account in Table 10.1, the net of tax figures are given in note 2.

Companies are allowed to compute an additional EPS based on the normal or maintainable profit. Generally this is known as the headline profit, the profit derived from the ongoing activities of the business prior to charging such exceptional or one-off expenses. The UK based Institute of Investment Management and Research (IIMR) has also made recommendations which seem to provide the basis for the method used by the market analysts. The figures in Table 10.1 for EPS give the EPS as calculated above after deduction of exceptional items and then state the per share cost of the exceptional items before arriving at the EPS based on the profit derived from ongoing activities, prior to the exceptional items. The calculations here for EPS will use the 'before exceptional items' profits, i.e. headline profits in line with the analysts' preferences.

The undiluted 'headline' EPS ratio for 2002 can be computed as follows:

		(£ million)
Profit for the financial year		202.9
Adjustments:		
Less preference dividends	0	
Add exceptional items (net)	71.4	71.4
		274.3

Average number of ordinary shares 490.4 million

$$\text{EPS} = \frac{274.3}{490.4} \times 100 = 55.94\text{p per share}$$

The exceptional items before tax amounted to £94.7 million which were adjusted for the impact of tax and minority interests to the net amount of £71.4 million. Earnings per share before exceptional items are presented in order to show the underlying earnings performance of the group. Note that this is consistent with the headline profit approach in calculating the ROCE and ROTA above.

For 2002, the cost per share for BOC's exceptional items was 14.58p which, when deducted from the headline EPS of 55.94p, gives a published profit basic EPS of 41.36p per share, in accord with FRS14 requirements.

Looking at the trend of EPS over the five years the significant effects caused by restructuring are obvious, as is the smoother pattern presented by the headline based EPS. The Accounting Standards Board would argue that when such a situation, such as restructuring, occurs the required method has served its purpose by highlighting to the market that the company has taken decisions which, in the short term have cost it money, but which it is hoped will have long-term benefits.

A second set of EPS figures must also be shown. This set is known as the diluted EPS. The calculations are similar to the basic EPS described, except that the denominator now reflects the number of shares that would be in issue if all of the options to take-up shares were to be exercised. Note 2 indicates the dilutive share option numbers, which for 2002 amounted to a further 1.8 million shares. If these options were exercised, then the existing equity base would be increased and the basic EPS diluted. The diluted EPS captures the effect of that adjustment.

So in spite of its widespread use, the EPS ratio does have several limitations. For example, if the ratio is used to compare the profitability of different companies, it may be misleading because it is based on the number of shares in issue. Two companies that are identical in every respect except for the nominal value of their ordinary shares will clearly have a different number of shares outstanding and will therefore have different EPS. If the profitability of the same company over time is being compared, the ratio will be affected by any bonus issues that have taken place. This has the effect of increasing the number of shares but does not provide any additional capital for the company. Also, because of the effect of retained earnings on the profit of a company, the EPS changes will be difficult to interpret correctly. For example, if a company has equity capital of £50,000 (in £1 ordinary shares) on which it currently earns an after-tax return of 20 per cent, then its earnings available to equity will amount to £10,000 and the EPS figure will be 20p per share. Of the earnings of £10,000, £2,000 might be distributed as dividends and the balance retained. The equity will now amount to £58,000 and, if the same return on equity is achieved in the next accounting period, then the earnings will be £11,600 and the earnings per share will increase to £11,600/50,000, i.e. 23.2p per share. Thus the EPS will have increased, although there has been no corresponding increase in the underlying performance of the company as measured by return on equity.

Price–earnings ratio (PER)

This ratio is calculated by dividing the market price of ordinary shares of a company by the EPS figure described above. The ratio is therefore made up of a component that reflects the expectations of the market concerning the future earnings of a company (i.e. the market price of the shares) and a component that reflects the earnings available for each ordinary share based on the results of the most recent past accounting period. For example, supposing the current market price of a BOC ordinary share is £8.85 and, using the EPS for the year ended 30 September 2002 of 55.94p, then the price–earnings ratio is

$$\text{PER} = \frac{8.85}{0.5594} = 15.82 \text{ times}$$

What this means is that if £8.85 is paid for these shares, then 15.82 years of earnings of 55.94 pence per share are being bought. Because the current market value of a share reflects the expectations of investors concerning the future profits of a company, the ratio is effectively measuring the market's anticipation of future earnings. If the price–earnings ratios of different companies are compared, then, all other things being equal, the company with the higher ratio will be the one that is expected to have the better prospects. Price–earnings ratios differ from other measures of profitability so far discussed in that the latter are based on the actual reported profit and financial position for a past period. Those might therefore offer a better basis for inter-firm comparisons than the price–earnings ratio, which is very much dependent on the subjective opinion of investors concerning future profitability.

A quick indication of whether the company is highly or lowly rated is obtained by computing the Price–Earnings Ratio relative (PER relative). This ratio is the result of comparing the PER of a company with the PER of the market, which is usually the FTSE All-share PER.

$$\text{PER relative} = \frac{\text{PER of BOC Group}}{\text{PER of market}}$$

For BOC, when its PER was 15.82, the FTSE All-share PER was 17.84, therefore

$$\text{PER relative} = \frac{15.82}{17.84} = 0.89 \text{ times}$$

Similar relatives can be computed using a company's industry PER, which was 15.8 giving a PER relative with the industry of 1.00. This implies the market is seeing BOC as an average member of its industry grouping. A high PER relative would suggest either a market leader or an overvalued share; a low PER relative the opposite. See the later analysis in Chapter 14 which does not report outstanding performance and growth by BOC, two signals which one would expect to find in a company with a PER relative greater than unity.

Return on sales and asset turnover

The profitability ratios that have been described so far relate profit earned to a specific investment base. An alternative way of examining the performance of a company is to make use of ratios that bring out the relationship between profit and sales, and the relationship between sales and capital employed. The first of these is the return on sales, or profit-margin, ratio and this is calculated as

$$\frac{\text{Profit}}{\text{Total sales}} \times 100$$

The purpose of this ratio is to indicate the performance of the company in achieving the maximum sales possible, while at the same time keeping costs to a minimum. The ratio can be thought of as expressing the profit in pence generated by each pound of sales; in general, the higher it is the better. However, such a ratio by itself may be misleading because it fails to take account of the assets or capital used to achieve the profit margin. In other words, a high return on sales may have been achieved, but only after making a considerable investment in resources, resulting in a low return on capital employed.

This problem can be overcome by introducing the asset-turnover ratio, which is calculated as

$$\frac{\text{Total sales}}{\text{Assets}}$$

This ratio is used to measure the performance of the company in generating sales from the assets at its disposal. It is described as the asset–turnover ratio because it is, in effect, expressing the number of times assets have been 'turned over' during a period to achieve the sales revenue. If one divided total sales by the capital employed the ratio could be called the capital-turnover ratio. The underlying principle is the same for both ratios.

The profit-margin ratio and asset–turnover ratio, if considered together, provide a useful means of breaking down the return on investment ratios described previously. The relationship between all three ratios can be seen to be

$$\frac{\text{Profit}}{\text{Total sales}} \times \frac{\text{Total sales}}{\text{Assets}} = \frac{\text{Profit}}{\text{Assets}}$$

Obviously, for such a relationship to hold, the numerator and denominator of each ratio need to be defined in a consistent manner. For example, if we refer to the return on capital employed ratios described earlier, several ways of defining both profit and capital employed were identified. The latter could be the total assets, the net total assets or, in the case of BOC, the net total assets after adjusting for short-term cash items. For the purpose of comparing the profit-margin and asset–turnover ratios of BOC in 2002 with the equivalent ratios for 2001, it will be convenient to use their own definition of capital employed.

From Table 10.1 it can be seen that the trading profit of £500.1 million in 2002 was earned from sales (turnover) of £4,017.9 million. Similarly, the 2001 trading profit of £530.6 million was earned from sales of £4,159.2 million. Both turnover and operating profit include the appropriate shares of the amounts made by the associated companies. Armed with this information, it is possible to calculate profit-margin ratios as follows:

$$\text{Return on sales (profit margin) } 2002 = \frac{500.1}{4,017.9} \times 100 = 12.45 \text{ per cent}$$

$$\text{Return on sales (profit margin) 2001} = \frac{530.6}{4,159.2} \times 100 = 12.76 \text{ per cent}$$

There has been a marginal decline between the two years in the profit margin which was not matched in the ROCE, as shown on page 126. This would suggest that the use of the capital employed in generating sales has improved. For confirmation of this it is necessary to calculate the asset–turnover ratios for each year. For consistency we use the BOC calculated capital employed figures in the denominator, see page 126 for explanation and pages 206–7 of the BOC five-year record for figures. The ratios are as follows:

$$\text{Asset–turnover ratio 2002} = \frac{4,017.9}{0.5(3,593.1 + 3,974.5)} = 1.06 \text{ times}$$

$$\text{Asset–turnover ratio 2001} = \frac{4,159.2}{0.5(3,974.5 + 4,453.2)} = 0.99 \text{ times}$$

The relationship between profit margin, asset-turnover rate and return on capital employed can now be expressed as follows:

	Profit margin	*Asset turnover*		*ROCE*
2002	12.45	× 1.06	=	13.22 per cent
2001	12.76	× 0.99	=	12.59 per cent

It is evident that the slight decline in the profit margin has been partially offset by the increase in the asset turnover to give a small increase in the return on capital employed. As the profit margin in 2002 has decreased proportionately less than the asset turnover has increased, the return on capital employed has increased only slightly.

Analysing the profitability of the company in this way therefore provides a better explanation of the change in return on capital employed. Comparisons can now be made with similar companies in the same industry to determine whether the trends isolated for BOC are repeated elsewhere.

Profit-margin ratios and asset–turnover ratios can of course be related to other returns on investment ratios, such as return on equity or earnings per ordinary share. Provided that the numerator and denominator of the ratios are calculated consistently, the break-down of these measures of return can provide a useful analysis of profitability for inter-firm and time-series comparisons.

Segmental analysis

So far the analysis of the profitability of BOC has made use of the figures contained in the consolidated financial statements. The process of consolidation involves the aggregation of the results of many subsidiary companies with those of the parent company to produce one single figure for trading profit, for tangible fixed assets and so on. However, with a diversified company such as BOC, the various companies making up the group are involved in a variety of lines of business or operate in different parts of the world and an analysis based simply on the aggregate position might fail to reflect the performance of the different industrial or geographical segments of the group. Differences in profitability and risk are likely to attach to different industries and to different geographical locations, and comparability, either with other companies or over time, will be improved by extending the analysis of profitability to the major segments of The BOC Group's activities.

Table 10.4   Return on capital employed

	2002	2001
Process gas solutions	$\dfrac{185.2}{1831.3} \times 100 = 10.11$ per cent	$\dfrac{156.5}{2004.9} \times 100 = 7.81$ per cent
Industrial and special products	$\dfrac{29.7}{179.4} \times 100 = 16.56$ per cent	$\dfrac{248.8}{1152.7} \times 100 = 21.58$ per cent

Segmental information concerning BOC is given in note 1 to its financial statements. The profit figure used is that described in Table 10.1 as 'operating profit' before exceptional items. The capital employed is the net total assets after adjusting for short-term cash items. Using this information, it is possible to isolate the profitability of each line of business or geographical location. For example, for two of the principal areas of business activity in terms of contribution to overall profit – process gas solutions and industrial and special products – the position is shown in Table 10.4.

Financial information for each region and segment is provided for three years but we shall use the year end capital employed for each of the two years in the example.

Such an analysis is useful for highlighting the changes that have taken place in the profitability of each major segment, and it may help to create a better picture of the performance of the company in past periods and also of the prospects for the future profitability of the group as a whole. Moreover, comparisons can now be made with companies in the same industry, e.g. with other companies, or segments of other groups, operating in the industrial gases industry.

Segmental analyses need not, of course, be limited to return on capital employed; they could also concentrate on profit-margin and asset–turnover ratios as described previously. Once again using the information contained in note 1 to the BOC financial statements, the picture that emerges for the two business segments of process gas solutions and industrial and special products is as shown in Table 10.5.

The improvement in the return of capital employed on process gas solutions can be seen to be due to the increase in both profit margin and asset turnover. For industrial and special products there was a decline in margins but an improvement in asset turnover. Further reading of the chairman's statement, the performance review of operations and note 1 of the financial statements, should provide some explanation for the changes highlighted by the ratios.

Obviously, where diversification does exist, the ability to be able to undertake this kind of detailed profitability analysis for the principal industrial and geographical segments should provide a useful supplement to the analysis of overall group profitability.

The segmental reports and their ratios help attest to the statements in the operating review of the annual report, helping to explain the much greater level of investment needed to support the process gas solutions division which then, over the longer term, brought improved turnover and profitability. Likewise the same ratios when computed for the geographical regions can help explain those regional differences. These are reproduced in Table 10.6 which serves to highlight the breadth of the dispersions of the regions' results from the overall range. The basic information was taken from note 1 to the financial statements (see pages 238–9). FAME, (see Appendix B, page 282)

Table 10.5   Profit-margin and asset-turnover ratios

	Profit margin (1)	Asset turnover (2)	ROCE (1) × (2)
Process gas solutions			
2002	$\dfrac{185.2}{1,200.6} \times 100 = 15.43$ per cent	$\dfrac{1,200.6}{1,831.3} = 0.66$ times	10.11%
2001	$\dfrac{156.5}{1,193.0} \times 100 = 13.12$ per cent	$\dfrac{1,193}{2,004.9} = 0.60$ times	7.81%
Industrial and special products			
2002	$\dfrac{248.0}{1,605.3} \times 100 = 15.45$ per cent	$\dfrac{1,605.3}{1,058.1} = 1.52$ times	23.44%
2001	$\dfrac{248.8}{1,573.9} \times 100 = 15.81$ per cent	$\dfrac{1,573.9}{1,152.7} = 1.37$ times	21.58%

Table 10.6   The BOC Group – regional profitability

		Europe	Africa	Americas	Asia/Pacific	Overall
2002	Profit margin (%)	14.51	12.86	9.39	13.73	12.45
	Asset turnover (×)	1.13	1.99	1.04	1.03	1.12
	ROCE (%)	16.43	25.63	9.75	14.10	13.92
2001	Profit margin (%)	16.51	13.73	9.89	12.54	12.76
	Asset turnover (x)	0.82	1.95	1.06	1.06	1.05
	ROCE (%)	13.55	26.80	10.51	13.33	13.35

provides general profitability ratios, but not the detailed segmental ratios. It has used the year end values for its capital and asset denominators and the net profit after interest but before tax for its numerators thus giving a different set of figures from those prepared here.

Cash flow returns

The publication of the consolidated cash flow statement (see Table 10.3 and Appendix A, page 232) is designed to aid users in making judgements on the amount, timing and degree of certainty of future cash flows. It has a further purpose, that of helping to indicate the relationship between profitability and cash generating ability, and thus the quality of the profit earned.

Quality of profit

The quality of profit earned ratio is expressed as a percentage and calculated as

$$\frac{\text{Net cash inflow from operations}}{\text{Operating profit}} \times 100$$

The ratio focuses attention on the company's ability to generate cash as opposed to profit and shows the proportion of profits actually earned as cash. This has obvious liquidity implications for interest, tax, dividend payments and future capital expenditure. These will be handled in Chapter 12. Given the relative size of the annual depreciation charge and various other non-cash expenses one would expect a company to have a quality of profit ratio in excess of 100 per cent. Note 14 to the financial statements of BOC provides the adjustments made to the operating profit to arrive at the figure for the net cash inflow from operations.

For the quality of profit ratios for BOC for 2002 the numerator is the amount of net cash inflow from operations, £759.3 million, which is taken from the consolidated cash flow statement. The denominator is the operating profit after exceptional items of £405.4 million in the profit and loss statement in Table 10.1.

$$\text{Quality of profit 2002} = \frac{759.3}{405.4} \times 100 = 187.3 \text{ per cent}$$

The ratio has increased marginally from the previous year, 2001, when it was 185.0 per cent. If turnover and profits start growing again, then as the ratio of annual depreciation charged to net profits declined, so too would the quality of profit ratio probably decline. If it ever came close to 100 per cent then analysts would start looking even harder at the company's liquidity ratios, though it is quite likely to occur in a business start-up situation.

Quality of sales

The quality of sales ratio is only possible if a company has chosen to use the direct method to report its net cash flow from operations, as this would include an amount for cash received from customers. The quality of sales ratio would be expressed as a percentage and calculated as

$$\frac{\text{Cash received from customers}}{\text{Sales}} \times 100$$

A ratio close to 100 per cent is desirable indicating that the company is keeping on top of the collection of cash from its debtors. Its value should be reviewed alongside any changes in the average collection period (see Chapter 11).

Cash return on capital employed

The cash return on capital employed is the cash equivalent measure of return on capital employed and is expressed as a percentage and calculated as

$$\frac{\text{Net cash inflow from operations}}{\text{Capital employed}} \times 100$$

To many users of financial statements it is the cash return on investment rather than the profit-based return on investment that is of greatest meaning and value. This is particularly so in the case of analysts using business valuation models and corporate projection models.

In the example here for The BOC Group the cash return on the average capital employed (calculated per BOC approach) will be shown. The BOC net cash inflow from operations is £759.3 million for 2002.

$$\text{Cash return on capital employed} = \frac{759.3}{0.5(3{,}593.1 + 3{,}974.5)} \times 100 = 20.07 \text{ per cent}$$

Like the profit-based ROCE, the cash return on capital employed (Cash ROCE) increased from 2001 to 2002, from 18.70 per cent to 20.07 per cent. It is still early days to report whether or not the cash ROCE has replaced the profit ROCE in terms of practical importance, even though the conceptual case is a strong one.

Cash flow per share

This ratio is the cash flow equivalent to the earnings per share. It indicates the amount of cash generated per share by the year's operations, together with dividends from joint ventures and associates and interest received from investments, less interest and tax payments. It is the cash generated by the business for the shareholders. The proportion of this that is paid out as dividends and the proportion that is kept for reinvestment in the business will be determined by the directors.

$$\text{Cash flow per share} = \frac{\begin{array}{c}\text{Net cash inflow from operating activities} \\ + \text{ dividends from joint ventures and associates} \\ - \text{ returns on investments and servicing of finance } - \text{ tax paid}\end{array}}{\begin{array}{c}\text{Weighted average number of ordinary shares} \\ \text{in issue during the year.}\end{array}}$$

The denominator of this ratio is exactly the same as that used in the calculation of earnings per share (see page 242). For BOC, all the elements of the numerator of this ratio for 2002 can be found in the cash flow statement in Table 10.3. In 2002, the net cash inflow from operating activities was £759.3 million, the dividends from joint ventures and associates were £33.9 million, the returns on investments and servicing of finance were an outflow of £90.7 million with the tax paid amounting to £96.2 million. The weighted average number of ordinary shares in issue in 2002 can be seen from note 2 (page 243) to be 490.4 million shares.

$$\text{Cash flow per share } 2002 = \frac{(759.3 + 33.9 - 90.7 - 96.2)}{490.4} = £1.24 \text{ per share}$$

The cash flow for 2002 has declined marginally from £1.28 per share in 2001. When compared to the dividend per share of £0.38 (page 266), (£0.37 in 2001) it can be seen that there is plenty of cash cover for the dividend.

11 Efficiency and effectiveness

The profitability ratios described in the previous chapter were concerned with the overall efficiency of a company in generating profits and cash from a given investment base. In addition it is often useful to calculate ratios that concentrate on the perform-ance of the management of a company in terms of specific resources such as stock, debtors, employees etc. This chapter considers how such ratios might be calculated and interpreted for The BOC Group plc.

Debtor turnover and collection

It is established practice in British industry for sales to customers to be made on credit terms. In other words, the goods or services supplied are not paid for immediately, but after an agreed period of time. Such a policy requires part of the capital of a company to be used to finance these unpaid sales; the total amount outstanding at the end of the financial year is recorded as debtors in the balance sheet. The questions then arising are concerned first with whether the amount of resources tied up in debtors is reasonable, and second with whether the company has been efficient in converting debtors into cash. Because the level of debtors at the end of the year might be expected to vary with the level of sales during the year, these questions are usually examined by calculating the following ratios:

$$\text{Debtor turnover} = \frac{\text{Sales}}{\text{Debtors}}$$

$$\text{Average collection period (in days)} = \frac{\text{Debtors}}{\text{Sales}} \times 365$$

The sales figures used in these ratios should, of course, reflect only the credit sales of the period. Where there is a marked seasonal variation in sales, then it would be more accurate to relate the year-end debtors to the sales of the last few months of the year. Some analysts prefer to use the average of the opening and closing debtors as the numerator, arguing that it has a slight smoothing effect. However, information on the distinction between cash and credit sales, or on the timing of sales, is not usually given in published annual reports, and the following ratios for BOC have been calculated by using the total figure for sales (Table 10.1). This does not include turnover of associated companies or joint ventures. Similarly, the debtors figure should ideally be the amount outstanding in respect of credit sales, i.e. the 'trade debtors'. Note 10 to the BOC financial statements (see pages 264–5) gives a break-down of the total debtors figures included in the balance sheet. The trade debtors for 2002 and 2001 were £601.2 million and £589.5 million respectively. If the notes to a company's financial statements do not give a detailed break-down of debtors, then the total debtors can be taken as an approximation.

	Debtor turnover	*Average collection period*
2002	$\dfrac{3,657.7}{601.2} = 6.08$ times	$\dfrac{601.2}{3,657.7} \times 365 = 59.99$ days
2001	$\dfrac{3,772.9}{589.5} = 6.40$ times	$\dfrac{589.5}{3,772.9} \times 365 = 57.03$ days

There has been some decline in the debtor turnover and an increase in the average collection period between 2001 and 2002. It would be helpful to compute the average collection period for the earlier trading periods to see whether this is a one-off decline or a deteriorating trend. Comparisons with similar companies will give some indication of relative performance. The movement in the quality of sales ratios should be computed and compared to see if it confirms the increase in the average time taken to collect the debts. The trend series can be seen in Chapter 14 (page 176).

The average collection period can also be compared with the stated credit terms of BOC. For example, if the credit terms are 'thirty days', then this is usually taken to mean thirty days from the end of the month in which the invoice is issued. This would imply an average collection period of about forty-five days. Any variation between the stated and actual credit duration might be thought of as an indication of inefficiency in the collection of amounts due from debtors. However, as was pointed out in the previous chapter, the trading operations of BOC are undertaken in many different parts of the world and credit terms may differ from country to country, depending on local customs and practice. The product trading mix of BOC is also changing and not all its lines of business have the same credit terms. This too will influence the overall average collection period. A more meaningful analysis would therefore be to calculate the average collection period for different geographical locations and by product groups. Unfortunately, this is not possible because a suitable breakdown of debtors is not provided.

Creditor turnover and payment

The system of supplying goods and services on credit terms also affects the purchases of a company. Any purchases that have not been paid for by the end of the year are shown as creditors in the balance sheet. The above exercise for debtors can therefore be repeated for creditors to show the average time taken to pay for the goods and services purchased. Information on purchases is not usually provided directly, but an approximate amount can be obtained from the cash flow statement providing the company uses the direct method which gives details of the net payments to suppliers. Unfortunately BOC uses the indirect method which does not give sufficient detail. If the information is available then the creditors turnover and payment period will be calculated in a similar manner to the debtors ratios.

$$\text{Creditor turnover ratio} = \frac{\text{Cash payments to suppliers during the period}}{\text{Trade creditors at the end of the period}}$$

$$\text{Creditor payment period} = \frac{365}{\text{Creditor turnover ratio}}$$

The creditor–turnover ratio is measured in times, with the payment period in days. In theory the turnover ratio is purchases divided by creditors, but because total purchases for the period are usually not published many approximations or surrogates are used. These surrogate measures used have included amounts for cost of sales, or cost of sales adjusted for changes in stock values and/or reduced by the depreciation expense.

The stock adjustment is to convert the expense into a purchase, whilst the depreciation adjustment is to remove some of the known non-purchase items from cost of sales. But whatever degree of improvisation is undertaken in the ratio components, the implications of it must always be borne in mind when interpreting the results.

An approximate 'purchases' figure for BOC for 2002 can be obtained by adjusting the cost of sales figures in Table 10.1 as follows:

		2002 (£ million)		2001 (£ million)
Cost of sales		2,104.8		2,208.8
Less depreciation	330.9		329.5	
increase in stocks	13.7		8.8	
		344.6		338.3
Approximate purchases for year		1,760.2		1,870.5

The depreciation and increase in stock figures have been taken from note 14 (page 269) where it indicates the adjustments to the operating profit for non-cash items and working capital changes. Since this approximate purchases figure includes trade purchases, wages and services purchased the creditors figure used will consist of the sum of the trade and other creditors as shown in note 10. Presumably the latter figure includes the amount unpaid on services received such as rates, electricity and so on.

Creditor turnover rate	*Average payment period*
2002 $\quad \dfrac{1,760.2}{367.3} = 4.79$ times	$\dfrac{367.3}{1,760.2} \times 365 = 76.16$ days
2001 $\quad \dfrac{1,870.5}{318.4} = 5.87$ times	$\dfrac{318.4}{1,870.5} \times 365 = 62.13$ days

Because of the imprecision in the calculation of the components of this ratio, it can be used only as an approximate indication of the creditor payment policy of BOC. Generally speaking, the longer the credit period achieved the better, because the operations of the company are being financed interest-free by suppliers' funds. However, if too long a period is taken to pay creditors, the credit rating of the company may suffer, thereby making it more difficult to obtain supplies in the future. A comparison of the average collection and payment periods is sometimes useful as a guide as to how a company is managing its short-term finances. Here the comparison indicates BOC takes somewhat more time to pay its creditors than it does to receive cash due from its debtors. For some companies this would be a worry, but for BOC it is probably due to the long-term contractual sales it has in its gas and related products segment. This ratio is computed less frequently than average collection period due to the lack of data available on the purchases of materials and services during the year. The implications of the degree of improvisation in the ratio components must always be borne in mind when interpreting the results.

Stock turnover

An important aspect of the management of a company concerns the levels of stocks that should be held. Very often a considerable amount of capital is tied up in the financing of raw materials, work in progress and finished goods. It is therefore important to ensure that the level of stocks is kept as low as possible. However, if the level falls too low there is the danger that customers' orders could not be fulfilled in time and sales may be lost to competitors. On the other hand it may be part of a company's marketing strategy that the level of stock required is sufficient to ensure that all customers are supplied within a stated time period. The shorter the time period the greater the stock to be carried. Similarly, the type of production system and type of product made have implications for the level of stocks held.

A sound system of stock management is therefore crucial. One way of assessing this is by calculating the stock–turnover ratio as follows:

$$\frac{\text{Cost of sales for the period}}{\text{Stock at the end of the period}}$$

If the closing stock figure is not typical of the amount of stock held during the period, an alternative way of arriving at the denominator of the ratio would be to use the average stock held. Because information is not given on the levels of stock held at different times of the year, a simple average of the opening and closing stock amount is sometimes used. It is important to use the cost of sales rather than sales as the numerator of the ratio, because stock is generally valued at cost. The following stock–turnover ratios for BOC have been computed from Tables 10.1 and 10.2 using year end stock figures.

	Stock–turnover rate	*Stock–turnover period*
	$\dfrac{\text{Cost of sales}}{\text{Stock}}$	$\dfrac{\text{Stock}}{\text{Cost of sales}} \times 365$
2002	$\dfrac{2{,}104.8}{260} = 8.10$ times	$\dfrac{260}{2{,}104.8} \times 365 = 45.09$ days
2001	$\dfrac{2{,}208.8}{275.2} = 8.78$ times	$\dfrac{275.2}{2{,}208.8} \times 365 = 45.48$ days

The stock–turnover period ratios reveal that the average period for which stock was held before sale in 2001 was 45.48 days, and that this has declined marginally to 45.09 days in 2002. Generally speaking the higher the stock–turnover ratio, or conversely the lower the stock–turnover period, the better, but whether these ratios should be classified as 'good' or 'bad' depends very much on the nature of the business. Manufacturing companies such as BOC might be expected to have longer stock–turnover periods than, say, a company primarily involved in food retailing. What is an optimal level depends on balancing such factors as the lead time for manufacturing processes, (e.g. zero for just-in-time – JIT) the need to hold reserve stock of raw materials to insure against uncertainties in supply, the length and types of the manufacturing process, the normal holding period of finished goods and the requirement to keep the amount of capital tied up in stock to a minimum. However, systematic changes over time, or deviations from the ratios of similar companies, might suggest that the stock position needs careful scrutiny, especially if it were a worsening situation. It would be useful to evaluate separately the levels of stocks held in raw materials, work in progress and finished goods, and thus highlight the area(s) causing the change in the overall picture. This point will be readdressed in Chapter 14 (see page 177) in more detail. At its simplest, purely from a cost of financing the stock, the lower the stock value, the lower the stock period.

In addition to the assessment of managerial performance in the use of resources and liabilities such as debtors, creditors and stock, these particular items also have important implications for the liquidity of the company and this will be considered in the following chapter. These resources can be combined into one ratio, the sales to working capital ratio, which is intended to indicate the adequacy of the total reservoir of liquid funds in supporting the level of sales.

Net working capital requirements

When the level of sales changes so does the amount of net working capital required. As this needs finance to support it then management will attempt to minimize its level or proportion of turnover. Net working capital is the sum of stock, plus trade debtors minus trade creditors.

$$\text{Net working capital to sales ratio} = \frac{\text{Stock} + \text{trade debtors} - \text{trade creditors}}{\text{Sales}} \times 100$$

When calculating this ratio, either the closing values for the numerator, or an average of the opening and closing values can be used. In this case the closing values are used. Note the bases for deriving stock, trade debtors and trade creditors are not all consistent with that for sales, since the sales figure has a profit element in it. Nevertheless it is the amount of funds needed for working capital compared to the total funds that would be generated if all sales were received in the year. In 2002 the turnover was £3,657.7 million (see Table 10.1) and the net working capital was as follows (see note 10, pages 264–5):

	(£ million)
Stock	260.0
Trade debtors	601.2
	861.2
Less Trade creditors	367.3
	493.9

Table 11.1 The BOC Group plc – employee ratios by line of business and by region

	Average number of employees		Sales		Sales per employee		Operating profit		Operating profit per employee		Capital employed		Capital employed per employee	
	2002	2001	2002 (£ million)	2001 (£ million)	2002 (£)	2001 (£)	2002 (£ million)	2001 (£ million)	2002 (£)	2001 (£)	2002 (£ million)	2001 (£ million)	2002 (£)	2001 (£)
Line of business														
Process gas solutions	5,979	6,076	1,200.6	1,193.0	200,802.8	196,346.3	149.3	124.2	24,970.7	20,441.1	1,697.6	1,878.2	283,927.1	309,117.8
Industrial and special products	14,681	14,201	1,605.3	1,573.9	109,345.4	110,830.2	225.3	229.0	15,346.4	16,125.6	982.4	1,080.6	66,916.4	76,093.2
BOC Edwards	5,186	4,916	688.2	873.1	132,703.4	177,603.7	12.3	62.7	2,371.8	12,754.3	545.1	543.6	105,109.9	110,577.7
Afrox hospitals	13,934	12,804	259.0	287.8	18,587.6	22,477.4	27.6	28.3	1,980.8	2,210.2	101.6	91.7	7,291.5	7,161.8
Gist	5,100	4,284	264.8	231.4	51,921.6	54,014.9	25.5	21.3	5,000.0	4,972.0	22.8	81.4	4,470.6	19,000.9
Corporate	376	296	—	—	—	—	-14.4	-7.1	-38,297.9	-23,986.5	-19.4	47.1	-51,595.7	159,121.6
Subsidiaries	45,256	42,577	4,017.9	4,159.2	88,781.6	97,686.5	425.6	458.4	9,404.3	10,766.4	3,330.1	3,722.6	73,583.6	87,432.2
Joint ventures and associates	4,324	4,558	360.2	386.3	83,302.5	84,752.1	74.5	72.2	17,229.4	15,840.3	263	251.9	60,823.3	55,265.5
Geographic region														
Europe	12,739	11,750	1,069.6	1,002.5	83,962.6	85,319.1	155.2	165.5	12,183.1	14,085.1	944.4	1,221.1	74,134.5	103,923.4
Americas	7,312	7,262	1,291.8	1,387.5	176,668.5	191,063.1	121.3	137.2	16,589.2	18,892.9	1,244.0	1,305.5	170,131.3	179,771.4
Africa	17,213	16,137	441.0	505.6	25,620.2	31,331.7	56.7	69.4	3,294.0	4,300.7	221.2	259.0	12,850.8	16,050.1
Asia/Pacific	7,992	7,428	1,215.5	1,263.6	152,089.6	170,113.1	166.9	158.5	20,883.4	21,338.2	1,183.5	1,188.9	148,085.6	160,056.5

$$\text{Net working capital to sales ratio } 2002 = \frac{493.9}{3,657.7} \times 100 = 13.5 \text{ per cent}$$

In 2001 the percentage of net working capital to sales was higher at 14.48 per cent of sales. The reduction in 2002 indicates that more of the current assets has been financed by short-term funds. It also indicates that it will require an amount of working capital equal to 13.5 per cent of any increase in turnover.

Employee ratios

Note 6 to the BOC annual accounts (see pages 252–9) provides details about the human resources used in the group. It gives a break-down by business and region of the year-end number of employees and the average number employed during the year. It also indicates both present and future costs arising from these employees. The note reveals that the total employment costs of 2002 amounted to £957.9 million. The significance of this amount in terms of the overall operations of BOC can be appreciated by relating it to the sales figure of £3,657.7 million. The wages to sales ratio is seen to be

2002   *2001*

$$\text{Wages to sales ratio} = \frac{957.9}{3,657.7} \times 100 \qquad \frac{908.8}{3,772.9} \times 100 = 24.09 \text{ per cent}$$

$$= 26.19 \text{ per cent}$$

In other words, for every £1 of sales achieved, almost 26p is paid in employee costs. Its significance is even more striking if it is related to the amount of value added by the operations of BOC. (The value added is the wealth created by the activities of a company, the difference between total amount paid for bought in materials and services and the total amount earned when the products of a company are sold on to third parties. This value added is shared out amongst the employees by way of wages, etc., the government by way of taxes, the lenders by way of interest, the shareholders by way of dividends and the company by way of retentions.) The employee costs take up a large proportion of the value added, so employees are an important part of the inputs of a company. The efficiency with which this particular resource is utilized needs to be carefully assessed. The methods, approach and ratios described below could be just as usefully applied to other important resources of a company, e.g. area of floorspace in a retail company.

There are a variety of ratios that could be calculated to focus attention on the utilization of labour, such as sales per employee, profit per employee, value added per employee and so on. In Table 11.1, employee ratios analysed by line of business and geographic region have been determined for BOC for 2001 and 2002. Information on average number of employees has been extracted from note 6 to the financial statements, and the sales, operating profit and capital-employed figures have been extracted from note 1. Note 6 also provides the year-end number of employees for both 2001 and 2002, which is also found in the five-year record from which the trend in employee numbers can be interpreted. There has been an overall increase in personnel involved in the continuing businesses of the group, both on the average and at the year-ends.

The segmental analysis in Table 11.1 does not reveal any major positive trends, though it does help to highlight those lines of business that are most capital and person intensive, e.g., process gas solutions for capital and industrial and special products and afrox hospitals for persons. Process gas solutions was the only line of business with a reducing head count and increasing profitability per employee.

In the regional analysis Europe was the only region with increasing turnover, but which was not converted into better sales or profitability per employee. Reasons for these changes can be found in the company's annual report or by taking the opportunity that shareholders have of attending the company's AGM and asking the appropriate questions.

The advantages of segmental analyses of this nature are obvious. Analysts can compare the employee ratios with other directly comparable firms operating in each line of business. Assessments of future profitability of the whole group will be facilitated by a knowledge of the position in the principal segments and the variations in performance over time can be more meaningfully evaluated.

Other ratios

There are several other aspects of operational efficiency that could be highlighted by the use of ratios. These usually consist of attempts to break down, by using the pyramid concept, some primary measure of profitability (such as return on sales) into its component parts to try to pinpoint the reasons for differences in the profit margin from that of previous periods or from that of other companies. For example, in order for BOC to sustain total sales of £3,657.7 million in 2002, it was necessary to incur expenditure on administration, distribution, research and development and so on. Ratios that relate these expenditure items to sales could be calculated from the profit and loss account (Table 10.1) and the information in note 2 (see page 241). From these two sources it was possible to compare these expenditure items with the turnover that was created by their expenditure since BOC provides information on turnover and costs for the continuing and new business acquired during the year, or when appropriate those businesses discontinued in a year.

The results from analysing the acquisitions and discontinued business cost ratios

Table 11.2   Cost ratios (proportion of sales)

	2002	2001
Wages to sales ratio	$\frac{957.9}{3,657.7} \times 100 = 26.19\%$	$\frac{908.8}{3,772.9} \times 100 = 24.09\%$
$\frac{\text{Cost of sales}}{\text{Sales}}$	$\frac{2,104.8}{3,657.7} \times 100 = 57.54\%$	$\frac{2,208.8}{3,772.9} \times 100 = 58.5\%$
$\frac{\text{Distribution costs}}{\text{Sales}}$	$\frac{344.1}{3,657.7} \times 100 = 9.41\%$	$\frac{339.3}{3,772.9} \times 100 = 8.99\%$
$\frac{\text{Administration costs}}{\text{Sales}}$	$\frac{814.4}{3,657.7} \times 100 = 22.27\%$	$\frac{814.4}{3,772.9} \times 100 = 21.59\%$
$\frac{\text{Research and development}}{\text{Sales}}$	$\frac{47.0}{3,657.7} \times 100 = 1.28\%$	$\frac{59.7}{3,772.9} \times 100 = 1.58\%$

have to be treated with some care. It has been argued by some that if a new company is acquired early in the financial year its first year's profits could appear better than previously due to the benefit of the new management, but if the acquisition is late in the financial year the benefits will not be seen until the following year. It has been argued that new management can and sometimes has influenced pre- and post-acquisition profits by use of accounting provisions and accounting conventions in order to present gains from an acquisition in the best light. Whether post-acquisition profits are influenced by pre-acquisition provisions is a moot point but it should ensure that the investor treats with caution any attempts to isolate the pre- and post-implications on profits of an acquisition (see Smith 1996).

Taking each cost as a percentage of the appropriate amount of turnover provides the results given in Table 11.2.

As the results indicate, there has been a small reduction in the proportion to sales of costs of sales, but not in distribution, administration and research and development costs to sales. This part of the analysis may be of more value when used internally by management on one company at a time and/or for those companies where a greater proportion of their costs are of a variable nature.

The asset–turnover ratio, as calculated in Chapter 10, could similarly be broken down to bring out the relationship between sales and specific categories of assets, such as plant and machinery, total fixed assets, total current assets and so on. Chapter 14 will include the values for these ratios in its structured review of The BOC Group plc's annual financial statements.

12 Liquidity and stability

An analysis of the profitability of a company may reveal a satisfactory position, and yet if there are insufficient funds available to pay bills as they fall due, the company will be unlikely to survive for very long. A problem that often faces highly profitable and fast-expanding companies is that of 'overtrading'. This situation arises when most of the profits are used to finance the additional fixed assets, stocks and debtors required to sustain the expanding level of business, producing a shortage of liquid resources for meeting short-term obligations. Therefore, it is important to assess not only the profitability of a company, but also its liquidity and stability. The principal methods adopted to focus attention on short-term liquidity are considered in this chapter.

Current ratio (working capital ratio)

The current ratio relates the current assets of a company to its current liabilities. Current assets consist of cash plus those items that can normally be expected to be converted into cash in the near future (i.e. debtors and stocks); together these are thought of as providing a reservoir of liquid resources for meeting the payments due to short-term creditors. The short-term creditors or current liabilities are defined as those requiring payment within twelve months of the balance sheet date. The working capital, or current ratio is calculated as

$$\frac{\text{Current assets}}{\text{Current liabilities}}$$

From the balance sheet shown in Table 10.2 it is possible to calculate ratios for The BOC Group plc as follows:

$$\text{Current ratio 2002} = \frac{1,246.4}{1,247.9} = 1.00 \text{ times}$$

$$\text{Current ratio 2001} = \frac{1,286.5}{1,281.7} = 1.00 \text{ times}$$

Thus between 2001 and 2002 there has been no real change in BOC's current ratio. As was pointed out in Chapter 9, it is not possible to state categorically what the ratio should be. Generally speaking, a ratio less than 1 might give cause for concern, because it would indicate that the liquid resources are insufficient to cover the short-term payments. Bearing in mind the time lag for converting debtors and stock into cash, it should perhaps be greater than 1. In the previous chapter it was shown that the average collection period for BOC's 2002 debtors was sixty days, and the average stock–turnover period was forty-five days. This compares with the somewhat imprecisely calculated average payment period of trade and other creditors of seventy-six days. In addition, an examination of note 10 to the financial statements reveals that a substantial part of the total current liabilities of £1,247.9 million is made up of items other than trade and other creditors.

The precise payment times for the loans and bank overdraft, taxes, dividends and so on may vary from almost immediately to several months in the future. Because of known and unknown variations in the time lags affecting the components of the working capital ratio, it might be considered safer for the ratio to be nearer to 2 than to 1. However, too high a ratio might be due to cash or stock levels being higher than is strictly necessary, and might therefore be indicative of the bad management of working capital requirements. Even a comparison with some 'standard' ratio for the industry might be misleading because of different circumstances facing individual companies.

Though the assets in the balance sheet are valued on a going concern basis, creditors are still interested in the value of the assets. They fear that if the company defaulted on its repayments of either capital or interest, the assets might not generate enough cash from an enforced sale to cover the amount outstanding. Hence, with a current ratio of 2:1 as a rule of thumb, the assets need only be realized for half their book value for the creditors still to recover their money. But since only debtors, stock and work in progress are likely to be sold off for less than book value, short-term creditors can still feel reasonably secure with a ratio between 2:1 and 1:1, but it does depend on the corporate circumstances.

Differences in accounting practices concerning the valuation of stocks and work in progress, and the susceptibility of the working capital ratio to 'window dressing', can cause problems with inter-firm comparisons. Window dressing involves manipulating the working capital position by accelerating or delaying transactions close to the accounting year-end. The following example shows how an inferior ratio could be improved by the use of window dressing, so that a healthier picture of the company's liquidity might be presented.

Supposing that, towards the end of the accounting period, a company forecast that if it follows its normal pattern of stock purchasing and creditor payment then the net current assets positions will be as follows:

Stock	£9,000
Debtors	5,000
Cash	6,000
	20,000
Less creditors	(15,000)
Net current assets	5,000

This will result in a current ratio of 20,000/15,000, i.e. 1.33.

This ratio could have been improved substantially by delaying stock purchases of, say, £4,000 until just after the end of the year. This would have reduced the stock figure to £5,000 and creditors to £11,000. The position could be further improved by using, say, £4,000 of the surplus cash to accelerate the payments to creditors, thereby reducing cash to £2,000 and creditors to £7,000. The net current assets would then appear as

Stocks	£5,000
Debtors	5,000
Cash	2,000
	12,000
Less creditors	(7,000)
Net current assets	5,000

Thus, although the net current assets position remains the same, the current ratio of 12,000/7,000, i.e. 1.71, would appear much healthier to external analysts.

Nevertheless, in spite of its imperfections, the working capital ratio is of use in providing an approximate indication of a company's liquidity, and is widely used as such.

Quick ratio (acid test ratio)

The working capital ratio is frequently criticized because the numerator includes items that are not very readily convertible into cash if the need arose to pay creditors at short notice. BOC is not untypical of manufacturing companies in having quite a lengthy stock–turnover period and therefore stock is generally thought of as lacking liquidity. The quick ratio overcomes this problem by excluding stock from the numerator. It is calculated as

$$\frac{\text{Current assets minus stocks}}{\text{Current liabilities}}$$

An examination of Table 10.2 reveals that the quick ratios for BOC are as follows:

$$\text{Quick ratio 2002} = \frac{1,246.4 - 260.0}{1,247.9} = 0.79 \text{ times}$$

$$\text{Quick ratio 2001} = \frac{1,286.5 - 275.2}{1,281.7} = 0.79 \text{ times}$$

From Table 10.2 it can be seen that the current assets totalled £1,246.4 million and stocks £260.0 million in 2002, with the current liabilities totalling £1,247.9 million for that year. This ratio, by concentrating on the more readily realizable of the current assets, is thought to provide a much stricter test of liquidity than does the working capital ratio.

The question of what is a 'good' or 'bad' ratio still depends on a variety of circumstances. In general, the quick ratio should not fall too far below 1 because this means that, if all of the creditors requested early repayment, there would be insufficient liquid, or nearly liquid, resources available to meet the request. In other words, the company will fail the 'acid test' of being able to pay the short-term obligations and would therefore be in danger of becoming insolvent. The ratio for BOC is unchanged between 2001 and 2002 but if the long-term trend is downwards the ratio of 0.79 might begin to give some cause for concern.

The quick ratio does provide a more useful indicator of potential liquidity problems and, because it avoids the distortions in stock valuation caused by different accounting practices, it gives a better basis than the current ratio for comparisons with other companies. However, the ratio can still be affected by 'window dressing' and it could be accused of oversimplifying the position. In reality the debtors of a company may not be very liquid. Certainly, the prepayments and accrued income may be difficult to convert quickly into cash and, at times of recession, the trade debtors may be seeking longer periods of credit because of their own liquidity problems. Attempts to press for earlier payment might force the debtors into bankruptcy. In fact, if recessionary conditions do exist, the raw materials component of the total balance sheet figure for stock may be more immediately realizable than the debtors. Even though the market for finished goods, and therefore work in progress, might be depressed, it should be relatively easy to sell raw materials, either back to suppliers or to other manufacturers.

One of the most important factors concerning liquidity appraisal is the extent to which loan and overdraft facilities are available. If a company has unused overdraft facilities that could be drawn on, then even in the extremely unlikely event of all of the creditors requiring immediate payment there would be a cushion to compensate for a low quick ratio. On the other hand, if overdraft facilities are currently being utilized up to the limit, a low quick ratio might be very serious. BOC indicate in note 3 to the financial statements (see page 246) that they have unutilized contractually committed facilities available to the group of $420 million (£267.5 million at balance sheet date). This has been available for a number of years and is still untouched. The facilities mature in 2002/2004. Though only 20 per cent of the current liabilities it is a substantial backup for the company in an emergency.

Cash flow analysis

A disadvantage of both the current and the quick ratios is that they measure liquidity at a single point in time rather than over a period of time. The liquidity position of a company such as BOC will be constantly changing in response to the flow of cash into and out of the company, and therefore a ratio that merely reflects the liquidity at the balance sheet date fails to capture the extremely important relationship between cash inflows and outflows.

As we explained in Chapter 4, it is now standard accounting practice for a consolidated cash flow statement to be included in the annual financial statements of a company. This statement is extremely useful in providing the external analyst with an explanation for the changes in liquidity over the year.

An examination of the consolidated cash flow statement for BOC in Table 10.3 shows how in 2002 there was a reduction in cash inflow over that of 2001. The funds generated from operations were sufficient to cover all the outgoings such as servicing loan and equity finance and payment of taxes, leaving enough to cover approximately most of the capital expenditure undertaken on new assets or businesses. This was also true in 2001. The balance of the funds needed to finance this capital expenditure has come both from borrowing and issue of shares. This too has declined annually with £342 million being borrowed in 1997. This will impinge on the company's gearing levels which will be investigated in the following chapter. Note 3 on pages 243–8 indicates that the types of loan used were predominantly of medium- to long-term maturity. This is a good sign because companies that consistently fund long-term investment from short-term funds run the risk of damaging the liquidity and eventually the viability of the company. A major purpose of liquidity analysis is to try to assess the potential cash flow problems that a company may face in the near future.

A careful review of the information in note 3 will help here, as will the table provided in BOC's Finance and Treasury Review. This table shows how the total debt has increased from £1,506.3 million in 2001 to the £1,511.1 million in 2002 with its maturity increasing slightly. Note 3 also provides information on the type of borrowing undertaken, its type, source, currency and maturity. This can be evaluated if desired when assessing future liquidity requirements, or when reviewing the foreign currency hedging and matching arrangements the company has, given that it is an international business with trade and investments sourced in many currencies.

Cash interest cover

The cash interest cover ratio is the preferred complement for the traditional interest cover ratio which will be described in the next chapter. This ratio states the number of times the cash flow from operations covers the interest payments to lenders. This is of obvious importance to both lenders and shareholders since non-payment of interest, when due, can precipitate a company's liquidation. Using the information from the cash flow statement the ratio is calculated as

$$\frac{\text{Net cash inflow from operations, dividends received and interest received}}{\text{Interest paid}}$$

In 2002 the net cash inflow from operations is £759.3 million, dividends from joint ventures and associates £33.9 million and interest received is £18.5 million, shown in the consolidated cash flow statement (Table 10.3). From the same statement the 2002 interest paid is £89.6 million. The cash interest cover ratios are:

$$\text{Cash interest cover 2002} = \frac{759.3 + 33.9 + 18.5}{89.6} = 9.06 \text{ times}$$

$$\text{Cash interest cover 2001} = \frac{787.8 + 23.5 + 23.1}{95.4} = 8.75 \text{ times}$$

The cushion on the interest payment has increased in 2002, but there is a long way to go before the company risks default on its interest payments. BOC has included in its interest payments both interest capitalized and interest charged to the profit and loss account. This is the correct way to test coverage. The true figure for interest must include all interest paid regardless of whether or not it is capitalized since the default risk is no different for either category of interest.

Cash dividend cover

The cash dividend cover ratio has a similar purpose to the cash interest cover in that it signals the ability, or lack of it, of the company to cover the cash dividend payout. In general, companies do not want to be paying dividends out of funds generated other than by earned profits. That would be a case of robbing Peter to pay Paul, i.e. of paying dividends out of capital flows.

The cash dividend cover is a multiple and is calculated as

$$\frac{\text{Net cash inflow after tax from operations} -}{\text{Dividends paid}}$$

Net cash inflow after tax from operations −
Returns on investments and servicing of finance +
Dividends received from joint ventures and associates
_____
Dividends paid

A multiple in excess of 1 indicates sufficient cash earned from operations and investment and after paying off the financing charges to provide for a dividend and for the reinvestment of cash to help maintain the physical and monetary capital of the company.

Taking the information from the cash flow statement for BOC (see page 232), the net cash inflow from operating activities for 2002 is £759.3 million, the net outflow for returns on investment and servicing of finance is £90.7 million and dividends from joint ventures and associates of £33.9 million. The tax paid is £96.2 million. The dividends paid in 2002 were £186.6 million.

$$\text{Cash dividend cover 2002} = \frac{759.3 - 96.2 - 90.7 + 33.9}{186.6} = 3.25 \text{ times}$$

$$\text{Cash dividend cover 2001} = \frac{787.7 - 100.6 - 87.2 + 23.5}{180.3} = 3.46 \text{ times}$$

The cash dividends paid in both 2001 and 2002 were well covered by the cash inflow from operations, leaving plenty of cash to be reinvested in the group for the maintenance of its capital.

Cash debt coverage

A company's ability to continue as a going concern is dependent not only on meeting its current interest payments but also on repayment of its loan capital. The cash debt coverage ratio can indicate how much of the maturing debt capital can be repaid out of the retained cash flow from operations. If the multiple exceeds unity the company will not need to reduce its asset base or raise additional external funds to repay the maturing loans.

The numerator is the net cash retained from operations after paying interest, tax and dividends. The denominator is the debt maturing in the next twelve months.

The cash debt coverage ratio is a multiple and is calculated as

$$\frac{\text{Net cash inflow from operations after interest, tax and dividends}}{\text{Debt maturing within the next twelve months}}$$

For the BOC group the numerator for 2002 is the net cash retained from that year's operations. This is made up of the £759.3 million net cash inflow from operations less the tax paid of £96.2 million and the net cash outflow from paying interest and dividends of £90.7 million and £186.6 million plus respectively the dividends from joint ventures and associates of £33.9 million. These amounts are found in the cash flow statement (see page 232). The denominator is the figure for loans maturing within the next 12 months which are given in note 3 (see page 245). For the BOC group in 2002 these maturing loans within a year total £390.1 million.

$$\text{Cash debt coverage 2002} = \frac{759.3 - 96.2 - 90.7 + 33.9 - 186.6}{390.1} = 1.08 \text{ times}$$

$$\text{Cash debt coverage 2001} = \frac{787.7 - 100.6 - 87.6 + 23.5 - 180.3}{486.4} = 0.91 \text{ times}$$

In 2002 the retained cash flow, earned through operations, is just sufficient to pay off the loans to be retired during the next 12 months. Link that fact with the fact that there is an increasing amount of cash reserved for capital expenditure highlighted in the cash flow statement and it will ensure analysts look carefully at the methods used by BOC to fund its cash flow needs. From note 3 we also learn that BOC has £185.5 million in cash and deposits of less than a year's maturity plus the previously mentioned $420 million (£267.5 million) unused credit facility. Before reaching for the panic button an historical review will indicate that the company has satisfactorily met its debt repayment requirements over the years in year-end situations not too dissimilar from the present.

As yet the definition of this ratio has not received widespread affirmation through usage and publication, unlike most others in this text. This is because it is only recently that data to compute the ratio have become available. Some writers have argued that all debt should be incorporated into the denominator, others would include creditors too while others would net off the cash and deposits held by the company. Each possible alternative has a logical rationale to support it. The logic supporting the ratio defined above is that the ratio matches the long-term source of cash that is derived from operations, with the requirement to repay the maturing element of long-term finances. Any loans maturing beyond twelve months will be repaid out of profits earned in the future, while cash presently held is in general needed for the day-to-day trading operations, though it has to be conceded that the cash may have been built up by the company for the purpose of the loan repayment.

Cash current and total liabilities coverage

A further pair of similar ratios are cash current liability and total liability coverage. The current liability coverage ratio shows the extent to which net cash from operations, after paying off the servicing of loans and tax, is available to pay off outstanding short-term liabilities. The total liability coverage ratio focuses on the ability of the net cash from operations after the servicing of loans etc. to meet all liabilities. They are further examples of the short- and long-term liquidity risks of the company.

$$\text{Cash current liabilities coverage} = \frac{\begin{array}{c}\text{Net cash inflow from operations and dividends}\\ \text{from joint ventures and associates} - \text{returns on}\\ \text{investments and servicing of finance} - \text{tax paid}\end{array}}{\text{Current liabilities}} \times 100$$

The BOC cash flow statement, Table 10.3, provides all the numbers for the numerator, and current liabilities are found in the balance sheet in Table 10.2. Current liabilities are £1,247.9 million in 2002.

$$\text{Cash current liabilities coverage 2002} = \frac{759.3 + 33.9 - 90.7 - 96.2}{1,247.9} \times 100 = 48.59\%$$

The cash current liability coverage for 2001 was virtually unchanged at 48.65 per cent, which according to some analysts is a healthy level to be at.

The cash total liability coverage ratio is very similar with the only difference being the replacement of current liabilities as the denominator by total liabilities. So for BOC the denominator is total liabilities of £2,834.4 million. Total liabilities can be derived from the balance sheet in Table 10.2 by deducting from the total assets of £4,893.1 million (fixed assets of £3,646.7 million plus current assets of £1,246.4 million), the capital and reserves of £1,802.0 million and the net pension liabilities of £256.7 million (pension assets of £54.3 million minus pension liabilities of £311.0 million), making £2,834.4 million.

$$\text{Cash total liabilities coverage } 2002 = \frac{759.3 + 33.9 - 90.7 - 96.2}{2,834.4} \times 100 = 21.39\%$$

The cash total liabilities coverage ratio for 2001 was slightly higher at 22.43 per cent. Both ratios would suggest a healthy coverage situation for BOC.

13 Capital structure and financial risk

In addition to an assessment of the short-term liquidity position of a company, it is also important to examine the overall means by which a company finances its operations. It is usual for a company to be financed partly by loans from banks and other lenders and partly by the funds of its ordinary shareholders. These two sources of finance are normally referred to respectively as debt and equity, and the relationship between the two gives a measure of the gearing of the company. Gearing has important implications for the long-term stability of a company because of its effect on financial risk. This is because debt and equity have quite different characteristics. The providers of loan capital require a fixed amount of interest to be paid to them each year, irrespective of the level of profits earned. The providers of equity capital do not enjoy a fixed reward each year, but are entitled to the residual profits after all other payments including interest charges have been met. This residual amount will vary depending on the fortunes of the company. Because the existence of loan capital imposes a fixed commitment in the form of interest charges, the higher the proportion of debt to equity in the capital structure of a company the more volatile the residual rewards available to equity will become and the greater will be the financial risk perceived by ordinary shareholders. For example, if an all-equity firm earns operating profits after tax of £200,000, then the amount accruing to ordinary shareholders, either as dividends or retained profits, will be £200,000. If in the next year the profits fall by 25 per cent to £150,000, then the amount accruing to ordinary shareholders will also fall by 25 per cent. However, if the company were geared, i.e. if it were financed partly by loans requiring an after-tax fixed-interest payment of, say, £75,000 per year, then the profits available to ordinary shareholders in the first year would be £125,000 (£200,000 minus interest of £75,000), but in the second year these would fall to £75,000 (£150,000 minus interest of £75,000), a decline of 40 per cent. Conversely, if profits had risen by 25 per cent to £250,000, the earning available to the ordinary shareholders in the geared company would have increased to £175,000 (£250,000 minus £75,000), an increase of 40 per cent.

A similar argument applies to the riskiness attached to capital repayments. In the event of the liquidation of a company, the providers of loan capital have priority over the ordinary shareholders as to capital repayment. Therefore, the higher the level of gearing, the greater is the chance of ordinary shareholders not being repaid in full.

It is not only the shareholders who are affected by gearing. Looked at from the point of view of creditors, it is clear that a high proportion of debt to equity will increase the risk of interest payments not being met, or the loan repayments and amounts owing to suppliers not being made in full. Even though lenders have the benefit of priority over shareholders for annual interest payments and on liquidation, the value of this benefit steadily declines as more and more of the operations of the company are financed by the lenders and the 'cushion' that the equity-financed part provides becomes less and less.

Nevertheless, gearing does have its advantages. It might be reasonable to expect that the benefits of a fixed amount of interest every year and priority over shareholders on liquidation should make the cost of debt capital cheaper than that of equity. In other words, the average return expected by lenders should be lower than the average return expected by shareholders. Furthermore, the interest payable on loan capital is an allowable expense when determining taxable profit, whereas dividends are a distribution out of the after-tax profits. Thus, for a company that pays corporation tax at the rate of, say, 35 per cent on its taxable profits, the after-tax cost of interest payments will be reduced in the same proportion, because every £100 paid in interest will reduce taxable profit by £100 and therefore tax payable by £35. To the extent that debt is a less expensive source of finance than equity, then initially the use of gearing might be beneficial, providing that the advantages of lower-cost debt more than compensate for the disadvantages caused by increased financial risk. However, as gearing increases, the financial-risk effect will begin to outweigh the benefits of low-cost debt. This implies the existence of some optimal level of gearing that a company should try to achieve. Empirical evidence would suggest that companies no longer assume that one specific level of gearing is appropriate all the time and in all the circumstances. For example, during the downturn of an economic cycle companies will attempt to reduce their gearing and then reverse it on the upturn. This will minimize the risks concerning non-payment of interest in poor trading conditions on the one hand, and on the other hand enable the company to gain the benefits of the gearing on the upturn in profits.

The ever widening portfolio of types of long- and short-term capital available to a company may make life more complex for financial managers, but at the same time it will hopefully reduce the financial risks by the better matching of fund type with corporate need. This financial engineering brings with it further problems for the analyst since a careful examination of gearing is obviously of crucial importance in an evaluation of the capital structure of a company. In the following sections of this chapter, the gearing position of The BOC Group plc is analysed.

Capital structure ratios

There are several ways of examining the gearing position of a company, depending on whether it is the long-term capital structure or the overall financial structure that is being analysed.

Long-term debt to equity ratio

From the point of view of long-term capital structure, the most widely used ratio is that of debt to equity. This is calculated as

$$\frac{\text{Long-term loans} + \text{Preference shares}}{\text{Ordinary shareholders' funds}} \times 100$$

Preference shares are usually included in the numerator because preference shareholders are entitled to a fixed rate of dividend. (It should be noted, however, that preference dividends are payable only if sufficient profits have been earned, therefore if a dividend has not been declared it might be more appropriate to exclude preference capital from the ratio.) FRS 4 ('Capital instruments') has stated that preference capital is non-equity capital and should be treated as a liability in this context. FRS 4 in dealing with accounting for capital instruments has as liabilities all capital instruments that contain an obligation to 'transfer economic benefits' (including contingent obligations). So convertible debt is treated the same as ordinary debt until it is converted. Ordinary shareholders' funds are usually taken to mean the ordinary share capital plus retained profits and reserves. The treatment of provisions can be somewhat problematical: depending on their nature, they might be thought of as part of ordinary shareholders' funds or as liabilities that should be included with long-term loans. In the ratios calculated for BOC, provisions have been excluded because they are non-interest bearing and have no gearing implications for the profits available to shareholders. Later in the chapter, when assessing the amount of asset coverage for the company's liabilities, provisions will be included, because, as defined earlier, they are a liability. The components of each ratio are made up as follows:

Long-term loans plus preference shares (see notes 11 and 12 to the financial statements).

	2002 (£ million)	2001 (£ million)	2000 (£ million)
Loans other than from banks	1,008.1	879.2	710.5
Bank loan	90.2	105.5	133.5
Financial leases	22.7	35.2	46.7
	1,121.0	1,019.9	890.7

Obligations under finance leases represent the present value of the future rental payments for assets financed under leasing agreements. Because this method of financing asset acquisitions gives rise to an interest payment that is included in the rental amount, the capital element has been included with long-term loans in accord with financial reporting practice. Up until 1997 BOC had £2.5 million of preference share capital which was repaid in 1998.

Ordinary shareholders' funds (the figures shown in the balance sheet in Table 10.2 have been used)

	2002 (£ million)	2001 (£ million)	2000 (£ million)
Equity called up share capital	124.3	123.6	123.1
Share premium account	362.1	335.8	317.1
Revaluation reserves	27.8	47.9	58.1
Profit and loss account	1,304.8	1,400.3	1,640.6
Pensions reserves	−256.5	47.1	0 *
Joint ventures' reserves	88.1	98.1	103.5
Associates' reserves	33.5	33.4	31.2
	1,684.1	2,086.2	2,273.6

*Not reported in 2000 accounts

The debt to equity ratios for BOC can now be calculated as

$$\text{Debt to equity ratio 2002} = \frac{1{,}121.0}{1{,}684.1} \times 100 = 66.56 \text{ per cent}$$

$$\text{Debt to equity ratio 2001} = \frac{1{,}019.9}{2{,}086.2} \times 100 = 48.89 \text{ per cent}$$

In the case of those companies, particularly small ones, that treat bank overdrafts as a form of long-term loan, then the value of a bank overdraft should be included as a long-term loan in the ratio calculations.

Long-term debt to total long-term finance ratio

An alternative way of considering the debt to equity relationship is to calculate the ratio in such a way that it expresses the amount of debt finance as a proportion of total long-term finance, i.e. by calculating

$$\frac{\text{Long-term loans + Preference shares}}{\text{Long-term loans + Preference shares + Ordinary shareholders' funds}} \times 100$$

Using this approach, the ratios for BOC are as follows:

$$\text{Long-term debt to total long-term finance ratio 2002} = \frac{1{,}121.0}{(1{,}121.0 + 1{,}684.1)} \times 100 = 39.96 \text{ per cent}$$

$$\text{Long-term debt to total long-term finance ratio 2001} = \frac{1{,}019.9}{(1{,}019.9 + 2{,}086.2)} \times 100 = 32.84 \text{ per cent}$$

Whichever method of comparing debt to equity is used, the resultant ratio is meant to clarify the relationship between funds requiring a fixed amount of interest and dividend to be paid each year and funds provided by ordinary shareholders. The higher the ratio, the higher the proportion of debt in the capital structure of a company, and therefore the higher the amount of interest charges that might be expected and the higher the level of financial risk.

In order to decide whether the level of gearing in 2002 and 2001 is appropriate or not, a knowledge of the optimal capital structure of the company is required. Although it is not possible to state precisely what this should be, a comparison with some industry 'standard' might give an indication of the appropriateness of the ratio. However, much depends on the individual circumstances facing each company. A company that experiences a low level of business risk, with operating profits tending to be stable from period to period, can withstand a higher level of financial risk, and therefore a higher level of gearing, than a company whose operating profits fluctuate widely. Companies that are well diversified might be expected to have relatively stable profits, because of the wide spread of activities, and so could operate at higher levels of gearing than non-diversified companies.

Total debt to total assets ratio

The gearing ratios that have been considered so far have concentrated on the long-term financial structure of BOC. An alternative way of examining gearing is to bring short-term debt into the picture to show the proportion of the total assets financed by borrowed funds, both short term and long term. This is the total debt to total assets ratio and is calculated as

$$\frac{\text{Long-term loans} + \text{Short-term loans}}{\text{Total assets}} \times 100$$

One advantage of including short-term loans is that this acknowledges that short-term bank loans and overdrafts are often almost automatically renewable, therefore being effectively a source of long-term finance.

To calculate the total debt to total assets ratio for BOC, the components of the ratio must be determined as follows:

	2002 (£ million)	2001 (£ million)
Total debt		
Long-term loans and obligations under financial leases (see note 3 to the financial statements)	1,121.0	1,019.9
Preference share capital	—	—
Short-term loans and obligations under financial leases (see note 3 to the financial statements)	390.1	486.4
	1,511.1	1,506.3
Total assets (obtained from the balance sheet [Table 10.2])		
Fixed assets	3,646.7	3,666.5
Current assets	1,246.4	1,286.5
	4,893.1	4,953.0

The following ratios can now be calculated:

$$\text{Total debt to total assets ratio 2002} = \frac{1{,}511.1}{4{,}893.1} \times 100 = 30.88 \text{ per cent}$$

$$\text{Total debt to total assets ratio 2001} = \frac{1{,}506.3}{4{,}953.0} \times 100 = 30.41 \text{ per cent}$$

This ratio shows that, of the total value of the assets of BOC at 30 September 2002, 30.88 per cent were financed by interest-bearing borrowed funds. This gives some indication of the extent to which interest payments will have to be made. Once again, it is not possible to state categorically whether this is 'good' or 'bad'. Another way of viewing the ratio is from the perspective of a possible liquidation. Were the total assets to be realized for less than 30.88p in the £1 then the lenders would not get all their money back. This is a little simplistic since there is a preferential payment ordering for creditor types in a liquidation or receivership and the interest-bearing loans would not necessarily be first in the queue. But at that level of 30.88 per cent, the lenders ought to feel comfortably secure. However, in BOC's finance and treasury review it quotes the gearing ratio as having grown from 32.0 per cent in 2001 to 36.9 per cent in 2002.

Notice that the BOC gearing ratios do not agree with any of the ones computed above. Its ratios are based upon information in note 3 to the financial statement (see page 245) and the five-year record (see page 207). The derivation of the net borrowings and capital employed was discussed earlier on page 126 and the ratio is calculated as follows:

$$\frac{\text{Net borrowings and financial leases}}{\text{'BOC capital employed'}} \times 100$$

BOC net borrowings to capital employed ratio 2002

$$= \frac{1{,}325.6}{3{,}593.1} \times 100 = 36.9 \text{ per cent}$$

According to the information in note 3 of the financial statements only £101.8 million of the £1,511.1 million borrowed is secured, i.e. tied to some identified asset. In the event of a receivership or liquidation, the proceeds from the sale of these specific assets would have to be used first to repay the £101.8 million, and only the surplus over and above this amount could be used for the benefit of other unsecured creditors. This is a low proportion of secured debt, approximately 7 per cent, and the unsecured lenders ought to feel reasonably safe, in that the book value of the total assets is approximately three times the total borrowings. However, these lenders should note that there are other creditors too, and that many analysts combine all forms of liabilities to third parties and calculate the ratio of total owing to total assets.

Total owing to total assets

This ratio is a better indicator for unsecured lenders, including trade creditors, that the book value of the assets gives a comfortable surplus over the amount owing. To differentiate it from previous ratios, all amounts included in the short- and long-term liabilities are combined to form the total amount owing. Preference-share capital is not included in this because it ranks after debt in a liquidation. The ratio is calculated as

$$\frac{\text{All creditors (less than one year)} + \text{Long-term liabilities}}{\text{Total assets}} \times 100$$

Provisions for liabilities have been included, because they represent liabilities which, although of uncertain amount, are reasonably likely to occur. The figures have been taken from the balance sheet in Table 10.2.

	2002 (£ million)	2001 (£ million)
Creditors: amounts falling due within one year		
Borrowings and finance leases	390.1	486.4
Other creditors	857.8	795.3
Creditors: amounts falling due beyond one year		
Borrowings and finance leases	1,121.0	1,019.9
Other creditors	58.0	59.4
Provisions for liabilities and charges	407.5	419.2
Net pension liabilities	256.7	−51.0
Total owing	3,091.1	2,729.2

The ratio for BOC can be calculated as follows:

$$\text{Total owing to total assets ratio 2002} = \frac{3{,}091.1}{4{,}893.1} \times 100 = 63.17 \text{ per cent}$$

$$\text{Total owing to total assets ratio 2001} = \frac{2{,}729.2}{4{,}953.0} \times 100 = 55.10 \text{ per cent}$$

The total owing to total assets ratio indicates that 63.2 per cent of the business has been financed by third parties, some of whom require interest payments on their loans. However, there is still a very reasonable surplus of book value of assets over the total amount owing to third parties.

Capital gearing

An alternative way of analysing gearing is to concentrate on the income position rather than on the capital structure. Under this approach, capital gearing, as it is sometimes called, is a multiplier or factor which, when applied to fluctuations in operating profit, shows the greater changes that would occur in profits available for the shareholders, thus highlighting the results of financial gearing. The concept of this capital gearing factor is similar to the gear-ratio principle of a car's gearbox. The ratio is calculated as follows:

$$\frac{\text{Profit on ordinary activities before interest} + \text{Interest received}}{\text{Profit on ordinary activities before taxation}}$$

Taking the figures in the profit and loss account in Table 10.1 and note 3(a) (page 243), the capital-gearing ratios for 2002 and 2001 are calculated as follows:

$$\text{Capital gearing 2002} = \frac{405.4 + 22.6}{335.3} = 1.28 \text{ times}$$

$$\text{Capital gearing 2001} = \frac{425.9 + 24.2}{362.2} = 1.24 \text{ times}$$

This means the proportionate change in profit before tax is 1.28 times that of a change in profit before interest paid. Thus if profit before interest paid rises by 20 per cent in 2003, i.e. £85.6 million, and if the amount of interest paid remains constant, the profit before tax will rise by the same £85.6 million, an increase of 25.5 per cent. This 25.5 per cent is 1.28 times the proportionate increase of 20 per cent in profit before interest paid. This relationship is only approximate because the level of gearing and interest paid on borrowing usually does not remain constant over the years. It holds for falls in profit before interest paid in exactly the same way. A similar ratio using profit after tax instead of profit before tax could be used, but its consistency could not be maintained because a company's effective tax rate changes from year to year. This change in the effective rate arises from tax allowances on changes in capital expenditure patterns, tax rate changes etc. Nevertheless, the capital gearing ratio does provide a rough guide to the extra change in profits attributable to the shareholders due to the level of gearing.

Interest cover

Before the cash flow statement was available this was the ratio calculated to focus attention on the relationship between interest payments and the profits available for meeting those payments. It showed the number of times interest is 'covered' by profits and therefore indicated the risk of non-payment of interest. The ratio, interest cover, is calculated as a multiple, as follows:

$$\frac{\text{Profit before interest and tax}}{\text{Gross interest payable}} =$$

$$\frac{\text{Profit on ordinary activities before interest } + \text{ Interest received}}{\text{Gross interest payable}}$$

The numerator is the profit available to pay the interest, and so includes both profit from operations and interest received. Note 3(a) to the financial statements reveals that the gross interest payable by BOC amounted to £103.2 million in 2002 and £125.2 million in 2001. The amount of profit before interest and tax that was available for meeting these interest payments is the profit on ordinary activities before interest for each year, as shown in Table 10.1. Interest receivable of £22.6 million in 2002 and £24.2 million in 2001 (see note 3(a) to the financial statements) would also be available to meet interest payments and should therefore be included in the numerator.

As profits from associated companies are combined in the total operating profits, so too should their interest proportion be included in interest payable. Any interest capitalized should be excluded. Thus, the gross interest payable net of interest capitalized in note 3(a) is increased by the associated company interest payable and reduced by the interest capitalized, leaving interest payable through the profit and loss account for 2002 at £125.7 million and for 2001 at £147.6 million.

$$\text{Interest cover ratio 2002} = \frac{405.4 + 22.6}{125.7} = 3.40 \text{ times}$$

$$\text{Interest cover ratio 2001} = \frac{425.9 + 24.2}{147.6} = 3.58 \text{ times}$$

An alternative way of looking at this is to say that as the profits available for paying interest in 2002 are 3.4 times the interest payable in that year, then the profits could fall by a factor of 2.4 times the interest payable and there would still be a sufficient amount of profit to cover the interest payable. The inference is that the smaller the multiple the smaller the amount of profit earned and therefore available for the equity owners of the company. The company's prime purpose is to generate profits for the ordinary shareholders. The ratio is giving an indication of the gearing relationship between profit and interest and how much of the profits are going in interest payments to service the requirements of the third parties who lent money to the company.

Prior to the publication of the cash flow statement this ratio was used as a surrogate for the cash interest cover described on page 151. From the point of view of providers of loan capital, the ratio indicates the protection they have if profits fall; therefore, the higher the ratio the better. Ordinary shareholders would also like to see a high interest cover ratio because this will indicate that the risk of non-payment of dividends is reduced. As with capital structure ratios, the adequacy of the interest cover is very much dependent on the business risk facing the company. For a company with high business risk whose profits fluctuate a great deal from period to period, a cover of 3.4 times might seem satisfactory. For a company that achieves stable profits over time, the cover might be very secure.

Dividend cover

Dividend cover is a ratio similar to the interest cover ratio. It involves examining the amount by which profits could fall before leading to a reduction in the current level of dividends. The dividend cover ratio is calculated as

$$\frac{\text{Profits available for paying ordinary dividends}}{\text{Ordinary dividends}} =$$

$$\frac{\text{Profit for the financial year} - \text{Preference dividends}}{\text{Ordinary dividends}}$$

The ratio is the reciprocal of the dividend payout ratio, the proportion of profits available to the equity owner paid out in dividends. Neither measures the company's actual ability to pay out the dividend in cash. This has already been calculated in the previous chapter as cash dividend cover.

The numerator of the dividend cover ratio should be the final amount of profit left after all other deductions have been made. The profits available to the ordinary shareholders of BOC in 2002 are therefore taken as profit for the financial year of £202.9 million. Details of the dividends paid and proposed are given in note 12 and indicate the ordinary dividends paid and proposed amount to £186.6 million for 2002. Even though some of the dividends were paid in scrip rather than cash it is the total dividend appropriated that is used to indicate the extent that profits have been used to reward the shareholder.

The dividend cover ratios are calculated as:

$$\text{Dividend cover ratio 2002} = \frac{202.9}{186.6} = 1.09 \text{ times}$$

$$\text{Dividend cover ratio } 2001 = \frac{224.1}{180.3} = 1.24 \text{ times}$$

At face value, these ratios show that ordinary dividends were covered 1.24 times in 2001 and that this declined in 2002 to 1.09 times. The cash dividend cover calculated in the previous chapter for each year indicated the considerable degree of safety in paying the dividend at that level in each of the two years. It was 3.25 times and 3.46 times for 2002 and 2001 respectively.

Some users of accounts prefer instead to use the payout ratio, defined as follows:

$$\frac{1}{\text{Dividend cover}} \times 100$$

For BOC the payout ratios of 2002 and 2001 are the reciprocals of the dividend cover ratios just calculated.

$$\text{Payout ratio } 2002 = \frac{1}{1.09} \times 100 = 91.74 \text{ per cent}$$

$$\text{Payout ratio } 2001 = \frac{1}{1.24} \times 100 = 80.65 \text{ per cent}$$

In 2002 BOC paid out 91.74 per cent of its available earned profits in ordinary dividends. It can also be said that BOC retained only 8.26 per cent of its profits for reinvestment in the business for 2002.

Questions

The following two questions provide examples of the techniques of ratio analysis that have been explained in the preceding four chapters.

Question 13.1

A summary of the profit and loss account of Diamond Ltd for year ended 31 December 20X3, together with the balance sheet as of that date and comparative data for the previous year are as follows.

31 December 20X2 (£000)		*31 December 20X3* (£000)
8,000	Turnover	9,200
7,500	Costs and expenses	8,620
500	Net trading profit	580
140	Interest charges	150
360	Profit for year	430
100	Corporation tax	125
260	Profit after tax	305
100	Proposed dividend	150
160	Retained profit for the year	155
1,885	Profit brought forward	2,045
2,045	Profit carried forward	2,200

Balance Sheets

31 December 20X2 (£000)		31 December 20X3 (£000)
3,600	Fixed assets at cost	4,600
1,080	*less*: Accumulated depreciation	1,660
2,520		2,940
	Current assets:	
800	Stock	950
1,100	Debtors	1,050
50	Cash and bank balances	—
1,950		2,000
	Current liabilities:	
100	Dividend	150
75	Corporation tax	125
650	Trade creditors	1,000
—	Bank overdraft	65
825		1,340
1,125	Current assets less current liabilities	660
3,645	Total assets less current liabilities	3,600
1,400	10% Debentures	1,200
2,245		2,400
	financed by:	
200	Ordinary shares of 25p each	200
2,045	Profit and loss account	2,200
2,245		2,400

Additional information

You have been able to obtain a number of financial ratios from the 20X3 accounts of a public limited company (PLC) which is in the same business as Diamond Ltd. The ratios are:

Total owing to total assets	50%
Sales growth (p.a.)	8%
Profit margin (return on sales)	7%
Interest cover	5×
Earnings per share	23p
Return on capital employed	21%
Current ratio	1.6
'Acid test'	1.1
Gearing (long-term debt to long-term debt + equity)	27%
Capital turnover	3×
Collection period	40 days
Stock period	20 days

Compute the twelve ratios given above for Diamond Ltd and discuss the performance of Diamond Ltd for the year ended 31 December 20X3.

Question 13.2

Playbus Ltd is a company established a few years ago to operate a small chain of retail toy shops in Wales. The chain was built up from the original shop by the present owners who continue to manage the business, but due to serious illnesses are considering putting the company on the market.

Extracts from the accounts of Playbus Ltd for the past two years ended 30 September 20X2 are as follows:

Profit and Loss Account for the year ended 30 September 20X2

	20X2 (£000)	20X1 (£000)
Turnover	15,000	12,000
Cost of sales	(9,500)	(7,000)
Gross profit	5,500	5,000
Administrative expenses	(3,200)	(2,900)
Interest	(300)	(100)
Profit before taxation	2,000	2,000
Taxation	(1,000)	(600)
Profit after taxation	1,000	1,400

Balance Sheet as at 30 September 20X2

		20X2 (£000)		20X1 (£000)
Fixed assets		4,400		2,000
Current assets				
Stock	1,500		1,000	
Debtors	800		500	
Cash	3,300		3,500	
	5,600		5,000	
Creditors due within one year (current liabilities)	(2,000)	3,600	(1,500)	3,500
		8,000		5,500
Long-term liabilities		(2,500)		(1,000)
		5,500		4,500
Share capital (£1 ordinary shares)		1,000		1,000
Retained profit		4,500		3,500
		5,500		4,500

Cash Flow Statement for the year ended 30 September 20X2

	20X2 (£000)	20X1 (£000)
Net cash inflow from operations	1,650	1,600
Servicing of finance		
Interest paid	(250)	(100)
Taxation paid	(600)	(1,000)
Capital expenditure		
Purchase of buildings	(1,800)	—
Purchase of vehicles	(700)	—
Financing		
Increase in loan	1,500	1,000
(Decrease)/Increase in cash	(200)	1,500

Childplay plc has a much larger chain of retail toy outlets and are looking to expand. An expansion either into Wales or into the north east would make a good strategic fit.

Childplay has already undertaken a financial analysis of another potential takeover target, Greattoys plc, which is quoted on the AIM market and is located in the north east. Greattoys shares are quoted giving a price–earnings ratio (PER) of 12× whilst the average PER for retail sector companies trading in similar products is 16×. Childplay has a PER of 20×.

The following financial statistics have been obtained for Greattoys for the same pair of time periods as Playbus.

Greattoys Plc Ratios

	20X2	20X1
Profitability		
Annual average sales growth over 5 years	34%	35%
Sales growth over previous year	30%	30%
Return on capital employed	30%	28%
Return on sales	15%	14%
Asset turnover	2×	2×
Return on equity	40%	40%
Earnings per share	£0.80	£0.60
Liquidity		
Current ratio	2.0×	2.2×
Quick ratio	0.7×	0.8×
Quality of profit	120%	115%
Efficiency		
Debtors period	15 days	15 days
Stock period	70 days	65 days
Capital Structure		
Long-term debt/Equity	60%	60%
Total debt/Total assets	50%	45%
Interest cover	4×	4×
Cash Flow		
Capital expenditure to free cash flow	50%	40%
Cash flow per share	£1.40	£1.20

The annual average sales growth of Playbus for the past 5 years in 20X2 was 30 per cent. The equivalent figure for 20X1 was 35 per cent. The sales growth from 20X1 to 20X2 was 25 per cent.

Compute not more than 10 ratios each year for Playbus which should be used in your report advising Childplay plc which of the two companies, Playbus or Greattoys, purely on financial grounds, would make the better takeover target. Use the ratios you have computed and the other information provided in the question. Mention some other pieces of information not available in the question which would be of use to you in your deliberations.

14 A structured approach to reviewing financial statements

The preceding four chapters have shown how financial ratios for The BOC Group plc could be derived from the published annual report to focus attention on different economic aspects of the group's activities. The purpose of ratio analysis is to provide a profile of the past performance and the present financial strength of a company that might be useful for decision making. The use that is made of ratios will vary, therefore, depending on the decisions faced by users and on the amount of detailed information available. Managers, for example, will be interested in comparing their actual performance with some predetermined budget performance, and also with the performance in previous years, or with that of other competing companies. Because managers have access to a great deal of detailed information about the company, the ratios they can calculate will range from those that reveal overall performance down to those that concentrate on specific manufacturing or internal processes. The information available to external users, on the other hand, is usually restricted to what is provided in the annual financial report, supplemented by other published data such as industrial or economic statistics.

This chapter, like the preceding five, is primarily concerned with the use of ratios by external users, although the ideas, concepts, approach and techniques could well be of use to management in their daily tasks. Whether the external reviewer is an existing or potential shareholder, an existing or potential creditor or lender, or even a major predator, they will still find it necessary to conduct some ratio analysis of the financial performance and position of the company. The emphasis of their goals will differ, some reviewers being more interested in explanations of profitability, or the lack of it, others being more interested in past or potential cash flows and yet others being interested in asset backing and loan security. All, though, will be helped by having a structure to their review indicating the various links between the different ratios.

The extent to which an examination of past data, through ratio analysis, can be incorporated into models for predictive purposes will be discussed at greater length in Chapter 15. Many financial reviewers use a more subjective approach and basis to their predictions but, nevertheless, are guided significantly by what they discover from their structured financial analysis.

It seems reasonable to suggest that a starting point in the predictive process would involve an assessment of the current performance of a company by the use of ratio analysis, together with an analysis of the position in previous years and a comparison with other companies.

The aim of this chapter is to put together those ratios, the underlying concepts and a series of key questions that ought to be asked, thus enabling the reviewer to obtain an overall view of the current corporate performance. Though there are ten stages to the review described here, the individual stages can be read and acted upon separately, should the reviewer only need to look at one aspect of a company's performance. However, the reviewer should be reminded that in many instances the corporate performance in one area will almost certainly have repercussions in another, e.g. increasing sales and profitability will bring with it funding decisions with implications for sources of finance and liquidity.

Main stages of review

It is suggested that the review should consist of a number of stages, the sequence of which does not necessarily have to follow that listed here, though it would be worthwhile to review the company in general in stages 1 and 2 before selecting the specific area of investigation. The ten stages are as follows:

1 SWOT analysis;
2 strategic and major features review;
3 profitability;
4 operating efficiency;
5 growth;
6 liquidity;
7 finance;
8 investment;
9 management of financial risk;
10 conclusions.

Each stage will be introduced in a separate section using ratios already computed, and where appropriate introducing new ones. These ratios will be used to provide answers to key questions posed during each stage. In the final section some general conclusions on the overall picture presented by The BOC Group plc annual report will be made. But we repeat here that the accounts are being used to help make a number of learning points, and that this chapter is not designed to provide a very critical analysis of The BOC Group, such as can be found in the financial pages of the press or in analysts' reports.

SWOT analysis

SWOT analysis – strengths, weaknesses, opportunities, threats – is an acronym taken from the four segments shown in Table 14.1. The analyst should attempt to identify characteristics of the company under each heading. Of course it is quite possible that an external reviewer may not have access to information that provides much depth for this analysis, though recourse to an analyst's report along with the annual report and items gleaned from the financial press during the year could be of great assistance.

This approach to analysis is just one of the number that strategic analysts offer as tools of analysis. One of its strengths is that it can be used as a basis for review in each

Table 14.1   SWOT

Strengths	Weaknesses (internal factors)
Opportunities	Threats (external factors)

of the narrower areas under review, e.g. under liquidity the reviewer can look at the system for generating, monitoring and controlling cash flows and thus identify operating as well as strategic attributes.

For BOC, under 'strengths' should be listed those areas of the firm's business where it is market leader, brand leader, etc. For example, it believes it is a world leader in its vacuum technology division, particularly in vacuum systems, equipment and components. Information such as this can be gleaned from a company's review of operations and from trade associations, though it does depend on the extent of detail required by the analyst as to how far afield an investigator has to go to complete this part of the analysis. The corporate long-range plan could well be a very rich source for the information sought.

The corporate strengths are not solely in the product or operations area, since a review of the annual report indicates that a significant proportion of the group's employees have some equity interest in the group's business thanks to the various employee share schemes. Thus it could be argued that the motivation and efforts of the workforce are the greater because of this.

Identifying the weaknesses, opportunities and threats is less easy, but still necessary. For example, over the past ten years, BOC had itself identified various parts of its business that no longer fit into its corporate strategy or are not profitable enough, because these have been included in the discontinued business section of the analysis. An example of this was the sale in 1992 of the Glasrock operations. A weakness in the vacuum technology segment could be the heavy dependence (50 per cent) on one industry, the semi-conductor industry. Another weakness the board identified in 1997 was the health care business which BOC sold off in 1998, registering a profit on sale of £144 million in the profit and loss account.

There will be the usual cost–benefit analysis of the information gathering, the direction of which will be influenced by the major area of interest of the investigator, e.g. a bank's loan officer considering a multi-million pound loan will need to spend more time than an employee considering the sale of two hundred shares gained through the employee profit-share scheme.

Financial Review Procedure

Before starting the ratio computations, gain an understanding of the events the company is reporting. As already described in the earlier chapters, the words of the chairman, chief executive officer and any other reporting person should be read carefully. They should provide some flesh to the bones prepared by your analysis; or put another way, your analysis should confirm what they have written.

Prior to reading the three main statements, it is important to read the note on accounting policies to obtain a feel for the approaches reflected in the figures presented.

It is also important to check for any changes in policies from previous years so that the implications and effects of these can be reviewed and assessed as the ratio analysis is worked through. In recent years there have been a number of scandals and corporate failures initially obscured by creative accounting practices.

Many executive compensation schemes are linked to figures such as earnings per share, net profit growth, share price movement, which are still open to manipulation despite the continuing efforts to tighten accounting standards. One way of improving profits is to capitalize costs. Some companies in the UK involved in private finance initiative (PFI) work in the public sector used to show, as an asset, costs incurred in the bidding process for substantial long-term contracts and then write them off, like depreciation, over the forecasted life of the project. Others would expense them immediately in the year they occurred. Cable and Wireless Plc controversially capitalized employee costs of £417 million in 2001; Amey Plc in 2001 had a profit of £55 million, which when it started expensing its PFI bid costs rather than capitalizing them became a loss of £18.3 million in 2002. Information about such things should be found in both the accounting policies and in the notes to the accounts. These examples reinforce the suggestions by many analysts that the accounts are best read back to front, i.e. read all the notes before the major statements. Capitalized costs can also be reflected in a weak cash flow; since employees still had to be paid even if the expenses did not go through the profit and loss account.

Profits can be influenced by stock write downs, inclusion of 'non-operating' activity income, imprudent revenue recognition and other measures. Major changes in gross margins – sales minus cost of sales – from one year to the next might bring stock write downs to light. For revenue recognition, review whether operating cash flows fall well short of operating profits. These are some of the areas that require review and analysis to check for malpractice or change in practice since the implication for the investor could be critical.

Strategic and major features review

In each of the next stages, a leading question will be put with a series of follow-up questions to provide the reader with a framework from which to work. Here the leading question ties in with the SWOT analysis, and asks what the major features of the business are and how the business has performed in the period just ended.

The follow-up questions may at times be more appropriate to a single-country, single-market company, but can easily be amended for use with a multinational enterprise such as The BOC Group plc.

Before the detailed analysis of the financial statements, a general review of the chairman's statement, the directors' report and any survey of operations should be read for answers and clues for further questions and analysis. The results of the SWOT analysis will be used in a strategy review of the company, its past and its future, and because the direction of the analysis is one of a financial nature the emphasis of the review questions, analysis and conclusions will be oriented in that direction. Some of the stock questions to be addressed are: Is the company in a vigorous and growing sector of the economy? What are the perceived trends in profitability, operating efficiency, liquidity, finance and investment? What significant events, occurrences or transactions, if any, have there been during the past year? What is the mood of the board and chairman concerning the past performance and the future forecast? Is the stated support of the company for the standards of corporate governance reflected in compliance with the Combined Code of the London Stock Exchange on governance and best practice in both substance and form?

Turning specifically, now, to the financial statements, there are some general questions here worth mentioning. Is the audit report clean or have the auditors qualified it? All qualifications should put reviewers on their guard and cause them to make substantial further enquiries into the area or item mentioned in the qualification. From a review of the company's accounting policies, have there been any changes during the year, and if so with what implications? Do the accounting policies have a critical bearing on profits, or any of the other reported items? Do the accounting policies bear the hallmark of a management trying to present an optimistic or pessimistic picture, or are they just the typical set of policies one would expect to find? See Smith (1996) for examples as well as discussion of the effects and implications of the use of various accounting policies.

During 1999 The BOC Group began to adopt a fundamentally different management and organizational structure, based upon four lines of business. Then in 2000 and 2001 these evolved into the five lines of today: process gas solutions; industrial and special products; BOC Edwards; Afrox hospitals; and Gist. The financial statements now reflect this change and provide segmental information for each of these five business segments. The basis for the regional analysis has not changed for a considerable number of years. Note 1 (pages 238–40) reflects this information for the past three years. The business analysis does not cover earlier periods than 2000 so earlier comparisons beyond 2000 are not possible. They are of course still possible for the regional analysis.

Not surprisingly, for The BOC Group plc the auditors gave a clean report. In the section on accounting policies, most of those reported would be considered typical of a company such as BOC.

Profitability

In Chapter 10 profitability was dealt with at considerable length, showing how various profitability ratios could be computed and interpreted. This section will use some of those ratios in an integrated manner, but first the leading question: is the reported profit real, adequate and maintainable? The first part of the question can be tackled by investigating the list of accounting policies to see if there have been any changes there and, if so, the implications these have for the profit figure. In the case of BOC there have been a number of new accounting standards over the past few years with which they have to comply. These are listed in the section of the accounts headed Accounting Policies, and have impinged on the reporting policies of the group, though there has been no material impact on the underlying results of the group in operating profits. However, both the profit and loss account and the balance sheet have had to be restated for both 2002 and 2001 to comply with FRS 17 concerning retirement benefits. This has required a separate section in the balance sheet, see Table 10.2, showing a total for both pension assets and liabilities with an explanation provided in note 6(e) (pages 254–9). As the pension fund is separate from the company and its trading assets, the net figure for assets or liabilities is not included in the capital employed figures used in any of the ratios. (See page 126 for the derivation of BOC's capital employed.)

The company indicated that it reviewed and then amended the lives of certain tangible assets but without making any material impact on total depreciation, operating profit or the net book value of these assets. When material impact occurs but is not reported, it is deemed an act of fraud on the part of management.

In earlier years, starting with 1990, there have been changes in many of the years. For example, in 1991 the first change was due to a change in translating foreign currencies. In 1991 profits and losses on disposals and closures of businesses were included as part of operating profit, while in 1992, to comply with the then new UTIF pronouncement 3 ('Treatment of goodwill on disposal of a business'), a charge against the profit was made to reflect the goodwill on acquisitions which had previously been written-off against reserves. This charge against profit had to be made because the undertaking for which the goodwill had been paid in the past was disposed of in 1992.

Annually, the Finance and Treasury review of BOC (see pages 208–14) highlights the new accounting standards that the company has followed in the preparation of its accounts. Another example was in the 1997 accounts, when for the first time, the US reporting requirements were incorporated due to the Group's listing in September 1996, on the New York Stock Exchange. We were also informed that the Group cash flow statement for 1997 was prepared in accordance with the revised FRS 1 and the comparative figures restated accordingly.

The five-year summary helps in a review of past trends and, with the future forecasts in the chairman's report, should help indicate whether the profit levels are maintainable and adequate, though confirmation of the latter ought to come from a comparison with profitability ratios of companies in the same industry.

Questions that also should be posed in this section include the following:

What is the company's return on capital?

What is the company's return on sales and its capital turnover?

What are the returns on capital and sales for the different product groups of the company?

What is the operating profit per employee?

How do the results compare with those of competing companies or with averages for the industry and with a trend over time?

What is the forecast for next year's profit and turnover?

The method of computation of these ratios was explained in Chapter 10 with the values for The BOC Group for 2002 and 2001 computed. Some comments were made on any perceived changes between each year's figures. An extended trend analysis of growth is provided later in this chapter. At this stage, however, it is useful to consider the level and trend of profitability and the relationship with each of the major inputs that helped to earn it.

A brief summary of the main profitability ratios for The BOC Group plc for the five years 1998–2002 is given in Table 14.2.

Though no obvious trends can be highlighted in the profitability ratios, the cash return on average capital employed has trended upwards over the five years, as has the cash flow per share. This is a good sign, particularly as the company has continued to annually increase the dividend paid per share. Over the five years, cash flow per share has risen by 24 per cent, cash return on capital employed by 26 per cent with dividends increasing at 23 per cent. Had it been the profitability ratios that had shown growth with stagnant, even declining, cash flow ratios the analyst would be less than sanguine about the continued dividend growth. See the earlier comments on the difficulties surrounding the discovery and interpretation of the effects of creative accounting (page

Table 14.2   The BOC Group plc – summarized profitability ratios

	1998	1999	2000	2001	2002
Return on sales (%)	13.5	14.5	12.8	12.8	12.5
Asset turnover (times)	0.99	0.93	0.95	0.99	1.06
Return on average capital employed (%)	13.4	13.5	12.1	12.6	13.2
Return on average equity (%)	15.2	17.2	18.8	14.7	16.4
Cash return on average capital employed (%)	15.9	18.5	17.3	18.7	20.1
Earnings per share (net)					
before exceptional items (p)	53.27	56.64	53.53	57.51	55.94
on published profit (p)	33.47	51.36	57.19	46.03	41.36
Dividends per share (p)	30.9	32.7	35.0	37.0	38.0
Cash flow per share (p)	100.0	86.0	114.8	128.0	124.0
Operating profit per employee (£)	11,863	13,048	10,499	11,257	10,087

172). Further analysis is provided in the next section in an attempt to explain the profitability performance. The segmental and regional analysis, particularly if traced back five years could be of help here.

Operating efficiency

This stage is dedicated to inquiring more deeply into the efficiency of the operations that gave rise to the overall profit picture of the previous stage. The leading question for this stage is concerned with the identification of all improvements in operating efficiency in all areas of the company's operations.

The sort of follow-up questions that should be included are: What is the cost structure of the business? Are costs mainly fixed or variable, or of what mixture? What is the gross profit ratio? Has it changed? If so, is the change material? Have there been any changes in the corporate strategy which have affected the operating policy and efficiency, e.g. in the area of marketing through pricing changes? Not available from the financial accounts, but nevertheless important, are ratios of strategic areas of management, concerning level of market penetration by product and by market, competitor performance, competitors' costs, effects of advertising policies, plus many other ratios. These latter examples simply serve to reinforce the point that ratio analysis is not limited to publicly available information but is also a valuable technique for use by internal management.

A useful tool for this section is the vertical analysis of the profit and loss account converted to a common size. This expresses the annual turnover as a basis of 100 and converts all other costs and revenues to percentages of turnover. Table 14.3 gives a five-year time series of the common-size profit and loss account for The BOC Group plc.

There are a number of discernible trends in Table 14.3, the first being the small decrease in cost of sales and operating profits. Strategically the declining research and development would be seen by some as a retrograde move. The growing contribution from associated companies and joint ventures will be seen as welcome, especially when seen in light of the trend in Table 14.5.

Table 14.3 The BOC Group plc – consolidated profit and loss account – common size vertical analysis, five years

	1998	1999	2000	2001	2002
Turnover*	100	100	100	100	100
Cost of sales	−58.6	−57.1	−56.9	−58.5	−57.1
Distribution costs	−9.2	−9.6	−9.1	−9.0	−9.4
Administration expenses	−24.4	−20.1	−21.8	−23.2	−23.6
Research and development	−2.0	−1.6	−1.7	−1.6	−1.3
Associated company profits	0.2	0.4	0.2	0.3	0.3
Joint venture profit share	1.2	1.3	1.3	1.5	1.7
Operating profits	14.6	15.7	13.9	14.1	13.7
Exceptional items	−2.9	−2.3	0.2	−2.8	−2.6
Interest	−2.5	−2.6	−1.8	−1.7	−1.9
Tax	−3.8	−2.8	−3.8	−2.8	−2.9
Dividend	−4.6	−5.2	−4.8	−4.8	−5.1
Profit retained	0.4	3.0	3.0	1.2	0.4

Note:
* Excluding associated companies' turnover

Table 14.4 The BOC Group plc – working capital management, five years

	1998	1999	2000	2001	2002
Average collection period (days)	56.5	70.3	66.1	57.0	60.0
Stock-turnover period (days)	41.6	47.8	50.0	45.5	45.1
Average payment period (days)	47.2	56.3	53.2	62.1	76.2
Net working capital to sales ratio (%)	13.5	16.5	16.6	14.5	13.5

Table 14.5 The BOC Group plc – consolidated profit and loss account items – common size horizontal analysis, five years

	1998	1999	2000	2001	2002
Turnover*	100	92.7	108.6	114.5	111.0
Cost of sales	100	92.2	108.1	114.9	111.0
Distribution costs	100	96.8	108.4	112.4	114.0
Administration expenses	100	76.3	89.7	100.3	98.8
Research and development	100	74.1	88.5	89.2	70.3
Associated company profits	100	140.8	111.8	173.7	140.8
Joint venture profits	100	85.6	104.8	128.5	139.0
Operating profits	100	100.0	103.4	110.6	104.2
Exceptional items – costs	100	38.2	−8.4	108.4	98.0
Interest	100	95.6	74.7	75.9	83.6
Tax	100	69.0	109.4	84.6	85.9
Dividend	100	105.8	113.0	119.7	123.9
Profit retained	100	743.4	888.5	359.0	133.6

Note:
* Excluding associated companies' turnover

In Table 14.4 the working capital ratios relating to debtors, stock and creditors are given. This series puts the efforts at efficiency by management into better perspective, and indicates a mixed set of results. The debtors or collection period has been materially reduced over the five years, with the creditor period allowed to rise, thus taking advantage of short-term financing from creditors. The stock–turnover period has partially recovered from the steady increase up to 2000, but is still 10 per cent higher than in 1998. Similarly the company's net working capital to sales ratio is back at 13.5 per cent of sales, a satisfactory level. As many companies provide a breakdown of stocks and work in progress it is possible to compute separate stock–turnover periods for each element if it is thought useful, e.g., raw materials can be compared with purchases, finished goods with sales.

Growth

The major issue at this stage is whether the business has achieved the desired and feasible growth rate. Of course, the two may be mutually exclusive if the desired rate is set too high. It is also probable that an external reviewer may be unable to answer that question because of lack of knowledge concerning the original growth targets.

Generally the two main targets are turnover and profit growth, and these can be computed as follows:

$$\frac{\text{This year's figures} - \text{Last year's figures}}{\text{Last year's figures}} \times 100$$

For example, the decline in turnover of BOC for 2002 on 2001 is

$$\frac{\text{Turnover (2002)} - \text{Turnover (2001)}}{\text{Turnover (2001)}} \times 100 = \frac{3{,}657.7 - 3{,}772.9}{3{,}772.9} \times 100$$
$$= -5.70 \text{ per cent}$$

The negative growth rate of operating profit in 2002 is computed using the same method, thus indicating that profits have declined like turnover, something that a simple visual comparison would confirm.

The follow-up questions will then be aimed at determining whether the decline was due to price changes; whether the annual change was a one-off or part of a trend; whether the decline in turnover and/or profits has been affected by internal growth or by external acquisition; and whether there are segmental differences (see pages 132–4).

Table 14.5 provides a horizontal analysis in common size for items in the profit and loss account for the five years 1998–2002. This gives an insight into the separate annual changes in the elements in the profit and loss account as well as the underlying trend in growth over the period.

The base year is 1998 and all other years' figures are related to this year and computed as in the following example:

$$\frac{\text{Turnover (2002)}}{\text{Turnover (1998)}} \times 100 = \frac{3{,}657.7}{3{,}294.8} \times 100 = 111.0$$

Table 14.5 presents a rather dismal picture with no major substantive trends showing except in dividends – upwards – and research and development costs – declining. There have been oscillations between years with falls and then rises in all the elements, but with the end of the period showing small overall gains. Unfortunately profits have not kept quite in line with turnover. In absolute terms the performance is not stunning but it is also necessary to take into account relative performance by undertaking comparisons with other companies in the same industry. Throughout the five years the company continued with its strategy of doing things to enhance shareholder value and thus maintained a growing dividend payout.

A review of the effects of price changes on growth is a useful tool but is not so straightforward for a multinational. This is because the sales and costs will be made up of many different currencies, each from a country with its own inflation rate. The approach adopted here has been to assume that the foreign exchange market is operating effectively and that all relative differences between the UK's rate of inflation and that of the foreign country are washed out by the change over the year in the foreign exchange rate, with the revised exchange rate being used as the basis for converting foreign transactions into sterling for consolidation purposes. Provided that assumption is a reasonably close approximation to the underlying reality, then the impact of price changes can be examined by using the annual average UK retail price index for all items for each year. Starting again with 1998, as 100, BOC's inflation-adjusted turnover and operating profit values are as follows:

	1998	1999	2000	2001	2002
Turnover	100	91.7	104.0	107.8	102.8
Operating profit	100	98.9	99.0	104.1	96.5

In real terms, even though turnover has increased marginally over the five years the growth has not really flowed through into the operating profits which still lag behind 1998, except for 2001. It has to be acknowledged that these adjusted figures for turnover and profits are only approximations, and care must therefore be taken in their interpretation.

Liquidity

The major question to be examined in terms of liquidity is whether the company is generating sufficient cash. In addition there are subsidiary questions concerned with the values of the current and quick ratios and the impact of changing working capital levels. Examples of the questions that might be asked are: Are there any trends or signals towards insolvency or poor asset management? Have there been any signs of attempted window dressing? Is there any information available suggesting possible changes in the liquid funds for the next year? For example, has the chairman announced a rights issue or new loan issue? Using data from BOC's financial statements for the years 1998–2002, a five-year analysis of the main liquidity ratios discussed in Chapter 12 can be constructed. This is shown in Table 14.6.

A look at the longer-term trend of five rather than two years can put into starker relief any recent changes in ratios. In the case of the current and quick ratios the company seems to be able to maintain a relatively low pair of ratios with a current ratio hovering around 1.0 times and a quick ratio continuing to decline and closing at 0.79 times; 1998 was an exceptional year for the quality of the operating profit even though the cash from operations had declined from 1997. The main reason was the large reduction in operating profit after exceptional items, since the exceptional items in that

Table 14.6   Five-year trend analysis of the main liquidity ratios

	1998	1999	2000	2001	2002
Current ratio (times)	1.21	1.09	0.94	1.00	1.00
Quick ratio (times)	1.00	0.91	0.76	0.79	0.79
Quality of operating profit (%)	173.0	127.9	124.0	127.9	127.9
Cash interest cover (times)	6.15	5.68	6.04	8.75	9.06
Cash dividend cover (times)	3.26	2.66	3.28	3.46	3.25
Cash current liabilities coverage (%)	45.97	33.40	35.97	48.65	48.59
Cash total liabilities coverage (%)	20.45	16.52	20.55	22.43	21.39

year were considerable. The cash interest cover and quality of operating profit are consistently at levels that engender confidence in the company, i.e. given the fact that over the year the company is receiving approximately 127 per cent of its profits in cash and that, in terms of cash, interest payable is increasingly well covered, rising to over nine times in 2002. Similarly dividends are well covered too. It is worth revisiting the earlier point about creative accounting and when and how it might be used. At times when turnover and profits are not increasing as well as management and the market would like to see, observation of cash based ratios help to flush out possible areas of concern. As already mentioned, quality of profit should be greater than 100 per cent, and not have significant annual fluctuations. The BOC Group has a steady quality of profit ratio around 127 per cent, with rising or steady cash interest and dividend cover. This is not a picture of a company trying to create book profits.

Finance

The finance stage follows on appropriately after the review of liquidity and prior to the consideration of investment. The major task of the analyst is to assess whether the financial structure of the company is both appropriate and adequate. Is the funding policy of the company broadly such that long-term commitments are financed by long-term finance? Do the ratios for the company's level of gearing, interest and dividend cover seem reasonable? Have there been any significant changes in the funding highlighted by the ratios and, if so, what do they indicate? Does the company appear to have plans to cope with the structural needs highlighted by the ratio changes? If so, what are the plans and are they appropriate? Finally, a question of increasing importance is whether there are signs of an expansion in the use of off-balance sheet finance, e.g. through increased numbers of operating leases of assets.

The mix of fixed and current assets will provide a starting point for the review of a company's financing needs. To calculate the ratio of fixed assets to total assets for BOC for 2002, the figures are obtained from the balance sheet in Table 10.2, giving fixed assets as £3,646.7 million and current assets as £1,246.4 million, which combine to give total assets of £4,893.1 million. The ratio is computed as follows:

$$\frac{\text{Fixed assets}}{\text{Total assets}} \times 100 = \frac{3,646.7}{4,893.1} \times 100 = 74.53 \text{ per cent}$$

The trend for this ratio is given in Table 14.7. The long-term funds invested in the company consist of the capital and reserves and the long-term liabilities. As can be seen

Table 14.7   Trend of finance ratios

	1998	1999	2000	2001	2002
Fixed assets to total assets (%)	71.3	71.6	72.2	74.0	74.5
Long-term funds to total assets (%)	76.3	74.0	70.5	74.0	74.5
Total owing to total assets (%)	53.4	52.6	51.6	55.1	63.2
Total debt to total assets (%)	28.8	29.5	30.1	30.4	30.9
Long-term debt to equity (%)	52.7	48.7	39.2	48.9	66.6
Capital gearing (times)	1.34	1.31	1.30	1.24	1.28
Interest cover (times)	3.96	4.20	5.10	3.58	3.40
Dividend cover (times)	1.08	1.57	1.92	1.24	1.09

from Table 10.2, these amount to £1,802.0 million and £1,843.2 million respectively, i.e. a total of £3,645.2 million. The ratio of long-term funds to total assets indicates how much of the total assets have been funded by long-term sources. Since there is also a long-term element in the need to carry stocks and debtors, many firms find it prudent to finance part of their current assets with long-term funds. The more conservative the funding policy, the higher the long-term funds to total assets ratio.

The ratio of long-term funds to total assets for 2002 is computed as follows:

$$\frac{\text{Long-term funds}}{\text{Total assets}} \times 100 = \frac{3,645.2}{4,893.1} \times 100 = 74.50 \text{ per cent}$$

This result of 74.5 per cent reinforces the point made earlier in the section on liquidity that the company depends increasingly on long-term funds but that it is quite aggressive in its funding since, effectively, none of its current assets are funded by long-term funds.

The five-year trend is given in Table 14.7. A more detailed break-down of the assets and fund structure can be found in Table 14.8, which uses the common-size approach in a vertical analysis of The BOC Group's balance sheets for 2002 and 2001. All items listed in the balance sheets in Table 10.2 have been converted to percentages of the *total* assets of that year.

Just as with the common-size profit and loss account in Table 14.5, the balance sheets for the past five years could be drafted to indicate the trends in the levels of different assets and liabilities over the period. This could be done by setting the 1998 figures equal to a base of 100 and computing the amount for the succeeding years in relation to 1998.

Though Table 14.8 only covers two years, 2001 and 2002, it clearly demonstrates the proportionate use of long- and short-term creditors, capital and reserves, as well as retained earnings in the profit and loss account and the total borrowings and finance leases. These latter two sources are shown as the major ones for the company.

Two other forms of commitment are the other form of leasing – operating leases and pension fund payments. The commitment to operating lease payments is shown in note 13(a) to the financial statements on page 268 as totalling £35.6 million, which is less than 0.8 per cent of total assets with further declining annual amounts continuing over a number of years. The pension fund payments are shown in note 6, (pages 254–9), which also provides information on the value of the pension fund's assets and liabilities. From this note it can be seen how the fund has moved from a surplus situation to a

Table 14.8   The BOC Group plc – consolidated balance sheets – common size vertical analysis

	2001	2002
Fixed assets		
intangible assets	0.97	3.08
tangible assets	63.97	61.87
investment in joint ventures		
share of gross assets	12.42	12.59
share of gross liabilities	−8.29	−8.39
loans to joint ventures	1.97	2.28
investment in associates		
share of net assets	0.95	1.18
loans to associates	0.18	0.13
investment in own shares	1.20	0.87
other investments	0.64	0.92
	74.03	74.53
Current assets		
stocks	5.56	5.31
debtors due within one year	14.40	15.00
debtors due beyond one year	0.43	0.58
investments	0.87	0.79
deposits and cash	4.71	3.79
	25.97	25.47
	100.0	100.0
Capital and reserves		
equity called up share capital	2.50	2.54
share premium account	6.78	7.40
revaluation reserves	0.97	0.57
profit and loss account	28.27	26.67
joint ventures' reserves	1.98	1.80
associates' reserves	0.67	0.68
pensions reserves	0.95	−5.24
Equity shareholders' funds	42.12	34.42
Minority interests	2.78	2.41
Creditors: amounts falling due after more than one year		
borrowings and finance leases	20.59	22.91
other creditors	1.20	1.19
Provisions for liabilities and charges	8.46	8.33
	75.15	69.25
Pension assets	−2.16	−1.11
Pension liabilities	1.13	6.36
	74.12	74.50
Creditors: amounts due within one year		
borrowings and finance leases	9.82	7.97
other creditors	16.06	17.53
	25.88	25.50
	100.00	100.00

deficit which is approximately equal to five years contributions to the fund. This large deficit has been caused primarily by the decline of the market values of the assets in which the fund is invested. The velocity and magnitude of the change is considerable and must give rise to questions and fears in the minds of employees and shareholders. This is new information provided by BOC in accord with FRS 17 requirements.

The trend in funding ratios is given in Table 14.7 and from this several points emerge: the first is that over 70 per cent of the assets are of a fixed nature and that these are all financed by long-term funds. The amount of long-term funds left to finance current assets is very small indicating a very aggressive funding policy by the company, a point reinforced by the low current ratio. The greater the proportion of funds in current liabilities the greater the financial risk from non-payment of debts on the due date. Unless the company wants to go out of business there is what might be termed an irreducible minima for both stock and debtors and these, it is argued, could or should be financed by long-term finance if the company is trying to match finance with the assets.

The long-term funds have remained around the same over the five years (save for 2000), with the gearing a little higher as the long-term debt, as a proportion of total long-term funds, increases marginally. The capital gearing has fluctuated a little, but shareholders could still benefit increasingly as turnover and profits improve. The decline in the dividend cover is because the annual dividend uplift, even though made conservatively, has not been matched by profit growth, which has been slow. However, although the company may be geared up, financially and operationally, the chairman in his 2002 report is guardedly optimistic about BOC's future.

Sometimes companies announce their future financial plans in the annual report, though not in great detail. In 1999 BOC took the opportunity to give explanations about what was a possible merger with Air Liquide and Air Products. Subsequently this did not occur. At present no future financial plans are given.

Investment

The next stage of the review examines the investment profile of the company and questions whether the company is making enough investments to ensure future profitability.

This is neither an easy question to answer nor is it easy to derive ratios and values which are of use in arriving at an answer. For example, how capital intensive an industry is the company in? What is the average age of its present assets? How does the annual amount of depreciation compare with the annual total new investment in fixed assets? Is there a change in the mixture of owning and hiring assets? Similarly, what investment is the company undertaking in its personnel?

Comparisons between capital expenditure and sales and the annual depreciation expenses are relatively straightforward to make. The sales turnover figure for 2002 can be found in Table 10.1, while the amount of depreciation written off can be found in note 8 on pages 261–2 along with the capital expenditure for the year. BOC's capital expenditure to sales ratio for 2002 is computed as follows:

$$\frac{\text{Capital expenditure}}{\text{Turnover}} \times 100 = \frac{354.3}{3{,}657.7} \times 100 = 9.69 \text{ per cent}$$

This percentage gives an indication of the level of capital expenditure undertaken to sustain the particular level of sales. Movements from the trend line should be particularly noted and investigated. An increasing trend line would indicate an increasing capitalization by the company and thus an increase in the fixed costs of the business. The capital expenditure to depreciation charge ratio for 2002 can be computed similarly:

$$\frac{\text{Capital expenditure}}{\text{Depreciation}} = \frac{354.3}{368.1} \times 100 = 96.25 \text{ pre cent}$$

Both these ratios are best reviewed as part of a time series, so that they place in perspective the changes over the past twelve months. Some analysts perceive deprecation as the setting aside of profits for the replacement of the asset being depreciated, rather than considering it as a matching of expired cost against the turnover it has helped to earn. The ratio of capital expenditure to depreciation does give an indication of the replacement rate of new for old assets, though it makes no allowance for price changes or for corporate growth. To help with the latter, a further ratio of capital expenditure to total tangible fixed assets can be computed using the information in note 8, pages 261–2. If possible the gross book value of the tangible assets should be used, but, failing that, the net book value can be used.

The capital expenditure to fixed tangible assets ratio for BOC for 2002 is

$$\frac{\text{Capital expenditure}}{\text{Gross book value, tangible fixed assets}} \times 100 = \frac{354.3}{6,025.3} \times 100 = 5.88 \text{ per cent}$$

Thus the capital expenditure is replacing fixed assets at a rate of once every seventeen years (i.e. 100/5.9) approximately, assuming there is no inflation and they are all assets of the same type. Note 8 also provides information on the proportion of leased to owned assets used by the company. Using the net book values given for leased assets of £71.5 million, and net tangible fixed assets of £3,027.4 million, the ratio can be computed as follows:

$$\frac{\text{Leased assets}}{\text{Net total tangible fixed assets}} \times 100 = \frac{71.5}{3,027.4} \times 100 = 2.36 \text{ per cent}$$

This indicates that the company leases a very small percentage of its fixed tangible assets. As further evidence of the company's commitment to future capital expenditure, the amount of the company's actual commitments is also given in note 8. The amount committed at the end of 2002 of £100 million was considerably smaller than any previous year-end commitments of the past five years, which could be construed as a negative sign, particularly if reinforced by comments in the performance review.

With the increasing pace of technological advancement, machinery is seen to be replacing people in manufacturing industry. A ratio comparing capital expenditure with the average number of employees can be calculated to identify the level of new investment per employee. The average number of employees is given in note 6 as 45,256 for 2002. The ratio can be calculated as follows:

$$\text{Capital expenditure per employee } 2002 = \frac{£354.3 \text{ million}}{45,256} = £7,829$$

The level of capital expenditure when compared with the employment costs of the workforce is approximately 37 per cent, which should reinforce the view about the

Table 14.9   Trend of important ratios of the BOC Group plc – capital expenditure

	1998	1999	2000	2001	2002
Capital expenditure to turnover (%)	18.1	16.56	11.56	9.3	9.69
Capital expenditure to gross fixed assets (%)	12.03	9.31	6.87	5.82	5.88
Capital expenditure to depreciation (times)	2.20	1.87	1.22	1.13	0.96
Capital expenditure per employer (£000)	14.74	13.74	9.76	8.28	7.83

degree of importance of the level of capital expenditure of the company. Again, a compilation of a trend series of the important ratios of BOC can be made and is given in Table 14.9. This provides a clear indication of the reducing amount being spent on capital expenditure, whilst in the performance review, the importance of maintaining continued investment in technology to develop business growth is stressed. The figures in this table and the declining amount spent on research and development highlighted in Table 14.5 ought to prompt questions of management. The report does note the very competitive as well as harsh economic conditions facing some of the segments, BOC Edwards and the problems in the semi-conductor manufacturing industry, being a specific example.

Although the financial report does not provide statistics concerning the age of the company's fixed assets, it is possible to see that it is turning over its fixed assets once somewhere between every seven to seventeen years. Given that many of the owned assets are land and buildings with a life well in excess of that, it would appear that no longer is BOC investing heavily in its plant and equipment. More detailed ratios using the information in note 8 would reinforce that statement. As with the profitability ratios it is worth computing the capital expenditure ratios for the business and geographical segments. The five-year trend figures are shown in Table 14.10.

By segmenting the data the analyst will get a more focused picture on the investment patterns across both business sectors and regional markets which will help reflect more precisely the statements made in the directors' review.

Capital acquisitions ratio

A company's ability to obtain or maintain its competitive advantage is partially due to its capital assets. The company must therefore have the necessary cash-generating ability in order to finance the acquisition of these investments. For the majority of companies cash generated by profitable operations is the major source of funds for reinvestment in the company. A comparison of the cash spent on new assets, either for replacement or for expansion, can be made to the amount of cash left from operations after payment of interest, tax and dividends. It is not possible to break down investment activity into consistent categories when making an external review, though internally it is easier but not necessarily completely straightforward. The ratio is the proportion of cash received net from operations to amount invested:

$$\frac{\text{Net cash inflow from operations after servicing of finance and payment of taxes}}{\text{Net amount invested}}$$

Table 14.10   The BOC Group plc – trend of investment ratios by business segment and geographic region

	1998	1999	2000	2001	2002
Business segments					
Capital expenditure to turnover (%)					
Process gas solutions			21.3	14.3	13.1
Industrial and special products			6.5	6.1	7.7
BOC Edwards			7.4	6.2	6.1
Afrox hospitals			5.3	3.6	3.6
Gist			7.4	7.7	7.2
Capital expenditure to capital employed (%)					
Process gas solutions			10.5	8.5	8.6
Industrial and special products			7.2	8.3	11.7
BOC Edwards			9.2	9.1	7.1
Afrox hospitals			12.9	10.5	8.8
Gist			13.1	22.0	83.3
Capital expenditure per employee (£000)					
Process gas solutions			36.5	28.1	26.3
Industrial and special products			6.9	6.7	8.4
BOC Edwards			14.6	10.9	8.1
Afrox hospitals			1.2	0.8	0.7
Gist			4.0	4.2	3.7
Geographic regions					
Capital expenditure to turnover (%)					
Europe	24.9	14.9	13.0	13.4	11.4
Americas	16.9	14.5	9.8	7.8	10.4
Africa	9.4	8.5	6.3	5.2	5.8
Asia/Pacific	12.8	19.1	11.5	6.6	6.0
Capital expenditure to capital employed (%)					
Europe	21.6	11.9	9.0	11.0	12.9
Americas	16.4	13.1	8.6	8.3	10.8
Africa	13.2	10.8	9.7	10.2	11.6
Asia/Pacific	13.4	16.5	10.3	7.0	6.1
Capital expenditure per employee (£000)					
Europe	19.7	11.7	11.1	11.5	9.5
Americas	24.7	21.5	17.7	15.0	18.4
Africa	3.2	3.0	1.9	1.6	1.5
Asia/Pacific	14.9	26.7	18.7	11.2	9.1

The cash inflow and outflow figures can be taken from the cash flow statement (see page 232), with the numerator in 2002 derived from the net cash inflow from operations of £759.3 million less the net cash outflow on interest and dividends of £243.4 million and less the tax paid of £96.2 million. The net cash outflow on investing of £324.5 million provides the denominator. The percentage capital acquisitions ratio for 2002 is computed as

$$\text{Capital acquisitions ratio 2002} = \frac{759.3 + 33.9 - 90.7 - 96.2 - 186.6}{324.5} \times 100$$

$$= 129.34 \text{ per cent}$$

In 2002, 129.3 per cent of the new investment was self-financed, with the surplus contributing to the financing of new business acquisition. The five-year summary of the capital acquisitions ratio indicates the swing from deficit to surplus funding of new investments. On its own this is a good sign, but not when the investigation highlights the declining trend in capital expenditure.

	1998	1999	2000	2001	2002
Capital acquisitions ratio (%)	64.6	58.4	95.2	142.1	129.3

Economic conditions will influence investment decisions and financing decisions and it is quite possible for this ratio to change considerably from one year to the next.

Table 14.10 provides a more detailed insight into the decline in capital expenditure, with the brunt of the decline coming in the process gas solutions segment. Afrox hospitals has also had a major reduction, relative to its starting point. Note that BOC have changed the basis of the segmentation of their business, so that now there are five segments. Because of this there are no comparable figures for capital expenditure for the new segments earlier than 2000. BOC have revised their databases so that for most of the important financial data of a business or regional segment there is a five-year profile. Not every company is so transparent and some in the past have changed their segmentation criteria to ensure it is not easy for trend analysis to take place.

The review of regional analysis highlights that over five years all regions have suffered a decline, though at different rates.

Capital market conditions may make the raising of new long-term funds much cheaper during some periods than during others. Thus a company may raise more capital than it needs for investment during a period. Conversely there may be market pressures that cause a company to make investments that require funding from short-term sources because there is no long-term capital available. For the first example the capital acquisition ratio may be low, while for the second the ratio could exceed 100 per cent.

Investment in employees

Companies are required by US and UK GAAP to provide some information about the pension schemes operated by the company and their net costs. In addition information is provided about the various share option schemes the company operates. (If all these options were exercised they could increase the nominal share capital by 5.9 per cent. Approximately 82 per cent of the options are available for the executive minority, but in total the various schemes include over 15 per cent of the employees. This does help indicate some idea of the possible size of employee committment to the company.)

In total the annual pension and social security costs amount to approximately 15 per cent of the total employment costs. In turn the employment costs amount to 26.2 per cent of turnover – a ratio that has remained reasonably consistent over the past five years. Though note 6 also includes average employee numbers, year end total remuneration, etc., it only provides a partial indication of the investment the company is or is not putting into its workforce. Though one can calculate the average remuneration per employee from the statistics provided, it is not very helpful given the range of jobs and the diversity of the locations of those jobs geographically. Nevertheless some useful general measures have been computed earlier in the efficiency section (see page 142).

Management of financial risks

Companies are becoming more and more multinational in their operations and the financial market place is becoming larger, wider and more sophisticated in its products and operations. Thus the need to assess a company's management of, and ongoing position in, its financial risks increases in importance.

The main risk areas arise in the currency, interest rate and credit dealings. To these three could be added the use of financial derivatives. Currency risk can arise from outstanding and future transactions and from the translation of the foreign currency values of assets and liabilities into sterling.

The main reason why differential interest rates exist between countries is because the market expects the exchange rate between those countries' currencies to move and counter the differential. Thus it is always possible to borrow in the lower interest rate currency, convert, and invest at the higher rate and thus make a 'profit', this of course is shown in the profit and loss account. At the same time there will almost certainly be a reduction in the capital value, but this will be passed through the balance sheet via the total recognized gains and losses statement. Thus profits could have been bolstered at the expense of the shareholders' equity. This can be checked by calculating the average cost of net borrowings and comparing it with the rates due on the portfolio of loans outstanding. From note 3 (see page 243) we obtain net interest payable of £80.6 million (interest payable £103.2 million minus interest receivable £22.6 million) with net borrowings and finance leases for 2002 and 2001 respectively of £1,325.6 million and £1,272.1 million. So the average cost of net borrowings for 2002 is:

$$\text{Average cost of net borrowings } 2002 = \frac{80.6}{0.5(1,325.6 + 1,272.1)} \times 100 = 6.21 \text{ per cent}$$

Comparing the average rate of 6.2 per cent and the rates quoted in note 3 (see page 245) for the outstanding loans, it can be seen that there is little difference between the two. Also compare the amount of the foreign currency net investment translation effect in the total recognized gains and losses with the size of the net borrowings. In 2002 the translation effect is a reduction of £136.6 million (10.3 per cent of net borrowings). This translation loss is not out of line with the size of annual gains or losses over the past few years.

The extent of the use of hedging mechanisms is also important information, particularly if the risks are left uncovered. At the end of 2002 BOC had 6 interest rate swap agreements with notional principal amounts of £420 million, which is 8.6 per cent of the group's total assets, while at the same point in time BOC had 8 currency swap agreements outstanding with a notional value of £360.7 million, (7.4 per cent of total assets). In each case the amount and proportion has marginally increased since 2001.

Conclusions

To reach a conclusion, the analyst has to make an overall review and decide whether or not the company is in good financial health. Here then, it is necessary to pull together the answers to all the main questions of each stage. From this the main lines of business will have been identified and assessed, and decisions made as to what should happen in the future. By reviewing the SWOT analysis in the light of the profitability assessment, and the operating efficiency in conjunction with the forecast needs for investment and the implications for liquidity and finance, it is possible to provide a very full report, the nature and direction of which will be determined in some way by the needs of the individual for whom it is prepared.

15 Other uses of financial ratios

So far the use of ratios has been to provide the basis for a subjective assessment of a business either as a whole and/or for some specific part of it. This chapter will address the use of ratios in more objective analytical structures which aim to provide specific recommendations to decision makers. Some results from research have proved to have a more practical application than others. For example, financial ratios have been found useful in forecasting potential corporate bankruptcies and in classifying a prospective customer's credit rating. Research is still continuing into the use of financial ratios in models to identify potential takeover targets, or to value shares. Two areas where the application of straightforward statistical techniques to financial ratios have helped improve the quality of the general picture of a company have been time series analysis and line-of-business analysis.

Time series analysis

Time series analysis involves the calculation of the ratios of a company not just for the current or preceding year but for a longer period of time, which may be five, ten or twenty years or more. The objectives of such an analysis are first to provide a 'standard' against which the current performance and financial stability of a company or business unit might be compared and, second, to attempt to isolate trends over time that might enable future values of the ratios to be predicted.

When conducting a time series analysis, it is obviously important to ensure that there has been consistency in accounting practices; where changes have occurred, these must be calibrated before the analysis is undertaken. It is also possible that the reasons for changes over time in a particular variable, such as sales or profits, may be due to economy – or industry-wide factors outside the control of a particular company. Simply to compare one period with another without adjusting for these factors may be misleading.

Two examples of where accounting alternatives can cause sizeable inconsistencies over time are foreign-currency translation and exceptional items. Care must be taken to ensure that exceptional items are what they say they are and thus are excluded from the annual profit figures while cognizance must be given to the influence of the foreign currency translation which will vary annually, sometimes materially. Material changes and influences should be excluded.

Time series analysis utilizes any systematic patterns in the behaviour of a financial series, such as revenue, costs, or profits, over time to generate forecasts of future values for the variable. It can also be used in non-forecasting contexts where management is looking for explanations of the values found in a series, e.g. if investigating whether profits have been 'managed' over the years or to provide a statistical model for executive compensation plans.

The statistical techniques used in time series analysis involve the isolation of four separate components of trends:

1 the secular component (the regular movement in trends caused by factors whose influence tends to be in the same direction over a long period);
2 the seasonal component (the short-term movement in trends caused by seasonal variations);
3 the cyclical component (the movement in trends caused by medium- and long-term cyclical fluctuations);
4 the residual component (the irregular movements in trends caused by random and unpredictable events).

Having identified the components of trends affecting a time series of past ratios, it is possible, through the use of the mathematical technique of least-squares regression, to determine a trend line for each ratio under consideration. (The statistical technique is not discussed here; readers are referred elsewhere, e.g. Foster (1986) for an introduction to an in-depth review.) It is this trend line that determines the yardstick against which the ratios of the current year should be compared and it provides the starting point for assessing whether the performance of the current period might be thought 'good' or 'bad'. The trend line also provides a base for predicting future values of the ratios.

This kind of analysis is, with the advent of spreadsheets, now an inexpensive and relatively easy procedure to conduct. In the previous chapter, ratios were calculated for The BOC Group plc for the past five years and, though they were not subjected to a rigorous time series analysis, a broad trend with apparent deviations was obvious in a number of instances. This was sufficient to provide some valuable commonsense observations but for a more rigorous approach recourse to time series analysis is advocated.

Line-of-business analysis

When time series analysis is used for prediction purposes, the examination of segmental, or line-of-business, information is crucial. The information for share-trading and lending decisions is drawn not only from a company's annual report but also from many other sources – forecasts of growth in particular industries and countries, general economic trends, details of major contracts awarded, details of major customers, the introduction of new manufacturing processes, new products, competitors' activities, changes in legislation, changes in key personnel and so on. Much of this information is specific to particular lines of business or geographical locations. The overall performance of a diversified group of companies is obviously affected by the individual performances of specific segments, which will in turn be affected by the environment in which they operate. Any prediction of overall performance will therefore require segmental information, so that all the factors that might have an effect on the performance of individual segments may be taken into account. In the earlier chapters it was plain to see the big differences in the profit margins of the different segments of The BOC Group and of their different returns on capital employed (see Chapter 10 and Table 11.1).

It must be noted that firms have considerable discretion over the line of business reporting; how the separate activities are combined and then described, how the intra-group transfers are calculated or transfer prices set. Many companies are sensitive about the economic value of this information to competitors and to governments of countries in which they trade and in which they wish to minimize taxes. They are therefore not as full in their disclosures as they could be. They can ensure a lack of consistency over time in the way in which the constituent parts of a company are grouped together. The constituent parts of a business can change over time through acquisition or divestment, or when the holding company makes major organizational and strategic changes. BOC changed its segmentation in 2001, and revised its 2000 comparative figures accordingly, but that meant that in 2002 there was still only a three-year sequence to review. Full and frank disclosure can provide a basis for very useful ratio analysis, especially when combined with the analysis of competing firms in similar areas of business. There is a substantial demand for information which compares the performance and financial position of different companies and there are several organizations which attempt to meet this demand by undertaking a cross-sectional ratio analysis.

Cross-sectional analysis – inter-firm comparison

Cross-sectional ratio analysis offers a further means of providing a 'standard' against which performance can be measured. A comparison of the ratios of a particular company, either with those of individual companies in the same industry or with some average of the group of companies in the industry, will be useful in assessing relative performance. Time series analysis using financial values or ratios has already been mentioned; it is used for comparing one entity at different points in time. Cross-sectional analysis compares different entities at the same points in time. To the extent that the investment decision facing shareholders and lenders involves choosing which companies to invest in, or which to lend to, the use of ratio analysis to compare the performance of different companies is helpful. A further example is the predictions of the financial distress of firms in the same or different industries. This we shall cover in more depth in the next section. There are, however, a number of problems associated with such inter-firm comparisons.

The first difficulty is in deciding on the appropriate industrial classification of a particular company. Many of the industrial groups contain companies that are surprisingly different. Moreover, diversified companies will, by definition, be involved in a range of quite different activities, each of which might belong to a different industrial classification. In the Stock Exchange industrial classification scheme, BOC is included in the 'general chemicals' sector, which places it among companies with which it has very little in common, such as ICI, Bayer, British Vita, Croda, Yule Catto and so on.

The second difficulty concerns the effects of corporate size. When comparing the results of individual companies, it is not sufficient merely to ensure that the companies operate in the same industry. They should also be more or less comparable in size. Even though one of the supposed benefits of ratio analysis is its ability to adjust for size differences, there are occasions when this breaks down. For example, many ratios make use of the annual sales figure. If company A has annual sales of £1.5 billion and these represent the major part of the total industry sales, an increase of 10.0 per cent may require a significant effort. If company B has annual sales of just £1 million, an increase of 10.0 per cent may be achieved much more easily. A further difference caused by size is the degree of risk associated with the company. Large companies usually have better access to the capital markets than their smaller competitors and find it easier to raise long-term finance; during particularly difficult periods, such large companies might often be supported by governments. In contrast, small companies are often restricted to the relatively riskier short-term credit and overdraft sources. Large companies might also be expected to benefit from the use of more sophisticated technology and superior marketing channels.

A further difficulty facing inter-firm comparison is that ratio analysis by itself may fail to reflect the true position of the different companies. For instance, the ratios of company X may be superior in every way to those of company Y, or superior to the industry average. However, if nine-tenths of the output of company X is taken up by just one customer, it may be more risky than its comparators. As with time series analysis, cross-sectional ratio analysis must be supplemented with information drawn from a variety of other sources.

Perhaps the most serious obstacle to perfect inter-firm comparison is the existence of variations in accounting policies and practices. Even though there are standards for accounting reporting which were discussed in the early chapters, a wide range of permissible accounting treatments still exist for such items as depreciation, stock valuation, intangibles and the like. Such differences obviously affect the validity of the comparison exercise. The only way that this particular problem can be overcome is through a standardized comparison scheme. The Centre for Interfirm Comparison operates one such scheme and seeks to ensure that the figures supplied by participant companies are truly comparable by providing detailed instructions – about the definition of terms, valuation principles and so on. Only by pursuing such an approach is it possible to attribute differences in ratios solely to differences in operational performance and economic position, rather than to differences in accounting terminology and treatment. Unfortunately, the information and data produced by the Centre for Interfirm Comparison are available only to participating companies and not to all external users of company reports. Appendix B gives details of a number of sources of comparative statistics and data.

One example of the use of publicly available financial ratios is the information provided by FAME which is produced by Jordans Ltd, and shown in Appendix B. Various consulting organizations make use of the financial values and ratios to build their own models from which they can then make recommendations to clients/public concerning the value of a particular company as a potential investment, or disinvestment. One such model that is cross-sectional is called market value added (MVA) which will be described briefly later in this chapter.

The prediction of corporate bankruptcy

An ability to predict the likelihood of the bankruptcy or failure of a company would be of obvious benefit to shareholders, lenders, suppliers and managers alike. Over the past forty years, a substantial amount of research has been undertaken on the extent to which ratio analysis might be useful in making such predictions. Much of the research effort has been based on US data, and the methodology generally adopted has involved the comparison of the ratios of failed companies for several years prior to failure with those of companies that did not fail.

The results of the research have been impressive, showing that significant differences were discernible between the ratios of failed and non-failed companies for up to five years before failure. Earlier research concentrated on the ability of a single ratio to predict failure – the 'univariate' approach – and perhaps the best known examples of the use of this approach are in the earlier work by Beaver (1966). He selected a sample of seventy-nine US companies that had either become bankrupt or had defaulted on the payment of interest or preference dividends. These he classified as failed companies; each failed company was then paired with a company from the same industry and of equivalent size that had not failed. For each of the pairs of companies, Beaver calculated thirty of the more conventional financial ratios for each of the five years prior to the demise of the failed company. He found that the mean ratios of the failed companies were substantially worse than those of the non-failed companies over the five-year period.

However, simply detecting differences in the mean values of ratios does not necessarily indicate predictive ability, and Beaver went on to test for that. He assumed that, for each pair of companies, the one with the poorer ratio would be the one most likely to fail, and made that the basis of his prediction. The prediction was compared with the actual outcome to determine the extent to which mis-classification occurred. Obviously, if this particular technique had no predictive ability at all, the classification would, at random, be correct for 50 per cent of the time and incorrect for 50 per cent of the time. Beaver found that, from the thirty ratios he used, a small number were particularly successful in predicting failure – success being measured in terms of the lowest number of incorrect classifications. The most successful of all was the cash-flow–total-debt ratio, with only 10 per cent of the companies incorrectly classified five years prior to failure. Somewhat surprisingly, the current ratio, which is often thought of as an important indicator of liquidity, was not a particularly good predictor: 20 per cent of the companies were incorrectly classified one year prior to failure and 31 per cent five years prior to failure.

An alternative and an improvement to the univariate approach is the 'multivariate' approach which considers several different ratios simultaneously. The seminal research work on the use of multivariate models to predict failure or non-failure was carried out by Altman (1968) in the USA. He used the statistical technique of multiple discriminant analysis, which is designed to classify observations into distinct groupings depending on the characteristics of the observations. In Altman's case, the observations were individual companies and he was seeking to classify them as 'failed' or 'non-failed', depending on the various financial characteristics of each company (size, profitability, liquidity and so on). The use of multiple discriminant analysis facilitates a linear combination of the economic characteristics that best discriminate between failed and non-failed companies. This linear combination is known as a discriminant function and is of the form

$$Z = b_1 X_1 + b_2 X_2 + b_3 X_3 + \ldots + b_n X_n$$

where X_1, X_2, X_3 etc. are the various financial ratios, b_1, b_2, b_3 etc. are the discriminant coefficients and Z is the discriminant score. It is the value of the discriminant score that is used to classify companies as either failed or non-failed.

Altman used the paired-sample method and selected thirty-three manufacturing companies that had failed and paired them with thirty-three manufacturing companies that had not failed. Size and industry were the criteria for pairing. For each company, he computed twenty-two accounting and non-accounting measures and then considered these in various combinations as predictors of failure. The following linear combination was found to be the best discriminator of the bankruptcy of a company, and it contained just five of the variables.

$$Z = 0.012X_1 + 0.014X_2 + 0.033X_3 + 0.006X_4 + 0.0099X_5$$

where X_1 is working capital/total assets, X_2 is retained earnings/total assets, X_3 is profit before interest and taxes/total assets, X_4 is market value of equity/book value of total debt and X_5 is sales/total assets.

This model is applied in solvency evaluation by calculating each of those five ratios for the company under consideration, feeding them into the discriminant function and calculating the discriminant score (usually known simply as the Z score). The value of the computed Z score is compared with the cut-off point that best discriminated between failed and non-failed companies.

Space precludes too detailed a discussion on the conceptual underpinning of the various models which have in general been devised from the original Altman approach. But it should be noted that the studies have pointed out that over a period of time, changes due to environmental changes do occur in the financial ratios. For example, levels of profitability and liquidity will tend to be lower during the downturn of the trade cycle. Thus lower ratios for a nevertheless successful company, when fed into the predictive model, could cause an erroneous prediction of failure, if the prediction model has been based on ratios achieved by companies during better economic times.

British research and commercial usage in this case has been spearheaded by Taffler with his first paper in 1977; he subsequently developed his model commercially. The methodology used by his company was very straightforward. It computed a Z-score for each company in its population and then ranked all the quoted companies in order of their Z-score. The coefficient and ratios incorporated in the model, though not publicly available, were rigorously tested over time and have been found to be very robust. Only four variables were used. The ranking positions of the companies were placed into percentiles and used to identify a cut-off Z-score.

If a company achieved a Z-value below this then it was deemed to be at risk. From this could be computed the percentage of companies with Z-scores below the cut-off, thus producing the quoted percentage of companies at risk. In 1977 there were approximately 11 per cent at risk, which increased with fluctuations to a peak of 29 per cent in 1992, whilst in 1998 it was around 22 per cent. Smith (1996) provides some good examples of how the model predicted the distress of Queens Moat House plc and Tiphook plc. An indication can be obtained of the industry average for a company, the percentage of companies at risk and the percentage point of the investigated company. Trends for each of the three variables can be portrayed graphically over time which will show the relative position of the client company, the industry and the at-risk stage with the changes in those positions. This clearly is of help to analysts, managers, investors, etc. because of the objectivity it provides in support of the signals it gives. Appropriate action can be taken by the individual concerned.

Though this version is no longer available commercially, other credit rating companies exist either as part of a larger group or separately and are using models which are similar to, or derived from, Taffler's original one.

The merits of not just concentrating on accounting data appealed to some, particularly if there was a possible use for commercial application. Argenti (1976), by combining quantitative and qualitative factors, developed a model which produced a score based on both financial statement data and qualitative assessments of management performance. More recently this work, too, has been extended to examine these issues in relation to small UK firms (Keasey and Watson 1987).

So although any particular predictive model may never be applicable at all times and under all circumstances, the models that have been developed do appear to have had quite definite predictive ability. Because of the potential payoff from being able to develop a proven predictive model, research continues apace. Most of the published research results have involved a retrospective analysis, being based on past data for firms that actually failed, and are subject to statistical shortcomings. A complete issue of the *Journal of Business Finance and Accounting* (vol. 17, no. 1, Spring 1990) was given over to financial statement analysis. It did include articles on takeover predictions as well as articles considering the *ex ante* predictive approach, the case of current cost accounting based ratios and the use of other statistical techniques than Z scores. The individual bibliographies to each article, when combined, provide a very full list of works on the use of financial ratios for anyone who wishes to follow up an earlier work, or who perhaps doubts the statements made here.

The evidence is impressive and has helped in the identification of those crucial ratios that have a strong measure of predictive ability. Thus, although the role of financial ratio analysis in the prediction of future profits, dividends and share prices may be somewhat unclear, its importance in the prediction of future solvency seems much clearer. So much so that there are commercial services available for those wishing to use Z-score analysis. In Appendix B (see page 283) the QuiScore and rating for BOC is given and for 2002 it was 72 and stable. The QuiScore in 2001 was 83 and secure. Below is the five year QuiScore for BOC abstracted from page 283.

Historical QuiScore and Rating for BOC

	1998	*1999*	*2000*	*2001*	*2002*
QuiScore	83	77	74	83	72
Comment	Secure	Stable	Stable	Secure	Stable

FAME publish the QuiScore for each company, which is a measure of the likelihood of company failure in the twelve months following the date of calculation. There are five distinct bands identified, secure, stable, normal, unstable and high risk. A company score is compared with the band range and an interpretation of the company's risk factor made. In the case of BOC, falling in the stable range is interpreted as a 'company failure is a rare occurrence and will only come about if there are major company or marketplace changes.'

Loan and credit-rating models

To potential lenders, the prediction of the future solvency of an aspiring client is extremely important and the use of models such as the bankruptcy or distress models, as they are sometimes called, is a vital cog in the decision-making machine.

Each bank has its own lending evaluation model which it uses to produce an assessment of a potential borrower, which it then uses in conjunction with other pieces of subjective and objectively measured data to help prepare the information dossier prior to the loan decision. Foster (1986) has an interesting, if a little dated, chapter on the types of models used in the USA.

Prediction of takeover targets

The prediction of takeover targets is another area where there are potentially large rewards for the model builder who can accurately predict companies that become takeover targets which are then successfully acquired. At present the work of researchers can be placed into two parts, either classificatory or predictive.

An article by Palepu (1986) reports a study using classificatory analysis. He took two samples of firms from the manufacturing and mining sectors. The first was a group made up of the 163 companies already taken over during the 1971–9 period under study. They were known as the targets. A second control sample of 256 companies was randomly selected from these sectors.

The mean values for each sample for ten different variables were compared on a univariable basis. It highlighted that, on average, the targets:

- had lower returns on the stock market over the four years prior to takeover;
- exhibited lower sales growth and greater resource surpluses, e.g. cash-rich firms;
- were not predominantly located in industries in which acquisitions had taken place in the previous year;
- were smaller in book-asset size than the average control sample firm.

These findings from the univariate comparisons reinforced some of the views already held by city individuals drawn from their own personal experiences. The more sophisticated multivariate analysis was then undertaken and Palepu (1986) reported that the likelihood ratio index never rose above 12.45 per cent, even though it was statistically significant. The likelihood ratio index is a measure of the overall explanatory power of the multivariate model. Such a low explanatory power suggests that any attempt at building a takeover predictive model upon which trading rules could be based is probably going to be unsuccessful.

The rationale behind attempts to build a predictive model for trading purposes is self-evident, and a number of authors have tried. Rege (1984) calculated financial ratios for liquidity, leverage, dividend payout, total asset turnover and profitability. He used these ratios to see if he could differentiate between those companies that are likely to be taken over and those that are not. His study was based on Canadian firms. His variables were unable to isolate potential takeover targets as they could not distinguish between taken-over and non-taken-over firms. Others, such as Bartley and Boardman (1990), have been marginally more successful, but results and methods are not yet commercially viable. However, since the benefits from the derivation of a model that could predict takeover targets are considerable, work will go on. Like the work in building models to forecast companies in financial distress, work in this area will continue, using expanded databases, longer time series, different groups of financial ratios, different statistical tools or perhaps the introduction of non-financial values, until it is felt either that the end result is not achievable or that a workable trading model is designed. For example, recent work has focused on utilizing financial ratios in models to predict corporate divestments, MBOs and the 'liquidation/merger' alternative (see Peel (1990) for a review of these).

Equity valuation models

Just as companies and other members of the investment community are interested in developing models for identifying takeover targets, and other corporate options, they have, from a much earlier time, been involved with the development of equity share valuation models for use in the selection of shares for buying or selling.

Underlying the development of these models is the belief that the market is not completely efficient in its pricing of shares, thus enabling some traders to gain better than average returns. These models are part of the fundamental approach to investment appraisal and are usually based on the use of data from the financial statements. They change over time as their relative effectiveness and reliability diminish, being replaced by new and different versions. As the models become part of the public domain through marketing by City firms, their effectiveness tends to depreciate due to the increased buying and selling pressures of the market arising from the ever-widening public knowledge of the model.

As an example, it is worth mentioning one model since it does appear to have had some limited success in detecting over- or undervalued shares. It is a US model called Value Line. Value Line uses a combination of three criteria to measure a share's price and profit characteristics against those of comparable shares in its listing. It then ranks the share on an expected 'relative price performance in the next twelve months' using this combination. Thus investors can select shares in the different groups which meet their risk and return needs, where the expected return for the group is indicated by the model. The three criteria are the non-parametric value position, the earnings momentum and the earnings surprise factor. These three do involve some financial statement information, predominantly profits related.

Many of the recommendations made by analysts concerning the under- or over-valuation of shares will be based to a greater or lesser extent on methods or models which combine objectively and subjectively based information. Financial ratios will have been used to derive some of the objective and some of the subjective elements incorporated in the model. Precisely which ratios, or with what weighting or in which combinations, will be dependent upon whose model. But no matter which model or approach is adopted there is a need to understand the financial information and ratios that are used in them. Jim Slater is regarded by many as a stock market investment expert, thanks to the success of both his advice and his commercial activities. His method for identifying undervalued shares, called 'the Zulu principle', still requires the 'analyst' to undertake some financial ratio analysis as part of the evaluation process (Slater 1996). The only certain thing is that no method yet has proved to be completely accurate in its predictions.

Asset-pricing models

A great amount of work by academics has been undertaken in empirically testing the asset-pricing models based on CAPM (capital asset pricing model) and APT (arbitrage pricing theory).

The two main parameters of interest are the beta (β) value of a security and the variances of its returns. The β value is a measure of a security's responsiveness to the movements of the market portfolio and is therefore a measure of the risk level of the security. It is also known as its systematic risk measure. β links the security's return with that of the market's risk premium over the risk-free rate through the expression

$$E(R_i) = R_f + \beta_i[E(R_m) - R_f]$$

where $E(R_i)$ is the expected return of the ith security, R_f is the return on the risk-free asset and $E(R_m)$ is the expected return on the market portfolio, which is the combination of the assets available in the market.

The Risk Measurement Service (RMS) of London Business School publishes a quarterly listing of the β values for shares traded on the London Stock Exchange, along with other linked parameters for those shares. With the ever-increasing size of the databases available, empirical research has discovered various specific effects in market operations, e.g. the small-firm effect, the weekend/Monday effect and so on. Details of these relatively specific and discrete effects can be incorporated into earlier, more general models, thus improving the accuracy of the inferences that can be made from patterns of past share returns or information gleaned from financial statements.

The derivation of a company's cost of capital through the CAPM approach which combined with the use of data from the balance sheet and profit and loss account of a company have helped produce a successful business for an American firm, Stern Stewart. Their conceptual approach derives two things, market value added (MVA) and economic value added (EVA). The former compares the total market value of the capital components of a company with the book value of the same components, shares, retained earnings, debentures, loans etc. found in the balance sheet – the difference between the two totals being the market value added. Effectively, the larger the positive MVA the more highly regarded the company in the market place. The computation of an annual EVA for the companies indicates historic support (or otherwise) for the futuristic view of the company from the MVA computation. EVA is a form of residual income for a company derived by deducting from a company's after-tax profit the capital cost of servicing its total sources of finance (debt and equity), the cost of equity being derived from the CAPM model. Thus an annual value of EVA is computed indicating historically the performance of the company in creating economic value. It is of course quite possible for a company to have a strong MVA and a negative EVA for a year. The concepts are an evolution from the shareholder value analysis (SVA) initiated by Rappaport (1986). Commercial interests abound that attempt to use financial and economic concepts with or without data obtained from the corporate accounts.

As described in the earlier sections of this chapter, links are still being investigated and developed between financial statement information or financial ratios and models designed for either predictive or explanatory purposes. It is clear, though, that at present research in these areas still has not reached a stage where systematic trading rules, built on financial statement information, can be used profitably by the investing public. Nevertheless the work continues to improve both the quality of the information reported in the financial statements and the sophistication of the models into which it is incorporated.

Valuation of BOC and the agreed share price

In July 1999 the BOC board announced that it had agreed terms for a cash offer for the company, to be made jointly by Air Liquide and Air Products at a price of £14.60 per ordinary share. Earlier in 1999 the BOC share price had been as low as £7.95. This had risen slowly over time to £10.20 and then, fuelled by speculation and rumour, rose to around £13.00 until the agreed price was announced. The magnitude of the change was considerable, with the agreed price showing a 43.1 per cent premium over the pre-bid price available in the late Spring of 1999 of £10.20. How do those various prices reflect the underlying shareholder value in the business? Many of the techniques mentioned in this chapter and the ratios discussed in earlier chapters can assist in answering this question.

The most simple and straightforward valuation method is to use the figures from the balance sheet, 30 September 1999, the date closest to the offer date. The original concept of the balance sheet was to provide the reader with a value for the entity. This method would therefore provide the Net Asset Value (NAV) or Net Book Value per share of the company.

$$\text{NAV per share} = \frac{\text{Total Net Assets} - \text{Minority equity interests}}{\text{Number of issued ordinary shares}}$$

$$\text{NAV} = \frac{2{,}284.0 - 270.9}{491} = £4.10$$

This value was based upon a mixture of depreciated historic cost and depreciated revalued amounts for fixed assets, and historic cost for current assets listed in the balance sheet and less any external sources of finance. This approach also failed to take into account any growth in earnings and dividends. Although BOC had not experienced particularly high earnings growth in recent prior years, there would have been expectations of future growth. This in turn should lead to further growth in dividends and this needs to be taken into account when assessing the value of BOC's shares.

One valuation model that does take growth in dividends into account is the Gordon Dividend Model. (See Gordon, 1962 for the original article or Samuels, Wilkes and Brayshaw, 2000, Chapter 15 for a more up-to-date description and critique.) The model can be expressed as follows:

$$P = \frac{D_1}{k - g}$$

where P is the price per share

$\quad D_1$ is the predicted dividend for next year

$\quad k$ is the cost of equity capital

$\quad g$ is the annual growth in dividends

Over the previous twelve years there had been a steady increase in annual dividends paid by BOC, even though the profits, in the form of EPS, have not grown at the same pace. [We had noted earlier that this situation has continued up to 2002.] The average annual rate of growth in dividends based on the previous twelve years had been 8.13 per cent, whilst for EPS it had only been 3.65 per cent. In the following illustration the figure that could be used for the predicted dividend for next year (D_1) is the *Investors Chronicle* (28 January 2000) estimate of 34.1p. Alternatively, if the 1999 dividend of 32.7p was grossed up at the 8.13 per cent growth rate then this results in an amount of 35.36p. The actual amount turned out to be 35.0p. In the four years to 2002 from 1998 the dividend grew by 23.9 per cent (see Table 14.5, page 176), i.e. an annual growth rate of 5.5 per cent. For consistency with the Gordon Dividend Model the amount of

35.36p was used as the estimate for D_1. It was then necessary to calculate the cost of equity capital (k). The capital asset pricing model (or CAPM), which was discussed earlier (see pages 197–8) is a widely used method for estimating cost of capital. The CAPM can be expressed as follows:

$$k = R_f + \beta(R_m - R_f)$$

where k is the equity return for BOC,

R_f was the projected risk free return, (the estimate for risk free UK Government stock was taken to be 5.75 per cent).

R_m was the projected stock market return, (the return on the FTSE Allshare index of 11.0 per cent was used here).

β was the equity beta for BOC (the appropriate Risk Measurement Service estimates this at 0.83).

If these values are applied to the CAPM model, then

$$k = 0.0575 + 0.83(0.11 - 0.0575)$$
$$= 0.1011 \text{ or } 10.11\%$$

Making use of the Gordon Dividend Model and substituting in these values, then

$$P = \frac{35.36}{0.1011 - 0.0813} = £17.86$$

If the *Investors Chronicle* value for the projected dividend of 34.1p had been used in the model, then this would have lowered the share price to £17.22. Both values considerably exceeded the offer price, which if based on the dividend and growth values of above, suggests that the company should be returning 10.55 per cent on its equity in order to be worth £14.60.

As mentioned on page 197, Jim Slater has developed an investment rule known as the 'Zulu principle'. One of the components of this is the relationship between the current price earnings ratio (PER) and the past growth rate in EPS. This relationship is the price earnings growth factor (PEG), where

$$\text{PEG} = \frac{\text{PER}}{\text{Past growth rate in EPS}}$$

For a share to be worth investing in, the PEG should be less than 1, the lower the better. For BOC Group, using the agreed shareprice of £14.60 the PER was 25.9 times, thus:

$$\text{PEG} = \frac{25.9}{3.65} = 7.1 \text{ times}$$

Even when the share price of BOC was at the lowest price it reached in 1999, its PEG would still have been 3.85 times, still very much higher than the recommended hurdle value of unity.

In summary, the shareholders' value, i.e. the share price, both in the past and even now has been driven primarily by the cash flows the company has generated for the shareholders. In the past this has been from dividends, and in the present from the cash offer. Had the company continued, the models suggest that continuing to increase dividends at the same rate ought to make the company worth even more than the agreed offer of £14.60, but the underlying profit fundamentals would not support that price. Similarly anyone following the 'Zulu' investment principle would not be prepared to pay anything like the agreed cash offer. However past growth in EPS is a backward looking measure and the PEG ratio is only relevant if past trends are expected to continue into the future. This may not be the case with BOC because of the major reorganization that was started in 1998. Even if the takeover bid did not go ahead the reorganization was expected to lead to significant improvements in future profitability and earnings per share. The value of the company's shares should reflect the stock market's belief, or otherwise, in those potential benefits.

As was pointed out above, a variety of approaches exist for determining the value of a company's shares. The NAV is based mainly on the historic cost of assets, appropriately depreciated, rather than the current market value of those assets, thus it is on the low side as the basis for determining an offer price. A potential purchaser therefore usually needs to offer a premium over the existing NAV in order to persuade the existing shareholders to agree to sell their holdings. Air Liquide and Air Products had offered a premium of over £10, or 250 per cent over the NAV, which would suggest that BOC had a range of intangible assets, the value of which had not been included in the Balance Sheet. For example the goodwill, brand names, patents, market share etc. of BOC were obviously of real value to the purchasing company. Presumably on merger the combined market share of the companies in the group was expected to reach a critical strategic level. Also, economies of scale might have been expected to reduce operational and overhead costs. Moreover, some of the tangible assets or individual subsidiary companies might have been perceived to have realizable values considerably in excess of book value, and these could then have been separately sold off post merger.

These are some of the reasons that might have provided a rationale for the proposed merger, and were also the reasons for the regulatory bodies in the USA and Europe taking such a close interest in the proposal. They were also possible explanations for the large price difference between the low NAV and the agreed bid price.

With the benefit of hindsight, Table 14.2 (page 175) indicates that from 1998 to 2002 there has been very little growth in EPS (5 per cent over the four years). Thus the recommended share price or the model generated price would not have been supported by the actual outcomes. The agreed offer was allowed to lapse in May 2000 once it had been announced that the US Federal Trade Commission (FTC) were unable to approve the proposed takeover.

Part Three

Appendices

Appendix A: Financial review of The BOC Group plc for the year ended 30 September 2002

Group five year record

Group five year record

Turnover[4]
£ million

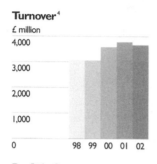

Profit before tax
(before exceptional items)
£ million

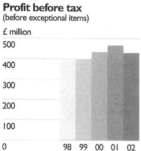

Profit and loss	1998 £ million	1999 £ million	2000 (restated) £ million	2001 (restated) £ million	2002 £ million
Turnover[1]					
Continuing operations	3,079.2	3,052.7	3,579.7	3,772.9	**3,657.7**
Discontinued operations	215.6	–	–	–	**–**
	3,294.8	3,052.7	3,579.7	3,772.9	**3,657.7**
Total operating profit before exceptional items[2]					
Continuing operations	473.9	479.9	496.4	530.6	**500.1**
Discontinued operations	6.0	–	–	–	**–**
	479.9	479.9	496.4	530.6	**500.1**
Exceptional items	(240.6)	(69.4)	(4.4)	(108.3)	**(74.5)**
Total operating profit	239.3	410.5	492.0	422.3	**425.6**
Profit/(loss) on termination/disposal of businesses	144.0	32.5	12.5	–	**(20.2)**
Profit on disposal of fixed assets	–	–	–	3.6	**–**
Profit before interest	383.3	443.0	504.5	425.9	**405.4**
Interest on net debt	(83.9)	(80.2)	(111.5)	(123.4)	**(103.1)**
Interest on pension scheme liabilities	–	–	(100.7)	(107.2)	**(106.1)**
Expected return on pension scheme assets	–	–	149.5	166.9	**139.1**
Net interest	(83.9)	(80.2)	(62.7)	(63.7)	**(70.1)**
Profit before tax	299.4	362.8	441.8	362.2	**335.3**
Tax on profit on ordinary activities	(123.6)	(85.3)	(135.2)	(104.6)	**(106.2)**
Profit after tax	175.8	277.5	306.6	257.6	**229.1**
Minority interests	(13.0)	(27.4)	(28.0)	(33.5)	**(26.2)**
Profit for the financial year	162.8	250.1	278.6	224.1	**202.9**
Earnings per 25p Ordinary share					
Basic:					
– on published profit	33.47p	51.36p	57.19p	46.03p	**41.36p**
– before exceptional items	53.27p	56.64p	53.53p	57.51p	**55.94p**
– on published profit, continuing operations	8.81p	51.36p	57.19p	46.03p	**41.36p**
Diluted:					
– on published profit	33.36p	51.17p	56.90p	45.87p	**41.21p**
– before exceptional items	53.09p	56.42p	53.26p	57.31p	**55.74p**
– on published profit, continuing operations	8.78p	51.17p	56.90p	45.87p	**41.21p**
Ordinary dividend per share[3]					
Actual	30.9p	32.7p	35.0p	37.0p	**38.0p**
Adjusted for inflation	33.4p	34.9p	36.2p	37.6p	**38.0p**
Number of fully paid Ordinary shares in issue at the year end (million)	489.0	491.0	492.2	494.4	**497.3**

1. Subsidiary undertakings only.
2. Including share of operating profit of joint ventures and associates.
3. Dividends paid in the calendar year.
4. Continuing operations.

Information for 2001 and 2000 has been restated to be on a comparable basis with 2002 following the adoption of FRS17 and FRS19 in 2002. Information for earlier years has not been restated. See also note 17 to the financial statements.

Capital employed
£ million

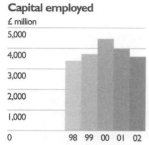

Capital expenditure
£ million

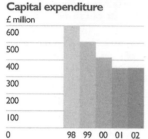

Balance sheet	1998 £ million	1999 £ million	2000 (restated) £ million	2001 (restated) £ million	2002 £ million
Fixed assets					
– intangible assets	4.2	36.5	49.2	48.1	**150.7**
– tangible assets	2,801.8	3,043.9	3,294.0	3,168.6	**3,027.4**
– joint ventures, associates and other investments	360.9	365.9	456.3	449.8	**468.6**
Working capital (excluding bank balances and short-term loans)	222.2	275.5	282.8	257.0	**203.1**
Deferred tax provisions	(30.5)	(36.4)	(295.8)	(294.3)	**(291.8)**
Other non current liabilities and provisions	(294.1)	(262.9)	(181.4)	(184.3)	**(173.7)**
Net borrowings and finance leases	(991.0)	(1,138.5)	(1,308.4)	(1,272.1)	**(1,325.6)**
Net assets excluding pension assets and liabilities	2,073.5	2,284.0	2,296.7	2,172.8	**2,058.7**
Pension assets[5]	–	–	402.0	107.0	**54.3**
Pension liabilities[5]	–	–	(31.1)	(56.0)	**(311.0)**
Net assets including pension assets and liabilities	2,073.5	2,284.0	2,667.6	2,223.8	**1,802.0**
Shareholders' capital and reserves	1,882.9	2,013.1	2,394.0	2,086.2	**1,684.1**
Minority shareholders' interests	190.6	270.9	273.6	137.6	**117.9**
Total capital and reserves	2,073.5	2,284.0	2,667.6	2,223.8	**1,802.0**

Other selected financial information
Total capital employed[6]

	1998	1999	2000	2001	2002
Total capital and reserves	2,073.5	2,284.0	2,667.6	2,223.8	**1,802.0**
Non current liabilities and provisions	324.6	299.3	477.2	478.6	**465.5**
Net borrowings and finance leases[7]	991.0	1,138.5	1,308.4	1,272.1	**1,325.6**
	3,389.1	3,721.8	4,453.2	3,974.5	**3,593.1**
Total assets	4,444.6	4,814.0	5,618.3	5,060.0	**4,947.4**
Long-term liabilities and provisions	1,316.4	1,278.7	1,399.0	1,554.5	**1,897.5**
Capital expenditure[1]	596.2	505.4	413.7	352.6	**354.3**
Depreciation and amortisation[1]	270.7	270.8	313.3	329.5	**330.9**

Employees

	1998	1999	2000	2001	2002
UK	11,107	10,067	9,929	10,597	**11,266**
Overseas	25,979	32,057	32,780	32,574	**35,014**
Continuing operations	37,086	42,124	42,709	43,171	**46,280**

Ratios

	1998	1999	2000	2001	2002
Return on average capital employed[8]	13.4%	13.1%	12.5%	12.9%	**12.3%**
Net debt/capital employed	29.2%	30.6%	29.4%	32.0%	**36.9%**
Net debt/equity	47.8%	49.8%	49.0%	57.2%	**73.6%**

5. Pension assets represents the excess of pension assets over pension liabilities in countries where pension assets exceed pension liabilities. Pension liabilities represents the excess of pension liabilities over pension assets in countries where pension liabilities exceed pension assets.
6. As defined in note 1 b) to the financial statements.
7. Analysed for 2002 and 2001 in note 3 c) to the financial statements.
8. Operating profit before exceptional items as a percentage of the average capital employed. The average is calculated on a monthly basis.

Information for 2001 and 2000 has been restated to be on a comparable basis with 2002 following the adoption of FRS17 and FRS19 in 2002. Information for earlier years has not been restated. See also note 17 to the financial statements.

Finance and treasury review

Net debt/equity

Percentage

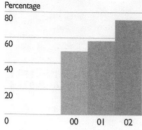

Net debt/capital employed

Percentage

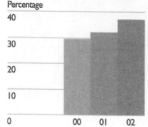

Restructuring

In August 2001 the company announced a business initiative with the objectives of releasing cash tied up in unproductive assets, improving cash generation and identifying restructuring opportunities. Programmes were implemented to divest some assets and to restructure and improve returns in the businesses being retained.

Divestments Proceeds of £39.0 million have been received in the year, in addition to the £41.2 million received last year, making a total of £80.2 million received to date. Management now expects further proceeds of some £30 million to be received in 2003. Proceeds from divestments will cover the cash costs of restructuring.

Restructuring Costs of restructuring programmes amounting to £47.2 million have been charged this year, in addition to the £35.8 million charged in 2001. The cost of restructuring this year includes £34.4 million related to the programmes announced in August 2001, which are now substantially complete with remaining costs of some £4 million expected to be charged in 2003. These programmes have resulted in 1,516 job losses with some 100 more expected. Further restructuring opportunities have been identified resulting in an additional cost of £12.8 million charged this year. Management expects the restructuring programmes to deliver efficiency and cost savings amounting to £55 million a year when completed, of which a run rate of £36 million has already been achieved.

Operational efficiency Operational efficiencies in Process Gas Solutions have been identified. These programmes were originally targeted to achieve further savings of some £50 million a year by the end of 2003, which has already been achieved. Further opportunities for savings from operational efficiencies in Industrial and Special Products have been identified.

Corporate transactions

In March 2002 BOC announced plans to merge its process plant operations with Linde Engineering in the US to form a new company, Linde BOC Process Plants LLC. The transaction was completed in September 2002. The costs of £21.3 million for closing BOC's Process Plants business have been charged this year as an exceptional item. Management expects cost savings to be worth some £15 million a year. This transaction is also explained in note 2 b) to the financial statements.

In September 2002 BOC and Air Liquide announced a conditional agreement to merge their industrial and medical gases businesses in Japan to form a combined company to be called Japan Air Gases. Valuations undertaken as part of the proposed business combination have resulted in an exceptional write down of £21.2 million in the profit and loss account in 2002. The transaction remains subject to approval by the Japanese competition authority. It is expected that Japan Air Gases will achieve synergy benefits estimated at £26 million a year by 2005. This transaction is also explained in note 2 b) to the financial statements.

Pre-conditional offer for the Group

As indicated last year, further costs associated with the pre-conditional offer for the Group were incurred during 2002. These were £6.1 million for share option and other costs related to the retention of key employees. All of the costs have been taken to the profit and loss account as exceptional items. There are no further costs to come.

Financial indicators

The trends of financial indicators which, taken together, are a measure of the performance and efficiency of the Group's finance and tax structures, are:

	2002	2001 (restated)	2000 (restated)
Interest cover (times)[1]	4.9	4.3	4.5
Interest cover (times)[2]	4.8	4.2	3.8
Net debt/equity (%)	73.6	57.2	49.0
Net debt/capital employed (%)	36.9	32.0	29.4
Average cost of net borrowings, before capitalised interest (%)	6.3	7.4	8.2
Average cost of net borrowings, after capitalised interest (%)	6.2	7.2	7.7
Group tax rate (%)[3]	30.0	32.5	33.4

1. Before exceptional and FRS17 financing items.
2. Before exceptional and FRS17 financing items and excluding interest capitalised.
3. Before exceptional items.

The ratios are commented on below in the appropriate section.

Financing

The Group has access to a range of funding. Debt finance is raised by issuing bonds, commercial paper, other obligations to investors and through borrowings from banks.

As well as medium and long-term borrowings, the Group maintains short-term borrowings, principally in the form of commercial paper and bank borrowings. The Group maintains US$420 million of committed multi-currency facilities with a group of relationship banks. These facilities mature between 2002 and 2004 and provide back-up for the issue of commercial paper. Additional committed facilities are maintained by the principal operating units in the Group.

Overall, net debt increased by £53.5 million as a result of a net cash outflow of £120.3 million offset by £25.0 million inflow from the issue of shares and £41.8 million for the effect of exchange rate and other movements. In 2001, net debt decreased by £36.3 million as a result of a net cash outflow of £2.3 million offset by £16.9 million inflow from the issue of shares and £21.7 million for the effect of exchange rate and other movements. During the year, borrowings by the parent company increased reflecting the company's effort to centralise its longer term funding needs.

The gearing ratio (net debt including finance leases as a percentage of capital employed) was 36.9 per cent in 2002 compared with 32.0 per cent in 2001 and 29.4 per cent in 2000. The decline in the value of pension fund assets following the fall in world equity markets accounted for some three per cent of the increase in 2002. The 2002 year end net debt/equity ratio was 73.6 per cent, compared with 57.2 per cent in 2001 and 49.0 per cent in 2000. As with the gearing ratio, the increase in the ratio in 2002 was mainly due to the decline in the value of pension fund assets.

The Group has access to a diverse range of debt finance including commercial paper, public bonds and bank borrowings which, it believes, will be available to meet long-term financing needs. The Group has sufficient facilities to cover likely borrowing needs. Management presently anticipates that capital expenditure in 2003 will be at a slightly higher level than in 2002 and will be covered by cash inflow from operating activities.

Management of financial risks

The board of directors sets the treasury policies and objectives of the Group which include controls over the procedures used to manage currency, interest rate and credit risk. The approach to managing risk is set out below. This approach is expected to continue during the next financial year. On a day-to-day basis, Group treasury carries out these policies, with regular review meetings with the Group finance director. Specific and significant activities need approval from the finance committee, which includes any two directors of the company.

Currency risk The Group faces currency risk principally on its net assets, most of which are in currencies other than sterling. Currency movements can therefore have a significant effect on the Group's balance sheet when translating these foreign currency assets into sterling. In order to reduce this effect the Group manages its borrowings, where practicable and cost effective, to hedge its foreign currency assets.

Where possible, hedging is done using direct borrowings in the same currency as the assets being hedged or through the use of other hedging methods such as currency swaps. Group borrowings are currently held in a wide range of currencies and, after swaps, 86 per cent of net debt (2001: 88 per cent) is denominated in the principal currencies affecting the Group: US dollars, Australian dollars, Japanese yen, South African rand and sterling. The aggregate of the notional principal values of currency swaps was £360.7 million (2001: £359.6 million) spread over a range of currencies. The fair value of such swaps is included in note 3 d) i) to the financial statements.

The balance sheets of overseas operations are translated into sterling at the closing rates of exchange for the year and any exchange difference is dealt with as a movement in reserves. This is explained more fully in the accounting policy note on page 71. The profit and loss accounts of overseas businesses are translated at average rates of exchange and this translation impact directly affects the profit and loss account of the Group.

The Group manages its currency flows to minimise currency transaction exchange risk and forward contracts are used as appropriate to hedge net currency flows and selected individual transactions. The Group's foreign exchange cover is mainly executed in the UK (which includes cover for exposures on net trade flows of the Group's companies in the US and certain other countries), Australia, Japan and South Africa. The aggregate principal amount of forward cover outstanding at 30 September 2002 amounted to £133.9 million (2001: £245.0 million).

Interest rate risk At 30 September 2002, the Group's net debt position after interest rate hedging activity included a net exposure of £497.3 million (2001: £379.4 million) to floating interest rates. Based on the Group's 2002 year end level and composition of net debt, an increase in average interest rates of one per cent per annum would result in a decrease in future earnings, before tax, of £5.0 million per annum (2001: £3.8 million).

Interest cover
(before exceptional and
FRS17 financing items)

Times

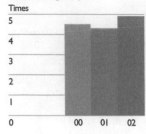

**Average cost of
net borrowings**[1]

Percentage

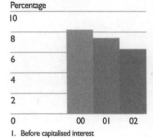

1. Before capitalised interest

In order to manage interest rate risk the Group maintains both floating rate and fixed rate debt. At 30 September 2002, there was a 38:62 ratio (2001: 30:70) between floating and fixed rate net debt. Underlying borrowings are arranged on both a fixed rate and a floating rate basis and, where appropriate, the Group uses interest rate swaps to vary this mix and to manage the Group's interest rate exposure.

At 30 September 2002, the aggregate of the notional principal values of swap agreements which affect the floating rate/fixed rate mix was £420.0 million (2001: £375.4 million). The fair value of such swaps is included in note 3 d) i) to the financial statements.

Foreign exchange risk At 30 September 2002, the Group had outstanding forward exchange contracts totalling £133.9 million (2001: £245.0 million) in respect of its actual and forecast transaction exposures. The fair value of these contracts at 30 September 2002 amounted to a gain of £4.9 million (2001: a loss of £9.1 million). A ten per cent appreciation of sterling would increase the fair value of these contracts by £7.4 million (2001: £19.2 million).

In addition to these forward contracts, the Group is exposed to foreign exchange movements on its net debt position. At 30 September 2002 net debt, after currency swaps, comprised net sterling liabilities of £345.2 million (2001: £298.2 million) and net currency liabilities of £980.4 million (2001: £973.9 million). Based on the Group's 2002 year end level and composition of net debt, a ten per cent appreciation of sterling would result in a reduction in the value of net currency liabilities of £89.1 million (2001: £88.5 million).

The Group does not undertake any trading activity in financial instruments nor does it enter into any leveraged derivative transactions.

Counterparty risk Cash deposits and other financial instruments give rise to credit risk on the amounts due from counterparties. Credit risk is managed by limiting the aggregate amount and duration of exposure to any one counterparty depending upon its credit rating and by regular reviews of these ratings. The possibility of material loss arising in the event of non-performance by a counterparty is considered unlikely by management.

The currency and interest rate hedging profile of the Group's borrowings at 30 September 2002 is shown in note 3 to the financial statements. Further information on financial risk management is also given in note 3 to the financial statements.

Interest on net debt
The net charge before deducting capitalised interest and before the Group's share of interest of joint ventures and associates was £80.6 million in 2002, which represented 6.3 per cent of average net borrowings during the year. After taking into account capitalised interest and the Group's share of joint ventures and associates the net charge was £103.1 million. Interest cover (the number of times that the interest charge on net debt is covered by operating profit before exceptional items) increased to 4.9 times (2001: 4.3 times, 2000: 4.5 times). The amount of interest capitalised in subsidiaries during the year was £2.0 million (2001: £2.5 million, 2000: £7.1 million). After deducting capitalised interest and excluding joint ventures and associates, the net charge was £78.6 million which represents 6.2 per cent of average net borrowings.

Net interest on pension financing items
The interest on pension scheme liabilities was £106.1 million in 2002 compared with £107.2 million in 2001. The expected return on pension scheme assets was £139.1 million in 2002 compared with £166.9 million in 2001. The decrease was due to the decline in world equity markets which has reduced the value of the pension scheme assets on which the expected return on assets is based.

Debt maturity profile
The maturity profile of the Group's gross borrowings is as follows:

	2002		2001	
	£ million	%	£ million	%
More than five years	549.5	36.4	630.1	41.8
Two to five years	390.6	25.8	237.0	15.7
One to two years	180.9	12.0	152.8	10.2
Within one year	390.1	25.8	486.4	32.3
Total	1,511.1	100.0	1,506.3	100.0

The lengthening of the maturity profile was accomplished primarily through the issuance of one bond and two smaller medium-term notes. These funds, raised by the parent company, were used to support acquisition activity and to re-finance existing short-term debt.

A portion of the debt which matures within one year is commercial paper issued by various Group companies. The Group maintains US$420 million of committed multi-currency facilities with a group of relationship banks. These facilities mature between 2002 and 2004 and provide back-up for the issue of commercial paper. Additional committed facilities are maintained by the principal operating units in the Group.

Group tax rate
(before exceptional items)
Percentage

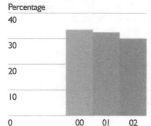

Other contractual obligations

The maturity of other contractual obligations of the Group is as follows:

	Operating leases £ million	Unconditional purchase obligations £ million	Total contractual cash obligations £ million
Due after more than five years	96.1	195.4	291.5
Due within two to five years	59.6	191.7	251.3
Due within one to two years	29.8	66.6	96.4
Due within one year	35.6	67.8	103.4
Total	221.1	521.5	742.6

In addition, the Group has provided guarantees to third parties of £158.0 million at 30 September 2002. These predominantly relate to guarantees of the borrowings of BOC's joint venture company which supplies nitrogen to the Mexican oil company, Pemex. These borrowings are scheduled to be repaid over the next eight years.

Inflation

Over the last three years, inflation has not had a material impact on the revenue or profit of the Group.

Taxation

The tax charge for 2002 of £106.2 million is calculated in accordance with UK accounting standards, including FRS19 (deferred tax), under which full provision is made for deferred taxes.

Excluding exceptional items, the effective tax rate in 2002 was 30 per cent, a reduction of 2.5 per cent from 2001. Including exceptional items, the tax rate was 32 per cent. The Group pays corporation tax in the UK at a rate of 30 per cent.

The Group is currently liable to pay federal tax at the rate of 35 per cent in the US. This is reduced by the existence of tax credits. In the other principal subsidiaries, the tax rate is typically between 30 per cent and 42 per cent.

Contingencies

The Group monitors all contingent liabilities including matters relating to the environment via a process of consultation and evaluation which includes senior management, internal and external legal advisers and internal and external technical advisers. This process results in conclusions with respect to potential exposure and provisions are made or adjusted accordingly by reference to accounting principles. Management believes that the Group has adequately provided for contingencies which are likely to become payable in the future. None of these contingencies is material to the Group's financial condition, results of operations or liquidity.

Legal proceedings

Group companies are parties to various legal proceedings, including some in which claims for damages in large amounts have been asserted.

The outcome of litigation to which Group companies are party cannot be readily foreseen, but the directors believe that such litigation will be disposed of without material effect on the Group's financial condition, results of operations or liquidity.

Similar to many other companies, BOC has been named, in the ordinary course of its business, in civil proceedings involving claims of toxic tort bodily injury related to asbestos and certain metals and arising out of the use of certain of the company's welding products.

Since BOC acquired Airco in 1978, all proceedings that have been concluded thus far have either been successfully defended or otherwise resolved on terms favourable to the company. To date, the costs of defending or otherwise resolving these proceedings, have not been material to the company's financial statements.

The company believes that it has strong defences to the claims asserted in these proceedings and intends to vigorously defend such claims. Based on the company's experience to date, together with the company's current assessment of the merits of the claims being asserted, and applicable insurance, the company believes that continued defence and resolution of these proceedings will not have a material adverse effect on its financial statements.

Insurance

Operational management is responsible for managing business risks. Several Group departments advise management on different aspects of risk and monitor results. Insurance cover is held against major catastrophes. For any such event, the Group will bear an initial cost before external cover begins.

Critical accounting policies

The principal accounting policies affecting the results of operations and financial condition are set out on pages 71 to 73 of the financial statements. The application of certain of these policies requires assumptions or subjective judgements by management. Management bases these on a combination of past experience and any other evidence that is relevant to the particular circumstances.

The application of these assumptions and judgements affects the reported amounts of profit during the year and the assets and liabilities at the balance sheet date. Actual results may differ from the estimates calculated using these assumptions and judgements. Management believes that the following are the critical policies where the assumptions and judgements made could have a significant impact on the consolidated financial statements.

Tangible fixed assets A significant part of the capital employed of the Group, particularly in the Process Gas Solutions and Industrial and Special Products lines of business, is invested in tangible fixed assets. The nature of the business demands significant capital investment to renew or increase production capacity or to enable the business to achieve greater productivity and efficiency.

It is the Group's policy to depreciate tangible fixed assets, except land, on a straight line basis over the effective lives of the assets. This ensures that there is an appropriate matching of the revenue earned with the capital costs of production and delivery of goods and services. A key element of this policy is the estimate of the effective life applied to each category of fixed assets which, in turn, determines the annual depreciation charge. In deciding the appropriate lives to be applied, management takes into account various factors including, among other things, the accumulated experience of the effective asset lives from historic business operations and an assessment of the likely impact of any changes in technology.

While Group earnings in any period would fluctuate if different asset lives were applied, in some cases the original estimated life of an asset is closely related to contractual arrangements with large customers. Some of the earnings impact of choosing a different asset life would be mitigated, as the different life may reflect different contractual arrangements with such customers. Nevertheless, variations in the effective lives could impact the earnings of the business through an increase or decrease in the depreciation charge.

Intangible fixed assets In a similar manner to tangible fixed assets, management uses its judgement to determine the extent to which goodwill arising from the acquisition of a business has a value that will benefit the performance of the Group over future periods. It is the Group's policy to amortise goodwill over its useful economic life. This takes into account, among other things, the maturity of the business acquired and its product and customer base. Any change in these assumptions would have an impact on the earnings of the Group.

Retirement benefits Results of the Group include costs relating to the provision of retirement benefits for employees. It is the directors' responsibility to set the assumptions used in determining the key elements of the costs of meeting such future obligations. The assumptions are based on actual historical experience and are set after consultation with the Group's actuaries. They include the assumptions used for regular service costs and for the financing elements related to the pension schemes' assets and liabilities. Whilst management believes that the assumptions used are appropriate, a change in the assumptions used would affect both the operating profit and net interest cost of the Group.

Environmental provisions In certain parts of the business, mainly in the US, the Group has obligations to carry out environmental clean-ups at former and current production sites. Many of these obligations will not arise for a number of years, and the costs are difficult to predict accurately. Management uses its judgement and experience to provide an appropriate amount for the likely cost of such clean-ups, and the amounts, if material, are discounted to present values. Both the amount of anticipated costs, and the interest rates used to discount such costs, are subjective. The use of different assumptions would impact the earnings of the Group.

Current asset provisions In the course of normal trading activities, management uses its judgement in establishing the net realisable value of various elements of working capital – principally stocks, work-in-progress and accounts receivable. Provisions are established for obsolete or slow moving stocks, bad or doubtful debts and product warranties. Actual costs in future periods may be different from the provisions established and any such differences would affect future earnings of the Group.

Accounting

The accounts this year comply with the requirements of the new UK accounting standard on deferred tax (FRS19). In addition, the UK accounting standard on retirement benefits (FRS17) has been fully adopted. Last year the Group applied the transitional arrangements permitted under this standard. Comparative figures for 2001 and 2000 have been restated for these two standards.

The report and accounts also continues to include US reporting requirements. The report on remuneration follows the disclosure requirements of the UK Listing Authority Listing Rules and the UK Companies Act 1985. Where appropriate, in order to improve clarity, voluntary disclosures are also given.

Average exchange rates:

US dollar

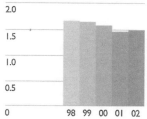

Australian dollar

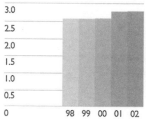

Japanese yen

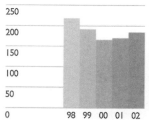

South African rand

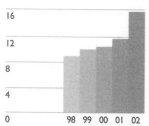

As a global business the Group supports initiatives to harmonise accounting standards. Its own accounting policies are based on accounting principles generally accepted in the UK (UK GAAP) but the Group also considers the implications of US GAAP and International Accounting Standards. The Group is planning for the move to report under International Accounting Standards in line with the timetable set out in European Union legislation. This will first apply to the report and accounts for the year ended 30 September 2006.

The Group plays an active part in accounting developments by responding to new proposals and by appropriate representation.

US GAAP

The financial statements of the Group have been prepared in accordance with UK GAAP, which differs in certain respects from US GAAP.

The US accounting information in note 16 to the financial statements gives a summary of the principal differences between the amounts determined in accordance with the Group's accounting policies (based on UK GAAP) and amounts determined in accordance with US GAAP together with the reconciliation of profit before tax and shareholders' funds from a UK GAAP basis to a US GAAP basis, presentation of the US GAAP measure of comprehensive income and a movement in shareholders' funds on a US GAAP basis.

The profit before tax for the year ended 30 September 2002 under US GAAP was £413.9 million (2001: £377.1 million, 2000: £417.7 million), compared with profit before tax of £335.3 million in 2002 (2001: £362.2 million, 2000: £441.8 million) under UK GAAP. Shareholders' funds at 30 September 2002 under US GAAP were £2,061.0 million (2001: £2,138.9 million), compared with £1,684.1 million (2001: £2,086.2 million) under UK GAAP. The difference primarily results from the differing accounting treatment of pensions, goodwill, financial instruments, restructuring costs, investments and fixed asset revaluations.

Exchange rates

The majority of the Group's operations are located outside the UK and operate in currencies other than sterling.

The effects of fluctuations in the relationship between the various currencies are extremely complex and variations in any particular direction may not have a consistent impact on the reported results. In 2002, sterling strengthened against three of the principal currencies affecting the Group: by two per cent against the US dollar, by eight per cent against the Japanese yen and by 36 per cent against the South African rand. Against the Australian dollar, sterling was almost unchanged.

In 2001, sterling weakened against the US dollar, but strengthened against the Australian dollar, the Japanese yen and the South African rand.

In 2000, sterling weakened against the US dollar and Japanese yen but strengthened against the South African rand. It was almost unchanged against the Australian dollar.

The rates of exchange to sterling for the currencies which have principally affected the Group's results over the last five years were:

	2002	2001	2000	1999	1998
US dollar					
At 30 September	1.57	1.47	1.48	1.65	1.70
Average for the year	1.47	1.44	1.56	1.63	1.65
Highest rate during year	1.58	1.50	1.67	1.72	1.71
Lowest rate during year	1.41	1.37	1.40	1.55	1.61
Australian dollar					
At 30 September	2.89	2.98	2.73	2.52	2.87
Average for the year	2.77	2.76	2.56	2.55	2.55
Highest rate during year	3.00	3.03	2.85	2.87	2.96
Lowest rate during year	2.54	2.62	2.45	2.33	2.19
Japanese yen					
At 30 September	191.45	175.09	159.77	175.34	231.32
Average for the year	184.34	170.04	166.03	191.43	218.08
Highest rate during year	193.05	181.26	178.67	230.73	240.27
Lowest rate during year	173.82	153.13	149.77	168.23	194.20
South African rand					
At 30 September	16.58	13.24	10.68	9.88	9.99
Average for the year	15.64	11.47	10.24	9.82	8.74
Highest rate during year	19.49	13.26	11.18	10.43	10.86
Lowest rate during year	13.00	10.54	9.92	9.12	7.53

On 12 November 2002, the latest practicable date for inclusion in this report and accounts, the rates of exchange to sterling for the principal currencies were as follows: US dollar 1.59; Australian dollar 2.83; Japanese yen 190.08; South African rand 15.59.

The highest and lowest rates of exchange for sterling against the US dollar for the last six months were:

	May	June	July	August	September	October
High	1.47	1.53	1.58	1.57	1.57	1.57
Low	1.45	1.46	1.52	1.52	1.53	1.54

Europe's single currency

Europe's single currency, the euro, was launched for business-to-business use on 1 January 1999. On 1 January 2002 the euro was adopted for all purposes in those countries participating. Sterling continued unaffected for use in the UK.

BOC businesses in Europe were able to operate in euros from January 1999. Subsequent system upgrades have provided for full euro functionality, and BOC suffered no issues with the full changeover. Costs to date have been fully expensed.

Principal operating companies

The following operating companies principally affect the amount of profit or assets of the Group:
- The BOC Group Inc, a wholly-owned Delaware corporation and a subsidiary of The BOC Group Inc, a wholly-owned Nevada corporation.
- BOC Limited, a wholly-owned English company.
- BOC Limited, a wholly-owned Australian company.
- Gist Limited, a wholly-owned English company.
- Osaka Sanso Kogyo KK, a Japanese company, in which the Group's shareholding is 97 per cent.
- African Oxygen Limited, a South African company, in which the Group's shareholding is 55 per cent.

Supplier payment policy

The Group applies a policy of agreeing and clearly communicating the terms of payment as part of the commercial arrangements negotiated with suppliers and then paying according to those terms. In addition the UK-based businesses have committed to the 'Better Payment Practice Code'. A copy of the code can be obtained from the Department of Trade and Industry, DTI Publications Orderline, Admail 528, London SW1W 8YT.

For UK businesses, of amounts owing to suppliers, trade creditors represents 52 days at 30 September 2002.

Going concern

The directors are confident, after having made appropriate enquiries, that both the company and the Group have adequate resources to continue in operation for the foreseeable future. For this reason, they continue to adopt the going concern basis in preparing the accounts. Management believes that its current credit facilities provide sufficient working capital to meet the present requirements of its existing businesses and that the gearing ratio is appropriate given the nature of the Group's activities.

Substantial holdings

Details of substantial holdings of Ordinary shares at 12 November 2002 are shown on page 115.

Corporate governance

The BOC Group is committed to business integrity, high ethical values and professionalism in all its activities. As an essential part of this commitment, the board supports the highest standards in corporate governance.

Board and committees

The board comprised five executive directors including the chief executive and six non-executive directors including the chairman at 30 September 2002. Roberto Mendoza was appointed as an additional non-executive director on 9 October 2002. Biographies of each of the directors and their board committee memberships can be found on pages 8 and 9. The non-executive directors bring a wide range of experience and expertise to the board and are all considered by the board to be independent. Göran Lundberg is the senior independent director, having been appointed to this role in November 2001. The roles of chairman and chief executive are separate. This has been the case since 1994.

There is a formal schedule of matters reserved to the board which includes the review of strategic and policy issues. These matters are reviewed annually at a combined board and strategy meeting lasting over a period of two days, with updates provided to the board on a regular basis. The board meets six times a year, with two meetings being held at major operating subsidiaries of The BOC Group, one at a location outside the UK.

There are six principal board committees and further details can be found on page 9. All the independent non-executive directors are members of both the audit and management resources committees with the exception of the independent non-executive chairman who attends by invitation. The nomination committee comprises all the independent non-executive directors and the chief executive.

In addition to ensuring the timely issue of board meeting papers, regular reports on the company and market sector activity together with updates on governance and regulatory matters affecting BOC are provided to the board.

All directors have access to the advice and services of the company secretary and there is a well established procedure enabling any director, in the furtherance of his or her duties, to seek independent professional advice at the company's expense.

The Group has long recognised the vital role that non-executive directors have in ensuring high governance standards and the BOC board has for many years had a significant non-executive element of high calibre. The nomination committee identify, evaluate and nominate candidates to fill vacancies for approval by the board as a whole. Non-executive directors are initially appointed for a three year term after which their appointment, whilst not automatic, may be extended subject to mutual agreement and shareholder approval.

The non-executive directors have full access to both management and internal and external auditors, and are encouraged to stay fully abreast of the Group's business through site visits and meetings with senior management. Training and briefings are available to all directors on appointment and subsequently, as necessary, taking into account existing qualification and experience.

During October 2002 the directors completed a self evaluation which included a review of processes and arrangements for the board and the audit, management resources and nomination committees. The findings and recommendations for change are currently being implemented including a more comprehensive training and induction programme for directors.

Directors and officers

The directors holding office at the date of this report are named on pages 8 and 9. Each of the following new non-executive directors were appointed: Rob Margetts on 4 October 2001, Fabiola Arredondo on 8 November 2001, Matthew Miau on 23 January 2002 and Roberto Mendoza on 9 October 2002.

At the conclusion of the Annual General Meeting held on 18 January 2002 Sir David John stepped down as chairman. He also retired as a non-executive director, as did Howard Macdonald and Harry Groome.

The officers of the company are the executive directors and other members of the executive management board as named on pages 10 and 11. All held office throughout the year ended 30 September 2002 and there have been no changes up to the date of this report.

Directors' remuneration

The management resources committee review and make recommendations to the board on remuneration policy. A report on remuneration is set out on pages 56 to 63.

Communications with shareholders

The board considers communications with shareholders, whether institutional investors, private or employee shareholders, to be extremely important. Results are published quarterly, and half year and annual reviews are sent to all shareholders. A copy of the full report and accounts is available by election or on request. The Annual General Meeting provides an opportunity for shareholders to question directors. The chairmen of each of the board committees are present at the meeting. During the year responses are given to letters received from shareholders on a variety of subjects. There is a programme of regular dialogue with major institutional shareholders and fund managers.

The company's website (www.boc.com) provides financial and other business information about The BOC Group.

Accountability and audit

Statements of the respective responsibilities of the directors and auditors for these accounts are set out on pages 64 and 65.

To enhance further the confidence of investors in the independence of the independent auditors and their report, the board of BOC has introduced a policy that defines which other services PricewaterhouseCoopers may or may not provide to BOC. The policy requires the provision of these services to be approved in advance by the audit committee of the board. A full statement of the fees paid for audit and non-audit services is provided in note 2 c) to the financial statements.

Risk management and internal controls

This statement of compliance with the Combined Code on Corporate Governance in respect of risk management and internal controls is in line with the arrangements set out by the UK Listing Authority.

The board has overall responsibility for the Group's system of risk management and internal controls.

The schedule of matters reserved to the board ensures that the directors maintain full and effective control over all significant strategic, financial, organisational and compliance issues.

Risk management The BOC risk management programme assists management throughout the Group to identify, assess and mitigate business risk.

Introduced in 2001, the risk management programme is supported by a dedicated central team of risk specialists. To ensure all parts of the Group have a firm understanding of risk, the central team has led over 100 risk workshops and reviews around the world in the past two years. These risk assessments have been broad, covering: risks in strategy; risks in achieving commitments contained in performance contracts; risks in organisational change; risks associated with major projects; and risks involving acquisitions. The risk management process operates throughout BOC and is applied equally to the global lines of business, the business units and corporate functions.

The output from each assessment is a list of prioritised risks with associated action plans to mitigate them. Line managers are responsible for these action plans and their progress is reported, as required, as part of their performance contract reviews.

As part of the strategy review conducted in 2002, BOC has identified six areas that have to be managed well to achieve our objectives. These are; managing growth within a competitive environment, managing the challenges in Asia, the semiconductor cycle, pricing and productivity, managing change successfully and understanding the global economic environment and its impact on BOC's plans.

A report is made to the board twice a year. Line of business chief executives made presentations to the board in May and October 2002, covering actions which had been completed and the status of continuing action plans to manage the Group's key risks. The risks reviewed include those described in the risk factors section on pages 29 and 30.

BOC views risk management as integral to good business practice. The programme is designed to support management's decision making and to improve the reliability of business performance. BOC will continue to embed the management of risk into all its management processes.

Internal controls The directors have delegated to executive management the establishment and implementation of a system of internal controls appropriate to the various business environments in which it operates. The Group operates under a system of controls that has been developed and refined over time to meet its current and future needs and the risks and opportunities to which it is exposed. These controls, which are communicated through various operating and procedural manuals and processes, include but are not limited to:

- the definition of the organisational structure and the appropriate delegation of authorities to operational management.
- procedures for the review and authorisation of capital investments through the investment committee including post-acquisition reviews and appraisals.
- strategic planning and the related annual planning and re-forecasting process including the ongoing review by the board of the Group's strategies.
- the establishment of individual business unit annual performance targets and the quarterly business review of actual performance.
- the monthly financial reporting and review of financial results and other operating statistics such as the health and safety reports as well as the Group's published quarterly financial statements, which are based on a standardised reporting process.
- accounting and financial reporting policies to ensure the consistency, integrity and accuracy of the Group's accounting records.
- specific treasury policies and objectives and the ongoing reporting and review of all significant transactions and financing operations.

The internal control system is monitored and supported by an internal audit function that operates on a global basis and reports its results to management and the audit committee of the board on the Group's operations. The work of the internal auditors is focused on the areas of greatest risk to the Group determined on the basis of a risk management approach to audit.

There have been regular reviews by the audit committee of the board of the effectiveness of the Group's overall internal control processes throughout the year and up to the date of this report and accounts.

The directors therefore believe that the Group's system of risk management and internal controls provides reasonable but not absolute assurance that assets are safeguarded, transactions are authorised and recorded properly and that material errors and irregularities are either prevented or would be detected within a timely period.

Having reviewed its effectiveness, the directors are not aware of any significant weakness or deficiency in the Group's system of internal controls during the period covered by this report and accounts.

Disclosure controls and procedures
The Group chief executive and Group finance director, after evaluating the effectiveness of the Group's disclosure controls and procedures (as defined in US Exchange Act Rules 13a-14(c)) within 90 days of the date of this report, have concluded that, as of such date, the Group's disclosure controls and procedures were effective to ensure that material information relating to the Group was made known to them by others within the Group particularly during the period in which this annual report and accounts was being prepared.

There were no significant changes in the Group's internal controls or in other factors that could significantly affect these controls subsequent to the date the Group chief executive and Group finance director completed their evaluation, nor were there any significant deficiencies or material weaknesses in the Group's internal controls requiring corrective actions.

Going concern
The directors' report on going concern is included in the finance and treasury review on page 50.

Compliance
The board has applied the principles contained in section 1 of the Combined Code on Corporate Governance appended to the UK Listing Authority Listing Rules and during the year has moved to a position of full compliance in the following areas:

a) on 8 November 2001 Göran Lundberg was appointed to the role of senior independent non-executive director; and
b) the share award plan, established in 2000 following the lapse of the offer by Air Liquide and Air Products to provide a mid-term incentive for senior managers, vested in June 2002. No further awards have been, or will be, made under the plan. Further details can be found on page 58.

With regard to executive directors' service contracts, the company has recently moved to a policy for all executive directors, which policy is in the course of being implemented, of service contracts that can be terminated by the company on one year's notice and an explanation can be found on page 58.

Directors submit themselves for re-election at regular intervals and at least every three years in accordance with the company's Articles of Association and the Combined Code.

Corporate social investment

In 2002, The BOC Group's corporate social investment programme had three key objectives. The first was to continue to focus on projects designed to improve environmental stewardship. The second was to continue to devolve the choices of social investment donations to our employees. The third was to broaden the organisation's involvement in social programmes around the world.

BOC made a number of positive contributions to environmental projects including the BOC New Zealand Community Environmental Grants Programme which provides assistance to schools and community groups. Together with the New Zealand Water Environment Research Foundation, we now manage a scheme providing funding to help communities maintain, protect and improve their water environment.

Our environmental flagship remains the UK-based BOC Foundation for the Environment, which was established with an initial injection of £1 million in 1990. The Foundation has so far supported 110 projects focusing on waste management, water quality and pollution control. This year, the Group contributed £214,000 to the Foundation and saw 11 new projects come on stream. Since the Foundation's inception BOC has donated £3.5 million. Combined funding from BOC and its co-sponsoring partners now exceeds £11 million.

As in previous years, BOC has managed a balanced charitable donations programme in which we direct our resources at areas where we feel we can make a difference or where our employees have a direct involvement. Social investment projects around the world have increased in number since last year and retain a local context.

In 2002, BOC made charitable donations totalling £1.28 million including £458,000 to UK-registered charities through direct donations from the company and matched giving. As in previous years, no political donations were made in the UK.

At a local level, BOC employees have continued to involve themselves in charitable fundraising and voluntary support. To this end, our matched giving scheme again proved its worth as a way of aligning corporate funding with the personal generosity of BOC employees. Matched giving schemes have been operating in the UK, the Americas and the south Pacific for some time, but this year there has been a marked increase in employee involvement. In the course of 2002, BOC in the UK donated a record £245,000 (included in the UK total above) through the Charities Aid Foundation to match employee beneficence – a rise of 38 per cent on the previous year. In the US, BOC's employees contributed a record sum equivalent to £80,000.

In addition to the numerous causes supported through matched giving, we also supported a number of projects on a Group basis, including the Royal British Legion, Children's Direct Aid and ProShare. We also launched the BOC Emerging Artist Award in March to encourage and support a committed UK-based artist for a year. We were delighted with the interest this received and are pleased to say the 2002 award was won by Royal College of Art graduate Simon Keenleyside, from Raleigh, Essex. Simon emerged as the overall winner of the £20,000 bursary from nearly 200 other young artists from across the UK.

Outside the UK, the development of community programmes also rests in the hands of our local companies, each one being responsible for its own project selection and funding. This devolved approach, both inside and outside the UK, has resulted in the funding of a rich variety of programmes that are truly relevant to the communities in which BOC companies operate.

In the US, through a combination of financial support and many hours of volunteer involvement, BOC and its employees continued to assist the United Way charitable appeal, helping to make a difference in many deprived sectors of the community.

BOC in the US also pursued a number of other projects including a Science Can Be Fun day for teenagers, a day spent building wheelchair access ramps to allow disabled girls to attend Girl Scout summer camps and a drive to collect used mobile phones to be distributed to local women at risk from domestic abuse.

In the south Pacific, our employees requested that the company matches their fundraising in relation to three charities a year. In Australia, employees chose the Salvation Army's Red Shield Appeal, Daffodil Day, a fundraising event for cancer research, education and patient support, and Jeans for Genes, an international campaign that raises funds for research into genetic disorders. In New Zealand, our employees selected Daffodil Day, the Westpac Rescue Helicopter and the Society for the Prevention of Cruelty to Animals.

BOC in Australia already has an established relationship with the Malcolm Sargent Cancer Fund for Children. BOC employees have renewed and deepened this relationship with additional financial contributions and employee support through volunteering and fundraising activities.

In South Africa, BOC's subsidiary Afrox and its staff continued to support the company's community involvement process, which includes the management of 115 projects to improve the lives of disadvantaged young people. Once more, the highlight of the year was Bumbanani (meaning 'let's build together') Day when 8,000 children attended events hosted by BOC staff. This year, in celebration of Afrox's 75th anniversary, the company contributed an additional £96,000 to its social investment fund, increasing its Bumbanani activities and lifting the sum spent on good causes to £192,000. This year's Bumbanani activities reached 1,000 more children than they did last year.

In addition, Afrox hospitals engage in a wide range of health care and safety initiatives, including sponsorship of the South African Heart Foundation. This year, the first Mended Hearts support group and cardiac rehabilitation team to assist people in their recuperation and rehabilitation after heart surgery, was launched in Cape Town from the Vincent Pallotti hospital.

Some Afrox hospitals have a special outreach in the form of rape crisis centres. Medical examinations are conducted in a non-threatening environment with the emphasis placed on maintaining the dignity of the victim. Preventive medication is given for the contraction of sexually transmitted diseases as well as antiretroviral drugs.

BOC and its employees have also been active in many other markets. BOC in Pakistan, for example, has been running a social investment programme for some time, particularly in support of leading medical institutions. This year, support continued for: the Layton Rehmatulla Benevolent Trust, an organisation dedicated to providing free eye care; the Marie Adelaide Leprosy Centre; the Shaukat Khanum Memorial Cancer Hospital, the first institution in Pakistan dedicated to cancer treatment; and the Aga Khan Medical Hospital and Foundation. BOC was one of the founding contributors to the Aga Khan Foundation which runs a world class university hospital affiliated to the Harvard Medical School.

In Venezuela, we donated funds and helium balloons to schools and orphanages and breathing oxygen to local fire stations. In Curacao, we channel support through the local Rotary Club and contributed to various youth education and care for the elderly projects. In India, we made a number of contributions across a range of community welfare interests.

Annual General Meeting

The Annual General Meeting will be held at the Institution of Electrical Engineers (Lecture Theatre), Savoy Place, London WC2R 0BL on Friday 17 January 2003 commencing at 11.00 am. The Notice of the Annual General Meeting, which includes explanations of all resolutions, is contained in a separate circular which is being sent to all shareholders more than 20 working days before the meeting.

Resolutions will seek approval to the following:
a) receipt of the report and accounts;
b) reappointment of Matthew Miau, Roberto Mendoza, Göran Lundberg, René Médori, and 'Raj' Rajagopal as directors;
c) reappointment of PricewaterhouseCoopers as auditors and granting authority to the directors to fix their remuneration;
d) the dividend policy;
e) the directors' remuneration report and the remuneration policy;
f) amendment to the rules of the all-employee share option scheme;
g) establishment of a new long-term incentive plan and executive share option scheme;
h) political donations and expenditure pursuant to the Political Parties, Elections and Referendums Act 2000;
i) renewal of the authority of the directors to allot shares;
j) renewal of the authority for the directors to allot shares for cash other than to existing shareholders in proportion to their holdings; and
k) granting of general authority for the company to purchase its own shares up to a maximum of ten per cent of issued share capital. No purchases were made following last year's authority.

The report of the directors has been approved by the board and signed on its behalf by:

Nick Deeming Secretary
Windlesham, 22 November 2002

Report on remuneration

The management resources committee
The management resources committee (MRC) comprises all the independent non-executive directors with the exception of the Group chairman, Rob Margetts. Its members are Göran Lundberg (Chairman), Fabiola Arredondo (appointed November 2001), Julie Baddeley, Matthew Miau (appointed January 2002), and Chris O'Donnell. Roberto Mendoza was appointed a non-executive director in October 2002 and has become a member of the MRC. Until their retirement on 18 January 2002 Harry Groome and Howard Macdonald had been members of the MRC. Whilst neither the Group chairman nor the chief executive are members of the MRC they both attend the meetings by invitation but are not present when their personal remuneration is discussed and reviewed. The Group human resources director, Rob Lourey, attends in an advisory capacity and acts as secretary.

Remuneration policy
The MRC sets the overall remuneration policy of The BOC Group and makes recommendations to the board on the framework of executive remuneration. It meets approximately six times a year. The terms of reference conform with best practice. The MRC determines, on behalf of the board, the detailed terms of service of the executive directors and other members of the executive management team including basic salary, performance-related bonus arrangements, benefits in kind, long-term incentives and pension benefits. The MRC does not retain remuneration consultants but appoints professional external advisors as it sees fit. During the year professional advice was sought from external consultants Deloitte & Touche. These advisors did not provide any other services to the Group. The MRC is also provided with information and data from national and international surveys on executive pay and conditions such as those provided by Towers Perrin, Mercer Human Resources consultants, Watson Wyatt and Monks Partnership Limited.

The MRC also reviews the remuneration of the Group chairman following a recommendation from the chief executive and senior independent director, though the board as a whole determine the non-executive directors' fees.

The fees of the non-executive directors are set at a level which will attract individuals with the necessary experience and ability to make a significant contribution to The BOC Group's affairs and are benchmarked with those fees paid by other UK listed companies. Non-executive directors' fees will be increased from £30,000 to £37,000 per annum and the committee chair fees increased from £5,000 to £8,000 per annum, effective 1 January 2003. These increases, after tax, will be used to acquire shares in the company which will be held by the non-executive directors for the remaining period of their term of office with the company.

BOC's remuneration policy for executive directors and other executive management is designed to attract and retain executives of the highest calibre so that The BOC Group is managed successfully to the benefit of its stakeholders. In setting remuneration levels the MRC takes into account the remuneration practices found in other UK listed companies of similar size, internationality and complexity and seeks to benchmark its whole remuneration at about the median level for this group.

During the year the MRC carried out a review of executive remuneration packages and decided that a realignment was necessary to support the company's business strategy to improve both earnings growth and capital efficiency and to ensure that the packages were market competitive. In reaching its conclusions the MRC took the view that performance related remuneration should form a substantial element of total remuneration thereby aligning the interests of directors with those of shareholders, which would be reflected through share price growth and dividends. As such, a proposal will be put to shareholders at the Annual General Meeting to adopt new long-term incentive arrangements. These arrangements are intended to encourage innovation and value-added growth and strengthen the link between short-term performance and sustainable improvement in shareholder value over the longer term.

The performance measures for the Long Term Incentive Plan (LTIP) will be based one third on Earnings Per Share (EPS) before exceptional items, one third on Return on Capital Employed (ROCE) before exceptional items and one third on the company's Total Shareholder Return (TSR) performance relative to industry based comparator groups – that is, an index of FTSE based manufacturing companies and a global industrial gases group. The performance measure for the Executive Share Option Scheme (ESOS 2003) will be assessed on the growth in basic EPS before exceptional items as reported in the annual report and accounts. The MRC consider these performance measures to be important drivers of sustainable improvement in shareholder value that focus executives' attention and effort on profitable growth and capital efficiency in both the short and long term.

Details of the arrangements are summarised in the chairman's letter and explanatory notes to the Notice of the Annual General Meeting. The MRC believes that executives' interests in long-term share price performance is an important link to future organisational performance. Additionally, the MRC encourages the executive management group to grow personal shareholdings in the business over time. It is anticipated that each executive would build towards a shareholding equivalent in value to one year's gross salary. The MRC believes that the vehicle of the long-term incentive package will facilitate the building of such a shareholding over a period of time.

Remuneration components

Basic salary Salaries for executive directors and executive management board members are based on median market rates drawn from external market data and take account of an executive's experience, responsibilities and performance. Performance is assessed both from an individual and business perspective. Executive salaries are normally reviewed annually by the MRC. Remuneration for those executives of businesses outside the UK is denominated in the local currency.

Benefits in kind Benefits in kind comprise company car benefits and membership of BOC's health care insurance scheme and, where appropriate, directors on international assignment receive overseas allowances such as housing and children's education fees. These allowances are on similar terms to those applying to other employees on the international assignment programme. Such benefits are in line with those offered by peer group companies. Benefits in kind do not form part of pensionable earnings.

Variable compensation plan The executive directors and senior management participate in the variable compensation bonus plan. The plan focuses on annual objectives and links individual performance with business plans. The financial targets for the executive directors and other executive management board members are set on an annual basis by the MRC and performance against these targets is reviewed by the MRC on a six monthly basis. The MRC considers that a six monthly review acts as a significant incentive and is conducive to sustaining performance throughout the year. The targets are based on EPS before exceptional items and ROCE before exceptional items at Group level. Bonuses are assessed two thirds on these financial targets with the remaining third based on personal objectives derived from BOC's strategic priorities, including safety and growth initiatives. Executives can be awarded an annual bonus of 80 per cent of salary for the achievement in full of both stretch financial targets and their personal objectives. Bonuses in excess of 80 per cent of salary can be paid for exceptional financial performance. There is a threshold performance level below which no bonus is paid.

The bonuses for the executive directors and other members of the executive management board are paid half yearly following the MRC review. Details of the payments to directors are included in the directors' remuneration for the year.

Retirement benefits Pension arrangements for executive directors are in line with those of comparable executives in the countries in which the directors are located.

In the UK, the BOC senior executive pension scheme is a funded, tax-approved, defined benefit pension arrangement. Where necessary, the director's pensionable pay is limited by the 'earnings cap' provisions of the Finance Act 1989. In such cases, the company pays the director a salary supplement on earnings above the pensions cap to reflect the loss of pension coverage. This supplement is recorded in the director's emoluments and is not taken into account in calculating bonuses or any other form of remuneration.

In the US, the BOC Top-Hat pension plan is an unfunded, non-tax-qualified, defined benefit pension arrangement.

Details of the individual directors' pension arrangements are shown on page 58.

Service contracts The company's policy is for all executive directors to have contracts of employment that terminate on the attainment of retirement age. In order to mitigate its liability on early termination, the company's policy is that it should be able to terminate such contracts on no more than 12 months' notice, and that payments on termination are restricted to the value of salary, and certain benefits, for the notice period.

All current executive directors have service contracts which are summarised on page 58.

The non-executive directors do not have contracts of service. They do not participate in the Group's variable compensation arrangements, its long-term incentive arrangements or its pension arrangements, nor do they receive any benefits in kind.

Share option plans Executive directors and other eligible employees participate in The BOC Group Executive Share Option Scheme (ESOS) which was introduced in 1995. The scheme uses newly issued and purchased shares. The MRC sets out the guidelines for the awards each year. The guidelines take account of personal performance and local market practice. Options are granted at the full market value of the company's shares at the time of grant and are exercisable between three and ten years from the date of grant subject to the performance condition, set by the MRC, being met. The options vest when the company's EPS growth (before exceptional items) is equal to, or exceeds, the growth in the Retail Prices Index (RPI) by three per cent per annum over any three year performance period. The MRC considers this performance condition to be a challenging performance hurdle when compared to the company's ten year EPS compound annual growth rate (before exceptional items) of around four per cent. The performance measure is assessed annually and is based on basic EPS before exceptional items as reported in the annual report. In countries where it is not appropriate to grant share options, grants are made as share appreciation rights and, on exercise, the gain is delivered in cash. The rules for such grants are similar to those for share options. Subject to shareholder approval of the proposed ESOS 2003 no further options will be granted under this scheme.

Prior to 1995 options were granted to executive directors under the Senior Executive Share Option Scheme, the 1994 Executive Option Scheme and the Executive Share Purchase Plan. In line with market practice at that time the vesting of these awards is not subject to performance conditions. UK based directors are also eligible to participate in the Inland Revenue approved BOC Savings Related Share Option Scheme which is open to all UK employees with one year's service or more.

Percentage

This graph shows BOC's TSR performance compared to the FTSE 100 index TSR over the last five years. TSR is defined as share price growth plus reinvested dividends. This provides a basis for comparison as a relevant equity index in which BOC is a constituent member. The company believes that other indices and time periods display aspects of relative performance on a more appropriate basis (see Group chairman's statement and LTIP proposals).

Other specific arrangements

Share award plan The awards made in June 2000 under the share award plan which was introduced as an immediate retention programme following the lapse of the offer from Air Liquide and Air Products vested in June 2002. Under the plan the shares awarded vested after two years provided a performance condition was met. The performance condition required EPS growth before exceptional items to equal, or exceed, the growth in the RPI by three per cent per annum over a two year period. Details of awards made to directors prior to their appointment to the board and which vested during the year are shown on page 63. No further awards will be made under the plan.

Share incentive unit plan Between 1989 and 1995 awards were made to executives under an incentive arrangement linked to the growth in the company's share price. No awards have been made under the plan since 1995. The final payment under the plan matured in November 2002.

Details of directors' individual remuneration, share options and share awards, share incentive units and share holdings are given on pages 59 to 63.

Individual pension arrangements

Mr Grant's pension is provided for under the US cash balance retirement plan and the US Top-Hat pension plan, which, in combination, entitle Mr Grant to a lump sum benefit on retirement at age 65 equivalent to a pension of approximately 72 per cent of final base salary. In accordance with local competitive practices existing in his country of operation prior to his appointment as a director, Mr Grant's bonus is pensionable.

Mr Isaac's pension to his contractual retirement age is being funded in the UK through a combination of a tax-approved personal pension plan and a funded unapproved retirement benefit scheme, which is underpinned by a guarantee for which provision will be made in the accounts if appropriate.

Mr Médori's pension benefits are funded under the UK senior executive pension scheme on earnings up to the 'pension cap' imposed by the Finance Act 1989. On retirement at age 60, he will be entitled to a pension of 57.5 per cent of capped earnings. In addition, he has a vested deferred benefit, under the US cash balance retirement plan, which he will be entitled to take as a lump sum on retirement at age 60.

Dr Rajagopal's pension benefits are funded under the UK senior executive pension scheme. On retirement at age 60, he will be entitled to a pension of two thirds of his final 12 months' salary.

Mr Walsh's pension is provided for under the US cash balance retirement plan and the US Top-Hat pension plan, which, in combination, entitle Mr Walsh to a lump sum benefit on retirement at age 65 equivalent to a pension of approximately 60 per cent of final base salary. In accordance with local competitive practices existing in his country of operation prior to his appointment as a director, Mr Walsh's bonus is pensionable.

Further details of the pension plans for executive directors are given on page 60.

Individual service contracts

Mr Grant has a contract effective from 1 May 1999 which expires on 1 April 2011. This contract can be terminated by the company on two years' notice, and provides for the payment of the value of base salary for the unexpired portion of the notice period. Additionally, the unexpired portion of Mr Grant's notice period would be added to his pensionable service in the calculation of his pension entitlement.

Mr Isaac has a contract effective from 19 November 2002 (which reflects the new arrangements announced on 21 May 2002) which expires on 30 June 2005 (subject to possible extension by mutual agreement). The contract can be terminated by the company on twelve months' notice. In the event of early termination, the contract provides for the payment of compensation based on the value of salary, car benefit and bonus entitlement (calculated on the basis of the average of actual payments over the preceding two years) for the unexpired portion of the notice period. Mr Isaac would also be entitled to a special contribution to his funded unapproved retirement benefit scheme amounting to the sum of 40 per cent of his pay above the 'pension cap' imposed by the Finance Act 1989 and 50 per cent (58.33 per cent from 6 April 2003) of his pay up to the cap for the unexpired portion of his notice period.

Mr Médori has a contract dated 21 November 2002, which expires on 23 September 2017. The contract can be terminated by the company on twelve months' notice. In the event of early termination, the contract provides for the payment of compensation based on the value of salary, car benefit and bonus entitlement (calculated on the basis of the average of actual payments over the preceding two years) for the unexpired portion of the notice period. Mr Médori would also be entitled (a) to have his capped deferred pension from the UK senior executive pension scheme paid without actuarial reduction from age 55; and (b) to an immediate payment representing the discounted value of the difference in the capital values of a pension calculated as in (a) and a pension calculated as in (a) but with the addition of the unexpired portion of his notice period in the calculation of pensionable service.

Dr Rajagopal has a contract dated 1 May 1999 (as amended by a deed of variation dated 22 November 2002) which expires on 14 December 2013. The contract can be terminated by the company on twelve months' notice. In the event of early termination, the contract provides for the payment of compensation based on the value of salary, car benefit and bonus entitlement (calculated on the basis of the average of actual payments over the preceding two years) for the unexpired portion of the notice period. Dr Rajagopal would also be entitled to have his deferred pension from the UK senior executive pension scheme (a) calculated with the inclusion of the unexpired portion of his notice period in the calculation of pensionable service; and (b) paid without actuarial reduction from age 55.

Mr Walsh has a contract dated 21 November 2002, which expires on 10 August 2015. The contract can be terminated by the company on twelve months' notice. In the event of early termination, the contract provides for the payment of compensation based on the value of salary, car benefit and bonus entitlement (calculated on the basis of the average of actual payments over the preceding two years) for the unexpired portion of the notice period. Additionally, the unexpired portion of Mr Walsh's notice period would be added to his pensionable service in the calculation of his pension entitlement.

All the above contracts can be terminated by the individual director on six months' notice (three months in the case of Mr Grant).

Remuneration and interests

a) Directors' remuneration

i) Charged against profit in the year	2002 £'000	2001 £'000
Salaries and benefits	2,586	2,292
Annual bonuses payable for the year	1,631	1,231
Other emoluments[4]	500	–
Fees to non-executive directors	352	179
	5,069	3,702
Company pension contributions to money purchase schemes	184	154
Company pension contributions to defined benefit schemes	927	793
Provision for share incentive scheme[1]	4	(203)
Provision for share award plan[1]	190	214
Payments to former directors and their dependants[2]	52	54
	6,426	4,714

	Year ended 30 September 2002					2001
ii) Individual remuneration	Basic salary/fees £'000	Allowances and benefits[3] £'000	Bonus payable £'000	Other emoluments[4] £'000	Total remuneration £'000	Total remuneration £'000
Chairman						
R J Margetts[5]	180	–	–	–	180	–
Executive directors						
R S Grant	385	16	325	–	726	681
A E Isaac[4]	623	147	536	500	1,806	1,231
R Médori	316	280	266	–	862	685
Dr K Rajagopal	311	16	263	–	590	502
J L Walsh[5]	285	131	241	–	657	113
Non-executive directors[6]						
F R Arredondo[5]	27	–	–	–	27	–
J M Baddeley	34	–	–	–	34	11
G U U Lundberg	34	–	–	–	34	30
M F C Miau[5]	21	–	–	–	21	–
C J O'Donnell	34	–	–	–	34	18
Chairman retiring in the year						
Sir David John	47	29	–	–	76	311
Non-executive directors retiring in the year						
H C Groome	11	–	–	–	11	35
J H Macdonald	11	–	–	–	11	35
Non-executive directors retiring in 2001						
R F Chase	–	–	–	–	–	29
Dr D Chatterji	–	–	–	–	–	10
C P King	–	–	–	–	–	11
Total	2,319	619	1,631	500	5,069	3,702

1. This represents the amount charged to operating profit during the year for those elements of the share incentive scheme and the share award plan relating to directors.
2. This represents payments to former directors and/or their dependants which were not provided for in previous years.
3. Includes overseas and relocation expenses.
4. Mr Isaac was the highest paid director in 2002. Mr Isaac's remuneration in 2000 included a payment of £250,000 which represented an additional discretionary bonus for his commitment and performance during the period of the offer. As part of the same arrangement, Mr Isaac received a further payment of £500,000 in 2002.
5. Mr Margetts was appointed to the board on 4 October 2001, Mrs Arredondo was appointed to the board on 8 November 2001, and Mr Miau was appointed to the board on 23 January 2002. Mr Walsh was appointed to the board on 11 July 2001. The remuneration above is the total remuneration earned since their appointment.
6. Non-executive directors do not normally participate in the Group's incentive programmes, nor is their remuneration pensionable. With the exception of the chairman, they were paid at the rate of £30,000 per annum, plus a further fee of £5,000 where they acted as chairman of a board committee.
7. The aggregate remuneration charged against profits for directors and members of the executive management board in the year was £9.4 million. Remuneration of members of the executive management board other than directors is given in b) below.

b) Executive officers

The aggregate remuneration of members of the executive management board, other than directors, for services in all capacities during 2002 was as follows:

Charged against profit in the year	2002 £'000
Salaries and benefits	1,637
Annual bonuses payable for the year	950
Provision for share award plan[1]	222
Company pension contributions	152
	2,961

1. This represents the amount charged to operating profit for the portion of the share award plan relating to executive officers.

c) Directors' pensions

Details of the executive directors' pension arrangements are given on page 58.

		Deferred benefit at 30 September		Increase in year net of inflation		Transfer value of increase less members' contributions		Defined contribution plans
		Pension £'000	Lump sum £'000	Pension £'000	Lump sum £'000	Pension £'000	Lump sum £'000	Company contributions in year £'000
UK-based directors								
A E Isaac	**2002**	–	–	–	–	–	–	**155**
	2001	–	344	–	307	–	303	147
Sir David John	**2002**	–	–	–	–	–	–	**–**
	2001	38	–	3	–	46	–	–
R Médori	**2002**	**7**	**153**	**3**	**2**	**17**	**2**	**–**
	2001	4	159	3	11	21	11	–
Dr K Rajagopal	**2002**	**137**	–	**21**	–	**152**	–	**–**
	2001	114	–	16	–	143	–	–
J L Walsh	**2002**	–	**376**	–	**142**	–	**142**	**13**
	2001	–	246	–	12	–	12	2
US-based directors								
R S Grant	**2002**	–	**1,607**	–	**423**	–	**423**	**16**
	2001	–	1,242	–	294	–	294	5

The transfer value equivalent excludes directors' contributions and has been calculated in accordance with Actuarial Guidance Note GN11.

In accordance with his original contract of employment, Mr Isaac's initial pension arrangements became payable on his 60th birthday at which time the combined value of the tax-approved personal pension plan and the funded unapproved retirement benefit scheme fell short of the amount guaranteed under Mr Isaac's contract. Accordingly, during the year, a payment amounting to £423,000 was made to Mr Isaac's funded unapproved retirement benefit scheme.

Sir David John retired during the year. As permitted by the terms of his contract of employment, he elected to commute his pension of £39,000 per annum for a cash payment of £708,000.

d) Directors' share interests

i) Directors' share interests at 30 September 2002

The directors of the company and their families had the following beneficial interests in the company's securities and rights under the share incentive scheme:

	At 30 September 2002				At 1 October 2001 (or at date of appointment if later)			
	Ordinary shares	Share options	Share awards	Share incentive units	Ordinary shares	Share options	Share awards	Share incentive units
F R Arredondo	500	–	–	–	–	–	–	–
J M Baddeley	500	–	–	–	500	–	–	–
R S Grant	62,803	542,697	–	–	40,000	510,000	15,000	–
A E Isaac	5,700	947,357	–	45,000	700	747,357	–	45,000
G U U Lundberg	5,000	–	–	–	5,000	–	–	–
R J Margetts	6,000	–	–	–	–	–	–	–
R Médori	16,772	367,112	–	–	4,772	287,112	12,000	–
M F C Miau	2,281	–	–	–	–	10,000	–	–
C J O'Donnell	2,081	–	–	–	2,000	–	–	–
Dr K Rajagopal	14,416	460,009	–	–	5,447	379,647	15,000	–
J L Walsh	8,175	387,500	–	–	1,000	312,500	12,000	–
Directors retiring in the year								
H C Groome	–	–	–	–	3,300	–	–	–
Sir David John	637	196,736	–	–	3,732	300,000	–	–
J H Macdonald	1,228	–	–	–	1,228	–	–	–

There has been no change in the interest of any of the directors between 1 October 2002 and 12 November 2002. No director had a non-beneficial interest at 30 September 2002 or between 1 October 2002 and 12 November 2002. Options are granted over Ordinary shares of 25p each under senior executive and general employee share option schemes.

Apart from the above and service agreements, no director has had any material interest in any contract with the company or its subsidiaries requiring disclosure under the Companies Act 1985.

At 30 September 2002, members of the executive management board, other than directors, had the following aggregate beneficial interests in the company's securities: 54,821 Ordinary shares; 1,064,015 share options; nil share awards and nil rights to share incentive units. The cumulative shareholdings of the company's directors and members of the executive management board represent less than one per cent of the company's outstanding Ordinary shares.

ii) Directors' share interests – movements during the year

Share options

	At 1 October 2001 (or at date of appointment if later)	Granted	Exercised	At 30 September 2002	Exercise price (pence)	Market price at date of exercise (pence)	Earliest exercise date	Latest exercise date	Notes
R S Grant	30,000	–	30,000	–	742	1081	12 Feb 1997	12 Feb 2003	b.
	30,000	–	10,104	19,896	677	1081	11 Feb 1998	11 Feb 2004	b.
	25,000	–	–	25,000	722		10 Feb 1998	10 Feb 2005	d.
	25,000	–	–	25,000	919		14 Feb 1999	14 Feb 2006	d.
	20,000	–	–	20,000	848		14 Aug 1999	14 Aug 2006	d.
	35,000	–	–	35,000	980		21 Feb 2000	21 Feb 2007	d.
	75,000	–	–	75,000	914		11 Feb 2001	11 Feb 2008	d.
	75,000	–	7,199	67,801	851	1081	10 Feb 2002	10 Feb 2009	d.
	120,000	–	–	120,000	937		26 May 2003	26 May 2010	
	75,000	–	–	75,000	993		7 Feb 2004	7 Feb 2011	
	–	80,000	–	80,000	1016		6 Feb 2005	6 Feb 2012	
	510,000	80,000	47,303	542,697					
A E Isaac	45,000	–	–	45,000	716		16 Nov 1998	16 Nov 2004	b.
	50,000	–	–	50,000	722		10 Feb 1998	10 Feb 2005	d.
	50,000	–	–	50,000	919		14 Feb 1999	14 Feb 2006	d.
	2,357	–	–	2,357	827		1 May 2003	31 Oct 2003	a. b.
	50,000	–	–	50,000	980		21 Feb 2000	21 Feb 2007	d.
	50,000	–	–	50,000	914		11 Feb 2001	11 Feb 2008	d.
	50,000	–	–	50,000	851		10 Feb 2002	10 Feb 2009	d.
	250,000	–	–	250,000	937		26 May 2003	26 May 2010	
	200,000	–	–	200,000	993		7 Feb 2004	7 Feb 2011	
	–	200,000	–	200,000	1016		6 Feb 2005	6 Feb 2012	
	747,357	200,000	–	947,357					

	At 1 October 2001 (or date of appointment if later)	Granted	Exercised	At 30 September 2002	Exercise price (pence)	Market price at date of exercise (pence)	Earliest exercise date	Latest exercise date	Notes
Sir David John	150,000	–	103,264	46,736	919	1067.5	14 Feb 1999	14 Feb 2006	d.
	75,000	–	–	75,000	980		21 Feb 2000	21 Feb 2007	d.
	75,000	–	–	75,000	914		11 Feb 2001	11 Feb 2008	d.
	300,000	–	103,264	196,736					
R Médori	10,000	–	–	10,000	742		12 Feb 1997	12 Feb 2003	b.
	20,000	–	–	20,000	677		11 Feb 1998	11 Feb 2004	b.
	15,000	–	–	15,000	722		10 Feb 1998	10 Feb 2005	d.
	15,000	–	–	15,000	919		14 Feb 1999	14 Feb 2006	d.
	15,000	–	–	15,000	980		21 Feb 2000	21 Feb 2007	d.
	30,000	–	–	30,000	914		11 Feb 2001	11 Feb 2008	d.
	30,000	–	–	30,000	851		10 Feb 2002	10 Feb 2009	d.
	100,000	–	–	100,000	937		26 May 2003	26 May 2010	
	2,112	–	–	2,112	870		1 Aug 2007	31 Jan 2008	a. b.
	50,000	–	–	50,000	993		7 Feb 2004	7 Feb 2011	
	–	80,000	–	80,000	1016		6 Feb 2005	6 Feb 2012	
	287,112	80,000	–	367,112					
M F C Miau	5,000	–	5,000	–	722	1044.5	10 Feb 1998	10 Feb 2005	c.d.
	5,000	–	5,000	–	919	1044.5	14 Feb 1999	14 Feb 2006	c.d.
	10,000	–	10,000	–					
Dr K Rajagopal	10,000	–	–	10,000	742		12 Feb 1997	12 Feb 2003	b.
	15,000	–	–	15,000	677		11 Feb 1998	11 Feb 2004	b.
	25,000	–	–	25,000	722		10 Feb 1998	10 Feb 2005	d.
	35,000	–	–	35,000	919		14 Feb 1999	14 Feb 2006	d.
	471	–	–	471	827		1 May 2003	31 Oct 2003	a. b.
	20,000	–	–	20,000	848		14 Aug 1999	14 Aug 2006	d.
	35,000	–	–	35,000	980		21 Feb 2000	21 Feb 2007	d.
	50,000	–	–	50,000	914		11 Feb 2001	11 Feb 2008	d.
	1,676	–	–	1,676	823		1 May 2003	31 Oct 2003	a. b.
	50,000	–	–	50,000	851		10 Feb 2002	10 Feb 2009	d.
	87,500	–	–	87,500	937		26 May 2003	26 May 2010	
	50,000	–	–	50,000	993		7 Feb 2004	7 Feb 2011	
	–	80,000	–	80,000	1016		6 Feb 2005	6 Feb 2012	
	–	362	–	362	914		1 May 2007	31 Oct 2007	a. b.
	379,647	80,362	–	460,009					
J L Walsh	5,000	–	5,000	–	627	1016	14 Feb 1996	14 Feb 2002	b.
	10,000	–	–	10,000	742		12 Feb 1997	12 Feb 2003	b.
	15,000	–	–	15,000	677		11 Feb 1998	11 Feb 2004	b.
	10,000	–	–	10,000	722		10 Feb 1998	10 Feb 2005	d.
	10,000	–	–	10,000	919		14 Feb 1999	14 Feb 2006	d.
	12,500	–	–	12,500	980		21 Feb 2000	21 Feb 2007	d.
	30,000	–	–	30,000	914		11 Feb 2001	11 Feb 2008	d.
	70,000	–	–	70,000	851		10 Feb 2002	10 Feb 2009	d.
	100,000	–	–	100,000	937		26 May 2003	26 May 2010	
	50,000	–	–	50,000	993		7 Feb 2004	7 Feb 2011	
	–	80,000	–	80,000	1016		6 Feb 2005	6 Feb 2012	
	312,500	80,000	5,000	387,500					

a. Options granted under the Save As You Earn scheme. All other options shown above are granted under the executive share option schemes.
b. Options with no performance conditions attached. All other options shown above have performance related conditions attached to them. These conditions are described on page 57.
c. At date of appointment, Mr Miau held 10,000 executive share options which had been granted to him in February 1995 and February 1996. He exercised the options and sold the resulting shares in March 2002.
d. The performance conditions attaching to these options have been satisfied.
e. No options have lapsed during the year.

The total gains made by directors on options exercised during the year were £354,000 (2001: £100,000).

At 30 September 2002, there were 2,319,210 options outstanding where the exercise price exceeded the market price of 867p. During the year, the share price ranged from a high of 1108p to a low of 836p.

Share awards

No awards under the scheme were made during the year to any executive director and there were no awards of shares outstanding at 30 September 2002. The following awards vested during the year:

Share awards — vested during the year	Number	Market price on vesting date (pence)
R S Grant	15,000	1001.5
R Médori	12,000	1001.5
Dr K Rajagopal	15,000	1001.5
J L Walsh	12,000	1001.5

Share incentive units

	Cash on deposit at 1 October 2001 £'000	Gain converted to cash in year[1] £'000	Paid in year £'000	Cash on deposit and not yet paid £'000	Number of units	Weighted average price (pence)
Current directors						
A E Isaac	–	–	–	–	45,000	716
Former executive directors						
Dr D Chatterji	144	49	(193)	–	–	–
A P Dyer	1,522	14	(1,536)	–	–	–

1. The amounts shown as converted to cash in the year include interest earned from the date of conversion.

The share incentive unit plan provides for cash payments to executives based on increases in the share price over a period of up to eight years from the time of grant. Grants under the plan were made between 1989 and 1995 to supplement or substitute for grants under the share option schemes. No grants have been made since 1995.

Executives may elect to convert share incentive units to cash provided that the units have been held for three years. The fixed cash sum, determined by reference to the share price on the date of election over and above the original grant price, will earn interest at one per cent above the HSBC base rate. A full cash payment can only be received by an executive after eight years but limited early payments may be made in certain circumstances between the fourth and eighth years, at the discretion of the management resources committee. The plan includes significant forfeiture penalties in the event that an executive leaves the company other than on retirement before the expiration of the eight year period.

On normal retirement, or earlier at the discretion of the management resources committee, an executive will normally continue to participate in the scheme so long as he observes a non-compete covenant in favour of the company. Full payment will be made at the eighth anniversary or earlier at the discretion of the management resources committee.

Former directors were granted their share incentive units when they were executive directors of the company.

The report on remuneration has been approved by the board and signed on its behalf by:

Nick Deeming Secretary
Windlesham, 22 November 2002

Responsibility of the directors

For preparation of the financial statements

Company law requires the directors to prepare financial statements for each financial year which give a true and fair view of the state of affairs of the company and of the Group at the end of the year and of the profit or loss for the year. In preparing those financial statements, the directors are required to:
* select suitable accounting policies and then apply them consistently.
* make judgements and estimates that are reasonable and prudent.
* state whether applicable accounting standards have been followed, subject to any material departures disclosed and explained in the financial statements.
* prepare the financial statements on the going concern basis unless it is inappropriate to presume that the company and the Group will continue in business.

The directors confirm that the financial statements comply with the above requirements.

The directors are responsible for keeping proper accounting records which disclose with reasonable accuracy at any time the financial position of the company and the Group and enable them to ensure that the financial statements comply with the Companies Act 1985. The directors also have general responsibility for taking reasonable steps to safeguard the assets of the company and the Group and to prevent and detect fraud and other irregularities.

A copy of the financial statements of the company is placed on the website of The BOC Group plc. The directors are responsible for the maintenance and integrity of statutory and audited information on the company's website. Information published on the Internet is accessible in many countries with different legal requirements. Legislation in the United Kingdom governing the preparation and dissemination of financial statements may differ from legislation in other jurisdictions.

Report by the independent auditors
To the members of The BOC Group plc

We have audited the financial statements which comprise the Group profit and loss account, the Group balance sheet, the Group cash flow statement, the total recognised gains and losses, the movement in shareholders' funds, the balance sheet of The BOC Group plc, Group undertakings, accounting policies and the related notes. We have also examined the amounts disclosed relating to the remuneration, share options and long-term incentive schemes' interests of the directors which form part of the report on remuneration.

Respective responsibilities of directors and auditors
The directors' responsibilities for preparing the Annual Report, Form 20-F and the financial statements in accordance with applicable United Kingdom law and accounting standards are set out in the statement of directors' responsibilities.

Our responsibility is to audit the financial statements in accordance with relevant legal and regulatory requirements, United Kingdom Auditing Standards issued by the Auditing Practices Board and the Listing Rules of the Financial Services Authority. This opinion has been prepared for, and only for, the company's members in accordance with Section 235 of the Companies Act 1985 and for no other purpose. We do not, in giving this opinion, accept or assume responsibility for any other purpose or to any other person to whom this report is shown or in to whose hands it may come save where expressly agreed by our prior consent in writing.

We report to you our opinion as to whether the financial statements give a true and fair view and are properly prepared in accordance with the United Kingdom Companies Act 1985. We also report to you if, in our opinion, the directors' report is not consistent with the financial statements, if the company has not kept proper accounting records, if we have not received all the information and explanations we require for our audit, or if information specified by law or the Listing Rules regarding directors' remuneration and transactions is not disclosed.

We read the other information contained in the Annual Report and consider the implications for our report if we become aware of any apparent misstatements or material inconsistencies with the financial statements. The other information comprises only the financial highlights, chairman's statement, chief executive's review, board of directors, executive management board, Group five year record, Group profile, employees, safety, health and the environment, research, development and information technology, risk factors, performance review, finance and treasury review, responsibility of the directors, dividends, nature of trading market, analysis of shareholdings, taxation, financial calendar, key contacts information, cross reference to Form 20-F and glossary of terms.

We review whether the corporate governance statement reflects the company's compliance with the seven provisions of the Combined Code specified for our review by the Listing Rules, and we report if it does not. We are not required to consider whether the board's statements on internal control cover all risks and controls, or to form an opinion on the effectiveness of the company's or Group's corporate governance procedures or its risk and control procedures.

Basis of audit opinion
We conducted our audit in accordance with Auditing Standards issued by the United Kingdom Auditing Practices Board and with Auditing Standards generally accepted in the United States. An audit includes examination, on a test basis, of evidence relevant to the amounts and disclosures in the financial statements. It also includes an assessment of the significant estimates and judgements made by the directors in the preparation of the financial statements, and of whether the accounting policies are appropriate to the company's circumstances, consistently applied and adequately disclosed.

We planned and performed our audit so as to obtain all the information and explanations which we considered necessary in order to provide us with sufficient evidence to give reasonable assurance that the financial statements are free from material misstatement, whether caused by fraud or other irregularity or error. In forming our opinion we also evaluated the overall adequacy of the presentation of information in the financial statements.

United Kingdom opinion In our opinion the financial statements give a true and fair view of the state of affairs of the company and the Group at 30 September 2002 and of the profit and cash flows of the Group for the year then ended and have been properly prepared in accordance with the United Kingdom Companies Act 1985.

United States opinion In our opinion the financial statements present fairly, in all material respects, the consolidated financial position of the Group at 30 September 2002 and 2001 and the results of its operations and its cash flows for each of the three years in the period ended 30 September 2002 in conformity with accounting principles generally accepted in the United Kingdom.

Accounting principles generally accepted in the United Kingdom vary in certain significant respects from accounting principles generally accepted in the United States. The application of the latter would have affected the determination of net income expressed in sterling for each of the three years in the period ended 30 September 2002 and the determination of shareholders' equity also expressed in sterling at 30 September 2002 and 2001 to the extent summarised in note 16 to the financial statements.

As shown in note 17 to the financial statements, the Group adopted two new accounting standards, for retirement benefits and deferred tax, in 2002. The change has been accounted for by restating comparative information at 30 September 2001 and 2000 and for the years then ended.

PricewaterhouseCoopers
Chartered Accountants and Registered Auditors
London, England
22 November 2002

Group profit and loss account
Years ended 30 September

	Notes	2002 Before exceptional items £ million	2002 Exceptional items £ million	2002 After exceptional items £ million	2001 (restated) Before exceptional items £ million	2001 Exceptional items £ million	2001 (restated) After exceptional items £ million	2000 (restated) Before exceptional items £ million	2000 Exceptional items £ million	2000 (restated) After exceptional items £ million
Turnover										
Continuing operations		3,890.8	–	3,890.8	4,159.2	–	4,159.2	3,878.8	–	3,878.8
Acquisitions		127.1	–	127.1	–	–	–	–	–	–
Turnover, including share of joint ventures and associates	1	4,017.9	–	4,017.9	4,159.2	–	4,159.2	3,878.8	–	3,878.8
Less: Share of turnover of joint ventures		324.1	–	324.1	340.0	–	340.0	258.0	–	258.0
Share of turnover of associates		36.1	–	36.1	46.3	–	46.3	41.1	–	41.1
Turnover of subsidiary undertakings	2(a)	3,657.7	–	3,657.7	3,772.9	–	3,772.9	3,579.7	–	3,579.7
Cost of sales	2(a)	(2,089.7)	(15.1)	(2,104.8)	(2,164.2)	(44.6)	(2,208.8)	(2,035.2)	(0.6)	(2,035.8)
Gross profit		1,568.0	(15.1)	1,552.9	1,608.7	(44.6)	1,564.1	1,544.5	(0.6)	1,543.9
Net operating expenses	2(a)	(1,142.4)	(58.9)	(1,201.3)	(1,150.3)	(61.1)	(1,211.4)	(1,104.7)	(3.8)	(1,108.5)
Operating profit										
Continuing operations		421.2	(67.8)	353.4	458.4	(105.7)	352.7	439.8	(4.4)	435.4
Acquisitions		4.4	(6.2)	(1.8)	–	–	–	–	–	–
Operating profit of subsidiary undertakings		425.6	(74.0)	351.6	458.4	(105.7)	352.7	439.8	(4.4)	435.4
Share of operating profit of joint ventures		63.8	(0.5)	63.3	59.0	(2.2)	56.8	48.1	–	48.1
Share of operating profit of associates		10.7	–	10.7	13.2	(0.4)	12.8	8.5	–	8.5
Total operating profit including share of joint ventures and associates	1	500.1	(74.5)	425.6	530.6	(108.3)	422.3	496.4	(4.4)	492.0
Loss on termination/disposal of businesses – continuing operations	2(b)	–	(20.2)	(20.2)	–	–	–	–	–	–
Profit on disposal of health care discontinued business	2(b)	–	–	–	–	–	–	–	12.5	12.5
Profit on disposal of fixed assets – continuing operations	2(b)	–	–	–	–	3.6	3.6	–	–	–
Profit on ordinary activities before interest		500.1	(94.7)	405.4	530.6	(104.7)	425.9	496.4	8.1	504.5
Interest on net debt	3(a)			(103.1)			(123.4)			(111.5)
Interest on pension scheme liabilities	6(e)			(106.1)			(107.2)			(100.7)
Expected return on pension scheme assets	6(e)			139.1			166.9			149.5
Net interest				(70.1)			(63.7)			(62.7)
Profit on ordinary activities before tax				335.3			362.2			441.8
Tax on profit on ordinary activities	4(a)			(106.2)			(104.6)			(135.2)
Profit on ordinary activities after tax				229.1			257.6			306.6
Minority interests – equity				(26.2)			(33.5)			(28.0)
Profit for the financial year				202.9			224.1			278.6
Dividends	12(a)			(186.6)			(180.3)			(170.2)
Retained profit for the financial year				16.3			43.8			108.4
Earnings per 25p Ordinary share, basic	2(d)									
– on published earnings				41.36p			46.03p			57.19p
– on exceptional items				14.58p			11.48p			(3.66)p
– before exceptional items				55.94p			57.51p			53.53p
Earnings per 25p Ordinary share, diluted	2(d)									
– on published earnings				41.21p			45.87p			56.90p
– on exceptional items				14.53p			11.44p			(3.64)p
– before exceptional items				55.74p			57.31p			53.26p

All turnover and operating profit arose from continuing operations.

Group balance sheet
At 30 September

	Notes	2002 £ million	2001 (restated) £ million
Fixed assets			
Intangible assets	7	150.7	48.1
Tangible assets	8	3,027.4	3,168.6
Investment in joint ventures			
– share of gross assets		616.2	615.2
– share of gross liabilities		(410.7)	(410.4)
		205.5	204.8
– loans to joint ventures		111.8	97.6
Investment in associates			
– share of net assets		57.5	47.1
– loans to associates		6.2	9.1
Investment in own shares		42.5	59.5
Other investments		45.1	31.7
Investments	9	468.6	449.8
		3,646.7	3,666.5
Current assets			
Stocks	10(a)	260.0	275.2
Debtors falling due within one year	10(b)	733.8	713.3
Debtors falling due after more than one year	10(c)	28.3	21.3
Investments		38.8	43.2
Cash at bank and in hand	10(d)	185.5	233.5
		1,246.4	1,286.5
Current liabilities			
Creditors: amounts falling due within one year			
Borrowings and finance leases	10(e)	(390.1)	(486.4)
Other creditors	10(f)	(857.8)	(795.3)
		(1,247.9)	(1,281.7)
Net current (liabilities)/assets		(1.5)	4.8
Total assets *less* current liabilities		3,645.2	3,671.3
Long-term liabilities			
Creditors: amounts falling due after more than one year			
Borrowings and finance leases	11(a)	(1,121.0)	(1,019.9)
Other creditors		(58.0)	(59.4)
		(1,179.0)	(1,079.3)
Provisions for liabilities and charges	11(b)	(407.5)	(419.2)
Total net assets excluding pension assets and liabilities		2,058.7	2,172.8
Pension assets	6(e)	54.3	107.0
Pension liabilities	6(e)	(311.0)	(56.0)
Total net assets including pension assets and liabilities		1,802.0	2,223.8
Capital and reserves			
Equity called up share capital	12(b)	124.3	123.6
Share premium account	12(c)	362.1	335.8
Revaluation reserves	12(c)	27.8	47.9
Profit and loss account	12(c)	1,304.8	1,400.3
Pensions reserves	12(c)	(256.5)	47.1
Joint ventures' reserves	12(c)	88.1	98.1
Associates' reserves	12(c)	33.5	33.4
Equity shareholders' funds		1,684.1	2,086.2
Minority shareholders' equity interests		117.9	137.6
Total capital and reserves		1,802.0	2,223.8

The financial statements were approved by the board of directors on 22 November 2002 and are signed on its behalf by:

A E Isaac Director **R Médori** Director

Group cash flow statement
Years ended 30 September

	Notes	2002 £ million	2001 (restated) £ million	2000 (restated) £ million
Net cash inflow from operating activities	14(a)	**759.3**	787.8	705.0
Dividends from joint ventures and associates				
Dividends from joint ventures		**30.5**	19.4	20.0
Dividends from associates		**3.4**	4.1	2.1
Dividends from joint ventures and associates		**33.9**	23.5	22.1
Returns on investments and servicing of finance				
Interest paid		**(89.6)**	(95.4)	(124.9)
Interest received		**18.5**	23.1	27.2
Dividends paid to minorities in subsidiaries		**(13.9)**	(7.7)	(6.1)
Interest element of finance lease rental payments		**(5.7)**	(7.2)	(1.4)
Returns on investments and servicing of finance		**(90.7)**	(87.2)	(105.2)
Tax paid		**(96.2)**	(100.6)	(62.8)
Capital expenditure and financial investment				
Purchases of tangible fixed assets		**(352.1)**	(349.8)	(405.8)
Sales of tangible fixed assets		**31.6**	47.1	24.2
Purchases of intangible fixed assets		**(0.1)**	(0.3)	(0.4)
Net sales/(purchases) of current asset investments		**4.3**	(6.5)	0.9
Purchases of trade and other investments		**(19.7)**	(10.2)	(29.8)
Sales of trade and other investments		**11.5**	7.8	2.6
Capital expenditure and financial investment		**(324.5)**	(311.9)	(408.3)
Acquisitions and disposals				
Acquisitions of businesses	15(a)	**(207.3)**	(145.9)	(32.1)
Net overdrafts acquired with subsidiaries		**(7.4)**	–	–
Disposals of businesses	15(a)	**10.6**	2.7	0.4
Investments in joint ventures		**(12.6)**	–	(33.6)
Divestments/repayments from joint ventures		**–**	10.8	3.0
Investments in associates		**(0.5)**	(2.7)	(0.7)
Divestments/repayments from associates		**1.7**	1.5	1.0
Acquisitions and disposals		**(215.5)**	(133.6)	(62.0)
Equity dividends paid		**(186.6)**	(180.3)	(170.2)
Net cash outflow before use of liquid resources and financing		**(120.3)**	(2.3)	(81.4)
Management of liquid resources				
Net sales of short-term investments		**52.6**	102.8	9.6
Financing				
Issue of shares		**25.0**	16.9	10.1
Increase/(decrease) in debt	14(d)	**64.1**	(51.3)	64.9
Net cash inflow/(outflow) from financing		**89.1**	(34.4)	75.0
Increase in cash		**21.4**	66.1	3.2

A reconciliation of the increase in cash to the movement in net debt in the year is given in note 14 b).

Liquid resources are defined as short-term deposits.

Total recognised gains and losses
Years ended 30 September

	Notes	2002 £ million	2001 (restated) £ million	2000 (restated) £ million
Parent[1]		**26.2**	12.1	129.7
Subsidiary undertakings		**170.1**	199.8	141.1
Joint ventures		**4.5**	10.3	6.5
Associates		**2.1**	1.9	1.3
Profit for the financial year		**202.9**	224.1	278.6
Actuarial (loss)/gain recognised on the pension schemes		**(431.2)**	(464.9)	114.2
Movement on deferred tax relating to actuarial loss/(gain) on pensions		**134.0**	154.5	(35.2)
Unrecognised loss on write down of revaluation reserve		**(11.5)**	–	–
Exchange translation effect on:				
– results for the year of subsidiaries		**(5.2)**	(3.9)	(2.2)
– results for the year of joint ventures		**(2.6)**	(1.5)	0.8
– results for the year of associates		**(0.3)**	(0.1)	0.2
– foreign currency net investments in subsidiaries		**(114.6)**	(55.8)	95.1
– foreign currency net investments in joint ventures		**(11.9)**	(1.6)	7.9
– foreign currency net investments in associates		**(1.7)**	0.4	6.8
Total recognised gains and losses for the financial year	12(c)	**(242.1)**	(148.8)	466.2
Prior year adjustment		**(220.1)**		
Total recognised gains and losses since last annual report		**(462.2)**		

1. In accordance with the concession granted under the Companies Act 1985, the profit and loss account of The BOC Group plc has not been presented separately in these financial statements.
2. There were no material differences between reported profits and losses and historical cost profits and losses on ordinary activities before tax for 2002, 2001 and 2000.
3. Profit attributable to the parent company includes dividends received from subsidiaries, joint ventures and associates, often through intermediate holding companies. These dividends may include the distribution of earnings of previous periods. As a result, the relationship of profit between parent, subsidiaries, joint ventures and associates may show fluctuations from year to year.
4. A current tax charge of £13.5 million (2001: £nil, 2000: £nil) has been recognised directly in the Group reserves.

Movement in shareholders' funds
Years ended 30 September

	2002 £ million	2001 (restated) £ million	2000 (restated) £ million
Profit for the financial year	**202.9**	224.1	278.6
Dividends	**(186.6)**	(180.3)	(170.2)
	16.3	43.8	108.4
Other recognised gains and losses	**(445.0)**	(372.9)	187.6
Shares issued	**24.6**	16.9	8.9
Credit in relation to share options	**2.0**	4.4	3.6
Net (decrease)/increase in shareholders' funds for the financial year	**(402.1)**	(307.8)	308.5
Shareholders' funds at 1 October – previously reported	**2,306.3**	2,273.6	2,013.1
Prior year adjustment	**(220.1)**	120.4	72.4
Shareholders' funds at 1 October – restated	**2,086.2**	2,394.0	2,085.5
Shareholders' funds at 30 September	**1,684.1**	2,086.2	2,394.0

Balance sheet of The BOC Group plc
At 30 September

	Notes	2002 £ million	2001 (restated) £ million
Fixed assets			
Tangible assets	8(e)	**14.0**	18.8
Investments	9(d)	**2,844.4**	2,702.0
		2,858.4	2,720.8
Current assets			
Debtors falling due within one year	10(b)	**515.6**	408.6
Cash at bank and in hand	10(d)	**—**	51.7
		515.6	460.3
Current liabilities			
Creditors: amounts falling due within one year			
Borrowings and finance leases	10(e)	**(178.9)**	(315.6)
Other creditors	10(f)	**(953.8)**	(717.3)
		(1,132.7)	(1,032.9)
Net current liabilities		**(617.1)**	(572.6)
Total assets *less* current liabilities		**2,241.3**	2,148.2
Long-term liabilities			
Creditors: amounts falling due after more than one year			
Borrowings and finance leases	11(a)	**(801.0)**	(570.4)
Other creditors		**(13.0)**	(16.5)
		(814.0)	(586.9)
Total net assets		**1,427.3**	1,561.3
Capital and reserves			
Equity called up share capital	12(b)	**124.3**	123.6
Share premium account	12(d)	**362.1**	335.8
Other reserves	12(d)	**113.7**	111.7
Profit and loss account	12(d)	**827.2**	990.2
Total capital and reserves		**1,427.3**	1,561.3

The financial statements were approved by the board of directors on 22 November 2002 and are signed on its behalf by:

A E Isaac Director **R Médori** Director

Accounting policies

General

- **Basis of preparation** These accounts are based on the historical cost accounting convention and comply with all applicable UK accounting standards.

  UK accounting standards differ in certain respects from those generally accepted in the US and the major effects of these differences in the determination of profit before tax and shareholders' funds are shown in note 16 to the financial statements. Disclosure requirements of both the UK and US are incorporated throughout the notes to these financial statements.

- **Basis of consolidation** The Group accounts include the accounts of the parent undertaking and of all subsidiaries, joint ventures and associates.

  The results of businesses acquired during the year are included from the effective date of acquisition. The results of businesses disposed of during the year are included up to the date of relinquishing control. Material, separately identifiable business segments disposed of are analysed as discontinued operations and prior years' analyses are restated to reflect those businesses as discontinued.

- **New accounting policies** This year, the Group has fully adopted the following two new accounting standards issued by the UK Accounting Standards Board:

  FRS17 – Retirement benefits

  FRS19 – Deferred tax

  For the year ended 30 September 2001, the Group followed the transitional arrangements permitted by FRS17 under which disclosure on retirement benefits was given in the notes to the financial statements. For the year ended 30 September 2002, the standard has been fully adopted and the accounting impact reflected throughout the financial statements. The impact of FRS19 is also reflected throughout the financial statements. The impact is explained further in note 17 to the financial statements.

  Comparative figures have been restated for both FRS17 and FRS19. Changes to existing policies as a result of adopting these new standards are described, where appropriate, below.

- **Exchange** Profit and loss and other period statements of the Group's overseas operations are translated at average rates of exchange. Assets and liabilities denominated in foreign currencies are translated at the rates of exchange ruling at the financial year end. Assets or liabilities swapped into other currencies are accounted for in those currencies. Exchange differences are dealt with as a movement in reserves where they arise from:

  i) the translation of the opening net assets of overseas operations;

  ii) the retranslation of retained earnings of overseas operations from average to closing rates of exchange; and

  iii) the translation or conversion of foreign currency borrowings taken to hedge overseas assets.

  All other exchange differences are taken to the profit and loss account. The principal exchange rates affecting the Group are shown on page 49.

Revenue recognition

Turnover is based on the invoiced value of the sale of goods and services, and includes the sales value of long-term contracts appropriate to the state of completion. It excludes sales between Group undertakings, VAT and similar sales-based taxes. Turnover for goods and services is recognised when delivery has occurred, title of the goods has passed to the purchaser, and where the price is fixed or determinable and reflects the commercial substance of the transaction.

Profit on contracts is only recognised close to contract completion and when profits can be reasonably determined. Provision is made for all losses incurred together with any foreseeable future losses.

Retirement benefits

Following the full adoption of FRS17, the regular service cost of providing retirement benefits to employees during the year is charged to operating profit in the year. The full cost of providing amendments to benefits in respect of past service is also charged to operating profit in the year.

A credit representing the expected return on the assets of the retirement benefit schemes during the year is included within net interest. This is based on the market value of the assets of the schemes at the start of the financial year.

A charge representing the expected increase in the liabilities of the retirement benefit schemes during the year is included within net interest. This arises from the liabilities of the schemes being one year closer to payment.

Differences between actual and expected returns on assets during the year are recognised in the statement of total recognised gains and losses in the year, together with differences arising from changes in assumptions.

Research and development

Revenue expenditure on research and development is written off when incurred.

Operating leases

The cost of operating leases is written off on the straight line basis over the period of the lease.

Intangible fixed assets

- **Goodwill** Goodwill arising on the acquisition of a business, being the excess of the fair value of the purchase price over the fair value of the net assets acquired, is capitalised and amortised on a straight line basis over its useful economic life, generally up to a maximum period of 20 years. An impairment review is carried out at the end of the first full financial year following acquisition. Any impairment in the value of goodwill, calculated by discounting estimated future cash flows, is dealt with in the profit and loss account in the period in which it arises. Negative goodwill, being the excess of the fair value of the net assets acquired over the fair value of the purchase price, is capitalised and amortised on a straight line basis, generally over a period equivalent to the realisation of the non-monetary assets acquired.

  Goodwill, both positive and negative, arising on acquisitions before 30 September 1998 was taken to reserves and has not been reinstated on the balance sheet. This is in line with the relevant accounting standard on goodwill, FRS10. This goodwill will remain in reserves until such time as it becomes impaired or the business or businesses to which it relates are disposed of, at which time it will be taken to the profit and loss account.

- **Intangibles** Other material intangible assets acquired, such as patents and trademarks, are capitalised and written off on the straight line basis over their effective economic lives.

Tangible fixed assets

No depreciation is charged on freehold land or construction in progress. Depreciation is charged on all other fixed assets on the straight line basis over the effective lives. Straight line depreciation rates vary according to the class of asset, but are typically:

	per annum
Freehold property	2% – 4%
Leasehold property (or at higher rates based on the life of the lease)	2% – 4%
Plant and machinery	3% – 10%
Cylinders	4% – 10%
Motor vehicles	7% – 20%
Computer hardware and major software	15% – 25%

- Until 30 September 1999, land and buildings were revalued periodically. Following the adoption of FRS15, land and buildings are no longer revalued. At 1 October 1999, the net book value of assets previously revalued is regarded as the historical cost.

- Interest costs on major fixed asset additions are capitalised during the construction period and written off as part of the total cost.

- Where finance leases have been entered into, the obligations to the lessor are shown as part of borrowings and the rights in the corresponding assets are treated in the same way as owned fixed assets.

- Any impairment in the value of fixed assets, calculated by discounting estimated future cash flows, is dealt with in the profit and loss account in the period in which it arises.

Investments

Investments which are held for the long term and in which the Group has a participating interest and exercises joint control with one or more other parties are treated as joint ventures and accounted for on the gross equity method. Investments which are held for the long term and in which the Group has a participating interest and exercises significant influence are treated as associates and accounted for on the equity method. In both cases, the Group's share of the results of the investment is included in the profit and loss account, and the Group's share of the net assets is included in investments in the balance sheet. Other investments are shown on the balance sheet at cost less any provision for impairment.

Stocks

Stocks and work in progress are valued at the lower of cost and net realisable value. Cost where appropriate includes a proportion of overhead expenses. Work in progress is stated at cost less progress payments received or receivable. Cost is arrived at principally on the average and 'first-in, first-out' (FIFO) basis. The amount of long-term contracts, net of amounts transferred to cost of sales and after deducting foreseeable losses and payments on account, is included in stocks as long-term contract amounts.

Deferred tax

Following the adoption of FRS19, the Group provides for deferred tax assets and liabilities arising from timing differences between the recognition of gains and losses in the financial statements and their recognition for tax purposes. Deferred tax assets are only recognised where it is more likely than not that they will be recovered. Deferred tax assets and liabilities are not discounted.

Provisions

Provisions are made when an obligation exists for a future liability in respect of a past event and where the amount of the obligation can be reliably estimated. Restructuring provisions are made for direct expenditures of a business reorganisation where the plans are sufficiently detailed and well advanced, and where appropriate communication to those affected has been undertaken at the balance sheet date.

Financial instruments

The Group uses financial instruments, including interest rate and currency swaps, to raise finance for its operations and to manage the risks arising from those operations. All transactions are undertaken only to manage interest and currency risk associated with the Group's underlying business activities and the financing of those activities. The Group does not undertake any trading activity in financial instruments.

- **Foreign exchange transaction exposures** The Group generally hedges actual and forecast foreign exchange exposures up to two years ahead. Forward contracts are used to hedge the forecast exposure and any gains or losses resulting from changes in exchange rates on contracts designated as hedges of forecast foreign exchange are deferred until the financial period in which they are realised. If the contract ceases to be a hedge, any subsequent gains and losses are recognised through the profit and loss account.

- **Balance sheet translation exposures** A large proportion of the Group's net assets are denominated in currencies other than sterling. Where practicable and cost effective the Group hedges these balance sheet translation exposures by borrowing in relevant currencies and markets and by the use of currency swaps. Currency swaps are used only as balance sheet hedging instruments, and the Group does not hedge the currency translation of its profit and loss account. Exchange gains and losses arising on the notional principal of these currency swaps during their life and at termination or maturity are dealt with as a movement in reserves. If the swap ceases to be a hedge of the underlying transaction, any subsequent gains or losses are recognised in the profit and loss account.

- **Interest rate risk exposures** The Group hedges its exposure to movements in interest rates associated with its borrowings primarily by means of interest rate swaps and forward rate agreements. Interest payments and receipts on these agreements are included with net interest payable. They are not revalued to fair value or shown on the Group balance sheet at the balance sheet date.

Notes to the financial statements

1. Segmental information

a) Turnover (including share of joint ventures and associates)

	Process Gas Solutions £ million	Industrial and Special Products £ million	BOC Edwards £ million	Afrox hospitals £ million	Gist £ million	Continuing operations Total Group by origin £ million	Total Group by destination £ million
2002							
Europe	**257.1**	**399.3**	**150.0**	—	**263.2**	**1,069.6**	**1,055.3**
Americas	**528.1**	**464.8**	**298.9**	—	—	**1,291.8**	**1,240.1**
Africa	**23.6**	**158.4**	—	**259.0**	—	**441.0**	**443.3**
Asia/Pacific	**391.8**	**582.8**	**239.3**	—	**1.6**	**1,215.5**	**1,279.2**
Turnover	**1,200.6**	**1,605.3**	**688.2**	**259.0**	**264.8**	**4,017.9**	**4,017.9**
2001							
Europe	240.2	375.3	157.4	—	229.6	1,002.5	979.6
Americas	529.7	464.5	393.3	—	—	1,387.5	1,326.1
Africa	25.6	192.2	—	287.8	—	505.6	504.9
Asia/Pacific	397.5	541.9	322.4	—	1.8	1,263.6	1,348.6
Turnover	1,193.0	1,573.9	873.1	287.8	231.4	4,159.2	4,159.2
2000							
Europe	226.6	357.3	171.3	—	225.3	980.5	948.9
Americas	433.3	428.5	378.1	—	—	1,239.9	1,160.6
Africa	26.7	181.3	—	292.8	—	500.8	499.9
Asia/Pacific	358.6	548.3	249.6	—	1.1	1,157.6	1,269.4
Turnover	1,045.2	1,515.4	799.0	292.8	226.4	3,878.8	3,878.8

b) Business analysis

	Process Gas Solutions £ million	Industrial and Special Products £ million	BOC Edwards £ million	Afrox hospitals £ million	Gist £ million	Corporate £ million	Continuing operations Total Group £ million
2002							
Total operating profit before exceptional items[1]	185.2	248.0	26.1	29.7	25.5	(14.4)	500.1
Operating exceptional items[1]	(24.0)	(18.7)	(27.5)	–	–	(4.3)	(74.5)
(Loss)/profit on termination/disposal of businesses[1]	(21.3)	–	1.1	–	–	–	(20.2)
Capital employed[2]	1,831.3	1,058.1	595.3	105.0	22.8	(19.4)	3,593.1
Capital expenditure[3]	157.3	123.6	42.0	9.2	19.0	3.2	354.3
Depreciation and amortisation[3]	167.7	96.8	41.1	7.2	16.1	2.0	330.9
2001 (restated)							
Total operating profit before exceptional items[1]	156.5	248.8	78.8	32.3	21.3	(7.1)	530.6
Operating exceptional items[1]	(52.8)	(21.8)	(16.1)	–	(0.7)	(16.9)	(108.3)
(Loss)/profit on disposal of fixed assets[1]	(0.3)	(3.1)	(1.3)	0.9	–	7.4	3.6
Capital employed[2]	2,004.9	1,152.7	589.9	98.5	81.4	47.1	3,974.5
Capital expenditure[3]	170.6	95.5	53.8	10.3	17.9	4.5	352.6
Depreciation and amortisation[3]	169.4	97.4	37.2	6.7	15.6	3.2	329.5
2000 (restated)							
Total operating profit before exceptional items[1]	127.2	254.6	71.1	27.2	18.6	(2.3)	496.4
Operating exceptional items[1]	(5.5)	(15.8)	(4.5)	–	1.5	19.9	(4.4)
Capital employed[2]	2,120.8	1,374.7	640.5	120.5	128.0	68.7	4,453.2
Capital expenditure[3]	222.2	99.1	59.1	15.5	16.8	1.0	413.7
Depreciation and amortisation[3]	157.9	93.8	33.3	7.2	17.1	4.0	313.3

1. Including share of joint ventures and associates.
2. Capital employed comprises the capital and reserves of the Group, its long-term liabilities and all current borrowings net of cash and deposits.
3. Subsidiary undertakings only.

1. Segmental information continued

c) Regional analysis

	Europe £ million	Americas £ million	Africa £ million	Asia/Pacific £ million	Total Group £ million
2002					
Total operating profit before exceptional items[1]	155.2	121.3	56.7	166.9	500.1
Operating exceptional items[1]	(38.4)	(8.1)	(0.4)	(27.6)	(74.5)
(Loss)/profit on termination/disposal of businesses[1]	(1.5)	(18.7)	–	–	(20.2)
Capital employed[2]	944.4	1,244.0	221.2	1,183.5	3,593.1
Capital expenditure[3]	121.4	134.7	25.6	72.6	354.3
2001 (restated)					
Total operating profit before exceptional items[1]	165.5	137.2	69.4	158.5	530.6
Operating exceptional items[1]	(42.9)	(40.5)	–	(24.9)	(108.3)
(Loss)/profit on disposal of fixed assets[1]	(2.2)	4.6	2.6	(1.4)	3.6
Capital employed[2]	1,221.1	1,305.5	259.0	1,188.9	3,974.5
Capital expenditure[3]	134.6	108.6	26.4	83.0	352.6
2000 (restated)					
Total operating profit before exceptional items[1]	171.3	117.3	66.1	141.7	496.4
Operating exceptional items[1]	22.9	(25.4)	(0.6)	(1.3)	(4.4)
Capital employed[2]	1,412.5	1,424.9	328.3	1,287.5	4,453.2
Capital expenditure[3]	127.2	121.9	31.8	132.8	413.7

1. Including share of joint ventures and associates.
2. Capital employed comprises the capital and reserves of the Group, its long-term liabilities and all current borrowings net of cash and deposits.
3. Subsidiary undertakings only.

d) Joint ventures and associates – business analysis

	Joint ventures			Associates			
	Process Gas Solutions £ million	Industrial and Special Products £ million	BOC Edwards £ million	Process Gas Solutions £ million	Industrial and Special Products £ million	BOC Edwards £ million	Afrox hospitals £ million
2002							
Turnover[1]	119.9	142.7	61.5	10.6	7.9	7.1	10.5
Operating profit before exceptional items[1]	30.9	20.8	12.1	5.0	1.9	1.7	2.1
Operating exceptional items[1]	(0.4)	(0.1)	–	–	–	–	–
Capital employed[2]	93.6	63.8	48.1	40.1	11.9	2.1	3.4
Capital expenditure	46.5	7.5	8.0	8.3	1.8	1.5	0.6
Group share	23.0	3.7	4.0	2.6	0.6	0.4	0.2
Other partners	23.5	3.8	4.0	5.7	1.2	1.1	0.4
Depreciation and amortisation[1]	20.9	8.2	6.1	2.9	0.7	0.1	0.2
2001 (restated)							
Turnover[1]	122.1	144.4	73.5	9.2	7.7	8.0	21.4
Operating profit before exceptional items[1]	28.2	16.8	14.0	4.1	3.0	2.1	4.0
Operating exceptional items[1]	(0.6)	(1.6)	–	(0.2)	(0.1)	(0.1)	–
Capital employed[2]	99.3	61.6	43.9	27.4	10.5	2.4	6.8
Capital expenditure	55.9	12.0	35.4	2.5	0.4	0.2	3.3
Group share	27.8	5.9	17.7	0.7	0.1	0.1	1.0
Other partners	28.1	6.1	17.7	1.8	0.3	0.1	2.3
Depreciation and amortisation[1]	20.5	7.9	5.4	2.5	0.5	0.1	0.6
2000 (restated)							
Turnover[1]	72.4	135.4	50.2	8.3	6.9	5.8	20.1
Operating profit[1]	19.6	16.9	11.6	1.6	2.5	1.2	3.2
Capital employed[2]	96.2	74.8	44.9	25.5	9.7	1.3	7.5
Capital expenditure	146.2	36.1	28.6	0.8	1.2	0.4	4.0
Group share	49.5	17.9	14.3	0.3	0.3	0.1	1.1
Other partners	96.7	18.2	14.3	0.5	0.9	0.3	2.9
Depreciation and amortisation[1]	9.9	10.1	3.8	2.3	0.5	–	0.5

1. Group share.
2. Capital employed comprises the Group's share of the net assets of joint ventures or associates.

1. Segmental information continued

e) Joint ventures and associates – regional analysis

	Joint ventures		Associates		
	Americas £ million	Asia/Pacific £ million	Americas £ million	Africa £ million	Asia/Pacific £ million
2002					
Turnover[1]	85.4	238.7	–	10.5	25.6
Operating profit before exceptional items[1]	21.9	41.9	–	2.1	8.6
Operating exceptional items[1]	–	(0.5)	–	–	–
Capital employed[2]	25.2	180.3	13.7	3.4	40.4
Capital expenditure	3.4	58.6	5.5	0.6	6.1
Group share	1.4	29.3	1.7	0.2	1.9
Other partners	2.0	29.3	3.8	0.4	4.2
Depreciation and amortisation[1]	14.6	20.6	–	0.2	3.7
2001 (restated)					
Turnover[1]	88.5	251.5	–	21.4	24.9
Operating profit before exceptional items[1]	18.5	40.5	–	4.0	9.2
Operating exceptional items[1]	–	(2.2)	–	–	(0.4)
Capital employed[2]	27.7	177.1	–	6.8	40.3
Capital expenditure	35.2	68.1	–	3.3	3.1
Group share	17.4	34.0	–	1.0	0.9
Other partners	17.8	34.1	–	2.3	2.2
Depreciation and amortisation[1]	14.7	19.1	–	0.6	3.1
2000 (restated)					
Turnover[1]	43.1	214.9	–	20.1	21.0
Operating profit[1]	12.6	35.5	–	3.2	5.3
Capital employed[2]	33.6	182.3	–	7.5	36.5
Capital expenditure	120.7	90.2	–	4.0	2.4
Group share	36.6	45.1	–	1.1	0.7
Other partners	84.1	45.1	–	2.9	1.7
Depreciation and amortisation[1]	6.5	17.3	–	0.5	2.8

1. Group share.
2. Capital employed comprises the Group's share of the net assets of joint ventures or associates.

f) Significant country analysis

	UK			US		
	2002 £ million	2001 (restated) £ million	2000 (restated) £ million	2002 £ million	2001 (restated) £ million	2000 (restated) £ million
Turnover	868.7	837.2	835.5	1,065.6	1,167.7	1,082.7
Total operating profit before exceptional items	115.2	125.5	136.4	50.5	66.9	77.6
Operating exceptional items	(36.5)	(41.9)	22.7	(25.7)	(34.5)	(24.8)
Exceptional (loss)/profit on disposal of fixed assets	–	(1.7)	–	–	4.6	–
Capital employed[1]	733.9	928.6	1,180.8	1,091.6	1,231.0	1,275.5
Capital expenditure	110.0	126.3	116.8	124.8	99.8	106.0

1. Capital employed comprises the capital and reserves of the Group, its long-term liabilities and all current borrowings net of cash and deposits.

2. Profit and loss

a) Analysis of costs

i) Expense category	2002 £ million	2001 (restated) £ million	2000 (restated) £ million
Cost of sales	(2,104.8)	(2,208.8)	(2,035.8)
Distribution costs	(344.1)	(339.3)	(327.2)
Administrative expenses[1]	(861.4)	(874.1)	(781.9)
Income from other fixed asset investments	4.2	2.0	0.6
Net operating expenses	(1,201.3)	(1,211.4)	(1,108.5)

1. Included in total administrative expenses is research and development expenditure of £47.0 million (2001: £59.7 million, 2000: £59.2 million).

2. Profit and loss continued

ii) 2002 analysis	Continuing operations £ million	Acquisitions £ million	Total before exceptional items £ million	Exceptional items £ million	Total £ million
Cost of sales	(1,998.2)	(91.5)	(2,089.7)	(15.1)	(2,104.8)
Distribution costs	(332.2)	(9.7)	(341.9)	(2.2)	(344.1)
Administrative expenses[1]	(783.2)	(21.5)	(804.7)	(56.7)	(861.4)
Income from other fixed asset investments	4.2	–	4.2	–	4.2
Net operating expenses	(1,111.2)	(31.2)	(1,142.4)	(58.9)	(1,201.3)

iii) 2001 analysis (restated)	Continuing operations before exceptional items £ million	Exceptional items £ million	Total £ million
Cost of sales	(2,164.2)	(44.6)	(2,208.8)
Distribution costs	(338.1)	(1.2)	(339.3)
Administrative expenses[1]	(814.2)	(59.9)	(874.1)
Income from other fixed asset investments	2.0	–	2.0
Net operating expenses	(1,150.3)	(61.1)	(1,211.4)

iv) 2000 analysis (restated)			
Cost of sales	(2,035.2)	(0.6)	(2,035.8)
Distribution costs	(327.2)	–	(327.2)
Administrative expenses[1]	(778.1)	(3.8)	(781.9)
Income from other fixed asset investments	0.6	–	0.6
Net operating expenses	(1,104.7)	(3.8)	(1,108.5)

1. Included in total administrative expenses is research and development expenditure of £47.0 million (2001: £59.7 million, 2000: £59.2 million).

b) Exceptional items analysis

	2002 £ million	2001 (restated) £ million	2000 £ million
(Charged)/credited in arriving at operating profit			
Restructuring costs	(47.2)	(35.8)	(18.8)
Write-down and impairment of assets	(21.2)	(24.5)	–
Write-down of unproductive assets identified for disposal	–	(21.0)	–
FRS17 retirement plan benefit amendments	–	(16.7)	–
Business systems investments	–	–	(6.0)
Costs of proposed takeover	(6.1)	(10.3)	(45.6)
Break fee	–	–	66.0
Total operating exceptional items	(74.5)	(108.3)	(4.4)

i) Restructuring costs
The business initiative announced in August 2001 included a number of restructuring programmes. The major programmes included the restructuring of BOC Edwards manufacturing capacity, closure of production at the Process Plants Edmonton site in the UK, investments in information technology and information management systems, restructuring to deliver operational efficiencies in Process Gas Solutions and restructuring of operational networks in Industrial and Special Products. Cash flow from operating activities includes an outflow of £48.0 million in 2002 in respect of these exceptional items.

ii) Write-downs of assets
In September 2002 BOC and Air Liquide announced a conditional agreement to merge their industrial and medical gases businesses in Japan to form a combined company to be called Japan Air Gases. The net assets of OSK (the existing BOC gases business in Japan), which had included an increase in the value of fixed assets through property revaluations in the 1980s and early 1990s, have been reduced to an appropriate amount based on valuations performed ahead of the merger. This has resulted in a write-down of £32.7 million, of which £11.5 million has been taken against the revaluation reserves, and the balance of £21.2 million has been charged as an exceptional item in the profit and loss account in 2002.

The write-downs in 2001 related to the business initiative announced in August 2001 with the objective of releasing cash tied up in unproductive assets and improving cash generation.

2. Profit and loss continued

iii) Costs of proposed takeover and break fee
The final costs associated with the pre-conditional offer for the Group have been incurred in 2002 in respect of share options and other costs related to the retention of key employees. There are no further costs to come. The break fee was received in 2000 from the potential bidders on the failure of the pre-conditional offer. Cash flow from operating activities includes an outflow of £4.5 million in 2002 in respect of these exceptional items.

	2002 £ million	2001 £ million	2000 £ million
(Charged)/credited after operating profit			
Closure of businesses – continuing operations	(21.3)	–	–
Profit on disposal of businesses – continuing operations	1.1	–	–
Profit on disposal of businesses – discontinued business	–	–	12.5
Profit on disposal of fixed assets – continuing operations	–	13.6	–
Loss on disposal of fixed assets – continuing operations	–	(10.0)	–
Total non-operating exceptional items	(20.2)	3.6	12.5

iv) In March 2002 BOC announced plans to merge its Process Plants business with Linde Engineering in the US to form a new company, Linde BOC Process Plants LLC. The costs of £21.3 million for closing BOC's Process Plants business have been charged as an exceptional item this year. This includes severance costs for 215 employees, the write-down of assets and the costs of winding down the business. Cash flow from operating activities includes an outflow of £12.5 million in 2002 in respect of these exceptional costs.
    In April 2002 BOC Edwards agreed the sale of its US glass coating business, resulting in a profit on disposal of £1.1 million.
v) The profit on disposal of the health care discontinued business in 2000 of £12.5 million arose from the release of provisions established at the time of disposal in 1998.
vi) In 2001, proceeds from the disposal of fixed assets were £41.2 million. Of this, £39.0 million was from those assets which were sold at a profit and £2.2 million was from those assets which were sold at a loss.

c) Fees to auditors

	2002 £ million	2001 £ million	2000 £ million
Audit fees (Parent: £0.3 million, 2001: £0.3 million, 2000: £0.3 million)	1.9	2.0	1.8
Non audit fees			
Tax advice and compliance	2.5	1.6	2.3
Expatriate tax administration	1.4	0.5	–
Acquisition related work	0.8	–	–
Other advice	0.4	0.1	1.0
Total non audit fees	5.1	2.2	3.3
Total fees paid to auditors	7.0	4.2	5.1

Tax compliance and expatriate administration work was outsourced following competitive tender processes. See also page 52 of the corporate governance report.

d) Earnings per share
Basic earnings per share is calculated by dividing the earnings attributable to Ordinary shareholders by the weighted average number of shares in issue during the year.
    For diluted earnings per share, the weighted average number of shares in issue is adjusted to assume conversion of all dilutive potential shares. The company has only one category of dilutive potential shares: those share options granted to employees where the exercise price is less than the average market price of the company's shares during the year and where any performance conditions have been met at the balance sheet date.
    Earnings per share before exceptional items are presented in order to show the underlying earnings performance of the Group.

i) Earnings	2002 £ million	2001 (restated) £ million	2000 (restated) £ million
Amounts used in computing the earnings per share			
Earnings attributable to Ordinary shareholders for the financial year	202.9	224.1	278.6
Adjustment for exceptional items[1]	71.4	55.9	(17.8)
Adjusted earnings before exceptional items	274.3	280.0	260.8

1. This comprises the exceptional items before interest of £(94.7) million (2001: £(104.7) million, 2000: £8.1 million) adjusted for the impact of tax of £22.8 million (2001: £46.9 million, 2000: £9.7 million) and minority interests of £0.5 million (2001: £1.9 million, 2000: £nil).

2. Profit and loss continued

ii) Average number of 25p Ordinary shares	2002 million	2001 million	2000 million
Average issued share capital	**496.0**	493.3	491.5
Less: Average own shares held in trust	**5.6**	6.4	4.4
Basic	**490.4**	486.9	487.1
Add: Dilutive share options	**1.8**	1.7	2.5
Diluted	**492.2**	488.6	489.6

3. Treasury information

a) Interest on net debt

	2002 £ million	2001 £ million	2000 £ million
Interest payable on borrowings totally repayable within five years	**47.5**	75.1	94.1
Interest payable on all other borrowings	**55.7**	50.1	41.4
Interest payable and similar charges	**103.2**	125.2	135.5
Interest capitalised	**(2.0)**	(2.5)	(7.1)
Interest payable (net of interest capitalised)	**101.2**	122.7	128.4
Interest receivable and similar income	**(22.6)**	(24.2)	(27.7)
Interest (net)	**78.6**	98.5	100.7
Share of interest of joint ventures (net)	**23.2**	22.6	7.9
Share of interest of associates	**1.3**	2.3	2.9
Total interest on net debt	**103.1**	123.4	111.5
Interest payable on finance leases	**5.3**	6.9	4.6
Interest payable on borrowings repayable by instalments	**19.5**	29.1	27.3

Share of interest of joint ventures and associates is after deducting capitalised interest of £nil (2001: £1.0 million, 2000: £12.9 million). The interest capitalised in 2000 was mainly in BOC's joint venture in Mexico.

b) Currency, interest rate and counterparty exposure

The Group's approach to managing currency and interest rate risk and its use of swaps in that process is described on pages 45 and 46 in the finance and treasury review under the heading 'management of financial risks'.

Interest rate swaps
At 30 September 2002, the Group had entered into six interest rate swap agreements (2001: five) with notional principal amounts of £420.0 million (2001: £375.4 million). The swaps' underlying currencies are sterling, US dollars and Japanese yen. The following table shows the maturity profile and weighted average interest rates payable and receivable on interest rate swaps at 30 September:

Maturity profile	2002 £ million	2001 £ million
Beyond five years	**295.0**	68.0
Four to five years	**–**	–
Three to four years	**–**	–
Two to three years	**–**	125.0
One to two years	**125.0**	–
Within one year	**–**	182.4
	420.0	375.4
	%	%
Average receivable swap rate	**5.5**	6.0
Average payable swap rate	**4.8**	5.2

The weighted average receivable/payable swap interest rate is calculated by applying the notional swap interest received or paid, using rates applicable at the financial year end, to the notional principal of outstanding swaps at the financial year end.

3. Treasury information continued

Currency swaps
At 30 September 2002, the Group had entered into eight currency swap agreements (2001: nine) with notional principal amounts of £360.7 million (2001: £359.6 million). The maturity dates range between one month and 33 months from the balance sheet date (2001: between one month and 24 months). The following table illustrates the impact of the currency swaps on the Group's net debt at 30 September:

				2002			2001
	Capital employed £ million	Gross borrowings £ million	Cash at bank and in hand £ million	Currency swaps £ million	Adjusted net borrowings £ million	Capital employed (restated) £ million	Adjusted net borrowings £ million
Sterling	781.7	(615.4)	13.6	256.6	(345.2)	1,103.0	(298.2)
US dollar	1,190.5	(327.2)	8.5	(185.7)	(504.4)	1,249.6	(469.5)
Australian dollar	263.1	(35.6)	71.2	(79.6)	(44.0)	268.5	(109.6)
South African rand	202.5	(46.6)	4.4	–	(42.2)	218.6	(47.8)
Japanese yen	237.4	(206.2)	51.5	(52.2)	(206.9)	260.8	(199.2)
Canadian dollar	85.8	(41.1)	1.0	–	(40.1)	80.9	(38.5)
Thai baht	120.6	(64.0)	6.3	–	(57.7)	73.7	(38.7)
Other	711.5	(175.0)	29.0	60.9	(85.1)	719.4	(70.6)
Total	3,593.1	(1,511.1)	185.5	–	(1,325.6)	3,974.5	(1,272.1)

The average receivable interest rate on currency swaps was 4.0 per cent (2001: 4.9 per cent) and the average payable interest rate was 2.8 per cent (2001: 3.5 per cent). The weighted average receivable/payable swap interest rate is calculated by applying the notional swap interest received or paid, using rates applicable at the financial year end, to the notional principal of outstanding swaps at the financial year end.

The currency and interest rate exposure of the net borrowings of the Group at 30 September, after taking into account interest rate and currency swaps entered into by the Group, is given in the table below.

			2002			2001
	Fixed rate £ million	Floating rate £ million	Total £ million	Fixed rate £ million	Floating rate £ million	Total £ million
Sterling	300.0	45.2	345.2	299.0	(0.8)	298.2
US dollar	225.5	278.9	504.4	241.2	228.3	469.5
Australian dollar	35.6	8.4	44.0	35.9	73.7	109.6
South African rand	23.7	18.5	42.2	78.0	(30.2)	47.8
Japanese yen	165.9	41.0	206.9	178.2	21.0	199.2
Canadian dollar	–	40.1	40.1	1.0	37.5	38.5
Thai baht	52.1	5.6	57.7	30.4	8.3	38.7
Other	25.5	59.6	85.1	29.0	41.6	70.6
Total	828.3	497.3	1,325.6	892.7	379.4	1,272.1

Counterparty risk
The Group is exposed to credit-related losses in the event of non-performance by counterparties to financial instruments, but does not expect any counterparties to fail to meet their obligations. There are procedures and policies in place limiting the Group's exposure to concentrations of credit or country risk.

3. Treasury information continued

c) Net borrowings and finance leases

i) Analysis

	Group 2002 £ million	Group 2001 £ million	Parent 2002 £ million	Parent 2001 £ million
Secured				
Finance leases	33.8	45.6	–	–
Other secured borrowings	68.0	71.7	–	–
Unsecured				
12¼% Unsecured Loan Stock 2012/2017	100.0	100.0	100.0	100.0
7¼% Notes 2002	–	150.0	–	150.0
6¼% Notes 2002	34.6	33.6	–	–
7.45% Guaranteed Notes 2006	159.2	170.0	–	–
Pollution Control and Industrial Bonds	19.3	39.2	–	–
European Investment Bank loans	82.8	85.1	–	–
6.75% Bonds 2004	125.0	125.0	125.0	125.0
1.00% Euroyen Bond 2006	130.6	142.8	130.6	142.8
5⅞% Bonds 2009	200.0	–	200.0	–
6.50% Bonds 2016	200.0	200.0	200.0	200.0
Medium term notes	57.4	–	57.4	–
Commercial paper	147.0	94.7	–	36.5
Other borrowings	153.4	248.6	166.9	131.7
Total borrowings and finance leases	1,511.1	1,506.3	979.9	886.0
Less: Cash at bank and in hand – due within one year	185.5	233.5	–	51.7
– due beyond one year	–	0.7	–	–
Net borrowings and finance leases	1,325.6	1,272.1	979.9	834.3

A reconciliation of net cash flow to the movement in net debt is given in note 14 b).

ii) Maturity

	Group 2002 £ million	Group 2001 £ million	Parent 2002 £ million	Parent 2001 £ million
Long and medium-term bank loans				
Repayable – beyond five years	11.5	7.3	–	–
– two to five years	41.8	58.2	–	–
– one to two years	36.9	40.0	–	–
Loans other than from banks				
Repayable – beyond five years	536.0	618.5	531.3	442.8
– two to five years	342.7	159.7	148.8	127.6
– one to two years	129.4	101.0	120.9	–
Finance leases				
Repayable beyond one year	22.7	35.2	–	–
Borrowings and finance leases (note 11 a))	1,121.0	1,019.9	801.0	570.4
Short-term – repayable within one year				
Bank loans and overdrafts	196.7	187.9	178.9	119.1
Loans other than from banks	182.3	288.1	–	196.5
Finance leases	11.1	10.4	–	–
Total borrowings and finance leases	1,511.1	1,506.3	979.9	886.0
Less: Cash at bank and in hand – repayable within one year	185.5	233.5	–	51.7
– repayable beyond one year	–	0.7	–	–
Net borrowings and finance leases	1,325.6	1,272.1	979.9	834.3

	2002 Finance leases £ million	2002 Borrowings £ million	2002 Total £ million	2001 Finance leases £ million	2001 Borrowings £ million	2001 Total £ million
Repayment profile of borrowings and finance leases						
Long-term repayable						
– beyond five years	2.0	547.5	549.5	4.3	625.8	630.1
– four to five years	2.0	142.5	144.5	2.2	31.6	33.8
– three to four years	2.4	179.7	182.1	2.4	33.3	35.7
– two to three years	1.7	62.3	64.0	14.5	153.0	167.5
– one to two years	14.6	166.3	180.9	11.8	141.0	152.8
Total	22.7	1,098.3	1,121.0	35.2	984.7	1,019.9

3. Treasury information continued

iii) Short-term interest rates
The average interest rate on commercial paper for the year to 30 September 2002 was 3.4 per cent (2001: 6.4 per cent) and on other short-term borrowings was 9.0 per cent (2001: 11.4 per cent).

iv) Facilities
The Group maintains a number of short and medium-term committed lines of credit. The main medium-term facilities are multi-currency agreements with a group of relationship banks, under which the Group may borrow up to US$420.0 million (2001: US$420.0 million) for general corporate purposes. These facilities were undrawn both at 30 September 2002 and 30 September 2001. The following table shows the maturity profile of these facilities.

	2002 $ million	2001 $ million
Within one year	200.0	–
One to two years	220.0	200.0
Two to three years	–	220.0
	420.0	420.0

Additional committed facilities are maintained by the principal operating units in the Group.

v) Security
The secured loans, maturing between 2002 and 2019, are principally secured by charges over the property, plant and machinery, stocks and trade debtors of certain overseas subsidiaries.

d) Fair value information

i) Fair values of financial instruments
Set out below is a comparison of the carrying amount of the Group's financial instruments (excluding short-term debtors and creditors) at 30 September 2002. Further details of the Group's financial instruments are given in notes 3 f) i) and ii).

	Note	2002 Carrying amount £ million	Fair value £ million	2001 Carrying amount £ million	Fair value £ million
Primary financial instruments					
Loans to joint ventures and associates	1	118.0	118.0	106.7	106.7
Other fixed asset investments	2	45.1	44.0	31.7	32.6
Current asset investments	3	38.8	39.5	43.2	44.1
Cash at bank and in hand	4	185.5	185.5	234.2	234.2
Borrowings and finance leases (excluding swap agreements)	5	(1,530.6)	(1,635.7)	(1,491.7)	(1,563.5)
Provisions for liabilities and charges	6	(16.9)	(16.9)	(21.7)	(21.7)
Derivative financial instruments held to manage the Group's interest rate and currency risk profile					
Foreign currency and interest rate swap agreements	7	19.5	31.1	(14.6)	(8.5)
Forward foreign exchange contracts	8	–	4.9	–	(9.1)
Net financial instruments		(1,140.6)	(1,229.6)	(1,112.2)	(1,185.2)
Financial assets		387.4		415.8	
Financial liabilities[9]		(1,528.0)		(1,528.0)	
Net financial instruments		(1,140.6)		(1,112.2)	

1. For those bearing either no interest or a floating rate of interest it is deemed that the carrying amount approximates to the fair value. For those bearing a fixed rate of interest an assessment of the interest rate at which the Group could make the same loan under current conditions has been made. Unless this differs significantly from the fixed rate it is also deemed that the carrying amount approximates to the fair value. Where this does differ significantly, the fair value is based on the discounted value of future cash flows.
2. For equity instruments listed on a recognised stock exchange the fair value is the quoted market price. For other equity instruments it is deemed that the carrying amount approximates to the fair value.
3. The fair value is the quoted market price.
4. As all bear either no interest or a floating rate of interest it is deemed that the carrying amount approximates to the fair value.
5. For those bearing a floating rate of interest it is deemed that the carrying amount approximates to the fair value. For those bearing a fixed rate of interest the fair value is either the quoted market price where a liquid market exists or has been calculated using well established pricing models.
6. Both the carrying amount and the fair value are based on current market prices and interest rates.
7. The fair value is the estimated amount the Group would receive or pay to terminate the agreements.
8. The fair value represents the net effect on the Group of closing out all outstanding contracts.
9. Includes foreign currency and interest rate swap agreements.

3. Treasury information continued

ii) Hedges
As explained on pages 45 and 46 of the finance and treasury review under the heading 'management of financial risks', the Group's policies are to use forward foreign exchange contracts to hedge transactional currency exposures (principally arising through anticipated sales and purchase transactions) and swap agreements to manage interest rate risks and hedge structural currency exposures.

Currency swaps are only held to change the currency of the Group's borrowings to match better its net investments in its overseas subsidiaries. In accordance with the Group's accounting policies, the assets and liabilities arising from these swap agreements are translated into sterling at the spot rate ruling at the balance sheet date. The resulting exchange gains or losses are recognised in the statement of total recognised gains and losses (to match the exchange gains or losses on the net investments in the overseas subsidiaries).

The carrying amount of the swap agreements (as shown in note 3 d) i)) is the result of the exchange gains and losses recognised in the statement of total recognised gains and losses, and is analysed in the deferred gains and losses table shown below.

	Swap agreements		
	Gains £ million	Losses £ million	Net £ million
Deferred gains and losses			
Deferred gains and losses on hedges at 1 October 2001	7.3	(21.9)	(14.6)
Gains and losses on hedges maturing in 2002	(5.0)	12.1	7.1
Deferred gains and losses on hedges recognised in the statement of total recognised gains and losses in 2002	23.6	3.4	27.0
Deferred gains and losses on hedges at 30 September 2002	**25.9**	**(6.4)**	**19.5**

The unrecognised difference between the carrying amount and the fair value of the forward foreign exchange contracts and the swap agreements (as shown in note 3 d) i)) is analysed in the unrecognised gains and losses table below.

	Forward foreign exchange contracts		Swap agreements		
	Gains £ million	Losses £ million	Gains £ million	Losses £ million	Net total £ million
Unrecognised gains and losses					
Unrecognised gains and losses on hedges at 1 October 2001	1.7	(10.8)	12.3	(6.2)	(3.0)
Gains and losses arising in previous years that were recognised in 2002	(1.5)	7.8	(4.3)	0.1	2.1
Gains and losses arising before 2002 that were not recognised in 2002	0.2	(3.0)	8.0	(6.1)	(0.9)
Gains and losses arising in 2002 that were not recognised in 2002	5.4	2.3	14.1	(4.4)	17.4
Unrecognised gains and losses on hedges at 30 September 2002	**5.6**	**(0.7)**	**22.1**	**(10.5)**	**16.5**
Of which					
Gains and losses expected to be recognised in 2003	5.2	(0.7)	0.8	(0.5)	4.8
Gains and losses expected to be recognised in 2004 or later	0.4	–	21.3	(10.0)	11.7

e) Currency exposures
As outlined on page 45 in the finance and treasury review under the heading 'currency risk', it is the Group's policy to hedge against the potential impact on its profit and loss account of the currency gains and losses arising from monetary assets and liabilities not denominated in the operating or functional currency of the operating unit involved.

After taking account of the hedging transactions, there was no significant net profit and loss account exposure to currency gains and losses arising from monetary assets and liabilities at 30 September 2002.

f) Financial instruments
i) Financial assets
The interest rate and currency profile of the Group's financial assets (excluding short-term debtors) at 30 September 2002 is shown below. The categories of the Group's financial assets are shown in note 3 d) i).

	2002				2001			
	Floating rate financial assets £ million	Fixed rate financial assets £ million	Financial assets on which no interest is received £ million	Total financial assets £ million	Floating rate financial assets £ million	Fixed rate financial assets £ million	Financial assets on which no interest is received £ million	Total financial assets £ million
Sterling	28.1	11.5	1.7	41.3	65.8	10.0	2.3	78.1
US dollar	10.4	123.4	21.3	155.1	13.9	115.8	21.2	150.9
Australian dollar	82.4	–	–	82.4	20.6	–	–	20.6
South African rand	9.0	–	1.6	10.6	44.4	–	2.3	46.7
Japanese yen	51.5	–	6.7	58.2	26.5	–	7.7	34.2
Other	39.2	–	0.6	39.8	85.2	–	0.1	85.3
Total	**220.6**	**134.9**	**31.9**	**387.4**	**256.4**	**125.8**	**33.6**	**415.8**

3. Treasury information continued

	2002 Fixed rate financial assets		2001 Fixed rate financial assets	
	Weighted average interest rate %	Weighted average period for which rate is fixed years	Weighted average interest rate %	Weighted average period for which rate is fixed years
Sterling	6.7	2.1	6.1	2.9
US dollar	10.3	4.8	10.1	5.4

Financial assets on which no interest is received comprise £30.3 million (2001: £31.7 million) of non-redeemable equity instruments in other companies and £1.6 million (2001: £1.9 million) of loans to joint ventures and associates which have no fixed date of repayment.

The floating rate financial assets, which principally comprise cash and deposits and loans to joint ventures and associates, carry interest based on different benchmark rates depending on the currency of the balance.

The principal benchmark rates for floating rate financial assets are LIBOR for sterling balances, US LIBOR for US dollar balances, Australian bank bill rate for Australian dollar balances, South African prime rate for South African rand balances and Japanese yen LIBOR for Japanese yen balances.

ii) Financial liabilities
The interest rate and currency profile of the Group's financial liabilities including swaps (excluding short-term creditors) at 30 September 2002 is shown below. The categories of the Group's financial liabilities are shown in note 3 d) i).

	2002							2001
	Floating rate financial liabilities £ million	Fixed rate financial liabilities £ million	Financial liabilities on which no interest is paid £ million	Total financial liabilities £ million	Floating rate financial liabilities £ million	Fixed rate financial liabilities £ million	Financial liabilities on which no interest is paid £ million	Total financial liabilities £ million
Sterling	58.8	300.0	–	358.8	66.6	299.0	1.9	367.5
US dollar	304.3	225.5	–	529.8	257.9	241.2	–	499.1
Australian dollar	79.6	35.6	–	115.2	83.4	35.9	–	119.3
South African rand	22.9	23.7	–	46.6	8.3	78.0	–	86.3
Japanese yen	92.5	165.9	–	258.4	47.5	178.2	–	225.7
Canadian dollar	41.1	–	–	41.1	39.3	1.0	–	40.3
Thai baht	11.9	52.1	–	64.0	11.5	30.4	–	41.9
Other	88.6	25.5	–	114.1	118.9	29.0	–	147.9
Total	699.7	828.3	–	1,528.0	633.4	892.7	1.9	1,528.0

	2002 Fixed rate financial liabilities		2001 Fixed rate financial liabilities	
	Weighted average interest rate %	Weighted average period for which rate is fixed years	Weighted average interest rate %	Weighted average period for which rate is fixed years
Sterling	8.3	13.9	8.4	14.9
US dollar	7.1	4.2	7.1	5.2
Australian dollar	6.2	0.2	6.2	1.3
South African rand	11.9	3.9	12.4	2.9
Japanese yen	0.9	3.8	1.0	4.2
Thai baht	4.0	1.8	6.2	0.4
Other	9.7	2.8	10.2	3.2

The floating rate financial liabilities principally comprise debt which carries interest based on different benchmark rates depending on the currency of the balance.

The principal benchmark rates for floating rate financial liabilities are LIBOR for sterling balances, US LIBOR for US dollar balances, Australian bank bill rate for Australian dollar balances, South African prime rate for South African rand balances and Japanese yen LIBOR for Japanese yen balances.

The maturity profile of the net borrowings is set out in note 3 c) ii). Other floating rate financial liabilities are mainly employee incentive provisions. These are expected to be utilised over the period to 2004 depending on the future choices of the relevant employees.

4. Tax

a) Tax on profit on ordinary activities

	2002 £ million	2001 (restated) £ million	2000 (restated) £ million
Current tax:			
Payable in the UK			
Corporation tax at 30% (2001: 30%, 2000: 30%)	**51.7**	60.4	54.8
Double tax relief	**(19.7)**	(17.0)	(16.3)
	32.0	43.4	38.5
Payable overseas			
US – Federal tax at 35% (2001: 35%, 2000: 35%)	**(1.0)**	–	2.1
– State and local taxes	**0.6**	1.3	1.6
– Prior year tax	**–**	(2.2)	(1.1)
Australia at 30% (2001: 34%, 2000: 36%)	**14.6**	14.0	18.2
South Africa at 30% (2001: 30%, 2000: 30%)	**18.0**	15.2	14.5
Japan at 42% (2001: 42%, 2000: 48%)	**8.3**	12.7	11.2
Other countries	**30.9**	27.3	20.3
	71.4	68.3	66.8
Total current tax	**103.4**	111.7	105.3
Deferred tax:			
Origination and reversal of timing differences	**3.4**	(7.1)	29.9
Effect of change in tax rate on opening liability	**(0.6)**	–	–
Total deferred tax	**2.8**	(7.1)	29.9
Tax on profit on ordinary activities	**106.2**	104.6	135.2
Analysis of charge in the period by entity type			
Subsidiary undertakings	**100.3**	97.6	121.6
Share of joint ventures	**3.6**	4.3	11.5
Share of associates	**2.3**	2.7	2.1
Tax on profit on ordinary activities	**106.2**	104.6	135.2

The tax charge includes a credit of £15.3 million for the operating exceptional charges (2001: £48.8 million, 2000: £12.4 million) and a credit of £7.5 million for the non-operating exceptional charges (2001: £1.9 million charge, 2000: £2.7 million charge). The effective rate of tax excluding exceptional items was 30.0 per cent (2001: 32.5 per cent, 2000: 33.4 per cent).

b) Deferred tax

i) Deferred tax – UK GAAP	2002 £ million	2001 (restated) £ million	2000 (restated) £ million
Analysis			
Arising from accelerated depreciation allowances	**362.1**	344.8	326.5
Other timing differences	**(53.5)**	(32.5)	(20.7)
Tax losses and other credits available	**(24.7)**	(26.4)	(18.5)
	283.9	285.9	287.3
Movement during the year			
At 1 October 2001	**285.9**	287.3	256.8
Exchange adjustment	**(8.6)**	(7.3)	10.6
Arising during the year[1]	**9.5**	(3.1)	23.7
Transfers to current tax	**0.8**	3.3	2.3
Other movements	**(3.7)**	5.7	(6.1)
At 30 September 2002[2]	**283.9**	285.9	287.3

1. Subsidiary undertakings only.
2. The balance at 30 September 2002 represents deferred tax assets of £7.9 million (2001: £8.4 million, 2000: £8.5 million) and deferred tax liabilities of £291.8 million (2001: £294.3 million, 2000: £295.8 million).

4. Tax continued

ii) Deferred tax – US GAAP

For US GAAP reporting, the Group follows SFAS109, Accounting for Income Taxes, in respect of deferred taxation. SFAS109 requires deferred tax to be fully provided on all temporary differences.

The table below provides a reconciliation of deferred taxes from a UK GAAP basis to a US GAAP basis at 30 September 2002.

	UK GAAP £ million	Adjustments to US GAAP £ million	US GAAP £ million
Accelerated capital allowances	362.1	–	362.1
Other temporary differences	(53.5)	72.7	19.2
Tax losses and other credits available	(24.7)	–	(24.7)
	283.9 [1]	72.7	356.6

1. The UK deferred tax balance of £283.9 million does not include the deferred tax asset of £106.4 million relating to the Group's net pension liabilities. As required by the applicable UK GAAP accounting standard, FRS17, this asset is set against the relevant retirement benefit liability to show the net position (see note 6 e)). If it was included above, it would be wholly reversed in the adjustments to US GAAP.

	US GAAP £ million
Movement during the year	
At 1 October 2001	333.8
Exchange adjustment	(7.2)
Arising during the year	37.5
Transfers from current tax	0.8
Other movements	(8.3)
At 30 September 2002	**356.6**

The components of deferred tax assets/(liabilities) at 30 September 2002 were:

	2002 £ million	2001 £ million
Long-term		
Asset	130.4	44.8
Liability	(507.0)	(399.3)
Net liability	(376.6)	(354.5)
Short-term		
Asset	25.5	22.8
Liability	(5.5)	(2.1)
Net asset	20.0	20.7
Total deferred tax assets	155.9	67.6
Total deferred tax liabilities	(512.5)	(401.4)
	(356.6)	(333.8)

4. Tax continued

c) Factors affecting the current and Group effective tax charge for the period

The table set out below provides a reconciliation between the UK corporation tax rate and the Group's effective tax rate, excluding exceptional items, computed by taking the various elements of the tax reconciliation as a percentage of the profit before tax, excluding exceptional items.

	2002 %	2001 (restated) %	2000 (restated) %
UK corporation tax rate	30.0	30.0	30.0
Difference in tax rates of overseas subsidiaries, joint ventures and associates	0.5	1.3	1.2
Excess of tax depreciation over book depreciation	(3.9)	(3.7)	(3.2)
Other timing differences	2.7	(1.5)	(2.0)
State and local taxes	0.5	0.7	1.0
Net utilisation of losses	(1.1)	(0.7)	(0.7)
Investment tax credits	(2.4)	(1.1)	(1.8)
Prior year tax	0.9	(0.6)	(1.3)
Permanent items and other items with less than a 5% net effect	0.1	1.1	2.5
Effective current tax rate before exceptional items	27.3	25.5	25.7
Timing differences	2.7	7.0	7.7
Effective Group tax rate before exceptional items	30.0	32.5	33.4

Profit on ordinary activities before tax (including exceptional items), as shown in the consolidated profit and loss account, is analysed over its component parts as follows:

	2002 £ million	2001 (restated) £ million	2000 (restated) £ million
UK	66.6	86.4	148.1
Overseas	268.7	275.8	293.7
	335.3	362.2	441.8

d) Factors that may affect future tax charges

The total charge in future periods will be affected by any changes to the corporation tax rates in force in the countries in which the Group operates. The current tax charges will also be affected by changes in the excess of tax depreciation over book depreciation and the use of tax credits.

e) Unused tax credits

On a consolidated basis, the Group has net operating loss carryforwards of £44.4 million. If not offset against taxable income, these losses will expire as follows:

Year	Net operating loss £ million
2003	—
2004	11.7
2005	—
2006	—
2007	—
Thereafter, or no expiry date	32.7

For US Federal tax purposes, the Group has investment tax credits and general business tax credits to carry forward of approximately £12.9 million, which are available to reduce income taxes otherwise payable. These do not expire until 2003 or thereafter.

In addition, the Group has alternative minimum tax credits for US Federal income tax purposes of approximately £27.7 million which can be carried forward to reduce regular tax liabilities of future years. There is no expiration date on these credits.

Investment tax credits are accounted for by the flow-through method whereby they reduce income taxes currently payable and the provision for income taxes in the period in which the assets giving rise to such credits are placed in service. Deferred tax assets, subject to the need for a valuation allowance, are recognised to the extent that the investment tax credits are not currently utilised.

5. Directors
Directors' remuneration and interests are given in the report on remuneration on pages 56 to 63.

6. Employees
a) Subsidiaries

	2002		2001	
	Year end	Average	Year end	Average
i) Employees by business				
Process Gas Solutions	5,806	5,979	6,037	6,076
Industrial and Special Products	15,266	14,681	14,369	14,201
BOC Edwards	5,367	5,186	4,830	4,916
Afrox hospitals	14,152	13,934	12,833	12,804
Gist	5,302	5,100	4,774	4,284
Corporate	387	376	328	296
	46,280	45,256	43,171	42,577
ii) Employees by region				
Europe	13,213	12,739	12,173	11,750
Americas	7,243	7,312	7,305	7,262
Africa	17,435	17,213	16,120	16,137
Asia/Pacific	8,389	7,992	7,573	7,428
	46,280	45,256	43,171	42,577

b) Joint ventures and associates

Joint ventures	3,570	3,596	3,595	3,874
Associates	742	728	712	684
	4,312	4,324	4,307	4,558

c) Employment costs

	2002 £ million	2001 (restated) £ million	2000 (restated) £ million
Wages and salaries	813.9	758.8	729.5
Social security costs	77.7	74.0	64.3
Other pension costs	66.3	76.0	54.4
	957.9	908.8	848.2

Other pension costs includes an exceptional charge of £nil (2001: £16.7 million, 2000: £nil). See also note 2 b).

6. Employees continued

d) Option and incentive schemes

BOC operates share option schemes for both executives and employees. The features of these are given in the report on remuneration and the employees report.

i) Summary of movements in share options	Employee options			Executive options[1]			Executive share award plan[2]
	Number of shares million	Range of option prices	Weighted average option price	Number of shares million	Range of option prices	Weighted average option price	Number of shares million
Outstanding at 1 October 1999	6.1	489p-882p	776p	16.7	532p-1119p	847p	—
Granted	1.3	870p	870p	6.7	937p	937p	0.8
Exercised	(1.1)	489p-762p	692p	(0.6)	536p-980p	670p	—
Lapsed	(0.4)	489p-882p	797p	(1.2)	722p-1119p	904p	—
Outstanding at 30 September 2000	5.9	610p-882p	810p	21.6	532p-1119p	877p	0.8
Granted	1.2	894p	894p	4.4	986p-1034p	994p	—
Exercised	(0.4)	610p-894p	765p	(2.5)	532p-980p	740p	—
Lapsed	(1.0)	610p-894p	830p	(1.8)	722p-993p	929p	(0.1)
Outstanding at 30 September 2001	5.7	610p-894p	835p	21.7	627p-1119p	914p	0.7
Granted	1.2	914p	914p	5.5	1016p-1079p	1016p	—
Exercised	(1.0)	610p-914p	787p	(3.1)	627p-980p	868p	(0.7)
Lapsed	(0.5)	610p-914p	857p	(0.6)	742p-1119p	957p	—
Outstanding at 30 September 2002	5.4	650p-914p	855p	23.5	677p-1119p	943p	—
Number of participants at 30 September 2002	6,100			1,097			—
Options exercisable:							
At 30 September 2002	—	—	—	8.6	677p-1119p	877p	—
At 30 September 2001	—	—	—	2.0	627p-742p	705p	—
Fair value of options granted during:							
Year ended 30 September 2002	**289p**			**242p**			
Year ended 30 September 2001	**264p**			**232p**			

1. Executive options include share options and rights and long-term share incentive units.
2. The executive share award plan was granted at an option price of £nil.

The weighted average fair value of options granted during the year was calculated using the Black-Scholes option pricing model. Details of the assumptions used are given in (ii) below.

ii) Analysis of share options	Employee options			Executive options[3]		
	Number of shares thousand	Weighted average option price	Normal exercisable date	Number of shares thousand	Weighted average option price	Normal exercisable date
Outstanding at 30 September 2002						
Date of grant						
1993	—	—	—	242	742p	1996-2003
1994	—	—	—	361	678p	1997-2004
1995	5	650p	2002-2003	712	722p	1999-2005
1996	270	827p	2001-2004	1,110	915p	1999-2006
1997	258	882p	2002-2005	1,276	981p	2000-2007
1998	843	823p	2001-2006	2,100	915p	2001-2008
1999	779	766p	2002-2007	2,809	860p	2002-2009
2000	1,090	870p	2003-2008	5,384	937p	2003-2010
2001	1,037	894p	2004-2009	4,126	994p	2004-2011
2002	1,147	914p	2005-2010	5,353	1016p	2005-2012
	5,429			23,473		

3. Executive options include share options and rights and long-term share incentive units.

6. Employees continued

Executive options are granted at the market price of the company's shares at the time of the grant and consequently there is no compensation expense under UK GAAP. The Group also takes advantage of the exemption granted under UITF17, Employee Share Schemes, whereby no compensation expense need be recorded for employee schemes.

For US reporting purposes the company applies APB Opinion 25, Accounting for Stock Issued to Employees and related interpretations in accounting for its plans. By applying this statement the employee share schemes are deemed non-compensatory and therefore do not result in an expense for financial reporting purposes. Under the executive schemes, grants of share options are at the market price of the company's shares at the time of grant.

If compensation cost for the Group's share option plans had been determined based on the fair value at the grant dates for awards under those plans consistent with the method of US SFAS123, Accounting for Stock Based Compensation, the Group's profit before tax under US GAAP would have been charged with an additional cost of £6.3 million (2001: £9.7 million, 2000: £8.3 million), basic earnings per share would have been 51.18p (2001: 46.71p, 2000: 53.99p) and diluted earnings per share would have been 50.99p (2001: 46.54p, 2000: 53.72p).

The Black-Scholes model was used to measure the compensation expense under US SFAS123. The assumptions used for grants in 2002 included a dividend yield of 4.0 per cent (2001: 4.0 per cent, 2000: 3.3 per cent), expected share price volatility of 31.0 per cent (2001: 30.0 per cent, 2000: 24.6 per cent), a weighted average expected life of 5.0 years (2001: 4.2 years, 2000: 4.2 years) and a weighted average interest rate of 4.9 per cent (2001: 5.1 per cent, 2000: 5.9 per cent). The weighted average interest rate is based on UK Gilts on the date of grant with a maturity similar to the related options.

e) Retirement benefits
i) UK GAAP FRS17 Retirement benefits – Group
The Group operates a number of pension schemes throughout the world. The majority of the schemes are self-administered and the schemes' assets are held independently of the Group's finances. Pension costs are assessed in accordance with the advice of independent, professionally qualified actuaries.

The Group operates defined benefit schemes in Europe, Americas, Africa and Asia/Pacific. The largest schemes are located in the UK, US, South Africa and Australia. The UK and South African schemes are based on final salary and the US on annual salary. With effect from 1 January 1998 the Australian scheme changed to operate primarily as a defined contribution scheme, although it retains some defined benefit guarantees. The geographical split of the pension schemes has been amended in 2002 to be consistent with the segmental analysis.

The most recent actuarial valuations have been updated by an independent qualified actuary to take account of the requirements of FRS17 in order to assess the liabilities of the schemes at 30 September 2002. Scheme assets are stated at their market value at 30 September 2002.

On the advice of the actuaries, company contributions to the principal UK scheme will resume from 1 October 2002 at a rate of 14.4 per cent of payroll. In accordance with South African legislation, contributions recommenced on 7 December 2001 at rates ranging from 10.5 per cent to 12 per cent. Contribution rates were increased in June 2002 and now range from 14.9 per cent to 19.5 per cent. As the South African schemes and the defined benefit guarantees of the Australian scheme are closed schemes, the current service cost as a percentage of pensionable salaries under the projected unit method will increase as the members approach retirement. Contributions recommended to the Australian scheme on 1 October 2001 at rates ranging from 11 per cent to 17 per cent. In the US, company contributions to the pension plan remain suspended.

During the year, the Pension Funds Second Amendment Act, 2001 was passed in South Africa. Under this Act, surpluses in pension funds have to be used in a manner specified under Regulations to the Act to improve current and former members' benefits prior to the employer obtaining any benefit from the surpluses. Consequently, it is considered unlikely that the company will obtain any benefit from the surpluses in the South African schemes. Therefore the surpluses at 30 September 2002 have been written off in the statement of total recognised gains and losses in accordance with FRS17.

Main assumptions for FRS17 purposes	Europe	Americas	Africa	Asia/Pacific
Date of latest actuarial valuation	31 Mar 02	1 Jan 01	30 Jun 01	31 Dec 00
2002				
Rate of increase in salaries	3.9%	3.75%	9.5%	3.5%
Rate of increase in pensions in payment	2.4%	–	6.8%	2.5%
Discount rate	5.5%	6.5%	12.0%	6.1%
Inflation	2.4%	2.5%	7.0%	2.5%
2001				
Rate of increase in salaries	4.55%	4.75%	7.5%	4.0%
Rate of increase in pensions in payment	2.5%	–	4.8%	3.0%
Discount rate	6.1%	7.25%	10.0%	5.75%
Inflation	2.5%	3.75%	7.5%	3.0%
2000				
Rate of increase in salaries	5.0%	4.85%	12.5%	3.5%
Rate of increase in pensions in payment	3.0%	–	9.4%	3.5%
Discount rate	6.2%	7.75%	15.0%	6.25%
Inflation	3.0%	3.75%	12.5%	2.5%

The assumptions used for the US health care benefits for FRS17 purposes are a discount rate of 6.5 per cent (2001: 7.25 per cent, 2000: 7.75 per cent) and an ultimate health care cost trend rate of 4.5 per cent (2001: 4.75 per cent, 2000: 5.25 per cent).

Contributions to non defined benefit schemes in the year were £9.6 million (2001: £6.3 million, 2000: £5.5 million) and are included in note 6 c).

6. **Employees** continued

The assets in the schemes and the expected rates of return were:

	Equities	Bonds	Other	Total
Long-term rate of return expected at 30 September 2002				
Europe	8.5%	4.9%	4.0%	–
Americas	9.5%	6.0%	–	–
Africa	14.0%	12.0%	8.5%	–
Asia/Pacific	7.7%	4.7%	5.7%	–
Value at 30 September 2002 (£ million)				
Europe	686.2	235.0	18.8	940.0
Americas	289.2	51.0	–	340.2
Africa	49.6	15.3	5.4	70.3
Asia/Pacific	89.8	16.3	16.7	122.8
Total	1,114.8	317.6	40.9	1,473.3
Long-term rate of return expected at 30 September 2001				
Europe	8.5%	5.2%	4.6%	–
Americas	9.5%	6.0%	–	–
Africa	12.0%	10.0%	8.4%	–
Asia/Pacific	7.4%	5.1%	6.1%	–
Value at 30 September 2001 (£ million)				
Europe	897.6	226.8	18.8	1,143.2
Americas	345.0	70.7	–	415.7
Africa	54.7	18.2	6.3	79.2
Asia/Pacific	92.3	18.0	17.3	127.6
Total	1,389.6	333.7	42.4	1,765.7
Long-term rate of return expected at 30 September 2000				
Europe	7.5%	5.0%	6.0%	–
Americas	9.0%	6.0%	–	–
Africa	15.5%	13.5%	12.2%	–
Asia/Pacific	7.5%	5.4%	5.9%	–
Value at 30 September 2000 (£ million)				
Europe	1,162.0	250.1	17.2	1,429.3
Americas	469.2	70.1	–	539.3
Africa	74.8	21.3	6.8	102.9
Asia/Pacific	111.7	18.4	18.9	149.0
Total	1,817.7	359.9	42.9	2,220.5

The following amounts at 30 September 2002 were measured in accordance with the requirements of FRS17:

	Europe £ million	Americas pensions £ million	Americas health care £ million	Africa £ million	Asia/Pacific £ million	Total £ million
2002						
Total market value of assets	940.0	340.2	–	70.3	122.8	1,473.3
Present value of scheme liabilities	(1,331.6)	(250.4)	(50.1)	(59.3)	(134.0)	(1,825.4)
Irrecoverable surplus	–	–	–	(11.0)	–	(11.0)
(Deficit)/surplus in the scheme	(391.6)	89.8	(50.1)	–	(11.2)	(363.1)
Related deferred tax asset/(liability)	117.5	(35.5)	19.8	–	4.6	106.4
Net pension (liabilities)/assets[1]	(274.1)	54.3	(30.3)	–	(6.6)	(256.7)
2001						
Total market value of assets	1,143.2	415.7	–	79.2	127.6	1,765.7
Present value of scheme liabilities	(1,172.0)	(258.2)	(52.0)	(66.4)	(130.8)	(1,679.4)
(Deficit)/surplus in the scheme	(28.8)	157.5	(52.0)	12.8	(3.2)	86.3
Related deferred tax asset/(liability)	8.6	(62.2)	20.5	(3.9)	1.7	(35.3)
Net pension (liabilities)/assets[1]	(20.2)	95.3	(31.5)	8.9	(1.5)	51.0
2000						
Total market value of assets	1,429.3	539.3	–	102.9	149.0	2,220.5
Present value of scheme liabilities	(1,161.9)	(233.0)	(43.7)	(70.8)	(146.6)	(1,656.0)
Surplus/(deficit) in the scheme	267.4	306.3	(43.7)	32.1	2.4	564.5
Related deferred tax (liability)/asset	(80.2)	(121.0)	17.3	(9.6)	(0.1)	(193.6)
Net pension assets/(liabilities)[1]	187.2	185.3	(26.4)	22.5	2.3	370.9

1. Included in the net pension (liabilities)/assets are assets of £54.3 million (2001: £107.0 million, 2000: £402.0 million) and liabilities of £311.0 million (2001: £56.0 million, 2000: £31.1 million).

6. Employees *continued*

Analysis of the amount charged to operating profit	Europe £ million	Americas pensions £ million	Americas health care £ million	Africa £ million	Asia/Pacific £ million	Total £ million
Year to 30 September 2002						
Current service cost	**(33.5)**	**(12.8)**	**(1.6)**	**(1.7)**	**(7.2)**	**(56.8)**
Past service cost[2]	**(0.6)**	**0.7**	**–**	**–**	**–**	**0.1**
Total operating charge	**(34.1)**	**(12.1)**	**(1.6)**	**(1.7)**	**(7.2)**	**(56.7)**
Year to 30 September 2001						
Current service cost	(35.8)	(8.6)	(1.3)	(2.2)	(4.7)	(52.6)
Past service cost	(0.4)	(16.7)	–	–	–	(17.1)
Total operating charge	(36.2)	(25.3)	(1.3)	(2.2)	(4.7)	(69.7)
Year to 30 September 2000						
Current service cost	(31.1)	(8.0)	(1.0)	(2.5)	(4.7)	(47.3)
Past service cost	(1.6)	–	–	–	–	(1.6)
Total operating charge	(32.7)	(8.0)	(1.0)	(2.5)	(4.7)	(48.9)

2. Two amendments have been made to the US pension plan in 2002 relating to the allocation of the interest credit to plan members, both retrospectively and in the future. The net impact of the amendments is a £0.7 million credit against past service cost in the year.

Analysis of the amount included in net interest	Europe £ million	Americas pensions £ million	Americas health care £ million	Africa £ million	Asia/Pacific £ million	Total £ million
Year to 30 September 2002						
Expected return on pension scheme assets	**87.4**	**36.2**	**–**	**7.2**	**8.3**	**139.1**
Interest on pension scheme liabilities	**(71.1)**	**(18.6)**	**(3.7)**	**(5.6)**	**(7.1)**	**(106.1)**
Net interest on FRS17 pension schemes	16.3	17.6	(3.7)	1.6	1.2	33.0
Year to 30 September 2001						
Expected return on pension scheme assets	99.3	46.7	–	11.9	9.0	166.9
Interest on pension scheme liabilities	(71.9)	(18.1)	–	(9.7)	(7.5)	(107.2)
Net interest on FRS17 pension schemes	27.4	28.6	–	2.2	1.5	59.7
Year to 30 September 2000						
Expected return on pension scheme assets	88.7	38.4	–	13.0	9.4	149.5
Interest on pension scheme liabilities	(69.4)	(13.7)	–	(10.3)	(7.3)	(100.7)
Net interest on FRS17 pension schemes	19.3	24.7	–	2.7	2.1	48.8

Analysis of the amount recognised in the statement of total recognised gains and losses	Europe £ million	Americas pensions £ million	Americas health care £ million	Africa £ million	Asia/Pacific £ million	Total £ million
Year to 30 September 2002						
Actual return less expected return on pension scheme assets	**(246.4)**	**(71.6)**	**–**	**3.0**	**(13.6)**	**(328.6)**
Experience gains and losses arising on the scheme liabilities	**(9.7)**	**6.7**	**5.8**	**(3.9)**	**(1.3)**	**(2.4)**
Changes in assumptions underlying the present value of the scheme liabilities	**(91.7)**	**(2.2)**	**(5.9)**	**–**	**5.5**	**(94.3)**
Irrecoverable surplus	**–**	**–**	**–**	**(11.6)**	**–**	**(11.6)**
Actuarial (loss) recognised in the statement of total recognised gains and losses[3]	**(347.8)**	**(67.1)**	**(0.1)**	**(12.5)**	**(9.4)**	**(436.9)**
Year to 30 September 2001						
Actual return less expected return on pension scheme assets	(346.2)	(156.4)	–	(11.9)	(13.3)	(527.8)
Experience gains and losses arising on the scheme liabilities	(7.6)	(0.9)	(6.9)	(0.3)	10.7	(5.0)
Changes in assumptions underlying the present value of the scheme liabilities	64.0	–	–	(2.9)	–	61.1
Actuarial (loss) recognised in the statement of total recognised gains and losses[3]	(289.8)	(157.3)	(6.9)	(15.1)	(2.6)	(471.7)
Year to 30 September 2000						
Actual return less expected return on pension scheme assets	109.0	57.2	–	8.5	9.0	183.7
Experience gains and losses arising on the scheme liabilities	22.2	(30.9)	(17.8)	3.9	(11.8)	(34.4)
Changes in assumptions underlying the present value of the scheme liabilities	(32.4)	–	3.0	–	–	(29.4)
Actuarial gain/(loss) recognised in the statement of total recognised gains and losses[3]	98.8	26.3	(14.8)	12.4	(2.8)	119.9

3. Included in the actuarial gain/(loss) for the year is £(5.7) million in respect of minority interests (2001: £(6.8) million, 2000: £5.7 million).

6. Employees continued

Movement in (deficit)/surplus during the year	Europe £ million	Americas pensions £ million	Americas health care £ million	Africa £ million	Asia/Pacific £ million	Total £ million
Year to 30 September 2002						
(Deficit)/surplus in scheme at 1 October	(28.8)	157.5	(52.0)	12.8	(3.2)	86.3
Movement in the year:						
Current service cost	(33.5)	(12.8)	(1.6)	(1.7)	(7.2)	(56.8)
Past service cost	(0.6)	0.7	–	–	–	0.1
Contributions	2.8	–	3.9	1.8	6.3	14.8
Other finance income	16.3	17.6	(3.7)	1.6	1.2	33.0
Actuarial (loss)	(347.8)	(67.1)	(0.1)	(12.5)	(9.4)	(436.9)
Exchange adjustment	–	(6.1)	3.4	(2.0)	1.1	(3.6)
(Deficit)/surplus in scheme at 30 September	(391.6)	89.8	(50.1)	–	(11.2)	(363.1)
Year to 30 September 2001						
Surplus/(deficit) in scheme at 1 October	267.4	306.3	(43.7)	32.1	2.4	564.5
Movement in the year:						
Current service cost	(35.8)	(8.6)	(1.3)	(2.2)	(4.7)	(52.6)
Past service cost	(0.4)	(16.7)	–	–	–	(17.1)
Contributions	2.4	–	3.7	–	–	6.1
Other finance income	27.4	28.6	–	2.2	1.5	59.7
Actuarial (loss)	(289.8)	(157.3)	(6.9)	(15.1)	(2.6)	(471.7)
Exchange adjustment	–	5.2	(3.8)	(4.2)	0.2	(2.6)
(Deficit)/surplus in scheme at 30 September	(28.8)	157.5	(52.0)	12.8	(3.2)	86.3

History of experience gains and losses	Europe £ million	Americas pensions £ million	Americas health care £ million	Africa £ million	Asia/Pacific £ million	Total £ million
Year to 30 September 2002						
Difference between the expected and actual return on scheme assets						
Amount (£ million)	(246.4)	(71.6)	–	3.0	(13.6)	(328.6)
Percentage of scheme assets	(26.2%)	(21.0%)	–	4.3%	(11.1%)	(22.3%)
Experience gains and losses on scheme liabilities						
Amount (£ million)	(9.7)	6.7	5.8	(3.9)	(1.3)	(2.4)
Percentage of the present value of scheme liabilities	(0.7%)	2.7%	11.6%	(6.6%)	(1.0%)	(0.1%)
Total amount recognised in the statement of total recognised gains and losses						
Amount (£ million)	(347.8)	(67.1)	(0.1)	(12.5)	(9.4)	(436.9)
Percentage of the present value of scheme liabilities	(26.1%)	(26.8%)	(0.2%)	(21.1%)	(7.0%)	(23.9%)
Year to 30 September 2001						
Difference between the expected and actual return on scheme assets						
Amount (£ million)	(346.2)	(156.4)	–	(11.9)	(13.3)	(527.8)
Percentage of scheme assets	(30.3%)	(37.6%)	–	(15.0%)	(10.4%)	(29.9%)
Experience gains and losses on scheme liabilities						
Amount (£ million)	(7.6)	(0.9)	(6.9)	(0.3)	10.7	(5.0)
Percentage of the present value of scheme liabilities	(0.6%)	(0.3%)	(13.3%)	(0.4%)	8.2%	(0.3%)
Total amount recognised in the statement of total recognised gains and losses						
Amount (£ million)	(289.8)	(157.3)	(6.9)	(15.1)	(2.6)	(471.7)
Percentage of the present value of scheme liabilities	(24.7%)	(60.9%)	(13.3%)	(22.7%)	(2.0%)	(28.1%)
Year to 30 September 2000						
Difference between the expected and actual return on scheme assets						
Amount (£ million)	109.0	57.2	–	8.5	9.0	183.7
Percentage of scheme assets	7.6%	10.6%	–	8.3%	6.0%	8.3%
Experience gains and losses on scheme liabilities						
Amount (£ million)	22.2	(30.9)	(17.8)	3.9	(11.8)	(34.4)
Percentage of the present value of scheme liabilities	1.9%	(13.3%)	(40.7%)	5.5%	(8.0%)	(2.1%)
Total amount recognised in the statement of total recognised gains and losses						
Amount (£ million)	98.8	26.3	(14.8)	12.4	(2.8)	119.9
Percentage of the present value of scheme liabilities	8.5%	11.3%	(33.9%)	17.5%	(1.9%)	7.2%

6. Employees continued

ii) UK GAAP FRS17 Retirement benefits – parent company
The pension rights of UK BOC Group employees are dealt with through a self-administered scheme, the assets of which are held independently of the Group's finances. The scheme is a defined benefit scheme that is funded partly by contributions from members and partly by contributions from Group undertakings at rates advised by independent professionally qualified actuaries. Acting on the advice of the actuaries, company contributions to the principal UK scheme will resume from 1 October 2002.

The company accounts for pension costs in accordance with UK Financial Reporting Standard 17 (FRS17) on retirement benefits. In accordance with the standard, the company treats contributions to the pension scheme as if it were a defined contribution scheme. This is because the underlying assets and liabilities of the scheme cover a number of UK BOC Group undertakings and cannot readily be split between each Group undertaking on a consistent and reliable basis.

iii) Pensions – US GAAP
For the purposes of US GAAP, the pension costs of the largest schemes have been restated in the following tables in accordance with the requirement of SFAS132. The changes in projected benefit obligation, plan assets and details of the funded status of these retirement plans, together with the changes in the accumulated other post-retirement benefit obligations of the Group's US business, are given below. The measurement date for UK and US pension plans is 30 June. The difference between the UK and US GAAP information, disclosed in note 6 e) i) and ii) is included in note 16.

	Pension benefits		Other benefits[1]	
	2002 £ million	2001 £ million	2002 £ million	2001 £ million
Change in benefit obligation				
Projected benefit obligation at 1 October	1,599.5	1,666.0	52.0	47.1
Change due to re-measurement	–	–	–	(3.4)
Exchange adjustment	(27.3)	(7.6)	(3.4)	0.3
Service cost	54.6	54.0	1.6	1.2
Interest cost	102.9	107.5	3.6	3.3
Plan participants' contributions	12.9	14.6	–	–
Actuarial losses/(gains)	44.7	(151.1)	0.2	7.2
Benefits paid	(91.9)	(86.6)	(3.9)	(3.7)
Other (income) less expenses	0.6	2.3	–	–
Curtailments, settlements, termination benefits	0.6	0.4	–	–
Plan amendments[2]	(0.7)	–	–	–
Projected benefit obligation at 30 September	1,695.9	1,599.5	50.1	52.0
Change in fair value of assets				
Fair value of assets at 1 October	1,995.7	2,203.4	–	–
Exchange adjustment	(39.8)	(24.9)	–	–
Actual return on plan assets	(180.4)	(115.5)	–	–
Employer contributions	8.9	2.4	–	–
Plan participants' contributions	12.9	14.6	–	–
Other income less (expenses)	0.6	2.3	–	–
Benefits paid	(91.9)	(86.6)	–	–
Fair value of assets at 30 September	1,706.0	1,995.7	–	–
Funded status and unrecognised (gains)/losses				
Funded status	10.1	396.2	(50.1)	(52.0)
Unrecognised net transition asset	(26.1)	(42.9)	–	–
Unrecognised prior service cost/(credit)	23.9	28.9	(3.4)	(4.1)
Unrecognised net loss/(gain)	195.5	(191.2)	9.3	10.1
Prepaid/(accrued) pension cost	203.4	191.0	(44.2)	(46.0)
Amounts recognised in the statement of financial position consist of:				
Prepaid benefit cost	183.0	191.0		
Accrued benefit liability	(1.5)	–		
Intangible asset	0.7	–		
Accumulated other comprehensive income	21.2	–		
Prepaid pension cost	203.4	191.0		

1. Other benefits relate to post retirement medical benefits.
2. Plan amendments relate to changes made to the US pension plan.

The fair value of plan assets exceeds the accumulated benefit obligation for all plans except the Australian plan, where the accumulated benefit obligation, projected benefit obligation and fair value of plan assets were £110.6 million, £110.6 million and £109.1 million respectively (2001: £108.4 million, £108.4 million and £112.5 million).

6. **Employees** continued

The main assumptions are as follows:

	Europe	Americas	Africa	Asia/Pacific
At 30 September 2002				
Discount rate	**5.8%**	**7.0%**	**12.0%**	**7.0%**
Expected return on plan assets	**7.7%**	**9.0%**	**12.0%**	**8.0%**
Rate of compensation increase	**3.9%**	**3.75%**	**9.5%**	**3.5%**
At 30 September 2001				
Discount rate	6.2%	7.25%	10.0%	5.75%
Expected return on plan assets	7.4%	9.0%	10.0%	6.5%
Rate of compensation increase	4.75%	4.75%	7.5%	3.0%

For the post retirement medical benefits plan at 30 September 2002, the initial health care cost trend rates for valuing the medical benefits and drug benefits were 10.0 per cent (2001: 9.0 per cent) and 2.4 per cent (2001: 2.0 per cent) respectively. These rates are assumed to reduce gradually to 4.5 per cent in 2009 (2001: 4.75 per cent in 2009) for valuing medical benefits but no reduction is assumed for valuing the drug benefits.

	Pensionable benefits			Other benefits[3]		
	2002 £ million	2001 £ million	2000 £ million	2002 £ million	2001 £ million	2000 £ million
Service cost net of employees' contributions	**54.6**	54.0	51.1	**1.6**	1.2	1.0
Interest cost on projected benefits obligation	**102.9**	107.5	99.5	**3.6**	3.3	1.8
Expected return on assets	**(156.7)**	(158.8)	(141.1)	–	–	–
Amortisation of net transition asset	**(14.7)**	(15.2)	(15.3)	–	–	–
Amortisation of prior service cost/(credit)	**3.5**	2.6	5.7	**(0.5)**	(0.5)	(0.4)
Amortisation of net (gain)/loss	**(7.2)**	(2.7)	–	**0.3**	–	(0.7)
Cost of special termination benefits	**0.6**	0.4	1.6	–	–	–
Net periodic pension (credit)/cost	**(17.0)**	(12.2)	1.5	**5.0**	4.0	1.7

3. Other benefits relate to post retirement medical benefits.

It is estimated that a one per cent change in the weighted average health care costs trend would have the following effects on the accumulated benefit obligation and net periodic pension cost at 30 September 2002:

	One percentage point	
	increase	decrease
Accumulated benefit obligation	6.0	(5.5)
Net periodic pension cost	0.9	(0.8)

7. Fixed assets – intangible assets

	Goodwill £ million	Negative Goodwill £ million	Other intangibles £ million	Total £ million
Gross book value				
At 1 October 2001	73.1	(20.4)	6.0	58.7
Exchange adjustment	(6.7)	(0.8)	(0.1)	(7.6)
Acquired during the year	117.3	(5.0)	0.6	112.9
At 30 September 2002	**183.7**	**(26.2)**	**6.5**	**164.0**
Amortisation				
At 1 October 2001	8.8	(1.1)	2.9	10.6
Exchange adjustment	(0.8)	–	(0.1)	(0.9)
Impairment	–	(3.8)	–	(3.8)
Provided during the year	8.8	(2.0)	0.6	7.4
At 30 September 2002	**16.8**	**(6.9)**	**3.4**	**13.3**
Net book value				
At 1 October 2001	64.3	(19.3)	3.1	48.1
At 30 September 2002	**166.9**	**(19.3)**	**3.1**	**150.7**

The increase in positive goodwill represents the excess of the fair value of the purchase price over the provisional fair value of the net assets of businesses acquired. The increase in negative goodwill represents the excess of the provisional fair value of the net assets of businesses acquired over the fair value of the purchase price. The most significant amounts are as follows:

Business acquired	Positive Goodwill £ million	Negative Goodwill £ million	Amortisation period Years
2002			
Seiko Instruments Inc – turbomolecular pumps business	**60.2**	–	**20**
Unique Gas and Petrochemicals Public Company Limited	**17.5**	–	**20**
Enron Teesside Operations Limited – industrial assets	**9.6**	–	**15**
Hydromatix Inc	**5.6**	–	**15**
Semco	**4.4**	–	**15**
Minorities in Osaka Sanso Kogyo KK	–	**(5.0)**	**10**
2001			
Remaining 50 per cent of joint ventures in Venezuela and Chile	7.5	–	12
UK Fluorogas	8.2	–	15
Minorities in Osaka Sanso Kogyo KK	–	(20.4)	10
2000			
Kachina Semiconductor Services	7.9	–	15
1999			
Chemical management division of FSI International Inc	16.4	–	15

Amortisation periods are those over which it is estimated that the value of the business acquired will exceed the value of the identifiable net assets of the business acquired.

8. Fixed assets – tangible assets

a) Group summary

	Land and buildings[1] £ million	Plant, machinery and vehicles £ million	Cylinders £ million	Construction in progress £ million	Total £ million
Gross book value					
At 1 October 2001	704.8	4,437.3	606.7	308.1	6,056.9
Exchange adjustment	(33.5)	(222.0)	(38.4)	(18.5)	(312.4)
Capital expenditure[2]	17.8	143.1	45.4	148.0	354.3
Disposals	(26.8)	(106.1)	(20.2)	(0.1)	(153.2)
Transfers	9.5	218.1	9.3	(236.9)	–
Acquisitions/disposals of businesses	42.9	19.2	17.3	0.3	79.7
At 30 September 2002	**714.7**	**4,489.6**	**620.1**	**200.9**	**6,025.3**
Depreciation					
At 1 October 2001	222.8	2,390.1	275.4	–	2,888.3
Exchange adjustment	(5.5)	(112.5)	(16.6)	–	(134.6)
Provided during the year	35.3	242.6	45.6	–	323.5
Impairment	37.4	7.2	–	–	44.6
Disposals	(13.4)	(89.8)	(16.0)	–	(119.2)
Disposals of businesses	(0.4)	(4.3)	–	–	(4.7)
At 30 September 2002	**276.2**	**2,433.3**	**288.4**	**–**	**2,997.9**
Net book value at 1 October 2001					
Owned assets	448.4	2,038.1	295.5	308.1	3,090.1
Leased assets	33.6	9.1	35.8	–	78.5
	482.0	2,047.2	331.3	308.1	3,168.6
Net book value at 30 September 2002[3]					
Owned assets	407.4	2,047.8	299.8	200.9	2,955.9
Leased assets[4]	31.1	8.5	31.9	–	71.5
	438.5	**2,056.3**	**331.7**	**200.9**	**3,027.4**

1. Net book value of land and buildings at cost was £405.4 million (2001: £407.6 million).
2. Subsidiary undertakings only. Capital expenditure of joint ventures and associates is given in note 1.
3. Net book value includes net interest capitalised of £63.8 million (2001: £67.7 million). The tax effect of this is included in the deferred tax provision.
4. Leased assets are shown net of accumulated depreciation of £111.0 million (2001: £105.6 million).

b) Depreciation and operating lease rentals

	2002 £ million	2001 £ million	2000 £ million
Depreciation on leased assets included above	**8.5**	6.8	6.7
Amortisation of capitalised interest included above	**4.2**	3.0	4.0
Operating lease rentals			
– hire of plant and machinery	**7.7**	15.0	8.1
– property rent	**23.1**	25.0	26.4
– other	**14.0**	11.9	10.8

c) Regional analysis

The Group has numerous manufacturing, distribution and office facilities which are located in some 50 countries. At 30 September 2002, the Group's property, plant and equipment, comprising land and buildings, plant, machinery, vehicles and cylinders was located regionally as follows:

	£ million	%
Europe (mainly the UK)	1,024.7	34
Americas (mainly the US)	978.4	32
Africa	178.3	6
Asia/Pacific	846.0	28
	3,027.4	100

The above amounts are stated at cost net of accumulated depreciation.

8. Fixed assets – tangible assets continued

d) Asset revaluations
Following the adoption of FRS15 – Tangible fixed assets in 2000, land and buildings are no longer revalued (see Accounting policies on page 72). The net book value of properties revalued in earlier years was £136.4 million. Properties not revalued were £302.1 million.

e) Parent summary

	Land and buildings £ million	Plant, machinery and vehicles £ million	Total £ million
Gross book value			
At 1 October 2001	14.3	18.9	33.2
Capital expenditure	–	0.1	0.1
Disposals	–	(3.3)	(3.3)
At 30 September 2002	**14.3**	**15.7**	**30.0**
Depreciation			
At 1 October 2001	3.3	11.1	14.4
Provided during the year	0.4	1.3	1.7
Disposals	–	(0.1)	(0.1)
At 30 September 2002	**3.7**	**12.3**	**16.0**
Net book value			
At 1 October 2001	11.0	7.8	18.8
At 30 September 2002	**10.6**	**3.4**	**14.0**

f) Net book value of land and buildings at 30 September 2002

	Group £ million	Parent £ million
Freehold property	407.4	10.6
Leasehold property – long-term	27.4	–
– short-term	3.7	–
	438.5	10.6

g) Capital commitments

	Group		Parent	
	2002 £ million	2001 £ million	2002 £ million	2001 £ million
Against which orders had been placed	**33.3**	96.0	–	2.5
Authorised but not committed	**66.7**	80.4	–	–
	100.0	176.4	–	2.5

The Group's share of its joint ventures' and associates' capital commitments was:

	2002 £ million	2001 £ million
Against which orders had been placed	**3.1**	2.4
Authorised but not committed	**8.6**	4.0
	11.7	6.4

9. Fixed assets – investments

a) Group

	Goodwill of associates £ million	Group share of net assets of joint ventures £ million	Group share of net assets of associates £ million	Group loans to joint ventures and associates £ million	Other investments at cost £ million	Own shares at cost £ million	Provisions against other investments £ million	Total £ million
At 1 October 2001								
– previously reported	–	212.2	47.1	106.7	33.5	59.5	(1.8)	457.2
Prior year adjustment	–	(7.4)	–	–	–	–	–	(7.4)
At 1 October 2001 – restated	–	204.8	47.1	106.7	33.5	59.5	(1.8)	449.8
Exchange adjustment	(0.6)	(12.7)	(4.1)	(7.8)	(2.8)	0.1	0.4	(27.5)
Acquisitions/additions	8.7	10.1	6.0	20.9	21.6	–	–	67.3
Associates becoming subsidiaries	–	–	(3.2)	(1.1)	–	–	–	(4.3)
Disposals/repayments	–	–	(0.3)	(0.7)	(6.9)	(17.1)	(0.2)	(25.2)
Increase in net assets	–	3.3	3.8	–	–	–	–	7.1
Other	–	–	0.1	–	1.8	–	(0.5)	1.4
At 30 September 2002	**8.1**	**205.5**	**49.4**	**118.0**	**47.2**	**42.5**	**(2.1)**	**468.6**

i) Joint ventures
The cost of investment in joint ventures was £116.9 million (2001: £107.6 million) and the attributable profit before tax was £40.1 million (2001: £34.2 million, 2000: £40.2 million). There were no significant fair value adjustments on acquisitions.

ii) Associates
The cost of investment in associates was £15.1 million (2001: £8.3 million) and the attributable profit before tax was £9.4 million (2001: £10.5 million, 2000: £5.6 million).

Goodwill of associates arose on the combination of the BOC Process Plants business with Linde Engineering. This represents the difference between the fair value of the consideration paid and the provisional fair value of the net assets acquired. This goodwill will be amortised over a period of 15 years. There were no significant fair value adjustments on acquisitions.

iii) Own shares
For share-based incentive schemes which do not use new issue shares, options are satisfied by the transfer of shares held in trust for the purpose. At 30 September 2002, options over 5.4 million shares were outstanding under these schemes, for which 4.6 million shares in the company were held pending exercise.

Loans and advances for the purchase of shares in trust have been made either by the company or its subsidiaries. If the value of shares in trust is insufficient to cover the loans, the company and its subsidiaries will bear any loss. The company also bears administrative costs on an accruals basis.

Based on the company's share price at 30 September 2002 of 867.0p, the market value of own shares held in trust was £39.5 million. This compares with the acquisition cost shown above.

Own shares are shown as fixed asset investments for accounting purposes, in accordance with FRS5 and UITF Abstract 13. Information on share option schemes appears in the report on remuneration and in notes 6 and 12.

Dividends waived on the shares held in trust amounted to £1.8 million (2001: £1.2 million, 2000: £1.5 million).

iv) Related parties
During the year, interest income of £8.3 million (2001: £6.9 million, 2000: £6.5 million) was received from the Cantarell joint venture, a related party.

9. Fixed assets – investments continued

b) Valuation

	2002 £ million	2001 £ million
Listed on stock exchanges in the UK and overseas	91.1	112.5
Unlisted – equity at directors' valuation	244.9	237.1
– other at directors' valuation	132.6	107.6
Total book value	468.6	457.2
Market value of listed investments	123.1	152.7

c) Income

	2002 £ million	2001 £ million	2000 £ million
Listed securities	7.5	6.0	2.2
Unlisted securities	30.6	19.5	20.5
	38.1	25.5	22.7
Less: Dividends receivable from joint ventures	30.5	19.4	20.0
Dividends receivable from associates	3.4	4.1	2.1
Income from other fixed asset investments	4.2	2.0	0.6

d) Parent

	Investments in subsidiary undertakings £ million	Investments in related undertakings £ million	Amounts due from subsidiary undertakings £ million	Own shares at cost £ million	Other investments £ million	Provisions £ million	Total £ million
At 1 October 2001	1,142.8	250.1	1,278.8	44.9	–	(14.6)	2,702.0
Additions	345.3	8.7	396.3	–	13.9	(1.9)	762.3
Disposals/repayments	(18.0)	(250.1)	(343.2)	(8.6)	–	–	(619.9)
At 30 September 2002	1,470.1	8.7	1,331.9	36.3	13.9	(16.5)	2,844.4

10. Net current assets/(liabilities)

a) Stocks

		Group
	2002 £ million	2001 £ million
Raw materials	67.8	81.2
Work in progress	47.8	59.5
Gases and other finished goods	159.0	164.7
Payments on account	(14.6)	(30.2)
	260.0	275.2

Amounts relating to long-term contracts included in work in progress were £0.2 million (2001: £1.3 million). There were no stocks held on the balance sheet of The BOC Group plc at either 30 September 2002 or 30 September 2001.

10. Net current assets/(liabilities) continued

b) Debtors falling due within one year

	Group		Parent	
	2002 £ million	2001 (restated) £ million	2002 £ million	2001 (restated) £ million
Trade debtors	601.2	589.5	–	–
Amounts due from subsidiary undertakings	–	–	485.8	382.1
Amounts due from joint ventures and associates	1.4	4.3	1.4	3.2
Other debtors	100.0	92.1	21.7	13.5
Prepayments and accrued income	31.2	27.4	6.7	9.8
	733.8	713.3	515.6	408.6

At 30 September 2002, trade debtors of £23.8 million (2001: £25.7 million) in subsidiary undertakings had been factored to third parties with limited recourse.

c) Debtors falling due after more than one year

	Group		Parent	
	2002 £ million	2001 (restated) £ million	2002 £ million	2001 (restated) £ million
Deposits	–	0.7	–	–
Deferred tax	7.9	8.4	–	–
Other debtors	20.4	12.2	–	–
	28.3	21.3	–	–

d) Cash at bank and in hand

Deposits	20.5	70.6	–	51.7
Cash at bank and in hand	165.0	162.9	–	–
	185.5	233.5	–	51.7

e) Borrowings and finance leases[1]

Bank loans and overdrafts	196.7	187.9	178.9	119.1
Loans other than from banks	182.3	288.1	–	196.5
Finance leases	11.1	10.4	–	–
	390.1	486.4	178.9	315.6

1. Details of borrowings and finance leases are given in note 3.

f) Other creditors

Deposits and advance payments by customers	41.5	46.0	–	–
Trade creditors	367.3	318.4	–	–
Amounts due to subsidiary undertakings	–	–	906.6	639.9
Taxation – UK	69.0	63.9	–	–
– Overseas	78.5	75.0	–	–
Other taxes and social security payable	27.3	25.5	–	–
Other creditors	130.0	128.4	2.0	38.6
Accruals and deferred income	144.2	138.1	45.2	38.8
	857.8	795.3	953.8	717.3

11. Long-term liabilities

a) Borrowings and finance leases[1]

	Group		Parent	
	2002￡ million	2001￡ million	2002￡ million	2001￡ million
Loans other than from banks	1,008.1	879.2	801.0	570.4
Bank loans	90.2	105.5	–	–
Finance leases	22.7	35.2	–	–
	1,121.0	1,019.9	801.0	570.4

1. Details of borrowings and finance leases are given in note 3.

b) Provisions for liabilities and charges

	Deferred tax￡ million	Incentive and other employee provisions￡ million	Uninsured losses￡ million	Restructuring provisions￡ million	Environmental￡ million	Other￡ million	Total￡ million
At 1 October 2001 – previously reported	37.0	84.2	23.9	11.6	26.9	21.7	205.3
Prior year adjustment	257.3	(43.4)	–	–	–	–	213.9
At 1 October 2001 – restated	294.3	40.8	23.9	11.6	26.9	21.7	419.2
Exchange adjustment	(8.6)	(2.7)	(0.1)	(0.2)	(1.7)	(0.5)	(13.8)
Provided in the year	9.5	4.6	–	5.0	0.9	12.6	32.6
Released in the year	–	(1.1)	(3.9)	–	–	(2.4)	(7.4)
Utilised in the year	–	(4.8)	(0.5)	(7.9)	(3.3)	(2.8)	(19.3)
Other movements	(3.4)	0.3	–	(0.8)	–	0.1	(3.8)
At 30 September 2002	291.8	37.1	19.4	7.7	22.8	28.7	407.5

Provision for uninsured losses covers third party liabilities or claims. Due to the time frame that is often involved in such claims, a significant part of this provision is subject to actuarial valuation. Where this is not appropriate, other external assessments are used.

The restructuring provision represents expenditure to be incurred on major reorganisations. This year £48.0 million was spent of which £4.2 million was provided for at 30 September 2001 and £3.7 million was provided for at 30 September 2000. The provisions remaining at 30 September 2002 consist mainly of redundancy costs and will be spent during 2003.

Incentive and other employee provisions include long-term share incentive units and deferred compensation plans. Note 6 d) contains further details of the long-term share incentive units.

Environmental provisions have been set aside to cover the costs of remediation for a number of hazardous waste sites. The costs are expected to be incurred between 2002 and 2030. Due to the period over which this expenditure is likely to be incurred, the provision has been discounted at a rate of four per cent. The effect of discounting is £6.7 million.

Other provisions are principally for warranty and legal costs.

Further information on deferred tax is disclosed in note 4.

12. Dividends and equity

a) Dividends

	Per share					
	2002 pence	2001 pence	2000 pence	2002￡ million	2001￡ million	2000￡ million
Ordinary						
First interim	15.5	15.5	15.5	75.8	75.5	75.6
Second interim	22.5	21.5	19.5	110.8	104.8	94.6
	38.0	37.0	35.0	186.6	180.3	170.2

12. Dividends and equity continued

b) Share capital

	Number of shares			
i) Analysis at 30 September	2002 million	2001 million	2002 £ million	2001 £ million
Equity capital:				
Issued capital – Ordinary shares of 25p each, called up and fully paid	**497.3**	494.4	**124.3**	123.6
Unissued capital – unclassified shares of 25p each	**92.7**	95.6	**23.2**	23.9
Authorised			**147.5**	147.5

	Number million
ii) Share issues	
Issues of Ordinary shares of 25p each during the year were:	
Under the savings related share option scheme	1.0
Under the senior executives share option scheme	1.9

c) Group reserves

	Share premium account £ million	Revaluation reserves £ million	Profit and loss account £ million	Pensions' reserves £ million	Joint ventures' reserves £ million	Associates' reserves £ million	Total £ million
At 1 October 2001 – previously reported	335.8	47.9	1,660.1	–	105.5	33.4	2,182.7
Prior year adjustment	–	–	(259.8)	47.1	(7.4)	–	(220.1)
At 1 October 2001 – restated	335.8	47.9	1,400.3	47.1	98.1	33.4	1,962.6
Total recognised gains and losses for the year	–	(20.1)	91.5	(303.6)	(10.0)	0.1	(242.1)
Share options	–	–	2.0	–	–	–	2.0
Dividends	–	–	(186.6)	–	–	–	(186.6)
Premium on share issues (net)	26.3	–	(2.4)	–	–	–	23.9
At 30 September 2002	362.1	27.8	1,304.8	(256.5)	88.1	33.5	1,559.8

The undistributed profits of Group undertakings may be liable to overseas and/or UK tax (after allowing for double tax relief) if distributed as dividends.

There are no material exchange control restrictions on the remittance of funds to the UK.

Goodwill written off against reserves in respect of continuing businesses acquired prior to 30 September 1998 amounts to £166.2 million (2001: £173.6 million). The movement in the year reflects exchange.

At 30 September 2002, in accordance with the Group's accounting policy, unrealised exchange gains (net of losses) on net borrowings at 30 September 2002 included in reserves amounted to £10.2 million (2001: £18.0 million).

There are no non-equity shareholders' interests in the share capital and reserves of the Group.

d) Parent reserves

	Share premium account £ million	Other reserves £ million	Profit and loss account £ million	Total £ million
At 1 October 2001 – previously reported	335.8	111.7	1,042.2	1,489.7
Prior year adjustment	–	–	(52.0)	(52.0)
At 1 October 2001 – restated	335.8	111.7	990.2	1,437.7
Profit for the financial year	–	–	26.2	26.2
Share options	–	2.0	–	2.0
Dividends	–	–	(186.8)	(186.8)
Premium on share issues (net)	26.3	–	(2.4)	23.9
At 30 September 2002	362.1	113.7	827.2	1,303.0

The premium on share issues represents amounts paid to The BOC Group plc for the issue of shares under the Group's share option schemes. Employees paid £23.9 million. The Group paid the balance of £2.4 million to a qualifying employee share ownership trust (Quest).

13. Commitments and contingent liabilities

a) Annual operating lease commitments

	2002		2001	
	Property leases £ million	Other operating leases £ million	Property leases £ million	Other operating leases £ million
On leases expiring:				
Within one year	2.9	1.3	2.4	1.3
Between one and two years	1.8	6.5	3.9	1.5
Between two and five years	5.7	8.5	7.8	13.2
Over five years	7.0	1.9	7.1	3.5
	17.4	18.2	21.2	19.5

	Operating leases £ million
Rentals are due under operating leases from 1 October 2002 to completion as follows:	
Year to 30 September 2003	35.6
Year to 30 September 2004	29.8
Year to 30 September 2005	23.7
Year to 30 September 2006	19.4
Year to 30 September 2007	16.5
Thereafter	96.1
	221.1

b) Contingent liabilities, legal proceedings and bank guarantees

	Group		Parent	
	2002 £ million	2001 £ million	2002 £ million	2001 £ million
Guarantees of joint ventures' borrowings	119.3	152.1	119.3	152.1
Guarantees of subsidiaries' borrowings	–	–	558.1	607.3
Other guarantees and contingent liabilities	38.7	37.9	22.3	20.4
	158.0	190.0	699.7	779.8

The guarantees of joint ventures' borrowings predominately represents guarantees of the borrowings of BOC's joint venture company which supplies nitrogen to the Mexican oil company, Pemex. These borrowings are scheduled to be repaid over the next eight years.

Various Group undertakings are parties to legal actions and claims, some of which are for substantial amounts. While the outcome of some of these matters cannot readily be foreseen, the directors believe that they will be disposed of without material effect on the net asset position as shown in these financial statements.

The Group is committed to make future purchases under take-or-pay contracts. Obligations under such contracts in effect at 30 September 2002 are as follows:

Year ending 30 September	£ million
2003	67.8
2004	66.6
2005	64.9
2006	62.9
2007	63.9
Thereafter	195.4
	521.5

For the years ended 30 September 2002, 2001 and 2000 total purchases made relating to these contracts amounted to £58.2 million, £53.5 million and £51.5 million respectively.

14. Cash flow

a) Net cash inflow from operating activities

	Notes	2002 £ million	2001 (restated) £ million	2000 (restated) £ million
Total operating profit before exceptional items		500.1	530.6	496.4
Depreciation and amortisation		330.9	329.5	313.3
FRS17 retirement benefits charge		49.9	53.0	48.9
Operating profit before exceptional items of joint ventures		(63.8)	(59.0)	(48.1)
Operating profit before exceptional items of associates		(10.7)	(13.2)	(8.5)
Change in stocks		13.7	8.8	(40.9)
Change in debtors		(38.4)	39.5	(24.5)
Change in creditors		57.3	(20.9)	(10.3)
Exceptional cash flows		(67.3)	(51.8)	0.5
Other		(12.4)	(28.7)	(21.8)
Net cash inflow from operating activities		759.3	787.8	705.0

b) Reconciliation of net cash flow to movement in net debt

	Notes	2002	2001	2000
Increase in cash		(21.4)	(66.1)	(3.2)
Increase/(decrease) in debt	14(d)	64.1	(51.3)	64.9
Decrease in liquid resources		52.6	102.8	9.6
Change in net debt resulting from cash flows		95.3	(14.6)	71.3
Net borrowings assumed at acquisition		0.5	–	21.8
Inception of finance leases		0.4	0.5	0.1
Exchange adjustment		(42.7)	(22.2)	76.7
Movement in net debt in the year		53.5	(36.3)	169.9
Net debt at 1 October		1,272.1	1,308.4	1,138.5
Net debt at 30 September		1,325.6	1,272.1	1,308.4

c) Analysis of net debt

	At 1 October 2001 £ million	Cash flow £ million	Acquisitions/disposals (excluding cash and overdrafts) £ million	Other non-cash changes £ million	Exchange adjustment £ million	At 30 September 2002 £ million
Deposits and cash due within one year	233.5	(43.5)	–	14.3	(18.8)	185.5
Deposits due beyond one year	0.7	0.5	13.1	(14.3)	–	–
	234.2	(43.0)	13.1	–	(18.8)	185.5
Borrowings and finance leases due within one year	(486.4)	208.8	(0.1)	(141.4)	29.0	(390.1)
Borrowings and finance leases due beyond one year	(1,019.9)	(261.1)	(13.5)	141.0	32.5	(1,121.0)
Net borrowings and finance leases	(1,272.1)	(95.3)	(0.5)	(0.4)	42.7	(1,325.6)

d) Increase/(decrease) in debt

	2002 £ million	2001 £ million	2000 £ million
5⅞% Bonds 2009	200.0	–	–
7¼% Notes 2002	(150.0)	–	–
Medium term notes	59.7	–	–
6.50% Bonds 2016	–	200.0	–
1.00% Euroyen Bond 2006	–	147.0	–
5⅞% Notes 2001	–	(138.9)	–
European Investment Bank loans	(5.0)	10.3	(5.7)
Pollution Control and Industrial Bonds	(18.5)	(2.4)	(5.3)
Net issues/(repayment) of commercial paper	59.5	(212.5)	68.6
Other (net)	(81.6)	(54.8)	7.3
Increase/(decrease) in debt	64.1	(51.3)	64.9

14. Cash flow continued

e) Consolidated cash flow statement: US format

	2002 £ million	2001 £ million	2000 £ million
Net cash provided by operating activities	620.2	631.2	565.2
Net cash used by investing activities	(540.0)	(445.5)	(470.3)
Net cash used by financing activities	(122.7)	(225.6)	(71.9)
Net (decrease)/increase in cash and cash equivalents	(42.5)	(39.9)	23.0
Cash and cash equivalents at 1 October	259.0	305.6	277.4
Exchange and other movements	(34.6)	(6.7)	5.2
Cash and cash equivalents at 30 September	181.9	259.0	305.6

The Group cash flow statement on page 68 has been prepared in accordance with UK accounting standard FRS1, the objectives and principles of which are similar to those set out in US accounting principle SFAS95, Statement of Cash Flows. The principal differences between the standards relate to classification of items within the cash flow statement and with regard to the definition of cash and cash equivalents.

Under FRS1, cash flows are presented separately for: a) operating activities; b) dividends from joint ventures and associates; c) returns on investments and servicing of finance; d) tax paid; e) capital expenditure and financial investment; f) acquisitions and disposals; g) equity dividends paid; h) management of liquid resources; and i) financing. Under SFAS95, however, only three categories of cash flow activity are reported: a) operating activities; b) investing activities; and c) financing activities. Dividends from joint ventures and associates, cash flows from returns on investments and servicing of finance (excluding dividends paid to minorities) and tax paid under FRS1 would be included in operating activities under SFAS95; capital expenditure and acquisitions and disposals would be included in investing activities under SFAS95; equity dividends would be included as a financing activity under SFAS95.

Under FRS1, cash is defined as cash in hand and deposits repayable on demand with any qualifying financial institution, less overdrafts from any qualifying financial institution repayable on demand. Under SFAS95, cash is defined as cash in hand and deposits but also includes cash equivalents which are short-term, highly liquid investments. Generally only investments with original maturities of three months or less come within this definition.

Set out above, for illustrative purposes, is a summary consolidated statement of cash flows under SFAS95.

15. Acquisitions and disposals

a) Cash flow

	2002 Acquisitions £ million	2002 Disposals £ million	2001 Acquisitions £ million	2001 Disposals £ million	2000 Acquisitions £ million	2000 Disposals £ million
Cash flow arising on the acquisition and disposal of businesses						
Intangible fixed assets	(0.5)	0.2	–	–	–	–
Tangible fixed assets	(85.7)	1.3	(34.8)	1.1	(37.9)	–
Joint ventures, associates and other fixed asset investments	(12.4)	0.2	20.7	0.4	7.3	–
Stocks	(20.9)	2.4	(2.4)	0.5	(3.7)	0.6
Debtors	(37.5)	0.7	(16.7)	1.1	(14.4)	0.9
Cash at bank and in hand	(13.5)	–	–	–	(2.2)	–
Creditors including taxation	55.7	(1.2)	4.7	(0.4)	13.6	–
Borrowings	21.4	–	–	–	24.0	–
Minorities	(8.6)	7.8	(117.5)	–	(6.5)	–
Net assets (acquired)/disposed of	(102.0)	11.4	(146.0)	2.7	(19.8)	0.4
Goodwill on acquisitions	(112.3)	–	(3.3)	–	(14.0)	–
Surplus over book value on disposals	–	2.5	–	–	–	–
(Acquisition)/disposal price	(214.3)	13.9	(149.3)	2.7	(33.8)	0.4
Deferred payments	7.0	(3.3)	3.4	–	1.7	–
	(207.3)	10.6	(145.9)	2.7	(32.1)	0.4

The Group purchased the vacuum and pressure business of the Smiths Group in December 2001. It also purchased Hydromatix Inc in January 2002 and the Semco business in April 2002. In March 2002 the Group acquired the turbomolecular pumps business of Seiko Instruments Inc. Purchases of products from Seiko Instruments Inc in the period from 1 October 2001 to the date of acquisition were approximately £3.0 million.

In May 2002 the Group purchased 79 per cent of Unique Gas and Petrochemicals Public Company Limited and acquired a further 20 per cent before the end of the year. In July 2002 the Group purchased the industrial assets of Enron Teesside Operations Limited.

During 2002 the Group acquired an additional three per cent of the minority interests in Osaka Sanso Kogyo KK.

The acquisitions in the BOC Edwards line of business contributed £55.5 million to turnover and £(0.8) million to operating profit before exceptional items. Acquisitions in the other lines of business did not have a material impact on turnover or operating profit before exceptional items.

Of the total acquisition expenditure, £48.1 million was in the Process Gas Solutions business, £57.3 million was in the Industrial and Special Products business, £86.2 million was in the BOC Edwards business and £15.7 million was in the Afrox hospitals business.

Businesses disposed of are detailed in note 2 b).

15. Acquisitions and disposals continued

b) Fair value of acquisitions

	Smiths Group book value £ million	Unique Gas and Petrochemicals Public Company Ltd book value £ million	Seiko Instruments Inc book value £ million	Other book value £ million	Total book value of businesses acquired £ million	Total adjustments £ million	Total fair value of businesses acquired £ million
Intangible assets	—	—	(0.5)	—	(0.5)	—	(0.5)
Tangible fixed assets	(9.0)	(25.3)	(2.9)	(44.9)	(82.1)	(3.6)	(85.7)
Joint ventures, associates and other investments	—	(0.6)	(0.1)	(12.3)	(13.0)	0.6	(12.4)
Stocks	(11.5)	(1.5)	(9.2)	(3.8)	(26.0)	5.1	(20.9)
Debtors	(12.6)	(9.7)	(4.6)	(11.1)	(38.0)	0.5	(37.5)
Cash at bank and in hand	—	(11.7)	(1.3)	(0.5)	(13.5)	—	(13.5)
Creditors including taxation	12.4	35.8	3.8	9.2	61.2	(5.5)	55.7
Borrowings	7.7	0.3	0.1	13.3	21.4	—	21.4
Minorities	—	0.2	—	(8.8)	(8.6)	—	(8.6)
Net (assets)/liabilities acquired	(13.0)	(12.5)	(14.7)	(58.9)	(99.1)	(2.9)	(102.0)
Consideration	6.6	39.7	72.1	88.9	207.3	—	207.3
Deferred consideration	—	—	2.4	4.6	7.0	—	7.0
	6.6	39.7	74.5	93.5	214.3	—	214.3
Goodwill on acquisitions	—	(17.5)	(60.2)	(34.6)	(112.3)	—	(112.3)
	6.6	22.2	14.3	58.9	102.0	—	102.0

The following fair value adjustments were made to the book value of the assets and liabilities of the businesses acquired:

	Smiths Group £ million	Unique Gas and Petrochemicals Public Company Ltd £ million	Seiko Instruments Inc £ million	Total adjustments £ million
Valuations				
Tangible fixed assets	—	(0.6)	—	(0.6)
Joint ventures, associates and other investments	—	0.6	—	0.6
Alignment of accounting policies				
Tangible fixed assets	1.5	(4.5)	—	(3.0)
Stocks	4.8	—	0.3	5.1
Debtors	0.1	0.4	—	0.5
Taxation	—	2.2	—	2.2
Other				
Creditors	—	(7.8)	0.1	(7.7)
	6.4	(9.7)	0.4	(2.9)

Fair value adjustments include some amounts which are provisional. No significant fair value adjustments were required in 2001 or 2000.

Group undertakings

A list of the Group's major operating undertakings, certain financing undertakings and undertakings in which the Group has a material interest is detailed below. All holdings shown are Ordinary shares. Undertakings are held either by The BOC Group plc directly (where indicated by*) or through other operating undertakings or through undertakings formed for the convenient holding of shares in certain subsidiaries, joint ventures or associates. The Group holding percentages shown below represent the ultimate interest of The BOC Group plc. All companies are incorporated and registered in the country in which they operate as listed below.

	Principal activity	Group holding %
Aruba		
BOC Gases Aruba NV	○	100
Australia		
BOC Ltd[3]	■○	100
Elgas Ltd[5]	○	50
Bangladesh		
BOC Bangladesh Ltd	○	60*
Belgium		
BOC Technologies NV	●	100
Hibon International NV[5]	●	100
Bermuda		
Priestley Insurance Company Ltd	◆	100
The Hydrogen Company of Paraguana Ltd	■	100
Brazil		
BOC Edwards Brasil Ltda	●◆	100
BOC Gases do Brasil Ltda[5]	■	100
Brunei		
Brunei Oxygen Sdn Bhd[(a),5]	○	25
Canada		
BOC Canada Ltd[3]	○	100
Hibon Inc	●	100
Chile		
Compania de Hidrogeno de Talcahuano Ltda[5]	■	100
Indura S.A., Industria y Comercio[5]	○	41
Colombia		
Gases Industriales de Colombia SA[5]	■○	74
Czech Republic		
3H Czech s.r.o.	●	100
Gist Czech Republic s.r.o.[5]	▶	100
England		
BOC Edwards Chemical Management Europe Ltd	●	100*
BOC Holdings[1,3]	◆	100*
BOC Ltd[3]	■○●	100
BOC Netherlands Holdings Ltd[3]	◆	100*
BOC Overseas Finance Ltd	◆	100*
Edwards High Vacuum International Ltd	●	100
Fluorogas Ltd	●	100*
Gist Ltd	▶	100*
Leengate Welding Group Ltd	○	100
Welding Products Holdings Ltd	○	100*
Fiji		
BOC Gases Fiji Ltd	○	90

	Principal activity	Group holding %
France		
Cryostar-France SA	■	100
Edwards SA	●	100
Hibon International SA[5]	●	100
Hibon SAS[5]	●	100
Société de Mécanique Magnétique	●	87
Germany		
BOC Edwards GmbH	●	100
Wilhelm Klein GmbH	●	100
Hong Kong		
Hong Kong Oxygen & Acetylene Co Ltd	■○	50
The BOC Group Ltd	●◆	100
India		
BOC India Ltd[5]	■○	55*
Indonesia		
PT BOC Gases Indonesia	■○	100
PT Gresik Gases Indonesia	■	90
PT Gresik Power Indonesia	■	90
Ireland		
BOC Gases Ireland Ltd[3]	■○	100
Italy		
BOC Edwards SpA	●	100
Japan		
BOC Edwards Technologies KK	●	100
BOC Japan Ltd	◆	97
Edwards Japan Ltd	●	100
Osaka Sanso Kogyo KK	■○●	97
Kenya		
BOC Kenya Ltd	○	65
Korea		
BOC Gases Korea Co Ltd	■	100
Songwon Edwards Ltd	●	97
Luxembourg		
BOC Luxembourg No. 1 Sarl	◆	100
BOC Luxembourg No. 2 Sarl	◆	100
Malawi		
BOC Malawi Ltd[(c)]	○	42
Malaysia		
Malaysian Oxygen Bhd[(a),3,4]	■○●	23
MOX Gases Bhd[5] (formerly NIOI)	○	23
Mauritius		
Les Gaz Industriels Ltée[(b)]	○	21
Mexico		
Compania de Nitrogeno de Cantarell, SA de CV[5]	■	35

	Principal activity	Group holding %
Namibia		
IGL Properties (Pty) Ltd	○	55
Netherlands		
BOC Edwards Pharmaceutical Systems BV	●	100
Gist BV	▶	100
The BOC Group BV[3]	◆	100
Netherlands Antilles		
BOC Gases Curaçao NV	○	100
New Zealand		
BOC Ltd	■○	100
Nigeria		
BOC Gases Nigeria plc	○	60
Pakistan		
BOC Pakistan Ltd	■○	60*
Papua New Guinea		
BOC Gases Papua New Guinea Pty Ltd	○	74
Peoples' Republic of China		
BOC (China) Holdings Co Ltd[3,5]	■	100
BOC Gases (North) Co Ltd[5]	■	100
BOC Gases (Shanghai) Corporation Ltd[5]	■	100
BOC Gases (Suzhou) Co Ltd[5]	■	100
BOC Gases (Tianjin) Co Ltd[5]	■	100*
BOC Gases (Wuhan) Co Ltd[5]	■	100
BOC TISCO Gases Co Ltd[5]	■	50*
BOC Trading (Shanghai) Co Ltd[5]	●	100
Nanjing BOC-YPC Gases Co Ltd[5]	■	50
Shanghai BOC Industrial Gases Co Ltd[5]	■	50*
Philippines		
Consolidated Industrial Gases Inc	■○●	100
Southern Industrial Gases Philippines Inc	○	100
Poland		
BOC Gazy Sp. z o.o.[3]	■○	98
Russia		
JSC Volgograd Oxygen Factory[5]	○	87
Samoa		
BOC Gases (Samoa) Ltd	○	96
Singapore		
BOC Gases Pte Ltd	◆	100*
Singapore Oxygen Air Liquide Pte Ltd	■○●	50
Slovakia		
BOC Plyny s.r.o.	■	100

	Principal activity	Group holding %
Solomon Islands		
BOC Gases Solomon Islands Ltd	○	100
South Africa		
African Oxygen Ltd[3]	■○□	55
Afrox Healthcare Ltd[(c),3]	□	39
Afrox Ltd	■○	55
Switzerland		
BOC AG	■	100
Taiwan		
BOC Lienhwa Industrial Gases Co Ltd	■○●	50
Thailand		
Thai Industrial Gases Public Co Ltd[3]	■○●	99
TIG HyCO Ltd	■	99
Unique Gas and Petrochemical Public Co Ltd	○	99
Turkey		
Birlesik Oksijen Sanayi AS	■○	50*
US		
BOC, Inc	◆	100
The BOC Group, Inc[3]	■○●◆	100
Linde BOC Process Plants LLC[(a)]	■	30
US Virgin Islands		
BOC Gases Virgin Islands Inc[5]	■	100
Venezuela		
BOC Gases de Venezuela, C.A.	■○	100
Vietnam		
North Vietnam Industrial Gases Ltd[5]	■	40
Zambia		
BOC Gases Zambia plc[(c)]	○	39
Zimbabwe		
BOC Zimbabwe (Pvt) Ltd	○	100

1. Unlimited company having share capital with registered office at the same address as The BOC Group plc.
2. Businesses where the Group percentage ownership is 50 per cent or less are accounted for as joint ventures, except as follows: (a) accounted for as associates, (b) accounted for as investment or (c) accounted for as subsidiary (controlled through partly owned intermediate undertaking). See also accounting policies on pages 71 to 73.
3. Group undertakings which made acquisitions or investments during the year.
4. Group holding for dividend purposes is 28 per cent.
5. Group undertakings with financial year ends other than 30 September.
6. The principal activity of each undertaking is indicated as follows:
   ■ Process Gas Solutions
   ○ Industrial and Special Products
   ● BOC Edwards
   □ Afrox hospitals
   ▶ Gist
   ◆ Corporate/holding company
7. * Indicates where investment is held directly by The BOC Group plc.

Appendix B: Sources of comparative statistics and data

The leading organization producing comparative statistics and data is the Centre for Interfirm Comparison (a non-profit undertaking jointly established by the British Institute of Management and the British Productivity Council). The Centre's main activity is the conduct of inter-firm comparisons as a service to management; it also advises on the use of management ratios within companies. It carries out comparative surveys and research activities in the field of performance assessment. For further information contact the Centre for Interfirm Comparison, 32 St Thomas St, Winchester, Hampshire SO23 9HJ (telephone 01962 844144).

One of the principal commercial organizations producing individual business ratio reports and financial surveys for each of a wide range of industrial sectors is ICC Information Ltd. The reports present details of profitability, liquidity and efficiency ratios for the main companies operating in each industry. For further information contact ICC Information Ltd, ICC Field House, 72 Oldfield Road, Hampton, Middlesex TW12 2HQ (020 8481 8800).

Other companies active in the field of comparative information provision include the following: Datastream (Thomson Financial), 1 Mark Square, Leonard Street, London EC2A 4EG (0870 1910581); Financial Times Interactive Data Ltd, 13–17 Epworth Street, London EC2A 4DL (020 7251 3333); Jordan and Sons Ltd, 21 St Thomas Street, Bristol, Avon BS1 6JS (0117 923 0600); Dunn and Bradstreet Ltd, Holmers Farm Way, High Wycombe, Buckinghamshire HP12 4UL (01494 422000); Standard and Poor Compustat, Broad Street House, 55 Old Broad Street, London E2M 1RX (020 7826 8580).

In addition to these services, there are several annual or regular directories and yearbooks that contain valuable financial, organizational and statistical data on relevant companies. The *Times 1000* is an annual publication giving details of the turnover and capital employed, profit margin and return on total capital employed ratios (in addition to a considerable amount of other information) for each of the 1,000 largest British industrial and commercial companies, and for a wide range of financial institutions. The *Stock Exchange Official Year Book* is an annual publication giving full corporate and financial information on all companies listed on the Stock Exchange, including a summarized balance sheet and capital formation details for each company. The Institute of Chartered Accountants in England and Wales issues *Financial Reporting*, an annual survey of published accounts which reports the results of detailed analyses of the reporting practices of a sample of 300 large industrial and commercial companies.

Government statistical bulletins and digests are useful sources of aggregated financial and performance data. The Office of National Statistics produces a monthly digest of financial information entitled *Financial Statistics*.

Finally, the directories, yearbooks and member publications of professional associations and trade bodies frequently provide financial and organizational information on their members and their activities. There are a considerable number of national and international directories and guides listing 'key' or sizeable enterprises; these entries are usually restricted to basic organizational and product information, but they form useful starting points for identifying appropriate companies and their activities.

In terms of examining the actual published annual reports and accounts of individual companies, a number of the largest municipal libraries throughout the UK maintain up-to-date collections of annual reports and accounts. The Guildhall Library in London has perhaps the largest accessible collection of such reports and accounts, while many university and business school libraries possess selective collections. For a considerable number of companies, key financial and operational data are available on a variety of computer tapes and information systems as, for example, the London Business School's or the Manchester Business School's computerized company records. The London Business School issues the quarterly *Risk Measurement Service* report, which details selected investment data for all quoted companies and provides risk measures for each company.

There are three major sources of computer-based financial information, FAME, Datastream and Extel. A copy of the FAME print-out for BOC is included in this appendix. This provides standard information about the company, name, address, SIC codes, etc., with five years figures for the profit and loss account, balance sheet, and the most recent cash flow statement. A selection of important ratios for the past five years is given including some trend ratios. A credit score and rating is given which is provided by QuiScore. Further information concerning directors, subsidiaries, etc. is provided by FAME but is not included here for space reasons. (The FAME print-out is provided by courtesy of Jordans Ltd.)

BOC GROUP PLC(THE)

R/O Address :	262958	**Registered No :**	00022096
	Windlesham	**Type of company :**	Public, Quoted
	Surrey	**ISIN Number :**	GB0001081206
		SEDOL Number :	0108120
R/O Phone :	01276 - 477222	**Date of incorporation :**	26/01/1886
R/O Post Code :	GU20 6HJ	**Accounting Ref.Date :**	30/09
		Accounts Type :	Group
		Company Status :	Live
Web site :	www.boc.com		

Latest Turnover :	3,657,700 th GBP	**Number of Holdings :**	
Latest No of Employees :	45,256	**Number of Subsid. :**	80

Activities :	Group are involved in process gas solutions for large customers, industrial & special products for smaller quantities of gas, manufacture of products & services for the semiconductor industry, logistics & supply of private health care in South Africa	
1992 SIC UK codes :	**Primary Code :**	2442 - Manufacture of pharmaceutical preparations
	Secondary Code(s) :	2411, 2442, 2912, 7415
1981 SIC UK codes :	**Primary Code :**	2511 - Inorganic chemicals except industrial gases
	Secondary Code(s) :	25110, 25670, 25700, 32893, 34350,
Standard Peer Group :	2442 - Manufacture of pharmaceutical preparations (VL : Very Large Companies)	

Main Exchange :	London SE SETS	**Ticker Symbol :**	BOC

USED PEER GROUP :	Standard PG	19 Companies

PROFILE	30/09/2002 12 months th GBP Cons.	30/09/2001 12 months th GBP Cons.	30/09/2000 12 months th GBP Cons.	30/09/1999 12 months th GBP Cons.	30/09/1998 12 months th GBP Cons.
Turnover	3,657,700	3,772,900	3,579,700	3,052,700	3,294,800
Profit (Loss) before Taxation	335,300	392,300	457,200	362,800	247,200
Net Tangible Assets (Liab.)	3,494,500	3,686,400	3,673,400	3,526,200	3,385,700
Shareholder Funds	1,684,100	2,306,300	2,273,600	2,013,100	1,840,500
Profit Margin (%)	9.17	10.4	12.77	11.88	7.5
Return on Shareholder Funds (%)	19.91	17.01	20.11	18.02	13.43
Return on Capital Employed (%)	9.2	10.5	12.28	10.18	7.29
Liquidity Ratio	0.79	0.83	0.76	0.91	1
Gearing Ratio (%)	139.61	83.02	94.51	98.88	99.72
Number of Employees	45,256	42,577	42,386	42,124	37,086

PROFIT & LOSS ACCOUNT	30/09/2002 12 months th GBP Cons.	30/09/2001 12 months th GBP Cons.	30/09/2000 12 months th GBP Cons.	30/09/1999 12 months th GBP Cons.	30/09/1998 12 months th GBP Cons.
Turnover	3,657,700	3,772,900	3,579,700	3,052,700	3,294,800
UK Turnover					
Overseas Turnover					
Cost of Sales	-2,104,800	-2,208,800	-2,088,700	-1,744,400	-1,938,200
Gross Profit	1,552,900	1,564,100	1,491,000	1,308,300	1,356,600
Other Expenses	-1,201,300	-1,121,600	-991,400	-897,800	-1,214,100
Total Expenses	-3,306,100	-3,330,400	-3,080,100	-2,642,200	-3,152,300
Operating Profit	351,600	442,500	499,600	410,500	142,500
Other Income	211,200	68,900	73,500	43,600	44,600
Exceptional Items	-20,200	3,600	12,500	32,500	144,000
Profit (Loss) before Interest	542,600	515,000	585,600	486,600	331,100
Interest Paid	-207,300	-122,700	-128,400	-123,800	-83,900
Profit (Loss) before Tax	335,300	392,300	457,200	362,800	247,200
Taxation	-106,200	-109,600	-103,700	-85,300	-114,000
Profit (Loss) after Tax	229,100	282,700	353,500	277,500	133,200
Extraordinary Items					
Minority Interests	-26,200	-30,400	-27,100	-27,400	-12,800
Profit (Loss) for Period	202,900	252,300	326,400	250,100	120,400
Dividends	-186,600	-180,300	-170,200	-159,400	-150,600
Retained Profit(Loss)	16,300	72,000	156,200	90,700	-30,200
Discontinued Operations					6,000
Depreciation	323,500	325,400	308,800	270,800	267,900
Audit Fee	1,900	2,000	1,800	1,600	1,600
Non-Audit Fee	5,100	2,200	3,300	1,000	

Amortisation of Goodwill	6,800	3,800	3,200		
Remuneration	957,900	823,500	786,800	747,000	851,000
Directors' Remuneration	6,426	4,714	3,863	4,611	5,269
Highest Paid Director	1,961	1,378	1,655	1,844	2,166
Number of Employees	45,256	42,577	42,386	42,124	37,086

BALANCE SHEET	30/09/2002 12 months th GBP Cons.	30/09/2001 12 months th GBP Cons.	30/09/2000 12 months th GBP Cons.	30/09/1999 12 months th GBP Cons.	30/09/1998 12 months th GBP Cons.
Fixed Assets					
Tangible Assets	3,027,400	3,168,600	3,294,000	3,043,900	2,801,800
Land & Building	438,500	482,000	522,000	482,800	
Fixtures & Fittings	0	0	0	0	
Plant & Vehicles	2,388,000	2,047,200	2,099,200	1,762,900	
Other Fixed Assets	200,900	639,400	672,800	798,200	
Intangible Assets	150,700	48,100	49,200	36,500	4,200
Investments	468,600	457,200	467,800	365,900	360,900
Fixed Assets	3,646,700	3,673,900	3,811,000	3,446,300	3,166,900
Current Assets					
Stock & W.I.P.	260,000	275,200	285,800	228,500	219,800
Stock	226,800	245,900	252,700	197,300	
W.I.P.	33,200	29,300	33,100	31,200	
Trade Debtors	601,200	589,500	648,300	587,700	510,000
Bank & Deposits	185,500	233,500	281,200	280,400	91,500
Other Current Assets	199,700	246,800	250,700	271,100	456,400
Group Loans (asset)	1,400	4,300	3,300	4,400	
Directors Loans (asset)	0	0	0	0	
Other Debtors	159,500	199,300	209,900	152,600	188,700
Investm. & Other Cur. Assets	38,800	43,200	37,500	114,100	267,700
Current Assets	1,246,400	1,345,000	1,466,000	1,367,700	1,277,700
Current Liabilities					
Trade Creditors	-367,300	-318,400	-341,400	-312,200	-284,500
Short Term Loans & Overdrafts	-390,100	-486,400	-699,800	-440,900	-285,900
Bank Overdrafts				-160,200	-110,500
Group Loans (short t.)					
Director Loans (short t.)					
Hire Purch. & Leas. (short t.)	-11,100	-10,400	-8,900	-400	-400
Hire Purchase (short t.)					
Leasing (short t.)	-11,100	-10,400	-8,900	-400	-400
Other Short Term Loans	-379,000	-476,000	-690,900	-280,300	-175,000
Total Other Current Liabilities	-490,500	-479,600	-513,200	-498,200	-484,300
Corporation Tax	-147,500	-138,900	-145,200	-129,200	-141,800

Dividends	0	0	0	0	0
Accruals & Def. Inc. (sh. t.)	-144,200	-138,100	-132,600	-108,700	-95,600
Social Securities & V.A.T.	-27,300	-25,500	-25,400	-34,100	-27,300
Other Current Liabilities	-171,500	-177,100	-210,000	-226,200	-219,600
Current Liabilities	-1,247,900	-1,284,400	-1,554,400	-1,251,300	-1,054,700
Net Current Assets (Liab.)	-1,500	60,600	-88,400	116,400	223,000
Net Tangible Assets (Liab.)	3,494,500	3,686,400	3,673,400	3,526,200	3,385,700
Working Capital	493,900	546,300	592,700	504,000	445,300
Total Assets	4,893,100	5,018,900	5,277,000	4,814,000	4,444,600
Total Assets less Cur. Liab.	3,645,200	3,734,500	3,722,600	3,562,700	3,389,900
Long Term Liabilities					
Long Term Debt	-1,121,000	-1,019,900	-890,700	-979,400	-991,800
Group Loans (long t.)					
Director Loans (long t.)					
Hire Purch. Leas. (long t.)	-22,700	-35,200	-46,700	-14,800	-11,800
Hire Purchase (long t.)					
Leasing (long t.)	-22,700	-35,200	-46,700	-14,800	-11,800
Other Long Term Loans	-1,098,300	-984,700	-844,000	-964,600	-980,000
Total Other Long Term Liab.	-722,200	-264,700	-275,800	-299,300	-367,200
Accruals & Def. Inc. (l. t.)	0	0	0	0	0
Other Long Term Liab.	-314,700	-59,400	-27,900	-30,500	-22,200
Provisions for Other Liab.	-407,500	-205,300	-247,900	-268,800	-345,000
Deferred Tax	-291,800	-37,000	-38,300	-36,400	-20,900
Other Provisions	-115,700	-168,300	-209,600	-232,400	-324,100
Balance Sheet Minorities	-117,900	-143,600	-282,500	-270,900	-190,400
Long Term Liabilities	-1,961,100	-1,428,200	-1,449,000	-1,549,600	-1,549,400
Total Assets less Liabilities	1,684,100	2,306,300	2,273,600	2,013,100	1,840,500
Shareholders Funds					
Issued Capital	124,300	123,600	123,100	122,700	122,300
Total Reserves	1,559,800	2,182,700	2,150,500	1,890,400	1,718,200
Share Premium Account	362,100	335,800	317,100	305,500	288,400
Revaluation Reserves	27,800	47,900	58,100	57,500	56,800
Profit (Loss) Account	1,304,800	1,660,100	1,640,600	1,422,800	1,282,400
Other Reserves	-134,900	138,900	134,700	104,600	90,600
Shareholders Funds	1,684,100	2,306,300	2,273,600	2,013,100	1,840,500

CASH FLOW STATEMENT	30/09/2002 12 months th GBP Cons.	30/09/2001 12 months th GBP Cons.	30/09/2000 12 months th GBP Cons.	30/09/1999 12 months th GBP Cons.	30/09/1998 12 months th GBP Cons.
Net Cash in(Out)flow Operat. Activ.	759,300	787,800	705,000	566,400	663,000
Net Cash In(Out)flow Ret. on Invest.	-56,800	-63,700	-83,100	-62,600	-107,500
Taxation	-96,200	-100,600	-62,800	-85,900	-98,400
Net Cash Out(In)flow Investing Activ.					
Capital Expenditure & Financ. Invest.	-324,500	-311,900	-408,300	-442,900	-517,100
Acquisition & Disposal	-215,500	-133,600	-62,000	88,000	447,800
Equity Dividends Paid	-186,600	-180,300	-170,200	-159,400	-122,900
Management of Liquid Resources	52,600	102,800	9,600	-26,700	-113,600
Net Cash Out(In)flow from Financing	89,100	-34,400	75,000	113,300	-114,300
Increase(Decrease) Cash & Equiv.	21,400	66,100	3,200	-9,800	37,000

FINANCIAL RATIOS	30/09/2002	30/09/2001	30/09/2000	30/09/1999	30/09/1998
Current Ratio	1	1.05	0.94	1.09	1.21
Liquidity Ratio	0.79	0.83	0.76	0.91	1
Shareholders Liquidity Ratio	0.86	1.61	1.57	1.3	1.19
Solvency Ratio (%)	34.42	45.95	43.09	41.82	41.41
Asset Cover	4.36	4.92	5.92	4.92	4.48
Gearing (%)	139.61	83.02	94.51	98.88	99.72
Shareholders Funds per Empl. (Unit)	37,213	54,168	53,640	47,790	49,628
Working Capital per Employee (Unit)	10,913	12,831	13,983	11,965	12,007
Total Assets per Employee (Unit)	108,120	117,878	124,499	114,282	119,846

FINANCIAL TRENDS & CHANGES	2002-01	2001-00	2000-99	1999-98	1998-97
Trends (%)					
Fixed Assets	-0.74	-3.6	10.58	8.82	-4.09
Current Assets	-7.33	-8.25	7.19	7.04	-19.98
Stock	-5.52	-3.71	25.08	3.96	-37.96
Debtors	1.98	-9.07	10.31	15.24	-27.43
Total Assets	-2.51	-4.89	9.62	8.31	-9.27
Current Liabilities	-2.84	-17.37	24.22	18.64	-29.99
Creditors	15.36	-6.74	9.35	9.74	-14.46
Loans/Overdraft	-19.8	-30.49	58.72	54.21	-53.92
Long Term Liabilities	37.31	-1.44	-6.49	0.01	3.33

Changes (th GBP)

Fixed Assets	-27,200	-137,100	364,700	279,400	-135,100
Current Assets	-98,600	-121,000	98,300	90,000	-319,100
Stock	-15,200	-10,600	57,300	8,700	-134,500
Debtors	11,700	-58,800	60,600	77,700	-192,800
Total Assets	-125,800	-258,100	463,000	369,400	-454,200
Current Liabilities	-36,500	-270,000	303,100	196,600	-451,900
Creditors	48,900	-23,000	29,200	27,700	-48,100
Loans/Overdraft	-96,300	-213,400	258,900	155,000	-334,500
Long Term Liabilities	532,900	-20,800	-100,600	200	50,000

PROFITABILITY RATIOS	30/09/2002	30/09/2001	30/09/2000	30/09/1999	30/09/1998
Profit Margin (%)	9.17	10.4	12.77	11.88	7.5
Return on Shareholder Funds (%)	19.91	17.01	20.11	18.02	13.43
Return on Capital Employed (%)	9.2	10.5	12.28	10.18	7.29
Return on Total Assets (%)	6.85	7.82	8.66	7.54	5.56
Interest Cover	2.62	4.2	4.56	3.93	3.95
Stock Turnover	14.07	13.71	12.53	13.36	14.99
Debtors Turnover	6.08	6.4	5.52	5.19	6.46
Debtor Collection (days)	59.99	57.03	66.1	70.27	56.5
Creditors Payment (days)	36.65	30.8	34.81	37.33	31.52
Net Assets Turnover	1	1.01	0.96	0.86	0.97
Fixed Assets Turnover	1	1.03	0.94	0.89	1.04
Salaries/Turnover (%)	26.19	21.83	21.98	24.47	25.83
Gross Margin (%)	42.46	41.46	41.65	42.86	41.17
EBIT Margin (%)	14.83	13.65	16.36	15.94	10.05
EBITDA Margin (%)	23.86	22.38	25.07	24.81	18.18
Turnover per Employee (Unit)	80,822	88,614	84,455	72,469	88,842
Average Remun. per Employee (Unit)	21,166	19,341	18,563	17,733	22,947
Profit per Employee (Unit)	7,409	9,214	10,787	8,613	6,666

PROFITABILITY TRENDS & CHANGES	2002-01	2001-00	2000-99	1999-98	1998-97
Trends (%)					
Turnover	-3.05	5.4	17.26	-7.35	-10.41
Profit before Taxation	-14.53	-14.2	26.02	46.76	-44.47
Interest Paid	68.95	-4.44	3.72	47.56	-30.14
Number of Employees	6.29	0.45	0.62	13.58	-10.36

Changes (th GBP)	2002-01	2001-00	2000-99	1999-98	1998-97
Turnover (th GBP)	-115,200	193,200	527,000	-242,100	-382,900
Profit before Taxation (th GBP)	-57,000	-64,900	94,400	115,600	-198,000
Interest Paid (th GBP)	84,600	-5,700	4,600	39,900	-36,200
Number of Employees	2,679	191	262	5,038	-4,288

CREDIT SCORE & RATING

Current QuiScore	(Year ending 30/09/2002)	72 Stable
Previous Period's QuiScore	(Year ending 30/09/2001)	83 Secure
QuiRating (£)		100000

The calculations are based on accounts for relevant periods.
The QuiScore and QuiRating have been devised by Qui Credit Assessment Ltd.
Ltd.

HISTORICAL QUISCORE & RATING

	30/09/2002	30/09/2001	30/09/2000	30/09/1999	30/09/1998
QuiScore	72	83	74	77	83
Comment	Stable	Secure	Stable	Stable	Secure
QuiRating (GBP)	100,000	100,000	100,000	100,000	100,000

CURRENT DIRECTORS

	Name	First Name	Date of Birth	Position
1	Dr K. Rajagopal	Krishnamurthy	14/09/1953	Director
2	Mr A.E. Isaac	Anthony	24/11/1941	Director
3	Mr C.J. O'donnell	Christopher	30/10/1946	Director
4	Mr G.U. Lundberg	Goran	11/12/1940	Director
5	Mr J.A. Bevan	John	01/09/1957	Director
6	Mr J.L. Walsh	John	08/10/1955	Director
7	Mr M.F. Miau	Matthew	14/09/1946	Chairman
8	Mr R. Medori	Rene	23/09/1957	Group Finance Director
9	Mr R. Mendoza	Roberto	09/03/1945	Chairman
10	Mr R.J. Margetts	Robert	11/10/1946	Director
11	Mr R.S. Grant	Richard	25/05/1946	Director
12	Mrs F.R. Arredondo	Fabiola	12/09/1966	Director
13	Mrs J.M. Baddeley	Julia	20/03/1951	Director
14	Mr N. Deeming	Nicholas		Company Secretary

Appendix C: Glossary of accounting terms

accounting concepts

The assumptions underlying the preparation of financial statements. The basic assumptions of going concern, accruals, consistency and prudence are included in this glossary.

accounting period

The period for which accounts are prepared, usually one year.

accounting policies

The specific accounting methods used by a business organization when preparing its accounts.

accounts payable

Alternative expression for *creditors*, i.e. amounts owing by a business to suppliers of goods and services.

accounts receivable

Alternative expression for *debtors*, i.e. amounts owing to a business by customers who have not yet paid for goods or services received.

accruals

The accounting concept which requires that revenues and expenses are recognized in the *accounting period* in which they are earned or incurred rather than in the period in which they are received or paid.

amortization

Alternative expression for *depreciation*, particularly that due mainly to the passage of time.

annual report

A report sent annually to the shareholders of a company. It contains the financial statements and explanatory notes, the report of the auditors, the chairman's statement and the directors' report.

asset

Any property or rights owned by a company that have expected future economic benefits.

associated company	A company over which another company or group of companies has a significant influence. An associated company is essentially the same as a *related company*. A company will normally be assumed to be an associated/related company if between 20 per cent and 50 per cent of its ordinary share capital is owned by another company or group of companies.
bad debt	An amount owing from *debtors* which is not expected to be received.
capital employed	Usually refers to the total of the funds invested by shareholders plus the long-term debt.
capital expenditure	Expenditure on fixed assets.
cash flow	The receipts of cash by and payment of cash from a business.
cash flow statement	A financial statement that reports the cash receipts and cash payments of an accounting period. Financial Reporting Standard No. 1 requires all companies to publish a cash flow statement.
close company	A UK company which is controlled by not more than five shareholders or their families or partners.
consistency	The accounting concept that a company should use the same accounting policies over time.
consolidated accounts	A set of financial statements which combine the accounts of a *parent company* and its *subsidiaries* as if they were a single entity.
contingencies	Conditions (usually liabilities) that are known at the date of balance sheet, but of which the future outcome (i.e. the amount of the liability) is not known for certain.
corporation tax	The tax that is payable by companies.
cost of sales/cost of goods sold	The costs of making the products that have been sold in a period (usually consists of raw material, labour and production overhead).
creditors	Amounts owing by a business to suppliers of goods and services.
current assets	Assets which are already in the form of cash or are expected to be converted into cash within one year from the date of the balance sheet.

current cost accounting	A system of accounting which adjusts for changing prices.
current liabilities	Amounts which a company owes which are expected to be paid within one year from the date of the balance sheet. (Also referred to as 'Creditors: amounts falling due within one year'.)
debentures	Long-term loans which are usually secured on the assets of a company.
debtors	Amounts owing to a business from customers.
deferred asset	An amount owed to a company that is not expected to be received within one year from the date of the balance sheet.
deferred taxation	An estimate of the tax liability payable at some future date that is due to timing differences in the accounting treatment and taxation treatment of some types of income and expenditure. For example, the depreciation allowed for tax purposes (*capital allowances*) may be greater than the depreciation used for accounting purposes in the early years of an asset's life, but the situation will be reversed in later years.
depreciation	A charge against the profit of an *accounting period* to represent the estimated proportion of the cost of a fixed asset which has been consumed (whether through use, obsolescence or the passage of time) during that period.
dividend	The amount distributed to shareholders out of the profits of a company. Large companies will normally pay an interim dividend part way through the financial year, with a final dividend paid after the end of the financial year when it has been approved by the shareholders.
equity method	A method of accounting for investments in *associated companies*.
equity share capital	An alternative expression for the normal type of ownership finance, i.e. ordinary shares. It is defined as any issued share capital which has unlimited rights to participate in either the distribution of dividends or capital.
exceptional items	Items appearing in the profit and loss account that arise within the ordinary course of business, but are of unusual size.

extraordinary items	Items of income and expenditure which are significant in amount and which are outside the normal activities of a business.
fixed assets	Assets such as land, buildings and machines which are intended for use on a continuing basis by the business rather than for sale.
gearing	The proportion of the *capital employed* of a company that is financed by lenders rather than shareholders.
going concern	An accounting concept which assumes that a business will continue in operation for the foreseeable future.
goodwill	The amount paid for a business which exceeds the fair value of the assets acquired.
gross profit	The difference between the value of sales and the *cost of sales*.
group accounts	The financial statements of a group of companies. These are usually presented in the form of *consolidated accounts*.
historical cost accounting	The conventional system of accounting under which assets are recorded at the original cost of acquiring or producing them.
holding company	A company which owns or controls other companies. (Control can occur through the ownership of 50 per cent of the voting rights or through the exercise of a dominant influence.)
inflation accounting	A system of accounting which, unlike *historical cost accounting*, takes account of changing prices.
insolvency	This occurs when a business is unable to pay debts as they fall due.
intangible assets	Assets such as *goodwill*, patents, trademarks, etc. which have no physical or tangible form.
interim report	A half-yearly or quarterly report issued by a company to its shareholders. *Listed companies* are required to publish an interim report.
issued share capital	The amount of the share capital of a company that has been issued to shareholders.
joint venture	An entity in which the reporting company holds an interest on a long-term basis and which is jointly controlled by the reporting company and

one or more other venturers under a contractual arrangement.

liabilities

The amounts owing by a company.

liquidity

The ability of a company to meet its immediate liabilities.

listed company

A public company listed or quoted on a stock exchange.

listed investments

Investments which are listed or quoted on a stock exchange.

loan capital

Alternative name for debt capital, i.e. the amounts borrowed by a company as a long-term source of finance.

materiality

An accounting concept which states that the normal rules of accounting concerning valuation or disclosure need only be applied to amounts that are significant or important.

minority interests

The share capital of a subsidiary company that is not held by the *parent* company. When consolidated accounts are prepared, 100 per cent of the assets, liabilities, revenues and expenses of all subsidiaries are normally included. However, not all subsidiaries are 100 per cent owned and in such cases a minority of the shares will be left in the ownership of what are known as minority shareholders. The interests of these minority shareholders in the capital of the group (i.e. the minority interests) are shown separately in the consolidated balance sheet.

net assets

The total of all the assets less liabilities to outsiders. This is equal to the *shareholders' funds*.

net current assets

An alternative name for *working capital*, i.e. the current assets less current liabilities of a company.

net realizable value

The amount at which an asset could be sold less the costs incurred in its sale.

off balance sheet financing

Financing operations in such a way that some or all of the finance does not appear as a balance sheet item.

operating profit

Profit before the deduction of interest and tax.

ordinary shares

Shares which entitle the owners to share in the profits remaining after deducting loan interest, taxation and *preference share* dividends.

parent company	Similar to a *holding company*, i.e. a company which owns, or has effective control over the activities of, another company (its subsidiary).
post balance sheet events	Events occurring after the date of the balance sheet but before the accounts are issued. These can be events that require adjustment of the financial statements ('adjusting events') and events that require disclosure but do not require adjustment to the financial statements ('non-adjusting events').
preference shares	Shares which normally have preference over *ordinary* shares for payment of dividends and for repayment of capital if a company is wound up. Preference shares are usually entitled to a fixed rate of dividend.
private company	A company that is not allowed to issue shares or loan stock to the public.
profit	The excess of the revenues earned in a period over the costs incurred in earning them.
provision	An amount charged against profit to provide for an expected liability or loss even though the amount or date of the liability or loss is uncertain.
prudence	An accounting concept which requires that provisions be made for all known liabilities or losses when calculating profit but that any gains or revenues should only be included when realized in cash or near cash (e.g. debtors).
public company	A company whose shares and loan stock may be publicly traded. A public company must have 'public limited company' (or plc) as part of its name.
registrar of companies	A government official who is responsible for collecting and arranging public access to the annual reports of all companies.
related companies	The Companies Act term for what are essentially *associated companies*.
replacement cost accounting	A system of accounting in which assets (and related expenses such as depreciation) are valued at what it would cost to replace them.
reserves	Reserves consist of the accumulated profits that have been retained by a company, plus any surplus from the revaluation of assets, plus any

share premium. Reserves belong to shareholders and are part of *shareholders' funds.*

retained profits

Profits that have not been paid out as dividends to shareholders, but retained for further investment by the company.

revaluation reserve

The gain or loss arising from the revaluation of assets.

rights issue

The issue of new shares by a company to existing shareholders. The 'rights' to buy the new shares are usually fixed at a price below the current market price.

share capital

The nominal value of the shares that have been issued by a company.

share premium

The amount received by a company for its shares that is in excess of their nominal value.

shareholders' funds

The total of the shareholders' interest in a company. It consists of share capital plus reserves and is equal to the *net assets* of the company.

short-term debt

A type of *current liability*. A loan that is repayable within one year from the date of the balance sheet.

solvency

The ability to pay debts as they become due.

statement of total recognized gains and losses

A statement of all the gains and losses (both realized and unrealized) of an accounting period that are attributable to shareholders. Financial Reporting Standard No. 3 requires all companies to publish this statement.

stocks and work in progress

This consists of items purchased for resale and includes raw materials required for production, partially completed products (work in progress) and finished products.

subsidiary

A company that is controlled by another company (a parent company). Control can occur because either more than 50 per cent of the voting rights are owned by another company or because a 'dominant influence' is exercised by another company.

tangible assets

Normally applied to those *fixed assets* that have a physical existence, such as land and buildings, plant and machinery.

total assets	The total of the fixed assets and current assets of a company.
turnover	The sales revenue of an accounting period.
unlisted investments	Investments which are not listed on a stock exchange.
window dressing	Manipulation of financial statements in order to give a misleading or unrepresentative impression.
working capital	An alternative name for *net current assets*, i.e. the current assets less current liabilities of a company.
written down value	The value of assets in the books of a company. This is usually the historical cost less the cumulative amount of depreciation written-off at the balance sheet date.

Appendix D: Glossary of ratios

A glossary of the ratios used in the text is given below. A more detailed explanation of the terms in these ratios can be found in either the glossary of accounting terms (Appendix C) or the appropriate chapters.

Profitability and performance

Return on capital employed (ROCE)

$$\frac{\text{Trading profit before interest, taxation and extraordinary items}}{\text{Average capital employed}} \times 100$$

measures the efficiency with which the long-term capital has been employed.

Return on total assets (ROTA)

$$\frac{\text{Trading profit before interest, taxation and extraordinary items}}{\text{Average total assets for the period}} \times 100$$

measures the efficiency of the overall trading return on the business as a whole.

Return on net total assets

$$\frac{\text{Trading profit before interest, taxation and extraordinary items}}{\text{Average net total assets for the period}} \times 100$$

measures the efficiency of the trading return on the net assets of the business.

Return on equity (ROE)

$$\frac{\text{Profit after interest and preference dividends but before tax and extraordinary items}}{\text{Average ordinary share capital, reserves and retained profit for the period}} \times 100$$

measures the company's efficiency in earning profits on behalf of its ordinary shareholders.

Earnings per share (EPS)

$$\frac{\text{Profit after interest, taxation and}}{\text{preference dividends but before extraordinary items}} \times 100$$
$$\frac{}{\text{Average number of ordinary shares outstanding in the year}}$$

measures the return per share of earnings available to shareholders. (Alternative methods of computation are given in the text.)

Price–earnings ratio (PE ratio)

$$\frac{\text{Market price per share}}{\text{Earnings per share}}$$

reflects the stock market's expectations of the future earnings of the company. The higher the number, the greater the expectations.

Return on sales (ROS)

$$\frac{\text{Trading profit before interest, taxation and extraordinary items}}{\text{Total sales}} \times 100$$

measures the profit margin on sales, i.e. on a company's trading activity.

Asset turnover

$$\frac{\text{Total sales}}{\text{Average (net) total assets}}$$

The asset figure can be either total or net total assets depending on which other profitability ratios are being calculated. The ratio measures the performance of the company in generating sales from the assets at its disposal.

Quality of profit

$$\frac{\text{Net cash inflow from operations}}{\text{Operating profit}} \times 100$$

Operating profit is net profit before interest, exceptional items and tax. This gives an indication of the amount of operating profit received in cash terms during the year.

Quality of sales

$$\frac{\text{Cash from customers}}{\text{Sales}} \times 100$$

gives the proportion of sales received in cash during the year.

Cash return on capital employed

$$\frac{\text{Net cash inflow from operations}}{\text{Average capital employed}} \times 100$$

Net cash inflow includes dividends from related undertakings during the year. This ratio measures the cash return generated by the long-term capital employed in the business (cash equivalent to ROCE).

Cash return on total assets

$$\frac{\text{Net cash inflow from operations and investments}}{\text{Average total assets for the period}} \times 100$$

measures the cash return from trading and investment by the business as a whole.

Cash flow per share

$$\frac{\text{Net cash inflow from operating activities} + \text{dividends from joint ventures and associates} - \text{returns on investments and servicing of finance} - \text{tax paid}}{\text{Weighted average number of ordinary shares in issue during the year}}$$

indicates the amount of cash generated per share by the year's operations. It is the cash flow equivalent to the earnings per share.

Efficiency and effectiveness

Debtor turnover

$$\frac{\text{Sales}}{\text{Trade debtors}}$$

The year-end debtors are taken. The ratio gives the number of times the debtors are turned over in the year, measuring efficiency of collection.

Average collection period

$$\frac{\text{Trade debtors}}{\text{Sales}} \times 365$$

is the average time it takes to collect the cash from the debtors.

Creditor turnover

$$\frac{\text{Purchases}}{\text{Trade creditors}}$$

gives the number of times the trade creditors are turned over in the year.

Creditor payment period

$$\frac{\text{Trade creditors}}{\text{Purchases}} \times 365$$

gives the average length of time the company is taking before it pays its creditors.

Stock turnover

$$\frac{\text{Cost of sales for the period}}{\text{Stock at the end of the period}}$$

gives the frequency with which the stock is turned over during the year.

Stock-turnover period

$$\frac{\text{Stock at the end of the period}}{\text{Cost of sales for the period}} \times 365$$

reveals the average period that items are held in stock.

Net working capital to sales ratio

$$\frac{\text{Stock and trade debtors} - \text{trade creditors}}{\text{Sales}} \times 100$$

gives the amount of working capital required per unit of sales.

Employee efficiency

$$\frac{\text{Wages for the period}}{\text{Sales for the period}} \times 100$$

gives the proportion of sales paid out in employee costs.

Sales per employee

$$\frac{\text{Sales for the period}}{\text{Average number of employees}}$$

measures the amount of sales generated per employee.

Return per employee

$$\frac{\text{Operating profit}}{\text{Average number of employees}}$$

gives the profitability of the company per employee.

Value added per employee

$$\frac{\text{Value added}}{\text{Average number of employees}}$$

provides the average value added by each employee.

Capital employed per employee

$$\frac{\text{Capital employed}}{\text{Average number of employees}}$$

states the average amount of assets employed in relation to the employees used by the company.

Specific costs to sales ratios

(a)
$$\frac{\text{Administration costs}}{\text{Sales}} \times 100$$

(b)
$$\frac{\text{Research and development costs}}{\text{Sales}} \times 100$$

(c)
$$\frac{\text{Manufacturing costs}}{\text{Sales}} \times 100$$

Each of these, and similar ratios for other costs, are primary measures of the impact of these different costs on profits.

Liquidity and stability

Current ratio (working-capital ratio)

$$\frac{\text{Current assets}}{\text{Current liabilities}}$$

measures the amount of liquid and near liquid resources available to meet short-term creditors.

Quick ratio (acid test ratio)

$$\frac{\text{Current assets minus stocks}}{\text{Current liabilities}}$$

i.e.

$$\frac{\text{Net monetary assets}}{\text{Current liabilities}}$$

This ratio concentrates on more readily realizable, or liquid, assets available to meet short-term creditors.

Cash interest cover

$$\frac{\text{Net cash inflow from operations and interest received}}{\text{Interest paid}}$$

measures the sufficiency of cash from operations from which the interest can be paid.

Cash dividend cover

$$\frac{\begin{array}{c}\text{Net cash inflow from operations and interest received} \\ \text{Dividends received from related undertakings} \\ -\text{Interest paid} - \text{Tax paid} - \text{Dividend paid to preference shareholders}\end{array}}{\text{Dividend paid to equity shareholders}}$$

measures availability of net cash from operations after payment of financing and tax charges for payment of ordinary dividends.

Cash debt coverage

$$\frac{\begin{array}{c}\text{Net cash inflow from operations} - \text{Tax paid} \\ - \text{ Interest and dividends paid} + \text{Interest and dividends received}\end{array}}{\text{Loans maturing within next year}} \times 100$$

This ratio states the percentage of loans to be repaid in the next year that can be met out of the net cash inflow from operating activities.

Cash current liabilities coverage

$$\frac{\begin{array}{c}\text{Net cash inflow from operations and dividends from joint ventures} \\ \text{and associates} - \text{returns on investments and servicing of finance} - \text{tax paid}\end{array}}{\text{Current liabilities}} \times 100$$

shows the proportion of current liabilities that could be paid off out of net cash from operations plus any dividends from associates and joint ventures after servicing the loans and paying off the taxes.

Cash total liabilities coverage

$$\frac{\begin{array}{c}\text{Net cash inflow from operations and dividends from joint ventures} \\ \text{and associates} - \text{returns on investments and servicing of finance} - \text{tax paid}\end{array}}{\text{Total liabilities}} \times 100$$

indicates the proportion of total liabilities that could be paid off out of net cash from operations plus any dividends from associates and joint ventures after servicing the loans and paying off the taxes.

Defensive interval

$$\frac{\text{Quick assets (net monetary assets)}}{\text{Average daily operating cash outflows}}$$

shows how many days a company could survive at its present level of operating activity if no inflow of cash was received from sales or other sources.

Capital structure, investment and financial risk

Long-term debt to equity ratio

$$\frac{\text{Long-term loans} + \text{Preference shares}}{\text{Ordinary shareholders' funds}} \times 100$$

measures the ratio of long-term borrowing to equity.

Long-term debt to total long-term finance ratio

$$\frac{\text{Long-term loans} + \text{Preference shares}}{\begin{array}{c}\text{Long-term loans} + \text{Preference shares and} \\ \text{ordinary shareholders' funds}\end{array}} \times 100$$

provides an alternative way of considering what is sometimes called the debt to equity ratio. It shows the amount of long-term debt finance as a percentage of total long-term finance.

Total debt to total assets ratio

$$\frac{\text{Long-term loans } + \text{ Short-term loans}}{\text{Total assets}}$$

provides a measure of asset coverage for all outstanding loans.

Interest cover
Traditional

$$\frac{\text{Profit before interest and tax and extraordinary items}}{\text{Gross interest payable}}$$

calculates the number of times the interest payable is covered by profits available for such payments.

Dividend cover

$$\frac{\text{Profit available for paying ordinary dividends}}{\text{Ordinary dividends (net)}}$$

gives an indication of the extent to which profits cover dividends. (It is the reciprocal of the payout ratio.)

Fixed assets to total assets ratio

$$\frac{\text{Fixed assets}}{\text{Total assets}} \times 100$$

gives the proportion of total assets that consist of fixed assets.

Long-term funds to total assets ratio

$$\frac{\text{Long-term liabilities } + \text{ Preference shares and ordinary shareholders' funds}}{\text{Total assets}} \times 100$$

measures the proportion of total assets funded by long-term funds.

Total owing to total assets ratio

$$\frac{\text{Short- and long-term creditors}}{\text{Total assets}} \times 100$$

provides the proportion of total assets financed by third-party funds.

Capital gearing

$$\frac{\text{Profit before interest, tax and extraordinary items}}{\text{Profit before tax and extraordinary items}}$$

highlights the effects on profits brought about by the interest paid on borrowings.

Capital expenditure to turnover

$$\frac{\text{Capital expenditure for the year}}{\text{Sales}} \times 100$$

gives an indication of the level of capital expenditure incurred to sustain the particular level of sales.

Capital expenditure to depreciation

$$\frac{\text{Capital expenditure for the year}}{\text{Annual depreciation expense}}$$

gives an indication of the replacement rate of new for old assets.

Capital expenditure to tangible fixed assets ratio

$$\frac{\text{Capital expenditure for the year}}{\text{Gross book value of tangible fixed assets}} \times 100$$

is a better ratio for giving an indication of the replacement rate of new for old assets.

Capital acquisitions ratio

$$\frac{\begin{array}{c}\text{Net cash inflow from operations}\\ - \text{ Net interest paid} - \text{Dividends paid} - \text{Tax paid}\end{array}}{\text{Net cash outflow on investment}} \times 100$$

indicates the proportion of investment expenditure on both new and replacement assets financed by internally generated funds.

Leased assets to tangible fixed assets

$$\frac{\text{Net book value of leased assets}}{\text{Net tangible fixed assets}} \times 100$$

indicates the proportion of tangible fixed assets which are leased rather than owned by the company.

Appendix E: Solutions to questions 4.1 and 4.2 (Chapter 4) and questions 13.1 and 13.2 (Chapter 13)

Question 4.1 (Poppy Field)

Cash Flow Statement for year ended 28 February 20X3

	(£)	(£)
Operating cash flow		
cash received from customers		102,120
Less		
shop rental	(18,000)	
wages	(14,680)	
flowers and other items for sale	(50,800)	
advertising charges	(3,800)	
heating, lighting, telephone, postage	(10,200)	
miscellaneous	(3,640)	(101,120)
Cash flow from operating activities		1,000
Returns on investment and servicing of finance		
interest paid (£200 per month × 11 months)		(2,200)
Capital expenditure and financial investments		
display counters, and fittings	(30,000)	
delivery van	(12,000)	(42,000)
Net cash out flow before financing		(43,200)
Financing		
owner's capital	25,000	
bank loan	24,000	49,000
Increase in cash		5,800

Note The above cash flow statement only includes the categories that are required for the data given in the question.

Profit and loss account for year ended 28 February 20X3

	(£)	(£)
Sales[1]		117,540
Cost of sales – purchases[2]	58,870	
– less closing stock	4,600	54,270
Gross profit		63,270
shop rental	18,000	
wages	14,680	
advertising charges	3,800	
heating, lighting, telephone, postage[3]	13,260	
miscellaneous	3,640	
interest on bank loan	2,400	
bad debts provision (£8,600 × 20%)	1,720	
depreciation		
delivery van[4]	3,500	
display counters and fittings[5]	5,000	66,000
Loss for year		(2,730)

Notes

(1) Sales consists of receipts of £102,120, plus £6,820 due from credit card companies and £8,600 due from customers who purchased flowers on credit.

(2) Purchases consists of payments of £50,800, plus £8,070 due to suppliers.

(3) Heating, lighting, telephone and postage consists of payments of £10,200, plus £420 for telephone charges and £2,640 for heating and lighting.

(4) Purchase price £12,000, disposal value £1,500, life 3 years. Depreciation is therefore (£12,000 − £1,500) ÷ 3 = £3,500 per year.

(5) Display counters and fittings cost £30,000, life 6 years, therefore depreciation is £30,000 ÷ 6 = £5,000 per year.

If Poppy wishes to show a profit rather than a loss then she might decide that the delivery van would be useable for 5 years rather than 3 and if the estimated disposal value was unchanged at £1,500 then the depreciation would be (£12,000 − £1,500) ÷ 5 = £2,100, a reduction of £1,400. Similarly, she might reconsider the likely life of the display counters and fittings and decide that 10 years is a more realistic estimate, in which case the depreciation charge would be £30,000 ÷ 10 = £3,000 per year, a saving of £2,000. Also she might decide that she had been too prudent in assuming that 20 per cent of the amount due from customers who had purchased flowers on credit might not be received and a provision of 10 per cent would be more appropriate. This would result in a saving of £860.

All of these adjustments could be argued to be legitimate revisions to assumptions about uncertain future events. The total value of these adjustments is £1,400 + £2,000 + £860 = £4,260 and if Poppy wished she could therefore turn the loss shown in the draft profit and loss account of £2,730 into a profit of £1,530 (£4,260 − £2,730).

Question 4.2 (Alibarba Limited)

Cash Flow Statement for year ended 30 April 20X3

	(£)	(£)
Operating cash flow		
cash receipts from customers[1]		59,840
Less		
rent	(9,000)	
wages	(13,060)	
advertising	(16,660)	
heating and lighting	(3,300)	
stationery and miscellaneous	(3,550)	(45,570)
Cash flow from operating activities		14,270
Returns on investment and servicing of finance		
net interest paid		(420)
Investing activities		
purchase of car	(7,200)	
lease on office premises	(7,500)	(14,700)
Net cash outflow before financing		(850)
Financing		
Capital from Ali and Barbara		4,000
Increase in cash		3,150

Notes

(1) Cash receipts from customers = (£4,680 × 12) + (£4,680 − £1,000) = £59,840. (Only the four categories of cash flow that are required for the data provided in the question are reported in the above cash flow statement).

Profit and loss account for year ended 30 April 20X3

	(£)	(£)
Sales[1]		67,860
less		
rent	12,000	
wages	13,060	
advertising[2]	18,080	
heating/lighting	3,300	
stationery and miscellaneous[3]	3,800	
net interest	420	
legal fees	300	
bad debts provision[4]	2,840	
depreciation on car[5]	1,200	
amortization of lease[6]	1,500	56,500
Profit for year		11,360

Notes

(1) Sales consists of $(£4,680 \times 14) + £2,340 = £67,860$.
(2) Advertising consists of payments of £16,660 plus invoice outstanding of £1,420 = £18,080.
(3) Stationery and miscellaneous consists of payments of £3,550 plus invoice outstanding of £250 = £3,800.
(4) Bad debts provision is 50% of the amount due from the Smythes (£2,340) plus 50% of the amount withheld for the dispute over the photographer (£500) = £2,840.
(5) Annual depreciation on the car = $£7,200 \div 3, = £2,400$, therefore for half a year the depreciation is £1,200.
(6) The lease on the office premises lasts for 5 years and so each year is charged one-fifth of $£7,500 = £1,500$ as an amortization charge.

The question does not ask for a balance sheet, but often it is useful to produce a balance sheet, to show the financial position of the business. A balance sheet at 30 April 20X3 could be prepared from the data provided and would be as follows:

Balance sheet as at 30 April 20X3

	(£)	(£)	(£)
Fixed Assets[1]			12,000
Current Assets			
debtors[2]	8,020		
less bad debts provision	(2,840)	5,180	
cash[3]		3,150	
		8,330	
less current liabilities[4]		4,970	3,360
			15,360
Owners' capital		4,000	
Profit for year[5]		11,360	15,360

Notes

(1) The fixed assets consist of the car £6,000 (purchase price £7,200 – depreciation £1,200), plus the lease on office premises £6,000 (acquisition cost £7,500 – amortization £1,500), i.e. a total of £12,000.
(2) Debtors consists of the £4,680 due from the Smythes, plus the £2,340 due from the 15th wedding plus the £1,000 from the couple in dispute over the photographer, i.e. a total of £8,020.
(3) The cash is the amount shown as increase in cash in the cash flow statement.
(4) Current liabilities consists of the outstanding amounts due for stationery (£250), advertising (£1,420), legal fees (£300) and the rent for the last quarter of the year (£3,000), i.e. a total of £4,970.
(5) The profit for the year is taken from the profit and loss account and assumes that no dividends have been paid or proposed to be paid out of the profit.

Question 13.1

Diamond Ratios

	20X2	Diamond 20X3	Plc 20X3
Profit margin	$\dfrac{500}{8,000} \times 100 = 6.25\%$	$\dfrac{580}{9,200} \times 100 = 6.3\%$	7%
Return on capital employed	$\dfrac{500}{3,645} \times 100 = 13.7\%$	$\dfrac{580}{3,600} \times 100 = 16.1\%$	21%
Capital turnover	$\dfrac{8,000}{3,645} = 2.2\times$	$\dfrac{9,200}{3,600} = 2.6\times$	$3\times$
Current ratio	$\dfrac{1,950}{825} = 2.4\times$	$\dfrac{2,000}{1,340} = 1.49\times$	$1.6\times$
Acid test	$\dfrac{1,150}{825} = 1.4\times$	$\dfrac{1,050}{1,340} = 0.78\times$	$1.1\times$
Collection period	$\dfrac{1,100}{8,000} \times 365 = 50.2$ days	$\dfrac{1,050}{9,200} \times 365 = 41.7$ days	40 days
Stock period	$\dfrac{800}{7,500} \times 365 = 38.9$ days	$\dfrac{950}{8,620} \times 365 = 40.2$ days	20 days
Gearing (long-term debt/ capital emp.)	$\dfrac{1,400 \times 100}{(2,245 + 1,400)} = 38.4\%$	$\dfrac{1,200 \times 100}{(2,400 + 1,200)} = 33.3\%$	27%
Total owing to total assets	$\dfrac{(725 + 1,400)}{(2,520 + 1,950)} \times 100 = 47.5\%$	$\dfrac{(1,190 + 1,200)}{(2,940 + 2,000)} \times 100 = 48.4\%$	50%
Earnings per share	$\dfrac{260}{(200 \times 4)} = 32.5$p	$\dfrac{305}{(200 \times 4)} = 38$p	23p
Interest cover	$\dfrac{500}{140} = 3.57\times$	$\dfrac{580}{150} = 3.87\times$	$5\times$
Sales growth	—	$\dfrac{(9,200 - 8,000)}{8,000} \times 100 = 15\%$	8%

Discussion

In the area of profitability, Diamond is not performing as well as its plc counterpart. It has a lower return on sales and its capital or asset turnover is lower which naturally combines to give a significantly lower return on its capital employed. But there is good news for Diamond, in that its sales growth in 20X3 is almost double that of the plc with a marginally improved profit margin and capital turnover. Thus overall the marketing strategy and management savings have produced an all-round improvement.

The growth in sales, linked to the investments in fixed assets in 20X3, has brought some liquidity pressures. The current ratio and acid test ratio have both declined and are now well below those of the plc. However, the company is improving its efficiency in managing its working capital. It has reduced its collection period to virtually the same as the plc, which is good, but it still needs to halve its stock period to be in line with the plc, which if it did would ease its liquidity problem. Of course it is possible that part of the company's marketing strategy is to offer a shorter delivery period, or 'off the shelf' type of service to its customers, and that is partially how it managed to facilitate the greater annual growth in sales than the plc.

The big increase in trade creditors shows how the expansion has been partially funded, and if a creditors or payment period were to be calculated it would show a substantial increase. The effect on total owing to total assets gearing has been marginal, leaving Diamond overall at a level below that of the plc, but in an improved long-term gearing situation. (That latter statement is a subjective one dependent on many things outside the knowledge of the reader since few environmental details have been given with the problem.)

As for the owners of the business, the shareholders will be pleased with the very satisfactory increase in earnings per share which have produced a 50 per cent increase in the dividend to be paid. Comparing Diamond's EPS with that of the plc is not a worthwhile exercise since the nominal value of each plc ordinary share is not given, nor is its price–earnings ratio.

Overall, Diamond started the year 20X3 clearly behind the plc in performance, but managed to get closer to its performance by the end of the year. It is, however, left with a liquidity problem, which though not yet a crisis could become one if the trade creditors start pressing, or if continuing to achieve above average growth in turnover without better margins if Diamond does not obtain appropriate funding.

Question 13.2

Palybus Ratios

	20X2	*20X1*
Profitability		
Return on capital employed	$\dfrac{(2,000 + 300)}{8,000} \times 100 = 28.75\%$	$\dfrac{(2,000 + 100)}{5,500} \times 100 = 38.18\%$
Return on sales	$\dfrac{2,300}{15,000} \times 100 = 15.33\%$	$\dfrac{2,100}{12,000} \times 100 = 17.5\%$
Asset turnover	$\dfrac{15,000}{8,000} = 1.87\times$	$\dfrac{12,000}{5,500} = 2.18\times$
Return on equity	$\dfrac{2,000}{5,500} \times 100 = 36.36\%$	$\dfrac{2,000}{4,500} \times 100 = 44.44\%$
Earnings per share	$\dfrac{1,000}{1,000} = £1.00$	$\dfrac{1,400}{1,000} = £1.40$
Liquidity		
Current ratio	$\dfrac{5,600}{2,000} = 2.8\times$	$\dfrac{5,000}{1,500} = 3.33\times$
Quick ratio	$\dfrac{4,100}{2,000} = 2.05\times$	$\dfrac{4,000}{1,500} = 2.67\times$
Quality of profit	$\dfrac{1,650}{2,300} \times 100 = 71.74\%$	$\dfrac{1,600}{2,100} \times 100 = 76.19\%$
Efficiency		
Debtors period	$\dfrac{800}{15,000} \times 365 = 19.47$ days	$\dfrac{500}{12,000} \times 365 = 15.21$ days
Stock period	$\dfrac{1,500}{9,500} \times 365 = 57.63$ days	$\dfrac{1,000}{7,000} \times 365 = 52.14$ days
Capital structure		
Long-term debt/equity	$\dfrac{2,500}{5,500} \times 100 = 45.45\%$	$\dfrac{1,000}{4,500} \times 100 = 22.22\%$
Total debt/total assets	$\dfrac{(2,000 + 2,500)}{(4,400 + 5,600)} \times 100 = 45\%$	$\dfrac{(1,500 + 1,000)}{(2,000 + 5,000)} \times 100 = 35.71\%$
Interest cover	$\dfrac{(2,000 + 300)}{300} = 7.67\times$	$\dfrac{(2,000 + 100)}{100} = 21\times$

Cash flow

Capital expenditure to free cash flow

$$\frac{(1,800 + 700)}{(1,650 - 250 - 600)} \times 100 = 312.5\% \qquad \frac{0 \times 100}{(1,600 - 100 - 1,000)} = 0\%$$

Cash flow per share

$$\frac{(1,650 - 250 - 600)}{1,000} = \pounds0.80 \qquad \frac{(1,600 - 100 - 1,000)}{1,000} = \pounds0.50$$

Report

Profitability

First, the sales growth of Greattoys, both in the past year and as an average over the past 6 years, has been greater than that of Playbus. Playbus, in going for turnover growth, seems to be losing profitability since both return on sales and return on capital employed have declined. Originally, in 2001, Playbus was the more profitable company both in terms of margins and efficiency in working its assets. (Asset turnover was 2.18 times versus 2×, return on sales was 17.5 per cent vs. 14 per cent). But for equity shareholders and in terms of capital employed, Greattoys is producing the better returns.

Comparisons of earnings per share are not relevant except for reviewing annual change or providing a base for calculating a company's share price. They should be compared to the company's cash flow per share, to provide an assessment of quality. This is similar to the quality of profit ratio. A healthy company would expect to have a quality of profit ratio greater than 100 per cent, and a cash flow per share ratio greater than earnings per share. This is true for Greattoys, but not for Playbus. In both years the quality of profit is below 100 per cent. This should provoke an investigation into the company's cash management and reporting procedures. Has the company been booking revenue (sales) which have not yet been achieved, or has the company been capitalizing payments which would usually be expensed? As the debtors period and stock periods of the two companies are not too dissimilar – suspicion should fall on the accounting practices.

Liquidity and efficiency

Playbus is certainly becoming less liquid. This can be seen from the decline in the current ratio, the acid test, the quality of profit ratio, and the increase in collection and stock periods. Greattoys, too, seem to follow the same trend, but not quite to the same extent. Clearly an area for investigation in the due diligence examination that will follow if Childplay goes further with its enquiries and makes a formal offer. Note the irregular capital expenditure pattern of Playbus vs. Greattoys. Greattoys is able to finance its capital expenditure from internally generated funds, whereas Playbus is not. Again the impact of the new investment of Playbus on its sales and profits needs to be investigated. When did the investment take place? Has it begun to have an impact on sales and profit yet?

Gearing and capital structure

Although Greattoys is the more heavily geared of the two companies, both have relatively high levels of gearing. If profits continue to grow then the gearing effect will mean that the profit available to shareholders, as measured by earnings per share, will grow faster than growth in operating profit. However, if profits fall then the existence of gearing will have the opposite effect, resulting in a greater fall in earnings per share. The profit growth prospects of the two companies are therefore important variables that require careful consideration.

Further reading

Accounting Standards Board (1999) *Statement of Principles for Financial Reporting*, London: ASB Publications.

Alexander, D. and Britton, A. (2001) *Financial Reporting* 6th edn, London: International Thomson Business Press.

Altman, E.I. (1968) 'Financial ratios, discriminant analysis and the prediction of corporate bankruptcy', *Journal of Finance*, September.

Altman, E.I., Haldeman, R.G. and Narayanan, P. (1977) 'Zeta analysis: a new model to identify bankruptcy risk of corporations', *Journal of Banking and Finance*, June.

Anderson, O.D. (1976) *Time Series Analysis and Forecasting*, London: Butterworth.

Argenti, J. (1976) *Corporate Collapse*, New York: McGraw-Hill.

Bartlett, S.A. and Chandler, R.A. (1997) 'The corporate report and the private shareholder: Lee and Tweedie twenty years on', *The British Accounting Review*, Vol. 29, 245–61.

Bartlett, S.A. and Chandler, R.A. (1999) 'The private shareholder, corporate governance and the role of the annual report', *The Journal of Business Law*, September.

Bartley, J.W. and Boardman, C.M. (1990) 'The relevance of inflation adjusted accounting data to the prediction of corporate takeovers', *Journal of Business Finance & Accounting* 17 (1), Spring.

Beaver, W.H. (1966) 'Financial ratios as predictors of failure', *Empirical Research in Accounting*, supplement to *Journal of Accounting Research*.

Beaver, W.H. (1981) *Financial Reporting: An Accounting Revolution*, Englewood Cliffs, NJ: Prentice Hall.

Belkaoui, A. (1983) *Industrial Bonds and the Rating Process*, Westport, CT: Quorum Books.

Bernstein, L.A. (1978) *The Analysis of Financial Statements*, Homewood, IL: Dow-Jones/Irwin.

Cadbury Report (1992) (The Committee on the Financial Aspects of Corporate Governance), *The Financial Aspects of Corporate Governance*, London: Gee.

Ellis, J. and Williams, D. (1993) *Corporate Strategy and Financial Analysis*, London: Pitman.

Ernst & Young (2001) *UK GAAP*, London: Butterworths Tolley.

Foster, G. (1986) *Financial Statement Analysis*, 2nd edn, Englewood Cliffs, NJ: Prentice Hall.

Gibson, C.H. and Boyes, P.A. (1979) *Financial Statement Analysis*, Boston, MA: CBI Publishing.

Gordon, M.J. (1962) *The Investment, Financing and Valuation of the Corporation*, Homewood, IL: Irwin.

Greenbury Report (1995) (The Study Group on Directors' Remuneration), *Directors' Remuneration: Report of a Study Group*, London: Gee.

Hampel Report (1998) (Committee on Corporate Governance) *Final Report*, London: Gee.

Ingham, H. and Harrington, L.T. (1980) *Interfirm Comparison*, London: Heinemann.

Institute of Chartered Accountants of Scotland (1988) *Making Corporate Reports Valuable*, London: Kogan Page.

Institute of Chartered Accountants of Scotland (1993) *Auditing into the Twenty-first Century*, a discussion document issued by the Research Committee of the ICAS, Edinburgh.

Johnson, B. and Patient, M. (1985) *Accounting Provisions of the Companies Act 1985*, London: Farringdon Publishing.

Journal of Business Finance & Accounting (1990) 'Special issue on financial statement analysis', 17 (1), Spring.

Keasey, K. and Watson, R. (1987) 'Non-financial symptoms and the prediction of small company failure: a test of Argentis Hypothesis', *Journal of Business Finance and Accounting* 14 (3).

Lee, T.A. (ed.) (1981) *Developments in Financial Reporting*, Oxford: Allan.

Lee, T.A. (1982) *Company Financial Reporting: Issues and Analysis*, 2nd edn, Wokingham: Van Nostrand Reinhold.

Lee, T.A. and Tweedie, D.P. (1977) *The Private Shareholder and the Corporate Report*, London: Institute of Chartered Accountants in England and Wales.

Lee, T.A. and Tweedie, D.P. (1981) *The Institutional Investor and Financial Information*, London: Institute of Chartered Accountants in England and Wales.

Lev, B. (1974) *Financial Statement Analysis: A New Approach*, Englewood Cliffs, NJ: Prentice Hall.

McLeay, S.J. (1991) 'International financial analysis', in C.W. Nobes and R.H. Parker (eds), *Comparative International Accounting*, Englewood Cliffs, NJ: Prentice Hall.

Mepham, M.J. (1980) *Accounting Models*, Stockport: Polytech.

Palepu, K. (1986) 'Predicting takeover targets: a methodological and empirical analysis', *Journal of Accounting and Economics*, March.

Parker, R.H. (1999) *Understanding Company Financial Statements*, 5th edn, Harmondsworth: Penguin.

Peel, M.J. (1990) *The Liquidation/Merger Alternative: Theory and Evidence*, Avebury: Aldershot.

Peel, M.J. and Peel, D.A. (1987) 'Some further empirical evidence on predicting private company failure', *Accounting and Business Research*, Winter.

Platt, H.D. and Platt, M.B. (1990) 'Developments of a class of stable predictive variables: the case of bankruptcy prediction', *Journal of Business Finance & Accounting* 17 (1), Spring.

Platt, H.D., Platt, M.B. and Pedersen, J.G. (1994) 'Bankruptcy discrimination with real variables', *Journal of Business Finance and Accounting* 21(4), June.

Porter, B., Simon, J. and Hatherly, D. (2002) *Principles of External Auditing*, 2nd edn, Chichester, Wiley.

Pratton, C. (1991) *Company Failure*, Financial and Auditing Group, London: ICAEW.

Rappaport, A. (1986) *Creating Shareholder Value – The New Standard for Business Performance*, New York: The Free Press.

Rege, U.P. (1984) 'Accounting ratios to locate take-over targets', *Journal of Business Finance and Accounting*, Autumn.

Samuels, J.M., Wilkes, F.M. and Brayshaw, R.E. (2000) *Management of Company Finance*, 6th edn, London: Thomson.

Slater, J.D. (1996) *The Zulu Principle*, 3rd edn, London: Orion Books.

Smith, T. (1996) *Accounting for Growth*, 2nd edn, London: Random House Business Books.

Stock Exchange (1979 *et seq.*) *Admission of Securities to Listing*, latest edn, London: Stock Exchange.

Swinson, C. (1990) *A Guide to the Companies Act*, 1989, London: Butterworth.

Taffler, R.J. (1983) 'The Z-score approach to measuring company solvency', *Accountant's Magazine*, March.

Taffler, R.J. (1984) 'Empirical methods for the monitoring of U.K. corporations', *Journal of Banking and Finance*, June.

Taffler, R.J. and Tisshaw, H. (1977) 'Going, going, gone – four factors which predict', *Accountancy*, March.

Tamari, M. (1978) *Financial Ratios: Analysis and Prediction*, London: Elek.

Tolley's Corporation Tax (annually) Croydon: Tolley.

Ward, T.J. (1994) 'An empirical study of the incremental predictive ability of Beaver's naive operating flow measure using four-state ordinal models of financial distress', *Journal of Business Finance and Accounting* 21(4), June.

Ward, T.J. and Foster, B.P. (1997) 'A note on selecting a response measure for financial distress', *Journal of Business Finance and Accounting* 24(6), July.

Index